WIELDING THE TRIDENT

WIELDING THE TRIDENT

Admiral Raymond A. Spruance and America's Victory in the Pacific

ANDREW K. BLACKLEY

Naval Institute Press
Annapolis, Maryland

Naval Institute Press
291 Wood Road
Annapolis, MD 21402

© 2026 by the U.S. Naval Institute
All rights reserved. No part of this book may be reproduced or utilized in any form or by any means, electronic or mechanical, including photocopying and recording, or by any information storage and retrieval system, without permission in writing from the publisher.

Library of Congress Cataloging-in-Publication Data

Names: Blackley, Andrew K. author
Title: Wielding the trident : Admiral Raymond A. Spruance and America's victory in the Pacific / Andrew K. Blackley.
Other titles: Admiral Raymond A. Spruance and America's victory in the Pacific
Description: Annapolis, Maryland : Naval Institute Press, [2026] | Includes bibliographical references and index.
Identifiers: LCCN 2025041707 (print) | LCCN 2025041708 (ebook) | ISBN 9798899190001 hardback | ISBN 9798899190018 ebook
Subjects: LCSH: Spruance, Raymond Ames, 1886–1969 | Admirals—United States—Biography | World War, 1939–1945—Campaigns—Pacific Area | World War, 1939–1945—Naval operations, American | United States. Navy—Biography
Classification: LCC D767.S72 B63 2026 (print) | LCC D767.S72 (ebook)
LC record available at https://lccn.loc.gov/2025041707
LC ebook record available at https://lccn.loc.gov/2025041708

♾ Print editions meet the requirements of ANSI/NISO z39.48-1992 (Permanence of Paper).
Printed in the United States of America.

34 33 32 31 30 29 28 27 26 9 8 7 6 5 4 3 2 1
First printing

Dedicated to the memory of
Cdr. Thomas B. Buell, USN

CONTENTS

MAPS AND TABLES

MAPS

TABLES

FOREWORD

IF ANY ADMIRAL of World War II deserves a new wartime biography, it is Raymond Spruance. For years, Thomas B. Buell's biography of the great admiral stood alone in the literature as the place to go to learn more about the "hero of Midway." However, scholarship has a way of losing its luster over time as new methods and sources (especially classified archives) emerge that give us a better picture of the man and his times. This is as true for Spruance as it is for anyone, although in his case, one wishes for more.

Andy Blackley builds on Buell's scholarship to give us a better, and more objective, picture of a man who was intensely private and reserved. From his early days as a child in Indiana to his final years in retirement in Monterey, California, Spruance maintained that separateness, that reserve—a sometimes cold intellectual aloofness that characterized him throughout his busy, eventful life. Spruance is thus a puzzle with many of the pieces still missing, but fortunately for us Blackley has used new sources, and the historian's trusty tool of inference, to give us a more complete picture of the man rather than simply an update of Buell's work. He adds more texture for the contexts that surrounded the man that Buell did not have access to—for example, the now declassified signals intelligence archives and sources.

Spruance's accomplishments in World War II were monumental. He acknowledged his good fortune to be in some of the most famous battles in naval history, including as a key partner with Frank Jack Fletcher and Chester Nimitz at Midway. This battle, in some ways, undermined his even more significant leadership of CTF-50 and the Fifth Fleet in the Central Pacific Campaign of 1943–44. This campaign culminated in a victory entirely his own, one of the most lopsided in history, at the Philippine Sea during the invasion of the Mariana Islands (Operation Forager). However, as Blackley shows, this victory was tarnished after the fact by second-guessing and jealousies, as well as the long shadow of Midway. Spruance's natural reserve led him to avoid the kind of self-aggrandizement one sometimes sees in great historical captains. Spruance was no Nelson, wearing his laurels for all to see with "victory" tours and public displays of bravado. After each victory, he simply returned to his methodical and unrelenting work.

Planning and staff work are fundamental to the prosecution and practice of operations in modern warfare, in the Second World War and today. However, military history—and especially its audiences—often neglect the details of these behind-the-scenes processes and the people who drive them. Accordingly, the period when Spruance returned from glory at Midway to become Chester Nimitz's chief of staff, confidant, and right-hand man has also been downplayed. It has been claimed that behind every great man stands a great woman, a somewhat dated aphorism. Modern warfare's analogy reads that behind great commanders are great chiefs of staff. Blackley's study brings out the opaque period when Spruance was that person, the unsung chief of staff articulating Nimitz's command decisions during the critical period of the Guadalcanal campaign and South Pacific Operations until Nimitz at last gave Spruance his heart's desire: perhaps the most important active fleet command then in existence for the Central Pacific campaign that began in the late fall of 1943. The Spruance of this period gives much more depth to the portrait offered, showing that he excelled not only in tactical and operational command, but at the staff processes and planning that undergird them.

The highlight of the book is the Battle of the Philippine Sea, a monumental victory that ironically resulted in much criticism of Spruance. Blackley pays particular attention to the intelligence that Spruance acted on: a purloined copy of the Japanese Plan Z (Z-Go) that led him to a more cautious approach in his decisions. The analysis on this point is fresh and original. The fallout of Spruance's failure to destroy more Japanese carriers (and battleships) may have been a factor in keeping him from getting a fifth star. It also absolutely framed the actions of Adm. William Halsey at the Battle of Leyte Gulf. I have always found Spruance's decision to focus on the defense of the invasion transports and successful conquest and occupation of the Marianas to be correct. The main thing was the seizure of islands and bases from which to bomb Japan. Spruance always kept the larger operational and strategic objectives in view. His operational command during Forager highlights this focus as a fine example for future joint force commanders.

However, the book is more than a World War II narrative centered on an important naval leader and his key campaigns. It looks closely at what made the man, and what became of him after the thrilling and terrifying operations of World War II in the Pacific. Especially noteworthy are the discussions of Spruance's time before the war, climbing the "fleet ladder" and serving multiple tours at the Naval War College, where he refined his already keen analytic mind on the problems of naval strategy for a war against "Orange" (the codename for Japan) in the Pacific. After the war Spruance naturally went to the Naval War College as its president and initiated the studies that both gleaned insights from World War II and established basic conceptual thinking about a war at sea against a new competitor—the Soviet Union. He then capped it all off as a diplomat admiral and served as ambassador to the Philippines, guiding that horribly damaged nation into independence, an event that gratified him in many ways as much as the part he played in the great naval victories of the war.

Spruance was that rare officer: both a hard-working staff officer and subordinate and a skilled commander of what we today would call Joint Task Forces. Spruance was a model for joint, and by the time of Okinawa coalition, command. Even though he did not begrudge others their fifth star, in my opinion Spruance too earned one, even though it was never awarded. He was a fighting, thinking admiral, and he shed honor and glory on the nation and Navy he served.

JOHN T. KUEHN
Professor, U.S. Army Command and Staff College,
and author of *Strategy in Crisis: The Pacific War, 1937–1945*

PREFACE

ON 21 FEBRUARY 1944, a blue ensign with four white stars unfurled for the first time on the foretruck of USS *New Jersey* (BB 62), anchored in the protected waters of Kwajalein Atoll, announcing that the newly promoted commander of the Fifth Fleet was aboard his flagship. Raymond Ames Spruance, at fifty-seven, was the youngest in an elite group of four-star admirals in the U.S. Navy. Besides the satisfaction of reaching the pinnacle of his profession, Spruance was deeply gratified by the most recent achievement of his fleet—the capture of the Kwajalein and Eniwetok Atolls in the Marshall Islands, in a combined operation described as "probably the most perfect operation of its kind in the war."[1]

After the bloody experience of Tarawa the previous November, Spruance and his staff had built on the hard lessons learned and organized a brilliant campaign to seize control of the Marshall Islands, deep in the heart of the Empire of Japan's defensive perimeter. It caught the Japanese unprepared, and the detailed planning by Spruance and his staff, as well as the near flawless execution by the fleet, resulted in a fraction of the casualties suffered previously.

Spruance had just returned from a devastating raid on Truk Island, the Japanese "Gibraltar of the Pacific," which was now rendered impotent. Spruance had hoped to meet the Japanese Combined Fleet at Truk to consummate the long-sought surface action between the respective battle lines, one that he had so often war-gamed at the Naval War College. But where in 1942 Admiral Yamamoto Isoroku and his Kidō Butai had commanded the seas, the tables had now turned, and the Japanese Combined Fleet was now on the defensive. Rather than meet the Americans, the Combined Fleet fled the area, declining battle.

In February 1944, the Fifth Fleet was the most powerful naval force ever assembled. After two years of war in the Pacific, the industrial might of the United States was at full flow, delivering an unprecedented number of the most technologically advanced ships, submarines, and aircraft, manned by highly trained crews and transporting the best light infantry in the world.

Under the direction of Adm. Chester W. Nimitz, Raymond Spruance and his Fifth Fleet would, over the next year and a half, advance through the Marianas, Iwo Jima, and Okinawa, and eventually arrive in Tokyo Bay. Rear Adm. E. M. Eller, USN (Ret.), the Navy's Director of Naval History in 1966, made the following observation about Spruance:

> Not an aviator, he nevertheless employed the powerful wings of the new trident Navy with devastating effect whether in fleet battle as at Midway or in an overwhelming sea assault from the Gilberts to Okinawa. Not a submariner, he nevertheless understood and reaped the benefits of the unique powers this undersea tine of the trident brings to navies in key fleet operations.[2]

The reference to the trident, the symbol of sea power, provides the title of the present work. The motto of the U.S. Naval Academy, *Ex Scientia Tridens*, "From Knowledge Sea Power," is personified in the person and career of Admiral Raymond Ames Spruance. His successful career as commander of the Fifth Fleet demonstrated that Spruance was a veritable Poseidon of the Pacific War.

The abundance of combat power in the American naval trident suited Spruance to a T. His philosophy of warfighting was to bring "violent, overwhelming force, swiftly applied" upon his enemy. His critics claimed he would "use a sledgehammer to drive a tack," a comment that he readily embraced. A fellow admiral once remarked to him that an effective commander had to be a gambler once in a while, to which Spruance replied that he only gambled when the odds were heavily in his favor. Spruance stacked the odds by carefully considering all the options and choosing the one he thought was likeliest to succeed, bringing his considerable intelligence to bear.[3]

Capt. Wayne P. Hughes Jr., USN, wrote, "Spruance had to an extraordinary degree the mental equivalent of peripheral vision. Not only did he visualize the situation he confronted in 360 degrees, but he did so in *n* dimensions—that is, in all aspects."[4] Fleet Adm. Ernest J. King called him the most intelligent man in the Navy, and others referred to him as the "electric brain." Admiral Nimitz best contrasted the character of command exemplified by his top commanders: "Bill Halsey was a sailor's admiral and Spruance, an admiral's admiral."[5]

Spruance did not seek fame or adulation; rather, his reward was knowing that he had done his best to achieve victory. As a result, he remains largely unknown to the public. Although seen as cold and aloof by some, a front that concealed his innate shyness, those who served with him found him worthy of intense loyalty. He inspired confidence in both his superiors and subordinates. He valued men whose personalities were quite different but complementary to his own, such as his old Naval War College comrade, the often acerbic Rear Adm. Richmond Kelly Turner, and the irascible Marine Maj. Gen. Holland "Howlin' Mad" Smith. Together they would form the nucleus of the team that helped bring down the might of the Empire of Japan.

The purpose of this work is to present the extraordinary career of Raymond Ames Spruance during the conduct of the Pacific War, reconsidered in light of recent scholarship, and make his achievements fresh to a new generation.

NOTES ON SOURCES AND PREVIOUS BIOGRAPHIES

Unlike many of his peers, Spruance was not a self-promoter and avoided interviews during his active career. He never wrote a memoir and was not a contributor to professional publications such as the U.S. Naval Institute's *Proceedings*, so his intimate thoughts on how the war was conducted are sometimes difficult to discern. Only after retirement did he grant a few interviews or respond to questions from eminent naval historians such as Samuel E. Morison and E. B. Potter, usually to set the record straight on something he thought had been misrepresented by others.

There are two major biographies of Spruance. The first, *Admiral Raymond A. Spruance, USN: A Study in Command*, was written for the U.S. Navy in 1966 by Vice Adm. Emmet P. Forrestel, USN (Ret.). Forrestel was on Spruance's staff during the Pacific War and was knowledgeable and sympathetic to his former boss. Forrestel's work was meant to be instructive for career naval officers; therefore, while reasonably concise, it reveals little about the man.

The second biography, *The Quiet Warrior: A Biography of Admiral Raymond A. Spruance*, was written by Cdr. Thomas B. Buell, USN, and published in 1974. It is considered to be the definitive work on Spruance. Buell had the good fortune to have met Spruance. Although their meeting was brief, Buell was so profoundly impressed, indeed moved by, that experience that it inspired him to study Spruance's life and career. Buell used primary sources almost exclusively. While he provides some excellent bibliographical notes for each chapter, the work is not otherwise annotated. Buell conducted extensive interviews and collected reminiscences from virtually everyone still living at that time who had known Spruance, including his wife and daughter, both named Margaret. Fifty years later, these options were not available to the present author.

Fortunately, Buell kept extensive notes and was scrupulous about preserving his research materials. These now reside at the U.S. Naval War College. The Naval War College Naval Historical Collection holds most of the available archival material on Spruance, including Buell's extensive collection of material. The Naval War College also holds archival material on Spruance's tours of duty there as a student, instructor, and president. These collections have provided the primary sources for this book, and I am deeply grateful to Commander Buell for his extensive research, which I used in the present work. This would not have been possible without the assistance of the archivists at the War College, especially Elizabeth M. Delmage and Stacie M. Parillo. Thank you both.

The Naval War College is also responsible for making an excellent and easily accessed version of *The Command Summary of Fleet Admiral Chester W. Nimitz, USN*, otherwise known as the Nimitz "Graybook," available to those researching the Pacific War. Following the progress of the war on a daily basis, it provides documentation of inestimable value and was used extensively in this work.

Since Buell's biography was published in 1974, a substantial amount of excellent scholarship on the Pacific War has emerged, including studies on cryptography and intelligence, fresh analyses of major battles and campaigns, and numerous new biographies of his fellow commanders, among other notable works. I have endeavored to incorporate this scholarship into the present work and am grateful to the historians responsible.

A WORD OF THANKS

I would like to take this opportunity to thank Cdr. John T. Kuehn, USN (Ret.) who generously provided much advice and encouragement. Thank you, John, for your confidence and friendship. Thanks also to Mr. Padraic (Pat) Carlin and the editors at the Naval Institute Press for guiding this first-time author to the finish line. Thanks also to Mr. Jon Parshall, who took time from his busy schedule to create the maps for this work, and the reviewers whose comments and suggestions were of great value. Finally, I must thank my loving wife, Deborah, for allowing me to devote nearly three years to this project.

PROLOGUE

APPOINTMENT WITH DESTINY

LATE IN THE FORENOON of 26 May 1942, USS *Northampton* (CA 26), the flagship of Rear Adm. Raymond A. Spruance, commander of Cruiser Division Five, completed her mooring at a buoy in the East Loch of Pearl Harbor. Earlier that day, she had been preceded into the base by the carriers USS *Enterprise* (CV 6) and USS *Hornet* (CV 8), the nucleus of Task Force 16, under the command of Vice Adm. William F. Halsey Jr. Spruance was anxious to report to Halsey for debriefing. The two admirals had just returned from a long deployment in the South Pacific, and Spruance wanted to discuss the disturbing intelligence reports he was getting about a possible Japanese attack in the North Pacific.

After he had exchanged his khakis for the white uniform required by Navy protocol, Spruance boarded his barge, accompanied by Lt. Cdr. Robert J. Oliver, his flag lieutenant. The lack of activity on *Enterprise*'s quarterdeck was disturbing. Usually, on the approach of a flag officer's barge, a boat gong sounded announcing his arrival. Now, no sideboys were waiting, and Halsey, who had always made a point of being present to greet Spruance, was not there either. Then they noticed that Halsey's pennant was not flying at her masthead, meaning he had already gone ashore to report to Adm. Chester W. Nimitz. As Spruance stepped onto the lower grating of the accommodation ladder, Halsey's flag lieutenant, William H. Ashford, bounded down the steps to meet him.

"Admiral Halsey is not aboard, sir," said Ashford. "We have been over to see Admiral Nimitz. As a matter of fact, Admiral Halsey is in the hospital. They want to see you at the Sub Base right away. You are going to take the Task Force out. Admiral Halsey told Admiral Nimitz that you are the only flag officer he would entrust his Task Force to. The Admiral says you are to have his staff, but would you please bring your own Flag Lieutenant because I am to stay with him." There was a moment of silence as Spruance let this sink in; then he turned and stepped back into the barge. "Let's go to the Sub Base," he said.[1]

When they reached Commander in Chief Pacific Fleet (CinCPac) Headquarters, Spruance said to Oliver, "I am going to see the Admiral. You go to the Fleet Intelligence Office and find out everything you can." Spruance entered Nimitz's office alone, and Oliver went to the basement, where he found Lt. Cdr. Edwin Layton. Layton assured Oliver that Spruance had the latest available information and would be apprised of any new developments. Based on the analysis of the available intelligence, it appeared that the Japanese intended to invade Midway Island on or about 4 June with a force that included four fleet carriers and supporting battleships. A messenger notified Oliver that Spruance was ready to depart, and as he turned to leave, Layton shook his hand and said, "Good luck and give them hell."[2]

Nimitz gave Spruance the news: Halsey was in the hospital with a severe case of dermatitis and was unfit for duty. Based on his recommendation, Spruance was to assume temporary command of Task Force 16 immediately. Rear Adm. Frank Jack Fletcher and Task Force 17 were expected to return shortly, and as soon as Fletcher arrived, they would hammer out a strategy to ambush the Japanese fleet. Nimitz also informed Spruance that upon his return, he would be detached from his cruiser command and replace Rear Adm. Milo Draemel as his chief of staff. This last piece of news did not thrill Spruance in the least. The last thing he wanted was another staff job on shore when there was an active shooting war at sea.[3]

Spruance and Oliver left the Sub Base and returned to *Northampton* to shift their gear into *Enterprise*. On the way, Oliver related what Layton had said. "Very well," replied Spruance. "Now, this is what I have. It appears that I am one of those commanders who have two sets of orders. I have written orders to meet and defeat the Japs. My oral orders are not to lose my force. If things go badly, I am to withdraw and let them have the place because they can't hold it and we can get it back." Spruance paused and said, "You and I had better get packed as soon as possible. Now, if I were you, I would not be taking anything I didn't need because we might get hit and lose everything."[4]

Before they returned to *Northampton* to pack, they visited Halsey in the hospital. They found him lying naked under a sheet, his body covered in ointment. Halsey was in good spirits, although in much discomfort. Spruance was relaxed as they chatted. Halsey eventually asked Oliver to leave the room, and he and Spruance conferred privately. Spruance never revealed what had passed between the old friends, and he and Oliver left shortly thereafter.

During the trip back across the harbor from the Sub Base, Spruance was deep in thought, his face displaying no emotion. Inside, he would have been simultaneously thrilled at the thought of leading the ships and men of Task Force 16 into the battle he had been preparing to fight his entire career but also saddened that his friend Bill Halsey would miss that opportunity. He later told Oliver that losing Halsey at a time like this was a shame. Nevertheless, no one reached flag rank without being ambitious, and Spruance was no different than his peers in that respect, even though his calm demeanor seldom revealed his emotions.

Early in the afternoon of 27 May, USS *Yorktown* (CV 5) returned to Pearl Harbor trailing oil from her ruptured storage tanks and immediately went into Drydock Number 1. She had been damaged during the Battle of Coral Sea (4 May to 8 May 1942), the first carrier against carrier battle in naval history. As soon as she was secured and the dock drained, Nimitz, in hip boots, led an inspection party to assess the damage to her hull and discuss the repairs needed with the dockyard engineers. The damage did not appear as bad as first feared. The wooden flight deck had been adequately repaired during the trip back, her elevators were working, and her machinery was undamaged. Nimitz told the yard to have *Yorktown* patched and ready for sea duty within three days. Round-the-clock repairs began immediately.[5]

When Nimitz returned to his office, he found Frank Fletcher ready to give his report. TF 17 had been in the South Pacific since early February and had scored a strategic, if not a tactical, victory against a superior Japanese carrier fleet at Coral Sea. Yet Fletcher had a black cloud hanging over his head, driven mainly by Admiral King's doubts about his perceived lack of offensive spirit during that battle. Nimitz had the distasteful task of evaluating Fletcher's performance and fitness for the major battle to come. After some uncomfortable discussion, Fletcher requested that he be given time to review his reports and provide a better answer to Nimitz's questions. The tension was broken when Spruance entered and inquired about the condition of *Yorktown*. "She'll be joining you," was Nimitz's reply.[6]

Later that afternoon, Nimitz called Spruance, Fletcher, and their staffs, together with Lieutenant Commander Layton, his war plans officer Capt. Charles "Soc" McMorris, and Rear Admiral Draemel to discuss the coming operation. Layton provided a detailed rundown of the Japanese forces based on the latest intelligence. The Japanese forces attacking Midway were estimated to be composed of an Occupying Force sailing due east from Saipan to conduct amphibious landings at Midway and a Striking Force, the Kidō Butai, sailing from the southern anchorage of Hashirajima in the Inland Sea of Japan. The latter, consisting of four to five carriers to provide air support for the landings, would be commanded by Admiral Nagumo Chuichi, the man who had led the Pearl Harbor attack. In addition to the carriers, there would be as many as four fast battleships, eight or nine cruisers, as many as two dozen destroyers, and a dozen submarines supporting the operation. Still unknown to American intelligence was the existence of a Main Force, led by Admiral Yamamoto Isoroku himself aboard his flagship *Yamato*, that would shadow the Kidō Butai from the north, ready to pounce on the unsuspecting Americans.

Layton reported that beginning as early as 30 May, the enemy would approach Midway from the northwest with the intent to neutralize its defenses with carrier air attacks, followed immediately by an amphibious assault to occupy the atoll and use it for future operations against Oahu. Layton informed the assembled commanders that he believed the attack would occur on 4 June, launched at approximately 0700 local time from a point 175 miles from Midway, on a relative bearing of 325 degrees. When the assembled team inquired about the accuracy and source of this information, Layton was reticent to provide any details, but Nimitz assured them that he was fully confident in its accuracy. Based on his experience at Naval Intelligence, Spruance was probably aware that it came from the Navy's code-breaking efforts. The general assumption was that it came from espionage at the source. A staffer quipped, "That man of ours in Tokyo is worth every cent we pay him."[7]

The conference worked into the evening, hammering out the details of what became Operation Plan 29–42. Under the overall command of Admiral Fletcher, TF 16 and TF 17 would take up positions northeast of the atoll at "Point Luck" with the intent of conducting a surprise attack "to inflict maximum damage on the enemy by employing strong attrition tactics" on the Japanese carriers as they were conducting operations against the atoll, but avoiding "such decisive action as would likely incur heavy losses on our carriers and cruisers." Finally, it was noted that "It is probable that if our carriers are spotted early in the operation, they will become the primary object of the enemy carriers."[8]

Spruance and Fletcher were both handed a Letter of Instructions for their eyes only that read: "In carrying out the task assigned in Operation Plan 29–42 you will be governed by the principle of calculated risk which you shall interpret to mean the avoidance of exposure of your force to attack by superior enemy forces without good prospect of inflicting, as a result of such exposure, greater damage to the enemy. This applies to a landing phase as well as during preliminary air attacks."[9]

Task Force 16 left Pearl Harbor in the forenoon of 28 May with Rear Adm. Raymond A. Spruance on the bridge of *Enterprise*. He headed north for Point Luck, accompanied by five heavy cruisers, one light antiaircraft cruiser, eleven destroyers, and two fleet oilers. Destiny was giving Spruance an unsought but welcome opportunity to prove himself in battle.

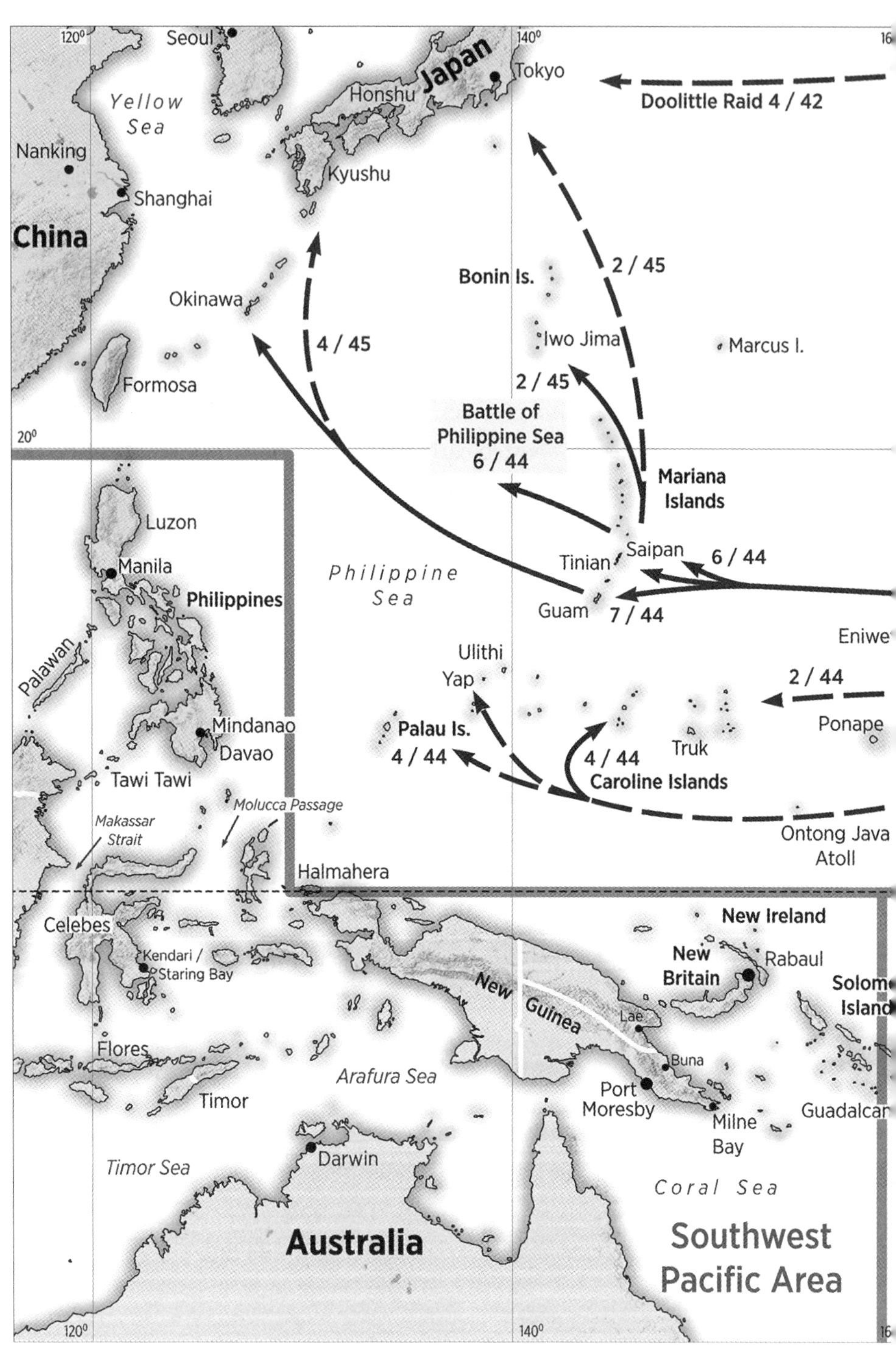

MAP 1. Spruance's Operations, 1942 to 1945

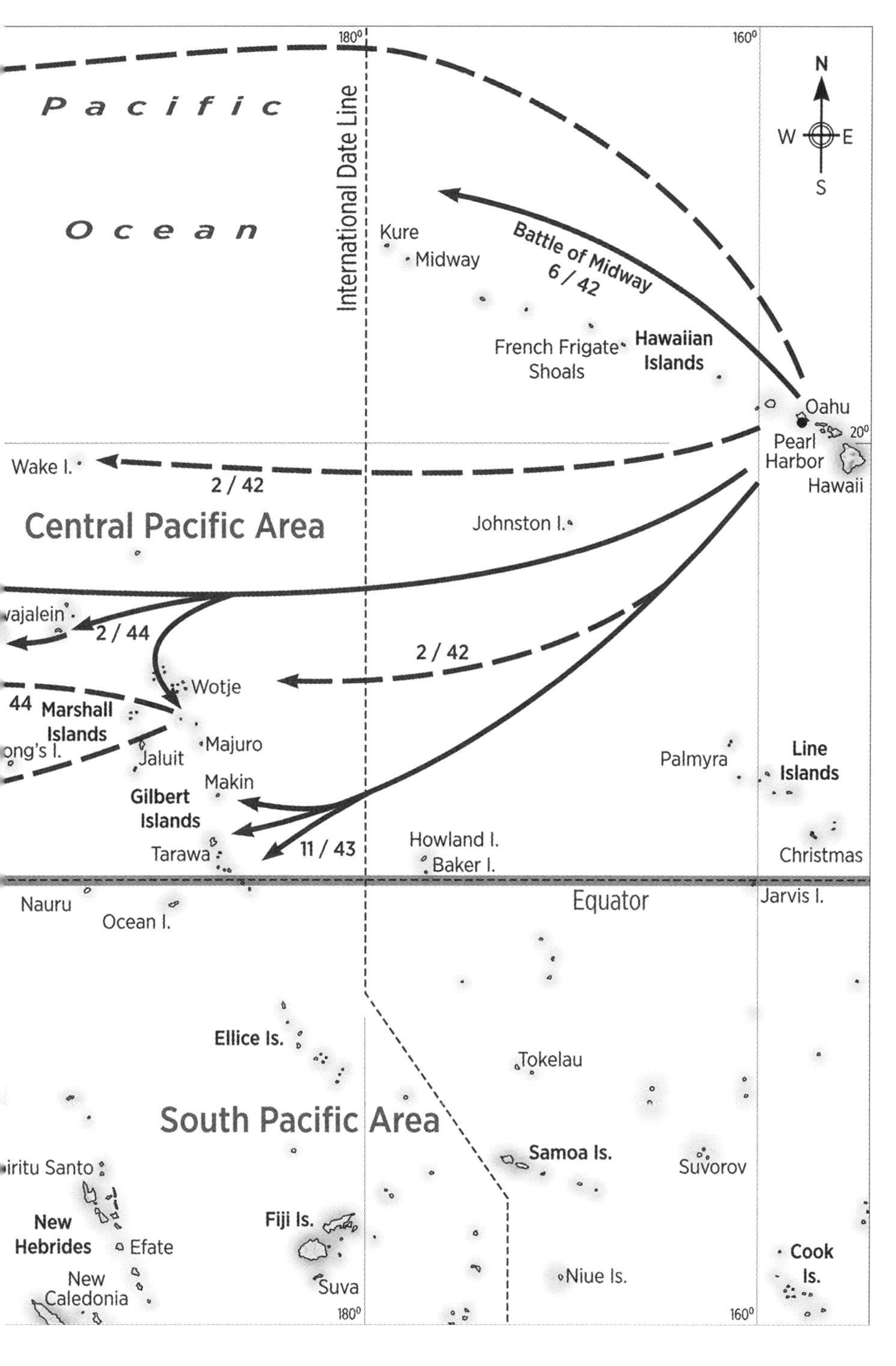
180°
160°
N
W
E
S
Pacific
Ocean
International Date Line
Kure
Midway
Battle of Midway
6 / 42
French Frigate
Shoals
Hawaiian
Islands
Oahu
Pearl
Harbor
20°
Hawaii
Wake I.
2 / 42
Central Pacific Area
Johnston I.
vajalein
2 / 44
2 / 42
Wotje
44
Marshall
Islands
ong's I.
Jaluit
Majuro
Palmyra
Line
Islands
Makin
Gilbert
Islands
Tarawa
11 / 43
Howland I.
Baker I.
Christmas
Nauru
Ocean I.
Equator
Jarvis I.
Ellice Is.
Tokelau
South Pacific Area
Samoa Is.
Suvorov
iritu Santo
New
Hebrides
Efate
Fiji Is.
Cook
Is.
New
Caledonia
Suva
Niue Is.
180°
160°

CHAPTER 1

LEARNING THE ART OF COMMAND

THE EMINENT NAVAL historian George W. Baer said of Adm. Raymond A. Spruance that he "perfectly characterizes Clausewitz's notion of military genius." The military theorist Carl von Clausewitz defined military genius as a harmonious combination of intuition and determination. The first is the product of a superior intellect that, coupled with acquiring knowledge through study and experience, could size up a problem or situation and resolve it almost instantly with the "inward eye," in what Clausewitz terms a *coup d'oeil.* Determination is a product of certain character traits, including courage, ambition, energy, endurance, and self-control, that give the commander the ability to remain cool-headed and take decisive action. Some of these traits could be learned or mastered with practice, but to a certain extent they are also inborn. As will be seen, with his combination of intelligence, knowledge, and courage, Raymond Ames Spruance very much fit the bill.[1]

Regarding command traits, Spruance would later write: "From my experience on the staff of the Naval War College going over the solutions to operations problems, I came to the conclusion that there are a considerable percentage of individuals whose imagination and reasoning power is definitely limited. This type may be a fine officer on the bridge of a ship, but he is unable to solve satisfactorily intricate problems whose solution is not obvious. These officers have what I like to call the tactical type of mind, in contradistinction to the strategical type. The Navy needs both types. Many people have a good combination of these two extremes. I believe the purely strategical type of mind might have great difficulty in making early decisions in a tight situation. The willingness to take responsibility and fight—the sine qua non of command in time of war—is something else again."[2]

Spruance told historian E. B. Potter that he considered himself a better strategist than a tactician. As his victories at the Battle of Midway and again at the Battle of the Philippine Sea demonstrate, he was no mean tactician either. To fully assess Spruance as a commander, it will be instructive to examine the knowledge and experience that he gained in the thirty-five-year period prior to his assuming command in the Pacific War, first learning the art of command as a junior officer and commander of destroyers and then the art of war during his many years at the Naval War College and participation in the interwar Fleet Problems exercises. His path to command began much as that of all his fellow admirals: through the portals of the United States Naval Academy at Annapolis, Maryland. But why did Spruance choose the Navy as his career path? The explanation is somewhat prosaic and is very much related to the finances of the Spruance family.

Raymond Ames Spruance was born in Baltimore, Maryland, the hometown of his mother Annie Ames Hiss Spruance, on 3 July 1886. She and the infant Raymond returned to Indianapolis, where she subsequently gave birth to two more boys, the youngest of whom had severe mental handicaps. Unable to cope with all three children, she sent young Raymond to live with her family, who had now relocated to South Orange, New Jersey, where Annie's three unmarried sisters raised him in the large Hiss household. There, Raymond was lavished with attention by his aunts. Spruance returned their love by supporting the spinster sisters out of his Navy pay for many years thereafter.

A gifted student, Spruance did well in school and, as an adolescent, was sent back to his parents' home in Indianapolis, where he graduated from high school in 1902. Spruance's father, Alexander, was a quiet and unassuming man, unsuccessful in business. Annie Spruance largely supported the family, working as an editor for the Bobbs-Merrill publishing house. Though not college-educated, Annie was well-read, intellectual, and a very social person. Unable to afford a private college education for her son, she was not shy about using her social and political connections, and through these she obtained an appointment for young Raymond to the Naval Academy.

Spruance reported to the United States Naval Academy on 2 July 1903, one day before his seventeenth birthday. If he could withstand the rigors of the Academy's discipline and maintain an average grade of at least 2.5 on a scale of 4.0, Spruance would graduate as a Passed Midshipman in June 1907. The midshipmen entered as "plebes" in the First Year, Fourth Class, and graduated in the Fourth Year, First Class. The midshipmen in each class all took the same subjects at the same time according to a strict schedule. Daily life was highly regimented, and the combination of tough academic standards and strict military discipline meant that more than a few aspiring naval officers "bilged," that is, were dismissed before graduation. The goal of the academy was not to pursue knowledge for its own sake or produce academicians, but to produce junior officers who obeyed their superiors without question and who could always be trusted to be loyal and honest, to do the right thing and do that thing right. At sea, whether combating an enemy or the forces of nature, nothing less would do.[3]

Thanks to his academic acumen, Spruance was consistently ranked in the upper third of his class and finished fifty-fourth out of 223 students at the end of his Fourth Year. His class of 1907 had started with 313 plebes, for an attrition rate of nearly 30 percent. While Spruance did well within this system, he hated it. He complained later that there was too much memorization and not enough theory. He recalled that once he provided an answer to a complex math problem that was correct but differed from the "book" solution, for which he was given a failing mark. For him, the academy was a necessary rite of passage toward the goal of becoming a commissioned naval officer. He never wanted to return there to teach or even attend a reunion, saying only that "four years had been enough."[4]

Spruance was never selected as an officer in the Brigade of Cadets, nor was he interested in sports, but he made a number of lifelong friends. He enjoyed the annual summer cruises, which gave him a chance to be at sea, which he loved. In the summer cruise of 1904, he sailed aboard the venerable USS *Hartford,* the steam sloop that had been Adm. David Farragut's flagship at the Battle of Mobile Bay some forty years earlier. Aboard *Hartford* that year were upperclassmen Chester W. Nimitz, William Calhoun, John S. McCain Sr., and Frank Jack Fletcher, all of whom rose to flag rank and served with Spruance in the Pacific. It was during these cruises that he acquired the unfortunate moniker of "Sprew," an obvious play on his name and his tendency to become seasick before he had gained his sea legs. Luckily for him, the name did not stick beyond his time at Annapolis.

Spruance was at Annapolis for less than four years, graduating as a Passed Midshipman on 12 September 1906. Being in the upper rank of his class, he was one of eighty-six midshipmen selected for early graduation so that they were immediately available for duty in the growing fleet. Less than two weeks after his graduation, Spruance reported for duty aboard USS *Iowa* (BB 4), a veteran of the Spanish-American War, beginning an apprenticeship of two years at sea before he could be commissioned as an ensign.

Spruance spent the next year in *Iowa* as she cruised the eastern seaboard and the Caribbean and then moved on to USS *Minnesota* (BB 22), carrying out maneuvers and gunnery practice with the Atlantic Fleet. The crew of a commissioned naval vessel, then as now, is divided into departments based on the major functional areas of a warship, such as navigation, weapons, communications, engineering, and others; these are further subdivided into divisions and then watches. All are under the eye of the executive officer, the second highest ranking after the captain. At each level, a junior officer is responsible for the good conduct and efficiency of the enlisted sailors under his authority. Spruance spent his time learning the job of a junior division officer, assisting the lieutenant who commanded the division. His duties did not only include performing the technical operations for which he was trained; he also had to become thoroughly acquainted with the personalities, abilities, and individual quirks of the enlisted men in his division if he expected to get the best performance out of them. It was an important but essential schooling in leadership.

On 16 December 1907, *Minnesota* and fifteen other battleships embarked on a world-spanning cruise known as "the Great White Fleet." Many of the senior officers who later fought the Pacific War were junior officers in one of the ships of this fleet, and the experience had a profound effect on them. They visited many of the ports they would come to know so well in the future, such as San Diego, San Francisco, Pearl Harbor, and Manila, for the first time. In October 1908, Spruance's squadron visited Yokohama, Japan, and he was among the officers invited to an elaborate celebration of mutual goodwill hosted by Admiral Togo Heihachiro, the victor of the Battle of Tsushima, aboard his flagship *Mikasa*. A young William F. Halsey Jr. was not impressed with the diminutive admiral, referring to him later as a "shrimp." Spruance, however, remembered him more fondly and helped preserve *Mikasa* from looting when he was headquartered with the Fifth Fleet at Yokosuka in September 1945 under very different circumstances.[5]

After the return of the Great White Fleet to the United States in February 1909, Spruance spent the next five years in a variety of engineering billets. In September 1911, Spruance sat for examination and was promoted to Lieutenant, Junior Grade. That October, he received orders to report to his next assignment as Senior Engineer in USS *Cincinnati* (CL 7), then at Mare Island, California, bound for duty with the Asiatic Torpedo Boat Flotilla based at Cavite, Philippines. Before he reported to Mare Island, Spruance was granted leave to visit his parents in Indianapolis. This visit home was perhaps the most important in his life, as he became reacquainted there with a lovely young woman destined to become his wife. Margaret Dean was the youngest daughter of a well-to-do family that resided in the same neighborhood as the Spruance family. Her father owned a successful business that built heavy-duty industrial pumps. She was attractive and athletic, enjoyed playing tennis and golf, and was educated at Lake Erie College in Ohio. They had first met when Spruance came home on leave during his plebe year when she was sixteen, but it was not until Spruance saw her on a tennis court in the autumn of 1911, nearly seven years later, that he resolved to ask her out formally.

Their first date, fittingly enough, was to see a performance of Gilbert and Sullivan's *HMS Pinafore* the night before he was scheduled to leave for the West Coast. She saw in Spruance a handsome, self-confident young man, intelligent, considerate, and thoughtful. He appeared reserved and aloof to some, but she found he had a "heavenly sense of humor," which he reserved for those closest to him. Although not formally engaged, they seemed to have a mutual understanding, and she agreed to wait for his return.[6]

After a year and more of cruising in the Philippines and along the coast of China in *Cincinnati* in March 1913, Spruance received orders to travel to Cavite and assume the command of his first ship, USS *Bainbridge* (DD 1), the Navy's very first destroyer. Spruance was assisted by Ensign Charles J. "Carl" Moore, the chief engineer, a highly intelligent young man who became his lifelong friend. Together, they would be called upon to show resolve, initiative, and no small amount of creativity in keeping this relic of an earlier era a seaworthy and happy ship. As commander, young Spruance was responsible for everything that happened aboard and the integrity and safekeeping of the ship and her people. Should his little ship run aground or otherwise fall victim to the poorly charted waters of the Philippine Archipelago, it would mean a mandatory court-martial. The Navy risked little by placing her in Spruance's hands but might reap great returns later by providing the young officer with an opportunity to show initiative and gain valuable experience. With a well-seasoned quartermaster at the helm, Spruance honed his ship-handling skills and took delight at being at sea aboard a ship of his own.

In May 1914, Spruance, now a lieutenant, was ordered to report to Newport News Shipyard in Virginia for duty as Assistant Inspector of Machinery in connection with the construction and fitting out of USS *Pennsylvania* (BB 38), the U.S. Navy's latest "superdreadnought." Before he reported for duty in Virginia, Spruance took a month's leave to visit his parents in Indianapolis and perform a task that he had been postponing for some time: proposing marriage to Margaret Dean. In his usual thorough fashion, Spruance prepared the ground ahead of time before commencing the operation. He told Margaret what life was like for the wife of a naval officer, giving her reasons in advance to reject his offer. His duty would have to take precedence over all—he could be at sea for months or even years at a time, and he was liable to be moved to a new posting at any time. Almost anywhere the U.S. Navy was, it was far away from Indianapolis. They might not have a permanent home of their own for a very long time. On top of all that, Spruance was sending a significant portion of his pay to support his maiden aunts, meaning married life on a very tight budget. In short, Margaret would not be living in the comfortable surroundings in which she was raised. None of this, however, fazed her, and she accepted his marriage proposal. A date was set for December of that year.[7]

Spruance reported to Newport News Shipyard on 24 July 1914. The keel for *Pennsylvania* had been laid on 13 October 1913, and work on the hull was well underway. Spruance's job would be to inspect and approve the machinery as it arrived from the various subcontractors before it was installed and then test it afterwards. She was launched on 16 March 1915 amid much fanfare, and her fitting out began immediately. The battleships of the early twentieth century were the most complex machines built up to that time, incorporating the latest technology, and *Pennsylvania* was the largest warship yet built by the United States. She had twelve 14-inch main guns, arranged in triples in four turrets, making her the most powerful warship afloat when commissioned in 1916. Unlike some previous ships that Spruance had served on, she was "state of the art" in every way.

Raymond Ames Spruance and Margaret Vance Dean were married in her family's home on 8 December 1914. Spruance was attired in his dress uniform, and his classmate Jonas Ingram was his best man. Ingram was the other midshipman from Indiana in the class of 1907 and he had also married a girl from Indianapolis, but his behavior at the reception gave Margaret's father the impression that "naval officers were just a bunch of drunken bums."[8]

After a honeymoon in Asheville, North Carolina, the newlyweds settled into an apartment in Newport News, a little town that Margaret found "forlorn." Nevertheless, they soon settled into a happy routine. Raymond came home daily for lunch to keep his wife company and reduce their expenses, perhaps an early sign of the self-imposed frugality that would rule his life. Margaret found her husband to be very sweet, unselfish, and affectionate, a hard worker who could also be stubborn when he believed he was in the right. He became more outgoing and relaxed with her, inviting friends from the office to their small apartment for dinner. Upon meeting Margaret for the first time, one complimented her for the change she had wrought on "old Frozen Face."[9]

Margaret quickly became accustomed to the personality traits and habits that would remain Raymond's lifelong proclivities. One was his penchant for long walks to help release stress and nervous energy. Another was his preference for meals including fish and fresh vegetables, followed by dessert and strong coffee. Raised a Presbyterian, Margaret enjoyed attending church, and Spruance would often accompany her, at least at first. He found the preaching to be trite and soon quit attending altogether. Although not a practicing Christian, he read the Bible frequently. Their marriage was happy, and their personalities complemented each other. On 24 October 1915 their first child, Edward Dean Spruance, was born.[10]

The inspecting officer of a newly built ship often remained aboard through commissioning and her first year at sea to help work out any problems that might arise, and Spruance was no exception. During the process of ensuring that the complex fire control apparatus functioned as designed, he became an expert in fire control and gunnery. *Pennsylvania* was commissioned on 20 July 1916 and began sea trials and training exercises immediately. On 12 October 1916, she became the flagship of the Atlantic Fleet, a status befitting the Navy's newest and most powerful battleship. While in *Pennsylvania* one of Spruance's shipmates was Lt. Richmond Kelly Turner, class of 1908, another young officer destined to become a close friend and comrade in arms in the years to come. Turner was the Assistant Gunnery Officer of the ship and an expert in ordinance. He and Spruance worked closely together.

In November 1917, Spruance was assigned to the Bureau of Steam Engineering, with duty at the New York Naval Yard as the senior engineering officer. Thanks to his experience, Spruance was made responsible for the installation of the latest fire control apparatus in the ships of the Atlantic Fleet. In the summer of 1918, Spruance traveled to Scapa Flow, the home of the Royal Navy's Grand Fleet and the U.S. Navy's Sixth Battle Squadron, reporting to Adm. Hugh Rodman aboard his flagship USS *Delaware* (BB 28) on 9 July. His activities there are not recorded, but he likely spent his time coordinating with the Fleet Gunnery Officer and examining the fire control equipment. It was during this period that Spruance told Margaret he had been responsible for designing a device that saved the U.S. Navy tens of thousands of dollars.[11]

Spruance was well rewarded for his good work when he received orders in March 1919 to proceed to the Bath Iron Works in Maine to take command of the newly built USS *Aaron Ward* (DD 132) and complete her fitting out. This was done with his usual efficiency, and she was duly commissioned on 21 April 1919, reporting immediately thereafter for duty with Destroyer Squadron Two of the Atlantic Fleet. After a brief sojourn in the western Mediterranean in September, *Aaron Ward* was ordered to join Destroyer Squadron Four, Division 15 of the Pacific Fleet, stationed at San Diego, California. As her husband and his crew sailed west, Margaret returned to her parents' home in Indianapolis, where she gave birth to their second child, Margaret Ames Spruance, on 19 September 1919.

In October 1919, Spruance's division received a new commander, William F. Halsey Jr., class of 1904. Halsey was senior to Spruance, and their personalities were quite opposite in many respects. Where Spruance was quiet, reserved, and self-effacing, Halsey was loud, gregarious, and given to telling funny, often profane stories. Nevertheless, the two men formed a fast friendship that would last for the rest of their lives. Spruance admired Halsey's seamanship and daring, and as his second in command, he would follow Halsey anywhere. Halsey appreciated Spruance's "electric brain," coolness under pressure, and dry sense of humor.

Margaret and the children had by now joined Raymond, taking up residence in the bustling community of Coronado Island. Bill Halsey and his wife Fanny lived nearby, and the young couples became close, enjoying the life of the "nine to five" Navy of the postwar 1920s. When not at sea, Navy officers could live in their own quarters and enjoy weekends off, entertaining themselves and their friends with picnics, beach parties, dinners, and cocktails. Heavy drinking was endemic; Spruance usually avoided it, but after a rare night of fun in a local tavern, he woke up the next day to find his favorite Panama hat was missing. When he inquired about it, the bar owner pointed to the top of a nearby palm tree. Halsey found this incident extremely amusing and continued to kid Spruance about it for some time.[12]

Spruance and Halsey had great fun putting their fast-moving ships through their paces during high-speed maneuvers and practicing the techniques of laying an effective smokescreen. This new tactical innovation for the Navy could only be reliably done by ships with oil-fired boilers. Instead of the usual three-hundred-yard spacing between ships underway, the distance was reduced to as little as fifty yards to keep the ship ahead somewhat visible in the resulting murk. To avoid serious mishaps, every skipper had to know instinctively how his ship and those of his section mates would react, something that could only be obtained through practice and experience.[13]

A crucial factor in the squadron's success was its ability to work together as a cohesive team. Halsey was a practitioner of the "conference style" of leadership, in which the commander laid out his ideas for an operation with his captains, who then gave their comments and feedback. Options were discussed, and a common plan was devised; in cases of disagreement, the commander made the final call. Every captain knew what was expected and how the plan was supposed to work. However, if an assumption made during planning proved false, they were expected to use their initiative and take action to ensure the plan's intent was achieved. This leadership style suited Spruance and became the cornerstone of his command philosophy in the future.

In the wardroom, Spruance entertained his messmates by introducing them to a variety of "delicacies," one such being the "alligator pear," more commonly known as the avocado, which was abundant in the San Diego area. Once Spruance was comfortable in their company, he displayed a keen wit and gently teased them and tolerated their card playing and occasional drinking to excess. Spruance obtained obedience by example, and his crew responded in kind. He was always loyal to his men, standing up for them if they got in trouble, and captain's masts were infrequent.[14]

In his last Fitness Report on Spruance, Halsey wrote, "Commander Spruance is one of the best all-around officers I have ever served with. He is quiet, efficient, always on the job, and with a clear thinking brain always working. His judgement is excellent and I invariably seek his opinion on any knotty problem. It is a pleasure having an officer of his caliber in my division."[15]

The happy times in Coronado soon came to an end in late June 1921 when Spruance received the order to report to the Chief of the Bureau of Engineering in Washington, DC, a duty that he dreaded. Working under the Chief Engineer, Rear Adm. John K. Robison, Spruance was placed in charge of the acquisition and installation of the vast array of electrical and mechanical gear found aboard a modern warship and made by a variety of contractors. He was often on temporary duty inspecting the fitting-out vessels then under construction, including the battleships USS *Colorado* (BB 45), USS *Maryland* (BB 46), and USS *West Virginia* (BB 48). His expertise in fire control also led to his appointment to a special board considering the problem of employing aircraft as aerial spotters for gunnery. In December 1921, he passed his physical and written examinations and was promoted to commander.[16]

On their Fitness Reports, officers could state a preference for their next assignment. Spruance usually indicated a desire to return to destroyer duty in the Pacific but now began to indicate a desire to attend the Naval War College in Newport, Rhode Island. His boss, Admiral Robison, was a proponent of officers attending the War College and may have influenced Spruance. Robison believed that line officers should have plenty of engineering experience in the first twenty years of their careers before moving on to higher command. Spruance had now reached a point in his career where he did not want to become pigeonholed as an engineering officer. He was indeed ready to move on.[17]

Many young officers left the Navy after World War I due to low pay and poor prospects for future advancement and sought more lucrative careers in business and industry. Spruance considered doing the same, but in March 1923, Margaret's father, Edward Dean, passed away, leaving his daughter a considerable sum. This inheritance alleviated their money woes, and Spruance decided once and for all that he could afford to pursue his naval career. In June 1924, he received orders to report for duty on the staff of Rear Adm. Philip Andrews, Commander, U.S. Naval Forces, Europe, in Cherbourg, France. Spruance was apprehensive about working with Andrews, who had a reputation for being irascible and argumentative. While there was some initial difficulty, this was overcome when Spruance made it clear that he would stand his ground. The Spruances ended up enjoying their time in Europe, where they lived in comfortable quarters, sent young Edward to a French-language boarding school, and engaged an Italian cook. They traveled with the admiral and his wife in France, Spain, and England. Spruance had the opportunity to improve his French skills during official calls. This was Spruance's first duty on a command staff, and Andrews gave him "excellent" ratings on his reports, commenting that Spruance was "a capable conscientious officer of great natural ability—industrious and hard working—of agreeable personality."[18]

In November 1925, Spruance relieved Bill Halsey as commander of USS *Osborne* (DD 295), then in Gibraltar. On his departure, Halsey told the wardroom what to expect from their new commander, warning them not to be fooled by his initial appearance of aloof reserve. With Halsey, the young officers were used to being boisterous and loud. At first they found Spruance to be a bit stiff, but "after things settled down we spotted the twinkle in his eye and soon he was part of the give and take at the table." Though Spruance and Halsey's personalities differed, the wardroom soon saw that "they both had the same warm regard and understanding of their shipmates."[19]

In late May 1926, Spruance finally received the orders he had longed for: to report to the U.S. Naval War College in Newport, Rhode Island, for "duties under instruction." Spruance and the crew of *Osborne* set sail for the New York Navy Yard, arriving there on 11 July 1926. A new phase in his career was about to begin.[20]

CHAPTER 2

LEARNING THE ART OF WAR

THE U.S. NAVAL WAR COLLEGE, located on Coasters Harbor Island in Narragansett Bay near Newport, Rhode Island, was founded in 1884 by Commo. Stephen B. Luce to provide for the professional military education of the officers of the United States Navy. Previously, officers were on their own when it came to educating themselves in the "higher arts" of naval strategy and tactics. Luce recognized that an institution of formal postgraduate education was necessary, especially in an era when the technical details of warships and gunnery were constantly evolving. The education officers received at the Naval Academy placed a heavy emphasis on engineering but gave very little instruction on how senior officers should best employ their marvelous new engines of war.

Spruance reported for duty "in instruction" at the Naval War College on 16 July 1926 as part of the senior class of 1927, consisting of forty-four students, mainly captains and commanders. Upon arrival, the staff distributed a reading list and a memorandum outlining the two primary areas of study for the upcoming year: naval operations and logistics. Spruance enjoyed the challenge of the coursework and the opportunity to read and think without the pressure of other duties. His study there provided intellectual stimulation and the chance to discuss strategy and tactics with his peers, which he could not find elsewhere. He also soon discovered the library, where he had access to a wide range of military thought and analysis.[1]

The class was divided into six committees, each required to study and then produce a report on a specific aspect of an assigned topic. The purpose of this exercise was to prompt students to consider naval strategy from the perspective of a potential adversary, thereby gaining insight into their mindset and methods of warfare. Spruance was assigned to Committee 3, which studied how the Japanese had defeated a numerically superior enemy during the Russo-Japanese War and considered what Japan might do if engaged in a war with the United States. The committee concluded that the Japanese would adhere to a strategy of a sudden surprise attack, working from interior lines, to attack the U.S. Navy's long lines of communication across the Pacific and then engage the weakened American fleet in a decisive battle. The committee concluded that "our lesson from all this is to be ready in peace and war to beat the 'Strike Sudden and Strike Hard' strategy of Japan."[2]

One of the early innovations at the War College was the use of naval war games, using miniature tokens representing warships and played on a scaled game board laid out on the floor of a classroom. In 1912 Capt. W. L. Rogers, the president of the War College, introduced the "Estimate of the Situation with the Order Form," a document that became the foundation of the U.S. Navy's method of military problem-solving before and during World War II. Given a general objective, the Estimate of the Situation provided the practitioner with a clear sequence of steps to solve the problem: first, clearly state the mission to achieve the objective; then analyze the capabilities of both the enemy's and one's own forces; and finally arrive at a decision on the best means and methods of completing the mission. The plan for obtaining the objective then had to be written in the Order Form format. Students used this rubric to solve a series of problems set by the War College staff, writing their operational plans and then testing them on the game board, with the staff observing and providing a critique. This activity could take days of meticulous setup and gameplay. The clarity and logical sequence of this methodology especially appealed to Spruance.[3]

A perennial problem that every class at the War College considered during the interwar period was the execution of War Plan Orange, the Navy's plan for a war with Japan. First conceived in 1907, it was continuously updated and modified. Plan Orange envisioned the necessity of seizing islands west of Hawaii as bases for American naval forces advancing from the east. The issue became more complicated after World War I when Japan was granted a mandate over the former German colonies in the Central Pacific. The so-called Mandate Islands, the Marshalls and

Carolines in particular, were identified as crucial for establishing advanced bases from which the U.S. Pacific Fleet could operate.[4]

Of particular interest is Operations Problem II-27, which examined how the forces of Blue (the United States) should respond to the actions of Orange (Japan) in the event of a war in the Western Pacific. The class was divided in late October into committees playing either Blue or Orange and had until the following March to study the problem and present their solutions. Spruance was assigned to the Orange team, which gave him valuable insight into how the Japanese might conduct a campaign to defeat an American fleet that was numerically superior. The Washington Naval Treaty, signed in 1922, imposed a ten-year moratorium on new capital ship construction and required the signatories to limit the total tonnage of such ships based on a ratio of 5:5:3, with the United States and Great Britain being equal and Japan limited to 60 percent. This meant that in a war against either Anglo-Saxon power, the Imperial Japanese Navy would have fewer battleships. At such a numerical disadvantage, their fleet was likely doomed to defeat unless they could even the odds before a decisive battle. With this in mind, the solution that the Orange team worked out was to establish air bases on the islands of the Central Pacific to weaken the Blue fleet as it moved west. The Orange fleet strength was concentrated at Truk, a large atoll in the Carolines, and at an opportune moment they would sortie and then engage the Blue fleet in a decisive battleship encounter in the western Pacific. The concept of a decisive battle was consistent with the strategy adopted by the Japanese Imperial Navy and was one to which they adhered for most of World War II. The correlation and relevance of this exercise to Spruance's campaigns in the Central Pacific is remarkable.[5]

In early January 1927, Col. Robert H. Dunlap, USMC, commander of the Marine School at Quantico, Virginia, gave the senior class a lecture based on the work of Maj. Earl H. Ellis, USMC, whose *Advanced Base Operations in Micronesia* was the first major study of amphibious warfare in the coral atolls and volcanic islands of the Central Pacific. Dunlap's lecture identified the very elements that were eventually vital to the success of the U.S. Navy's amphibious operations in the Pacific War: intense training of the landing forces, offshore naval gunfire support, the use of aircraft for bombing and strafing the defenders, and above all the need to create advanced bases to establish secure lines of communications.[6]

Students in the senior class were also required to write two papers: one on "Policy" and the other on "Command." In his paper on command, Spruance emphasized the importance of the chain of command, noting that freedom of action decreases as a commander advances through the ranks. They can delegate authority to subordinates but never responsibility. The orders given to subordinates must be clear and in harmony with directives given to others. There should be a common system of doctrine and training, as doctrine without training was useless; therefore, practical experience in the application of doctrine was a must. Spruance wrote that to be successful, a commander must combine leadership qualities with knowledge of his profession. Leadership was comprised of certain moral qualities: force, initiative, a strong sense of justice, good judgment, generosity, self-possession, energy, decisiveness, and above all, loyalty—loyalty to not only the nation and the Navy but to both subordinates and superior officers. Loyalty engendered reciprocal loyalty and, in a crisis, would be rewarded by men willing to do the near impossible. According to Spruance, "it requires both the moral qualities and the brains and knowledge to make a great leader. Both may be improved by application, study, and reflection." For Spruance, great leaders are made as least as much by self-improvement as innate genius.

Spruance also discussed the importance of a good staff for planning, writing, and executing orders. He believed the commander's staff should not exceed ten individuals, as anything larger made it difficult for a commander to provide personal guidance. If the commander's staff required more help, it would have to be provided by delegation to their own or other lower-echelon staff. This idea became a central tenet of Spruance's philosophy of command.[7]

In October 1929, Spruance reported for duty as the executive officer of USS *Mississippi* (BB 41), homeported in San Pedro, California. Such a posting was a real plum as there were but sixteen battleships in the U.S. Navy, and this kind of duty was a prerequisite for any officer who wanted to command one, as Spruance most certainly did. "Ole Miss," as she was nicknamed, was a *New Mexico*–class superdreadnought commissioned in December 1917. She was one of the "standard-type" battleship designs, having an "all or nothing" armor citadel protecting the ship's machinery, her magazines, and the plotting room, the combat nerve center located deep in the bowels of the ship. Spruance was entirely at home aboard his new billet, having fitted out four previous ships of similar design. The real challenge came from dealing with a crew of more than one thousand enlisted and fifty-five officers, nearly ten times the size found in his previous destroyer commands.[8]

The executive officer is the second in command of a warship, and it has been said that while the "Ex-O" runs the ship, the captain runs his executive officer. By all accounts, Spruance got on well with his commander, Capt. Harry L. Brinser, class of 1899. Brinser had been at the Battle of Santiago, still a cadet-midshipman, and was awarded the Navy Cross for his service during World War I. Barring any mishaps during his tenure as captain, he was in a position to be promoted to flag rank at the conclusion of the ship's commission. Having climbed so close to the pinnacle of a naval career made some captains extraordinarily nervous and fearful of any "screw-up" that could jeopardize their ascension. This fear could make life hell for their executive officer. Captain Brinser, however, was not a worrier and saw in Spruance a calm competence and capability that he could depend upon. As one shipmate put it, they worked "hand in glove." Thanks in no small part to Spruance, "Ole Miss" was a happy ship with high morale and achievement.[9]

Discipline and good order in a warship started at the top with the officers, and Cdr. Raymond A. Spruance was the model of self-discipline and naval bearing. He was strict but never unfair. Criticism was done in private, and Spruance never raised his voice. He was described as having a natural dignity and reserve that discouraged familiarity; hence he was seen as "aloof" and "stand-offish" by some. On the other hand, he was readily accessible and friendly with those officers who came to him for advice and counsel, creating some lasting friendships, especially with those who joined Spruance for long walks on deck during the first watch when they carried on lengthy conversations about the naval profession and human nature.[10]

Spruance at this time was still very much a "black shoe" line officer, that is, a member of the "gun club" of battleship proponents that the "brown shoe" naval aviation officers saw as old-fashioned, looking to refight the Battle of Jutland. For the small but growing cadre of aviation officers, the future of naval warfare was to be found in the air. From the perspective of the "gun club," however, the purpose of naval aviation was to be the eyes of the battlefleet: to spot the enemy first and then direct naval gunfire on his ships from over the horizon. If bombers managed to whittle away some of the opposing fleet's gun power, so much the better, but aircraft carriers were still seen as the handmaidens of the battle line.

This was the verdict reached at the conclusion of Fleet Problems X and XI, which occurred in March and April of 1930. Instituted in 1923, the annual "Fleet Problem" tested the theories of War Plan Orange and the results of the War College's simulations using naval maneuvers at sea. The existing fleet was divided into opposing forces, often augmented by "notional" forces that existed only on paper. In Problem X, the forces of Black, a coalition of European naval powers, sought to wrest control of the Caribbean from Blue, the United States. The Blue fleet, consisting of the seven newest battleships, the carriers USS *Langley* (CV 1) and USS *Saratoga* (CV 3), and a collection of cruisers and destroyers, sailed east through the Panama Canal from the West Coast. The Black Fleet, composed of the seven oldest battleships, including *Mississippi* and the carrier USS *Lexington* (CV 2), moved from north of Haiti and sailed west to meet the Blue Fleet. The exercise aimed to refine the battle tactics of two roughly equal fleets, explore the use of light forces in scouting, and experience operations in a tropical climate.[11]

This exercise placed carriers in independent task groups ahead of the battle line. *Lexington*'s scouts found Blue's carriers just west of Haiti on the third day. Some *Lexington* bombers were already spotted and their subsequent strike resulted in the referees ruling *Saratoga* and *Langley* hit and disabled, leaving Black with control of the air. Subsequently, Black's bombers "damaged" three of Blue's battleships with their 30-pound bombs. With an advantage in guns and the ability to deploy aerial spotters, the Black battle line overwhelmed and defeated the Blue battle line. Several features of future naval battles were apparent: the value of detaching carriers into fast, independent task groups and the paramount importance of finding and striking the enemy first. During these Fleet Problems, Spruance had a front-row seat to witness how the Navy explored, refined, and developed its tactical doctrine.

In March 1931, *Mississippi* headed east to the Norfolk Navy Yard, where she arrived for a major refit and modernization. Spruance left "Ole Miss" in Norfolk on 7 June and reported for duty on the staff of the Naval War College with the assignment to run the Correspondence Course, an early version of what is now termed "distance learning." The course focused on the study of strategy and tactics, and successful completion depended largely on a student's self-motivation and ability to concentrate on the assignments while also performing their day jobs as serving officers. Although Spruance had an assistant, he found himself busy reorganizing the course to his satisfaction and then evaluating and grading the work submitted. Spruance put a lot of effort into the course but was disappointed that some students were not giving it their best efforts. Some may have had duties light enough to allow successful completion, while others, such as Spruance's old shipmate Charles J. Moore, may have found that their dedication to their primary jobs prevented them from completing the course.[12]

Despite such occasional disappointments, Spruance very much enjoyed his second stint at the War College, as it allowed him time to concentrate on his study of war in an atmosphere of collegiality among officers who were, for the most part, genuinely interested in the subject. As part of the teaching staff, Spruance commented on and assisted with the problems being played out on the game board. These continued to include lessons from the Battle of Jutland. When Spruance took the Senior Course in 1927, the battle, then just ten years old, was becoming less relevant due to the introduction of new technologies in the form of vastly improved radio communications and aircraft. Arguably this was even more the case in 1932, but the idea of the exercise was not how to refight Jutland per se, but how *not* to fight a major battle-line engagement. The British Grand Fleet had had numerical superiority, a superior tactical position, and an element of surprise, yet failed to achieve a decisive result. This was understood to be due to a combination of poor communications and a lack of initiative by Admiral Sir John Jellicoe's subordinates. The U.S. Navy intended to inculcate in its officers a doctrine that emphasized aggressive action and individual initiative: they would know how to act even if they were not receiving directions from the fleet commander.

The War College's class of 1933 included two captains who were destined to have a significant influence on Spruance's future career: Ernest J. King and William F. Halsey Jr. It is not surprising then that a highly ambitious officer like King, himself a proponent of advanced officer education and a prior graduate of the Correspondence Course, eagerly sought a place in the senior class of 1933. Coming off his brilliant stint as commander of *Lexington*, he had much tactical acumen to contribute to solving the problems that the staff had set forth. Likewise, Bill Halsey was attracted to War College as a savvy career move and entered the junior class of 1933.[13]

Spruance and Margaret were delighted to have their old friends Bill Halsey and his wife Fran in Newport, and they socialized regularly. Halsey was always known as "Billy" to them, and Margaret was particularly fond of his affection for the Spruance children. Despite his gruff exterior on the bridge of a ship, he was a warm, thoughtful man among his good friends. Their families became entwined when Lou Spruance, Raymond's cousin and a successful executive with the DuPont Corporation, married Halsey's daughter, also named Margaret, in the chapel of the Naval Academy in June 1932.[14]

In early May 1932, Spruance easily passed the professional examination for captain, to which grade he was officially promoted on 6 July 1932. In Spruance's Fitness Report for 1933 Adm. Harris Laning, the president of the War College, wrote, "Captain Spruance is an officer of superior intelligence, excellent judgement, and high military character. He is a sound strategist and tactician. He has performed his duties in charge of the Correspondence Course in a highly satisfactory manner. With further experience he will be well suited for flag rank and I recommend him for selection and promotion when due."[15]

On that Fitness Report, Spruance indicated a preference that his next duty assignment be in command of a ship with the Battle Force (formerly known as the Battle Fleet). Spruance was ordered instead to report by 31 May 1933 to the Commander, Destroyers, Scouting Force, to be the chief of staff. While he might have been disappointed at not having a ship to command, as chief of staff his work placed him at a higher level of command, writing operational plans and training schedules for one of the largest destroyer forces in the world. Acting as the watchdogs of the surface fleet, the destroyers of the Scouting Force looked for signs of the enemy's fleet, warned of attacking aircraft, and hunted enemy submarines looking for a kill. It turned out to be a valuable move for him.

Spruance's new boss, Rear Adm. Adolphus E. Watson, was reputed to be difficult to work with, but Spruance found him personable and easygoing, perhaps a bit too easygoing as Watson quickly delegated most of the administrative chores and operational planning to him. Spruance enjoyed the freedom from interference and could often be found working long hours, standing at a drafting table and doing his paperwork. Spruance preferred to work while standing, as it freed him to pace the room and think, discouraging visitors from staying long and distracting him with useless chitchat. If you wanted to engage Spruance in a discussion, the best way was to accompany him on one of his long walks.[16]

In the spring of 1934, the Battle Force moved east to engage in the next Fleet Problem, Number XV. Aboard Watson's flagship USS *Raleigh* (CL 7), Spruance had an active hand in planning one of the most intense fleet problems to date, an experience he put to good effect as Nimitz's chief of staff eight years later. Naval air superiority again played a crucial role, and the analysis of the exercise recommended that if carriers were to become the offensive weapon their proponents envisioned, then dive bombers needed to carry a heavier payload of 500- and 1,000-pound bombs to be truly effective. The Battle Force spent the next six months on the East Coast before returning to California, one of the longest deployments in the interwar period. In his Fitness Report, Watson was effusive, describing Spruance as "an outstanding officer. As chief of staff, he displayed exceptional administrative abilities. Well qualified for command. Will be exceptionally well qualified for promotion when due."[17]

On the same Fitness Report, Spruance indicated that his preference for his next duty assignment was at the Naval Mine Depot located in Yorktown, Virginia. This was an unusual request, as he typically preferred sea duty. The explanation was that he wanted to be close to Annapolis and his son Edward, who had secured an appointment to the Naval Academy. His wife Margaret was looking forward to moving into comfortable government quarters for a change and had already measured the windows for new curtains. Spruance was surprised and maybe a little disappointed when his orders instead sent him back to the Naval War College once more. This may have been at the request of Adm. Edward C. Kalbfus, the new president of the War College, who had also been a member of the class of 1927 and had been impressed with Spruance.[18]

It turned out to be a blessing in disguise, as Spruance was joined by two friends upon whom he came to rely heavily during his tenure as commander of the Fifth Fleet: Capt. Richmond Kelly Turner and Cdr. Charles "Carl" J. Moore. Besides Turner and Moore, staff included Robert A. "Fuzzy" Theobald, Milo F. Draemel, Robert L. Ghormley, and Aubrey W. Fitch, officers that Spruance knew from his Annapolis days and who later served with him in the Pacific War. The new assignment gave Spruance nearly three years to think about and study naval warfare with some of the most intelligent and talented officers in the U.S. Navy.

These years also witnessed an inexorable movement toward another world war. When Spruance arrived at the War College in April 1935, the world was still at peace, at least as far as the United States was concerned. The Second Sino-Japanese War was still a year away, but the Imperial Japanese Army was carefully pursuing its long-term strategy to dominate Northeast Asia, known as *hokushin*, or "northward advance." This stood in stark contrast to the Imperial Navy's strategy of *nanshin*, or "southward advance" into what was loosely termed the "south seas," as the means to ensure Japan's security. These fundamental and long-held policy differences led to a vicious interservice rivalry for material and financial resources and eventually to a competition for political control that later seriously undermined Japan's ability to wage war.[19]

When Rear Admiral Kalbfus arrived at the War College the previous year, he decided to combine the "Estimate of Situation and Order Form" with his own treatise on the theory of war, a distillation of Clausewitz's *On War*, into a comprehensive document entitled *Sound Military Decision*. When Spruance and Theobald arrived in late spring 1935, Kalbfus tasked them with reviewing it and making suggestions for improvement before the class of 1936 convened in July. Critiquing the cherished work of one's immediate superior is seldom an amenable assignment, to say the least. Spruance found the sections that Kalbfus had written to be an unnecessary clutter of "words, words, words" that obfuscated rather than clarified a most important subject—how to think clearly to analyze a situation, arrive at a "sound decision" for action, and then write orders to see that the action is carried through to a successful end. Spruance did not pull any punches in his review. If Spruance's candor about *Sound Military Decision* bothered Kalbfus, it was not evident in his evaluation of Spruance on his Fitness Reports for the period, as Kalbfus gave Spruance uniformly excellent marks and described him as "a very intelligent, conscientious officer of the superior type. A clear and independent thinker with a strong character. Always willing and cheerful. Fine personal and professional character. Well qualified for promotion."[20]

Spruance taught Tactics and Minor Strategy to the junior class of 1936, Tactics to the senior class of 1937, and advanced to be the head of the Department of Operations for 1938. In his lectures on Tactics to the senior class of 1937, Spruance quoted Clausewitz, Jomini, Mahan, and Corbett, among others, on the subject of objectives and the employment of force in attaining them. He stressed the importance of correctly selecting the primary objective, citing the example of a mission to intercept an escorted convoy. In this case it is the convoy and not the escorts that should be the object, foreshadowing another of his command tenets, that the assigned mission always takes precedence. Spruance told his students, "The most important thing in obtaining tactical success is *superiority*; to be superior to the enemy at the decisive point." This, too, remained one of his basic command philosophies.[21]

Kelly Turner had been in the senior class of 1937, and his performance was so strong that he was asked to join the staff to teach Strategy to the senior class in 1938. He and Spruance made an impressive teaching team. Vice Adm. George H. Fort recalled many years later that the duo put him and the other students of the senior class through the wringer: "Spruance and his right-hand man Kelly Turner *were* the Naval War College. . . . They worked our pants off. It was the hardest year I ever spent. Turner corrected every Estimate of the Situation and final Decision with red ink, or pencil, and his caustic comments saturated it."[22]

Their teaching styles reflected their personalities. One of Spruance's students recalled that he "was an excellent instructor. Quiet and courteous, he had answers, reasons, and patience. You had to like him. . . . We always listened to him because he made you think." Another recalled that "Spruance demanded and received respect. He was always ready to make a decision in handling our problems on and off the game board. . . . Students recognized this brilliant tactician and officer."[23]

Margaret Spruance recalled that their last three years in Newport before the war were some of the most enjoyable of their married life. The Spruances socialized with their friends the Moores and the Turners, who lived nearby, and exchanged calls with the other staff officers and students. Spruance could relax, walk and swim for exercise, and study without the pressure of command or an overbearing superior officer. Their son Edward graduated from Annapolis in June 1937, finishing with a respectable class rank of 88 out of 323. Their daughter Margaret left home to attend Vassar College later that fall. When Spruance escorted young Margaret to a waiting car, she was surprised to see tears in his eyes, a rare and unexpected display of emotion.[24]

However, this chapter of their lives came to a close when, in the spring of 1938, Spruance received orders to report back to the Battle Force, San Pedro, California, to take command of *Mississippi*, a ship he knew well and loved. Spruance's nearly eight years at the Naval War College had given him a deep intellectual understanding of the art and science of naval warfare, which was complemented by his experience in the annual Fleet Problems. When faced by a resourceful and intelligent enemy, this proved to be of inestimable value.

CHAPTER 3

REAR ADMIRAL SPRUANCE

DURING THE INTERWAR PERIOD, the road to flag rank crossed the bridge of a battleship. Spruance was well on his way to this goal when, on 20 April 1938, he relieved Captain F. L. Reichmuth and once more crossed the quarterdeck of *Mississippi*, this time to assume command. She had come out of her modernization program much transformed from when Spruance had last trod her decks. Sturdy tower masts incorporating a new bridge and mounting fire-control directors replaced her distinctive cage masts. Additional armor and underwater protection against torpedoes had been added, and her gun mounts were modified to increase the range of her 14-inch guns. Her engines and boilers had been replaced, and new amenities, such as a cafeteria-style galley with an ice cream machine, improved habitability. And there was something else entirely new: recently installed radio direction-finding equipment mounted on her foredeck that hinted at a new age of electronic warfare to come.[1]

The years before the Pearl Harbor attack witnessed the apogee of the battleship era of the U.S. Navy. *Mississippi* was part of Battleship Division 3 (BATDIV 3) of the Battle Force, homeported at San Pedro, California, a suburb of the growing city of Los Angeles. The fleet of battleships, cruisers, and auxiliaries rode at anchor in neat rows behind the Los Angeles Harbor breakwater, which had been extended recently to provide better protection from attacks from the sea. Rear Adm. John D. Wainwright commanded the three ships of BATDIV 3 aboard his flagship USS *Idaho* (BB 42). The other ship in the division was USS *New Mexico* (BB 40). All three were of the same class: improved versions of *Pennsylvania*, identical in size (33,000 tons), speed (twenty-one knots), and firepower. Together with three other battleship divisions, they formed the backbone of the interwar navy, the battle line of the U.S. Fleet.

The officers and men of *Mississippi* had heard rumors that their new skipper was a cold fish. They encountered something much different: a man of above average height, lean and fit, whose calm, gray eyes locked onto yours, sizing you up. He was a man of few words but whose every word conveyed his intelligence and self-confidence. He smiled seldom but exhibited a dry wit; as always, the sparkle in his eye betrayed his true feelings. Spruance was not one to fraternize, but he was always approachable and friendly. He made an immediate and positive impression on his crew. When Spruance first inspected his division, one junior officer instinctively reached out for a friendly handshake instead of saluting. Spruance returned the handshake and thought nothing of such a serious breach of protocol.[2]

Spruance ran a taut but happy ship. He was a stern but fair disciplinarian, and captain's masts for serious infractions were few and far between. As in his previous commands, Spruance engaged with his crew with mutual respect. He knew the details of the ship's engineering plant, hull, and armaments as few others did, and if need be, he patiently explained how some apparatus worked or how some evolution could be improved. Spruance demanded that everything be kept in top condition, and an inspection by the captain could be a real cause for anxiety for a junior officer.

One such occasion occurred when Spruance and an inspection party arrived in the powder-handling room at the base of one of "Ole Miss'" turrets. Robert J. Oliver, the young lieutenant responsible for that zone, suggested that he and the captain should do the inspection, leaving the rest below. The path to the gun house from the lowest handling room involved climbing a series of rung ladders, hand over hand, passing through shell and powder-bag handling platforms and electric machinery spaces, past the huge gearing that turned the turrets and elevated the three 14-inch guns, through flash-proof hatches, up four deck levels, for a distance of nearly forty feet before finally reaching the gun house. The lieutenant had perhaps thought that a middle-aged captain might politely decline such an offer, but he hadn't counted on the fact that his captain kept himself in top physical condition. The lieutenant kept a rapid pace, thinking he could put the Old Man through the wringer, but Spruance deftly followed his lead, sometimes crawling on hands and knees, finally exiting through a trap door in the turret's rear overhang and onto the weather deck. While Spruance emerged "fresh as a daisy," the lieutenant, thirty years his junior, was "one whipped puppy." Spruance thanked him for a fine job and strode off smartly for his cabin while Oliver headed for a shower.[3]

One former ensign recalled how Spruance came onto the bridge and quietly observed those standing watch, seldom interfering or finding it necessary to give orders. By comparison, the previous captain had spent most of his time on the bridge, nervous that something was about to go wrong. "When (Spruance) took command, the atmosphere in the ship turned from fog to bright sunshine. . . . Everyone appeared to relax and become interested in doing his job. (Spruance) took over the ship like it was his life's project. Everyone appeared delighted that this C.O. knew exactly what he was doing."[4]

The Battle Force began concentrating in the Caribbean on 1 February 1939 for Fleet Problem XX, an exercise to demonstrate the Navy's ability to defend American interests in the Caribbean and Central America. The scenario for the exercise was that a pro-fascist coup had occurred in "Green," a Latin American country clearly intended to represent Brazil, and a European power, "White," was sending warships to the Caribbean in support of the insurgents. "Black," the United States, was tasked with defending against the incursion and preventing an invasion of Puerto Rico. Spruance explained the goals of the exercise and BATDIV 3's part in the operation as he always did before fleet maneuvers, returning to the role of teacher. One of his officers recalled that "the operations plans were discussed at length with the Captain doing most of the talking. . . . It was the best instruction of this nature that I experienced during my naval career."[5]

Two of Spruance's old bosses commanded the opposing fleets, with Adm. Edward C. Kalbfus in command of White and Adm. Adolphus Andrews in command of the Black forces. Vice Adm. Ernest J. King, once more flying his flag aboard *Lexington,* commanded the White carrier force, while Bill Halsey, as his subordinate, commanded Carrier Division 2 (CARDIV 2), consisting of the carriers *Yorktown* and *Enterprise.*

The Black force had only one carrier, USS *Ranger* (CV 4), but boasted a considerable force of PBY scout seaplanes and land-based Marine aircraft.[6]

Both commanders made air attack and achieving air superiority the central strategy of their plans. Beginning on 20 February, the fight primarily pitted the surface and aerial scouting forces of the two fleets against each other. Kalbfus released King to operate his carriers as an offensive task force independent of the battle line. However, on 24 February, a force of PBYs led by Capt. Marc Mitscher located *Lexington* and "damaged" her with scores of hits. The next day *Ranger*, using her top secret radio direction-finding equipment, located *Enterprise* and launched a successful strike, "sinking" her. Notably, the two battle lines never engaged before the exercise was halted.

Fleet Problem XX reinforced the lessons from earlier exercises in the use of carrier aviation as a major offensive element in fleet tactics. It also reinforced the importance of locating the enemy and striking first, as well as the fact that land-based aircraft posed a serious threat. Although he was not an aviator, Spruance recognized the potential for naval aviation to be a game changer, and showed genuine interest in the rapid advances in aviation technology. His aviation officer, Clifford H. Duerfeldt, had been a test pilot for multiengine flying boats. Whenever Duerfeldt wanted additional flight time, he was sent to Spruance to ask permission. He always found Spruance standing at his desk as usual, and on each occasion, Spruance discussed aviation with him at length. Duerfeldt recalled, "Knowing that I had been in the testing game and was familiar with all of the latest aircraft either flying or on the drawing boards, he picked my brains. Before long, I felt that he knew all I knew about the capabilities of all current aircraft."[7]

After Fleet Problem XX, *Mississippi* traveled north for a fleet review in New York City before returning to the West Coast. The Battle Force spent the summer and fall of 1939 exercising tactical formations, conducting gunnery drills off San Clemente Island or cruising the eastern Pacific and out to Hawaii. When at sea, Spruance continued to engage in his preferred exercise by walking the foredeck, usually in the company of the officer of the deck. In the tropics, he escaped the heat of his cabin by sleeping on the quarterdeck next to the aircraft catapults. In the morning, Spruance prepared his own coffee, first grinding the fresh roasted beans himself and then brewing a potent concoction using a small four-cup Silex vacuum percolator, which required careful timing to get the drink just right. He then offered a cup to anyone who wished for something stronger than the usual Navy drink.[8]

War was now raging in Europe following the German invasion of Poland on 1 September 1939. The Third Reich had been busy rebuilding its navy, the Kriegsmarine, and its new U-boats and surface raiders roamed the Atlantic, attacking British and Allied shipping. The dramatic Battle of the River Plate in December 1939 and the subsequent scuttling of the pocket battleship *Graf Spee* outside Montevideo Harbor added to the growing fear that the interwar scenarios of a hostile European power meddling in the Western Hemisphere had been all too plausible.

Fleet Problem XX also revealed the need for improved facilities for aircraft and warships in the Caribbean. Mitscher's PBY seaplanes had been dependent on tenders for refueling and maintenance. The Marine aviation facility on Culebra was little more than a dirt airstrip. There were no drydocks or fuel storage facilities for the surface fleet. The Roosevelt administration's remedy was to launch a major program of public works and naval infrastructure construction in Puerto Rico to reinforce America's strategic posture in the Caribbean and improve the lives of the territory's citizens by providing them with good-paying jobs. By 1943, the planned work had created the largest naval facility outside the continental United States.[9]

Late in 1939, Spruance received a letter from Rear Adm. Chester W. Nimitz, now the head of the Bureau of Navigation, inquiring whether he was interested in being the commandant of the soon-to-be-reactivated Tenth Naval District, with headquarters in San Juan, Puerto Rico. An assignment to head a naval district was usually reserved for a rear admiral, one headed into the waning years of his career. Spruance had already been selected for flag rank, but in those prewar days the number of flag billets was limited, and he could not ascend to the rank of rear admiral until someone with more seniority retired or died. Despite his dislike for hot climates, Spruance recognized the importance of this assignment and accepted Nimitz's offer. He knew that the Navy and the president had a keen interest in developing new bases in the Caribbean and would be watching the project closely. Adm. William D. Leahy, previously the Chief of Naval Operations (CNO), had recently been appointed governor of the territory and was already in San Juan, a fact that may have also influenced his decision.[10]

On 30 October 1939, the Bureau of Docks and Yards awarded the contract to construct Naval Air Station San Juan on a 340-acre site on Isla Grande, located west of the old city and across the San Antonio Canal, utilizing the small airport previously built by Pan American Airways. Most of the island consisted of tidal mudflats and mangrove swamps, hardly suitable ground for a major air base. The proposed expansion was built using fill material dredged from the adjacent canal and harbor to prepare the area for the construction of a 5,400 by 500-foot runway, hangars, workshops, and seaplane ramps. A large housing area and a naval hospital were also slated for construction, but first additional clean fill had to be trucked into the site, spread, and compacted. Owing to the very poor deep-soil conditions, the site experienced repeated consolidation and settlement, requiring every structure, including underground utility lines, to be built on driven pile foundations.

Spruance arrived in San Juan on 22 February 1940 to assume command of the Tenth Naval District. After settling in and getting acquainted with the massive project, he was less than pleased. He found the entire concept of building on a swamp to avoid taking sugar plantation land out of production offensive and a massive waste of money. While the land had cost the Navy practically nothing, the development cost was five to ten times the cost of purchasing more suitable ground. But as he had no say in the matter, Spruance got on with the work. On the plus side, Spruance quickly learned the ins and outs of major base construction, which he later found very useful. He soon discovered that he had a major asset on his staff in the form of Cdr. Harold W. Johnson, CEC, the Officer in Charge of Construction (OICC). Technically, as the OICC, Johnson did not answer to Spruance but to his boss, Rear Adm. Ben Moreell, CEC, the Bureau of Yards and Docks chief, and the head civil engineer of the Navy. However, in Spruance Johnson found another like-minded engineer and an able administrator with whom he was pleased to work in close collaboration. Spruance, Johnson later recalled, "was an entirely practical thinker and often went on reconnaissance of the swamps and rough country to select sites and on inspection of the work in progress. He was truly an 'Engineer's Admiral' and was able to see our problems as we did."[11]

In early January 1941, Adm. Ernest J. King, slated to become the new commander of the revived U.S. Atlantic Fleet, invited Spruance to observe the upcoming Fleet Landing Exercise, FLEX 7, to be staged from 22 January through 10 February. The exercise was led by Brig. Gen. Holland M. Smith, USMC, commander of the newly created First Marine Division. FLEX 7 demonstrated several innovations in amphibious operations that were eventually used throughout the Pacific War. Present were three of the Navy's new "attack transports," former civilian mail ships modified to accommodate the new shallow-draft landing craft. These were designed by Andrew Higgins of the Eureka Boat Company and were designated Landing Craft, Vehicle, Personnel (LCVP), but were more generally known as the "Higgins boat." Also present for evaluation were several strange new tracked amphibious machines called "alligators" as a nod to their origin as rescue vehicles in the Florida Everglades. These still had problems to work out, but the Landing Vehicle, Tracked (LVT) and its variants eventually developed into the Marine Corps' primary amphibious assault vehicle. It was during this exercise that Spruance first met Smith; the crusty general evidently made an impression as Smith was Spruance's first pick to lead his amphibious operations in the Central Pacific.[12]

In March, Spruance received a letter from Nimitz informing him that he was to be relieved from his present duty on or about 1 August and instructing him to report to the Chief of Naval Operations for further duty. King was copied on the letter, as were the Commander-in-Chief, Pacific Fleet (CinCPac), and Commander, Aircraft, Battle Force, both located at Pearl Harbor. The latter was none other than his old friend Bill Halsey. It appeared that Spruance was going to be assigned to the Pacific Fleet.[13]

By this time, Spruance was glad to be relieved as the commandant of the Tenth Naval District, but duty in Washington, DC, was far from his ideal assignment. On his Fitness Reports for the last several years, Spruance had indicated that his preferred next duty assignment was to command a cruiser division. In March 1941, Spruance specifically requested duty with Cruiser Division 5 (CRUDIV 5) at Pearl Harbor. CRUDIV 5 was assigned to be the scouting and screening force for TF 2, commanded by Bill Halsey. Spruance felt certain that a war with Japan was imminent, and he wanted to be at sea, fighting under a commander he knew and respected. He must have communicated this wish to Halsey, who likely pulled some strings to make it happen. Halsey was well aware that the current commander of CRUDIV 5 was about to be rotated back to Washington for shore duty, and doubtless saw this as an opportunity to bring Spruance on board.[14]

The Spruances boarded the Army transport *Oriente* and sailed from San Juan on 7 August, arriving at the Brooklyn Navy Yard four days later. They met their daughter Margaret, who had just graduated from Vassar College, and immediately headed south to Washington, DC. Spruance must have gone straight to Nimitz to discuss his new assignment and request new orders. His orders were duly changed to match his preferred duty and signed by Nimitz on 12 August: he was to report to Pearl Harbor to assume command of CRUDIV 5.[15]

It has been written that Spruance wanted to command a battleship division and was disappointed by his new assignment. This seems unlikely, as he had explicitly requested the cruiser assignment six months earlier. If his experience in the Fleet Problems was any indicator, the battleships would be little more than spectators, sailing in column formation and waiting for their chance to engage from a safe distance. A junior rear admiral in the battleship force had little room for initiative; however, commanding the scouting screen for Bill Halsey's carriers would put Spruance at the tip of the spear in a major battle, a position that greatly appealed to him. Although not an aviator, Spruance was keenly interested in carrier operations, and the assignment offered him an opportunity to watch and learn.[16]

Spruance's orders required him to report to Pearl Harbor by 15 September, and as usual, he was expected to keep the Bureau of Navigation informed of his movements along the way. However, Spruance had heard a rumor in Washington that Admiral King, knowing that he was available, was looking to make him the chief of staff of the newly created Atlantic Fleet. By custom, King would have asked Spruance beforehand if he wanted the assignment, and while Spruance certainly respected and liked King, he had no desire to serve in another staff job in the wrong ocean. Spruance had been preparing for years for a war in the Pacific and fighting the relatively weak surface force of the Kriegsmarine looked to be a sideshow by comparison. Spruance did not relish turning down a direct request from King, however, so he simply kept mum as he, his wife, and daughter drove cross-country once more to San Francisco before boarding a liner for Hawaii.

When Spruance and his family arrived in Honolulu on 10 September, they were met by Edward Spruance and his wife Josephine. Edward was now the executive officer in USS *Tambor* (SS 198), one of the Navy's newest fleet submarines, based at Pearl Harbor. Edward and Josephine took the newly arrived trio on a sightseeing tour of Oahu, ending at the top of a mountain. Below, the Pacific Fleet was in full view at its moorings. Young Margaret remarked to her father, "What's to stop the Japanese from bombing our ships in Pearl Harbor?" Her father replied with a tone of sarcasm that was rare for him, "They are not supposed to do it that way." He explained that the current thinking was that the Japanese planned to station submarines around Hawaii and attack the fleet as it steamed out. She noted that her father was evidently concerned that war was imminent and that the Navy was not adequately prepared.[17]

Cruiser Division 5 was composed of the heavy cruisers *Northampton*, USS *Chester* (CA 27), and USS *Salt Lake City* (CA 25). Built in the late 1920s as "treaty cruisers," they had been designed to stay within the 10,000-ton displacement limit of the Washington Treaty. Relatively fast and well-armed with nine 8-inch guns, their armor protection was notably light for their type, making them more akin to a heavily armed light cruiser. Their lack of underwater protection also made them highly vulnerable to torpedoes and bomb attacks. These ships carried scout planes in hangars located amidships, and many of the later losses in this class were caused by the ignition of the highly flammable aviation fuel stored there.[18]

After settling into new quarters, Spruance relieved the outgoing commander, Rear Adm. Sherwoode Taffinder, aboard the division flagship *Northampton* on 17 September. Owing to the short notice given by the change in his orders, Spruance had made no arrangements to bring his own staff aboard but was content to inherit and retain the staff left by Taffinder, all of whom he found to be competent career officers. His flag secretary recalled that Spruance read through the daily mail and dispensed with routine paperwork as quickly as possible. When Spruance was a captain, he had been deeply involved in the day-to-day running of his ship, but as the cruiser division commander, *Northampton* was not his ship, and its daily running was not his problem. He was freed from such worries and instead spent his mental energy on bigger things. Likewise, Spruance expected that the division staff had seen to the daily training schedule, and he rarely interfered with their work unless absolutely necessary. In port, he could be found in his cabin reading, but at sea he was always on the bridge, watching the operations quietly and directing the staff to transmit his orders to the division during task force operations. Following the lead from some of his former bosses, Spruance's style as a flag officer was not to do anything that his subordinates could do for him, giving them great latitude as long as the desired results were achieved.[19]

As before, the staff had heard that Spruance was a "cold fish," and their first impressions seemed to confirm this. However, once they got to know him better, they found a warm human being under the stoic exterior. He got along particularly well with his flag lieutenant William M. McCormick, whom he found a willing companion for his customary long walks and discussions. One of the first orders of business coming aboard *Northampton* was to install the usual standing desk on the bulkhead of his cabin. The cruiser force spent the next few weeks in training exercises with TF 2, spending weekdays at sea but returning to Pearl Harbor on weekends for liberty and resupply.[20]

One of Spruance's captains was Ellis M. Zacharias, skipper of the *Salt Lake City*. A fluent speaker of Japanese and former assistant naval attaché to Japan, Zacharias had been the head of the Far East Division in the Office of Naval Intelligence in 1928 and was well known to Spruance. In early October, Zacharias, alerted by his intelligence contacts in Hawaii, came to Spruance to discuss his fears of an impending aerial attack on Pearl Harbor. Spruance listened carefully to Zacharias' concerns and, satisfied that they merited further discussion, together they went to see Adm. Husband E. Kimmel, commander of the U.S. Pacific Fleet. Zacharias repeated his warning to Kimmel and his staff, but as far as Spruance and Zacharias could see they listened politely and did nothing about it.[21]

In fact, Kimmel was well aware of such a possibility, and such reports had become almost routine. In Washington, DC, peace negotiations with the Japanese embassy were making little progress. Secretary of State Cordell Hull and his team were reading the Japanese diplomatic traffic in nearly real time, thanks to the efforts of the "Magic" cryptoanalysis. They were well aware that the militarists of the Imperial Army who controlled the Japanese government would never accede to American demands that Japan abandon its war in China and withdraw from French Indochina. While the Japanese ambassador to the United States, Admiral Nomura Kichisaburo, may have been genuine in his desire to find a peaceful solution, his diplomatic efforts provided a convenient smokescreen that bought time for Admiral Yamamoto Isoroku's plan to attack Pearl Harbor to unfold. While Yamamoto had long opposed war with the United States as essentially unwinnable, he nevertheless acquiesced to the prevailing winds in the Imperial Naval General Staff and saw a sudden strike as Japan's best option. The Kidō Butai, the First Mobile Fleet, consisting of six aircraft carriers and other elements of the Combined Fleet under the command of Admiral Nagumo Chuichi, sailed from its anchorage in northern Japan on the morning of 25 November (Hawaii time), heading for a station northeast of the Hawaiian Islands.[22]

That same day Kelly Turner, now the director of the War Plans Division of Naval Operations, drafted a dispatch for review by CNO Harold Stark and the president, which started with the never-before-seen phrase "This dispatch is to be considered a war warning." It stated that "an aggressive move by Japan is expected within the next few days" and went on to say that the likely target for such a move was the Philippines, Thailand, the Malay peninsula, or possibly Dutch Borneo. It ordered the recipients to "execute an appropriate defensive deployment" in accordance with the Navy's Basic War Plan. After some editing, it was sent out late on the day of 27 November.[23]

Even before this dispatch had been received, Admiral Kimmel, Vice Admiral Halsey, and Lt. Gen. Walter Short, the Army's commander in Hawaii, had been meeting to discuss how to best prepare for what now seemed to be an inevitability. Station Hypo, the Navy's cryptoanalysis office at Pearl Harbor, headed by the brilliant Lt. Cdr. Joseph Rochefort, had been intercepting and deciphering Japanese diplomatic messages and monitoring the radio communications of the Japanese navy. Although the Imperial Japanese Navy's main code, JN-25, had not been broken by the U.S. Navy, radio traffic analysis provided valuable information about possible movements and intentions. The Japanese were on the move, and the Pacific Fleet had to prepare. While an air attack on Pearl Harbor was a possibility, it did not seem probable. Instead, they discussed reinforcing the bases on both Midway and Wake atolls with troops and aircraft. They considered sending Army P-40s, but ultimately decided to keep these on Oahu and send Marine F4F Wildcats instead. Halsey and TF 2 were assigned the task of ferrying the Marine squadron to Wake.[24]

TF 2 was centered on the carrier *Enterprise* and, in addition to Spruance's cruisers, included the three battleships of BATDIV 1, USS *Arizona* (BB 39), *Pennsylvania*, and USS *Nevada* (BB 36), under the command of Rear Adm. Isaac Kidd. This impressive task force sailed out of Pearl Harbor on the morning of 28 November, but once over the horizon, Kidd's battleships left the formation. Their slow speed was a hindrance to the mission and a liability if the task force chanced to meet a superior enemy force. *Enterprise* and the cruisers of Spruance's division were henceforth known as TF 8.[25]

Two Army P-40s had been loaded on the flight deck of *Enterprise* as part of the effort to mislead any watchers, and once the carrier was at sea, these flew off back to Hickam Field while *Enterprise*'s air groups flew out to join the task force, joined by the Marine squadron destined for Wake. Once the air groups had landed aboard, the carrier shaped a course for Wake Island. Although Spruance had been briefed, his staff and the rest of the men of the TF 8 had assumed this was another training operation. But Halsey soon revealed their true mission. He immediately ordered that the force be placed on a war footing, "ready for instant action": aircraft spotted on the flight deck, torpedoes armed with live warheads, and guns manned and loaded, with orders to shoot down any "hostile" aircraft or sink any snooping submarine. Antisubmarine patrols were conducted, the ships darkened at night, and absolute radio silence was maintained.[26]

The wording of the war-warning dispatch appeared to confirm the belief that the Japanese intended to strike south to seize the oil fields of Borneo. No mention had been made of an attack on Pearl Harbor, and no one in TF 8 believed it to be a real possibility. Reinforcing Wake and Midway were sound precautionary moves, but secrecy was needed to avoid these moves becoming a provocation. A fleet of Japanese warships and troop transports were known to be heading south, but the whereabouts of their carriers remained unknown. As Halsey's task force moved west, far to the north the Kidō Butai was steaming east. Admiral Nagumo received the order "Climb Mount Niitaka," the code to proceed with the attack on Pearl Harbor, on 2 December. The die was cast.

At dawn on 4 December, the Marine Wildcats flew off the flight deck of *Enterprise* and headed for Wake with a navigational escort. The task force then turned east and headed back at high speed for Hawaii, now running on a parallel course with the Japanese fleet to the north. Storms and high seas afflicted both the TF 8 and the Kidō Butai, but the dangerous weather was a blessing in disguise for both. It helped hide the Japanese fleet from observation as they approached Oahu and began their turn to the southwest. The rough seas did little to hamper the big Japanese carriers and cruisers, but they played hell with the American destroyers and their fuel consumption. The task force had sailed without a fleet oiler, so *Enterprise* had to refuel the "tin cans" while underway, a time-consuming process that ended up saving her from certain destruction. Halsey's ships had been scheduled to return to Pearl Harbor on 6 December, but the refueling delayed their return by at least a day.

The first wave of Kate B5N bombers struck Pearl Harbor at 0757 local time on 7 December 1941. At 0815, the message "Air raid on Pearl Harbor. This is no drill" was received on *Northampton*'s flag bridge. McCormick, who was on duty, telephoned Spruance, who was having breakfast in his cabin, and read him the message. He took the news calmly and told McCormick, "Thank you, you know what to do." The crew sprang into action, stripping the ship for combat. At Halsey's order, the national ensign was hoisted on the mainmast of every ship in the task force. Spruance came to the bridge and stayed there until the ship reentered Pearl Harbor the next day.[27]

Spruance and his cruisers were detached to conduct a search pattern southwest of Oahu, based on what were later learned to be erroneous radio direction-finding bearings. The southwest made sense, as the Marshall Islands were the logical and expected source for an attack by the Imperial Japanese Navy. In the forenoon, the Scout Observation, Curtiss (SOC) float planes of VCS-5, the cruiser's scout observation squadron, launched from their catapults and began an extended search. At this time, the task force was south of Ni'ihau, the westernmost island of the Hawaiian chain. The scouts were assigned a search pattern to the north and east, out to 200 miles. They found no sign of the Japanese fleet, which was fortunate since *Enterprise* had already flown off most of her fighters to Pearl Harbor and was low on fuel. Against the Kidō Butai she was also outnumbered, one against six. Nor were Spruance's three cruisers a match for the two fast battleships and two heavy cruisers that screened the Japanese strike force.[28]

Spruance's cruisers entered Pearl Harbor in the forenoon of 8 December. The crew of *Northampton* stood dumbfounded along the lifelines, gazing upon the terrible devastation. The reality looked far worse than the early reports had led them to expect. *Nevada*, blackened from fire and beached on the east side of the harbor entrance near Hospital Point, was the sight that first greeted them. At the end of Battleship Row, *Arizona* was still burning, shattered beyond any possibility of salvage. Rear Adm. Isaac Kidd was killed on her bridge when her magazines exploded; his body vaporized so that only his Annapolis class ring was found, embedded in the bulkhead. BATDIV 1 was no more; Spruance was now second in command to Halsey.[29]

The ships of TF 8 resupplied and refueled as quickly as possible. Hundreds of sailors from the stricken ships came aboard for temporary duty, as there was no other place to house and feed them. The officers not on watch went ashore as soon as possible to check on their families in Honolulu. Spruance reported to Admiral Kimmel and told him Halsey and *Enterprise* would enter later that day, then headed home. He found his wife, daughter Margaret, daughter-in-law Josephine, and several other Navy wives safe but understandably nervous and anxious. When he tried to talk about what he had just seen, his usual façade of stoicism dissolved. "He was very emotional, had tears in his eyes, and forced himself to talk about what he had seen and felt. . . . He was trying to talk about it, but he just couldn't. Apparently, they had no idea about the extent of the damage, and when they first saw it, it was a terrible shock." The sight of the ships of his beloved Navy still burning shook Spruance to his core; his wife had never seen him so upset. He appeared as if he had aged twenty years. But after a good night's sleep, he shook off the horror of it all and was ready for duty, his emotional discharge over and the stoic façade back in place. The immense strain of waiting for the attack he knew was coming was over. Curiously, unlike his friend Bill Halsey and many others, Spruance did not react to the attack with a visceral hatred for the Japanese; instead, he had a grudging admiration for them and attempted to understand their mindset. He never used the racist nicknames that were popular. In his mind, hatred served only to cloud his thinking. He could now get on with the business of war.[30]

TF 8 stood out from Pearl Harbor early the next day. Kimmel had recovered from his profound shock enough to order the *Enterprise* to leave as soon as possible to patrol the seas around Oahu, as he fully expected the Japanese to return and finish the job they had started. Many auxiliary ships, including the fleet oilers, came off relatively unscathed, and the vast fuel-oil tank farms were intact. But Admiral Nagumo had no intention of making a second strike and had already ordered the Kidō Butai to withdraw at high speed along the route from which they had arrived. While disappointed that the American carriers had not been present in Pearl Harbor as expected, Nagumo was unsure of their current location, which made him nervous. He decided to withdraw with his fleet intact and return to Japan immediately, even forgoing a scheduled attack on Midway Atoll. The Imperial Naval General Staff was anxious to make an expeditious conquest of the Dutch East Indies, and his fleet was needed in the south. Time was of the essence.[31]

Hours after the Pearl Harbor attack, Wake Island suffered an attack by a large bomber force, and on 11 December a Japanese invasion force arrived to stage an amphibious assault. The Marine shore batteries, however, inflicted heavy losses on the invasion force, sinking two destroyers and forcing the Japanese to withdraw. On 16 December, TF 14, commanded by Rear Adm. Frank Jack Fletcher and centered on *Saratoga*, was sent to relieve Wake Island. TF 17, under Rear Adm. Wilson Brown, centered on *Lexington*, would raid Jaluit in the Marshall Islands as a diversion. On 19 December, Halsey's TF 8 left Pearl Harbor and steamed toward a position west of Johnston Island where it could assist either task force if they found themselves pursued by a superior force. Halsey, however, was too far from either to provide immediate support.

Unknown to CinCPac or Fletcher, Yamamoto had sent his Carrier Division 2, consisting of the carriers *Soryū* and *Hiryū*, along with cruisers and destroyers, to finish off Wake once and for all. The Japanese assault rebounded on the heroic defenders with even greater fury on 21 December. Unaware of these developments, Fletcher had paused to refuel his destroyers, causing a day's delay. He could not arrive before 23 December, by which time the island had fallen to the troops of the Japanese Special Naval Landing Forces. Vice Adm. William S. Pye, who had relieved Kimmel on 17 December, had no choice but to issue a recall, and Fletcher reluctantly followed his orders. The three American carrier task groups, widely separated as they were, would have been ripe for destruction in detail had Pye ordered them to support Wake Island.[32]

The success of carrier aviation in the prewar Fleet Problems may have made the U.S. Navy's carrier advocates somewhat complacent about the soundness of their doctrine and blind to the possibility that their foe might be better at the game. In this war, however, they faced an opponent to whom victory was not just a way to burnish their career but a do-or-die-trying affair. The admirals of the U.S. Navy assumed their enemy had reached the same conclusions they had concerning the number of carriers that should operate as a group and that American aviation technology was superior. In the war games and the fleet exercises, they "fought" against their own weapon systems, oblivious to the idea that the enemy might have a technological edge. The superiority of Japanese carrier tactics, carrier aircraft, and pilot training in the first months of the war came as a great surprise. It would take many months of heavy fighting and heavy losses before the Japanese onslaught could be slowed and then reversed.

Spruance and his three cruisers spent the next week and a half following the movements of Halsey and the *Enterprise* patrolling the areas north and west of Midway, covering the flank of the Wake mission, and chasing false reports. They reentered Pearl Harbor on 31 December for several days of refueling and resupply. Spruance went home to his family for a brief respite.[33]

While TF 8 was at sea, President Roosevelt selected Adm. Chester W. Nimitz as the new commander in chief of the Pacific Fleet. Nimitz arrived on 25 December, a fitting Christmas present for the men of his new command. On that same day that TF 8 returned, Ernest King became CINCUS, an acronym that he quickly changed from "Sink us" to the better sounding COMINCH: Commander in Chief, U.S. Fleet. Spruance was elated by these changes and felt that, with King in overall command and Nimitz in command in the Pacific, the naval war was now directed by forceful, aggressive leaders who shared his vision of naval warfare. With Nimitz's arrival, they stopped hanging around Oahu—"We commenced to go places and fight."[34]

CHAPTER 4

THE EARLY CARRIER RAIDS

WHEN HITLER'S THIRD REICH declared war on the United States on 11 December 1941, the two-year-old European war that Spruance had observed with interest now became a world war. In the early months of 1942, that war unquestionably favored the Axis. The Third Reich and its allies controlled most of Europe. They were on the verge of crushing the Soviet Union, which greatly influenced Japan's decision to start a war of conquest in the Western Pacific. Japan's rapid success in the initial phases of the war did not come as a great surprise to Spruance or, indeed, to any of his contemporaries who had spent time at the Naval War College. Japanese operations generally conformed to events predicted by Plan Orange; the great surprise was that the Imperial Navy could simultaneously launch an undetected attack as far east as Pearl Harbor and manage to cripple the U.S. Pacific Fleet.

The new Allies met at the first Washington Conference (code-named Arcadia) in late December 1941 and decided that the primary goal for the war was the defeat of Hitler in Europe. Recognizing that the stunning Japanese successes necessitated a response, however, they established the American-British-Dutch-Australian (ABDA) Command on 1 January 1942, almost as an afterthought. The primary task of ABDA was to hold the "Malay Barrier" centered on Singapore, to keep Japanese forces out of the Indian Ocean, and to keep the sea lanes to Australia open until resources became available for a general offensive. While this was the correct strategy, it effectively ignored the defense of the Philippines, which by now looked increasingly hopeless, as the prewar planners had predicted.

Adm. Ernest J. King was not content with the idea that the Pacific Fleet should remain on the defensive. On 2 January, he sent a dispatch to

Nimitz advising that he should give "thorough consideration of expedition of (a) raid against enemy bases in the Gilbert Islands probably Makin," to be coordinated with a planned reinforcement of Samoa. King concluded with a directive to "undertake some aggressive action for effect on general morale." King's stipulation of Makin Atoll indicates how little the Americans knew about the Mandates. As a later raid showed, the Japanese had no significant installations there.[1]

Fortunately, the CinCPac staff had studied the problem and provided Nimitz with a reply. Their report deemed the close defense of Oahu unnecessary as long as the line from Midway to Johnston Atoll was secure. It was recommended that offensive actions be taken immediately against the Japanese bases in the Gilbert and Marshall Islands. At that time, Nimitz had at his disposal four carriers, each the center of a Task Force:

- TF 8: *Enterprise*, three cruisers, nine destroyers. Commanded by Bill Halsey.
- TF 11: *Lexington*, two cruisers, five destroyers. Commanded by Wilson Brown.
- TF 14: *Saratoga*, one cruiser, one light cruiser, five destroyers. Commanded by Herbert F. Leary.
- TF 17: *Yorktown*, one cruiser, one light cruiser, and four destroyers. Commanded by Frank Jack Fletcher.

TF 14, under the command of Rear Admiral Fletcher, departed San Diego on 6 January, shepherding a convoy of transports headed for Samoa. The task forces under Brown and Leary had defended the Midway and Johnston Atolls line since the Pearl Harbor attack. Nimitz ordered Halsey and TF 8, including Spruance and CRUDIV 5, to sail south to attack the Gilberts, while Brown and TF 11 went west to attack the Marshalls. He planned on having Leary's TF 14 remain on defensive patrol, but a Japanese torpedo damaged *Saratoga*, sending her to the Bremerton Navy Yard for repairs. The revised plan called for Halsey and Fletcher to attack the Marshalls in two thrusts, with TF 8 hitting Maloelap and Wotje and TF 17, once its duty in Samoa was complete, Jaluit and Mili. Nimitz kept Brown and TF 11 on the defense in the North Pacific, awaiting further orders.[2]

On 11 January, Halsey's force stood out from Pearl Harbor to join Fletcher's TF 14 en route to Samoa. In the convoy were three ocean liners transporting several battalions of the 2nd Marine Division, as well as cargo ships carrying coastal artillery, antiaircraft guns, construction supplies, and equipment. Spruance's cruisers kept their scout planes in the air daily, conducting long-range searches. Lookouts sighted Savaii Island of the northern Samoa group on 21 January, and as the convoy unloaded, the two carrier groups kept station to the north and west. When the troops had been disembarked, the two task forces, now under the overall command of Halsey, the senior officer, departed Samoa on 25 January, bound for their respective targets in the Marshall Islands. In mid-January, under pressure from King, Nimitz issued an operation order for Brown's TF 11 to attack Wake Island, but once again his plans were disrupted by the exigencies of war when, on 22 January, the submarine *I-72* sank the oiler USS *Neches* (AO 5) en route to refuel the force. The task force had no choice but to return to Pearl Harbor, postponing the attack on Wake Island to a future date. It would now be up to Halsey and Fletcher to raise the "general morale."[3]

Allied radio traffic analyses indicated that the main elements of the Combined Fleet were either in Truk, far to the west, or conducting operations in the southwest Pacific. Apart from some submarine reconnaissance of the islands, the Marshalls remained an enigma to the CinCPac planners, who believed the bomber force that had attacked Wake Island a month earlier originated there, which was enough to make them a target. Halsey split his task force into three task groups. TG 8.1, consisting of Spruance in *Northampton*, accompanied by *Salt Lake City* and the destroyer USS *Dunlap* (DD 384), was to bombard Wotje. TG 8.3, comprising the cruiser *Chester* and the destroyers USS *Balch* (DD 363) and USS *Maury* (DD 401), was to bombard Maloelap. In support, TG 8.5, consisting of *Enterprise* and four screening destroyers, would launch air attacks on both the target atolls plus Kwajalein Atoll. Halsey's chief of staff, Miles Browning, added the latter to the target list as the available intelligence indicated that the entire Marshall group was lightly defended. It was a calculated risk, but offered the chance to hit the enemy while its main forces were elsewhere.[4]

The task groups moved into place and began their attacks as scheduled early on 31 January. To escape the tropical heat, Spruance had a cot set up on the bridge wing, where he slept all night. Awakened before dawn, he ordered all eight of the task group's SOCs from VCS-5 into the air to scout the atoll, report on any shore batteries, and spot the fall of the cruiser's shells during his carefully planned bombardment. Fighters from *Enterprise* were already on their way to flush out and destroy any enemy air cover before VCS-5 arrived, but despite Wotje having a large airstrip, no Japanese fighters appeared to defend the island.[5]

As the scouts approached, they reported a small patrol vessel about eight miles south of the atoll. Spruance ordered *Dunlap* to take it under fire, which she did, and ten minutes later, only an oily spot remained where the patrol boat had been. Over the atoll, the scouts did not spot any shore batteries but reported that several ships were anchored in the lagoon. When VCS-5 began to draw heavy antiaircraft fire, they ascended to a range beyond the guns' reach. The cruisers opened fire at 0715 at a range of 27,000 yards, and with the scouts directing fire, several of the Japanese auxiliaries were hit and forced to beach, and a large merchantman was set ablaze.

Northampton and *Salt Lake City* drew close ashore during their bombardment. Once they came within range, several concealed shore batteries made themselves known and began to take the cruisers under fire. Several shots landed close aboard, spraying the ships with shell fragments. Spruance stood on the open wing of *Northampton*'s bridge, taking it all in, remaining cool and unperturbed. Fearful for his commander's safety, McCormick asked Spruance if he shouldn't be in the armored conning tower. Spruance replied, somewhat annoyed, "No, but maybe you'd better as you have so much longer to live than I do."[6]

Over a period of forty-five minutes, each cruiser fired about 360 rounds of 8-inch armor-piercing (AP) shell, while *Dunlap* fired about 500 rounds of 5-inch, on the island and its air base. After lifting their fire at 0855, the ships withdrew, and the scouts went in to photograph the installations and drop the two 100-pound bombs they carried. The scout planes of *Salt Lake City* carried an improvised gasoline bomb nicknamed "the Zacharias Zombie" and dropped those. Neither did much damage. By 1230, the scout planes had been recovered, and the task group sailed north to rejoin the *Enterprise*.[7]

The bombardment of Maloelap was cut short when several high-level bombers attacked *Chester.* The bombers missed their target, but one bomb delivered by a single determined fighter landed in her well deck, killing eight men and doing considerable damage. Halsey's TG 8.5 had done better with their air attacks on Kwajalein Atoll, the home of the Imperial Navy's Sixth Fleet, the primary Japanese submarine command in the Central Pacific. The carrier bombers hit the submarine base on Kwajalein Island and the airfields on Roi-Namur and claimed to have sunk a number of ships, including two submarines and four auxiliaries, and damaged the light cruiser *Katori.* Over a nine-hour period, the air groups of *Enterprise* had launched twenty-one attacks in the Marshalls, damaging runways and destroying radio transmission facilities, antiaircraft batteries, hangars, and other buildings. Shortly after 1300 Halsey, sensing that he had been pushing his luck for long enough, ordered the entire task force to retire to the northeast at high speed, thereby creating the fraternity known as the "Haul Ass with Halsey Club."[8]

Fletcher's TF 17 was not so lucky. Bad weather and severe storms greatly hampered their attacks on Jaluit, Makin, and Mili. The raid caused only moderate damage, and a total of eight aircraft were lost, primarily due to the weather, against a paltry tally of four enemy planes. Fletcher had sailed into a literal black cloud that continued to dog him in the Pacific. Running low on fuel, he retired at nightfall, and after refueling the next day he shaped a course to follow TF 8 back to Pearl Harbor. Halsey and TF 8 were given a raucous welcome when they entered the East Loch on 5 February. Sailors lined the lifelines of their ships and cheered them in with sirens blaring. The attacks in the Marshalls became national news, blown far out of proportion compared to their actual military value but seen as a great and welcome victory during a time of constant defeats elsewhere. Halsey was well on his way to becoming a national icon.

Later that evening, Robert J. Oliver reported aboard *Northampton* as McCormick's relief. The haggard appearance of his old captain came as a shock. Spruance looked tired and low in spirits. Spruance had found the hullabaloo greeting their return that morning to be depressing, given what he considered the raid's rather meager results. He had another good reason for feeling down: his wife, daughter, and daughter-in-law had been evacuated to the West Coast during his absence. The family car went with them. Spruance's son Edward was also gone, as his sub *Tambor* had developed engine trouble and was on its way to Mare Island for repairs. Rather than rattle about an empty rented house, Spruance chose to remain aboard *Northampton*, relying on his Filipino steward to look after his needs.

Spruance warmly greeted his old *Mississippi* shipmate. Instead of turning in as Oliver suggested, he wanted to discuss the Wotje operation. Spruance was bitterly disappointed at what he perceived to be the poor performance of his cruiser division. When a periscope had been reported, all tactical discipline had been lost and the ships scattered, upsetting his carefully laid out bombardment plan. It turned out that it was nothing more than an empty powder canister. The task force's antiaircraft fire had also been ineffective due to inexperience and lack of training. As Halsey said later in his memoir, they might as well have been using water pistols. But as Spruance talked, his attitude brightened. Although Spruance was never overtly demonstrative in his affection for Oliver, it was real, and having the young man back at his side pleased him. Overall, the Marshall raid had been a success, he told Oliver, and he was gratified to be fighting alongside his friend Bill Halsey and under the capable command of Chester Nimitz. He told his new flag lieutenant not to be discouraged; while things might look bad, he was confident that the war would be won in time. After a good night's sleep aboard ship, the next morning Spruance appeared to Oliver to be back to his old self, vigorous and bright-eyed.[9]

Appearances may have been deceiving. Spruance wrote to Margaret a few days later that he was sad to have missed the women's departure. "Life has certainly lost its interest for me since you left," he wrote, "and the worst of it is that I have no definite date to look forward to when I shall see you again." Turning to more practical matters, he gave her instructions on how to deal with their finances, taxes, and the registration of their car in California. He indulged in some gossip about which of their friends had made the selection for rear admiral and told her to keep an eye out for a newsreel about their latest raid. Spruance didn't know it then, but he would not see his wife again for another ten months.[10]

After the Marshalls raid, Admiral Yamamoto had briefly directed two of his carriers to pursue Halsey, but after two days he redirected them south to support the ongoing operations against the Dutch East Indies. Clearly it would take more than a few nuisance raids to relieve the beleaguered Allies fighting in the southwest theater. Under pressure from King, the CinCPac staff resurrected the operations plan for the attack on Wake Island. When Soc McMorris handed Halsey the orders, he was aghast. His task force had been redesignated Task Force 13 in keeping with COMINCH's directives for task force numbering, and his orders directed him to sail on Friday, 13 February. Having an old salt's superstition about the number thirteen, Halsey successfully argued to change his task force designation to TF 16, with orders to sail one day later. After a short period of rest and resupply, Halsey's task force went to sea again in the afternoon of 14 February.

The original operations plan called for TF 16 to attack Eniwetok Atoll, requiring them to sail even deeper into the Mandates, while Fletcher and TF 17 attacked Wake Island several days later. The attacks were timed to occur simultaneously on 24 February, but larger strategic events intervened. The British fortress of Singapore fell on 15 February, freeing up Japanese forces for further moves south to threaten the lines of communication with Australia. Fletcher was then ordered to proceed south to Canton Island to cover the operations of Brown's TF 11, which was about to attempt a raid on Rabaul. On 16 February, Halsey was ordered to abandon the Eniwetok operation and conduct the planned raid on Wake Island instead. TF 16 then shaped a course west toward Wake, a distance of more than 2,000 miles, arriving at a point several hundred miles northeast of the island on the afternoon of 23 February. Halsey's operation plan called for an air assault from *Enterprise* to be timed to occur at the same time that Spruance's bombardment group began their attack, just after dawn.[11]

The next day, Spruance's cruisers approached Wake Island from the northwest. At 0705, his task group came about, heading due east to launch the scout planes and begin their bombardment run. Bad weather delayed the arrival of the carrier planes, and the Japanese air cover soon made its presence known. While the VCS-5 scouts were still at low altitude, three Japanese floatplanes of the same type as the SOC, Nakajima E8N Type 95s, appeared out of the broken clouds and dived to attack *Northampton*. Spruance and Oliver, standing together on the bridge, looked up just as the second plane in the formation pushed over and dived straight for them. "I was sure I could see the (Japanese) pilot's eye through his telescope," Oliver recalled. "I looked around for something to get under. Spruance did not move. Completely exposed, he watched the plane grow larger and larger. Then the bomb started on its course, and it became clear that Spruance had no intention of taking cover. At the very last instance, the rudder came over just enough to get us out from under the bomb." The Type 95 was an obsolete biplane, relatively slow and poorly armed. Their slow speed kept them exposed for an extended period to all the antiaircraft fire CRUDIV 5 could produce, and yet, for all that, only one was brought down. Additional antiaircraft armament and training were clearly needed.[12]

Shortly thereafter, the cruisers began their bombardment from 16,000 yards, just beyond the range of 4.7-inch shore batteries. As with the Wotje attack, the scouts of VCS-5 spotted the warships, but they had a tough time reporting on the results as the AP ammunition they used tore through the wooden structures with little visible effect unless they hit something readily flammable, such as aviation fuel storage. By now, the carrier planes had arrived and begun a methodical bombing of the island. In the lagoon, four multiengine Kawanishi H6 seaplanes were seen taking off to make their escape. These "snoopers" were the eyes of the Imperial Japanese Navy, especially valuable in the time before the Japanese deployment of operational radar, but also highly vulnerable to attack. As it turned out, only one was shot down. *Enterprise*'s scout bombers cratered the runway, damaged buildings, and set fire to two aviation storage tanks. They found no ships in the lagoon to attack, and other than the flying boats, no aircraft either, limiting the overall impact of the raid. The destroyers managed to sink two small patrol boats operating offshore. As the carrier planes flew off, the scouts of VCS-5 had the final say by dropping their 100-pounders, but again, to no visible effect.[13]

Enterprise and her destroyer escorts retired to the northeast, and after CRUDIV 5 had recovered the scout planes they also withdrew at high speed to join up. During this time, the cruisers were shadowed by the flying boats that had escaped destruction earlier. Near dusk, one of them closed the distance as if to attack. With all eyes on the flying boat, no one saw the two twin-engine bombers overhead until it was almost too late. *Northampton*'s air search radar had been damaged and knocked out of service from the shock of her main guns during the bombardment. These were land-based aircraft, and somewhat ironically, they had likely originated from Eniwetok, the original target of the raid. The attack happened so quickly that none of the ships had time to develop effective antiaircraft fire. They proceeded to drop their bombs from 13,000 feet, which gave the ships below ample time to maneuver out of the way. Both sides in this war would learn that horizontal bombing from high altitude was unlikely to score a hit on a ship capable of movement.[14]

The cruisers rendezvoused with *Enterprise* the next morning. CinCPac gave Halsey a new mission: attack Marcus Island, located some 760 miles to the northwest. Little was known about the Japanese military installations on this island, located only 1,000 miles from Tokyo Bay, but planners suspected that they included a radio station and an airstrip. This was to be strictly a hit-and-run air attack, with the cruisers and escort destroyers standing by as aircraft guards, ready to pick up any downed flyers. Halsey positioned the task force at a point some 125 miles northeast of the island and began launching aircraft in the predawn darkness of 4 March. At 0630, the raiders spotted the island through a break in the clouds, and the attack began. The dive bombers of Lt. Richard H. Best's Bombing Six (VB-6) led the charge, followed by the planes of Scouting Six (VS-6) which attacked in a combination of dive and glide bombing. Six F4F fighters flew above as cover, but there were no Japanese aircraft in the air or on the ground. Unlike the previous raids, no preplanning could be done, so the attackers hit what seemed best: the runway, the hangars, and fuel storage. The raid caught the Japanese completely by surprise. After the bombing runs some limited strafing was conducted, but by now the defenders were awake and mounting a spirited antiaircraft defense. Halsey recalled that the attack force were back aboard *Enterprise* by 0800.

During these early raids, Spruance observed the carrier operations with great interest. As he explained to Oliver, a classic battle-line fleet engagement seemed unlikely; rather, the carrier task force was going to be the primary method of force projection in this war. He read all the air tactical instructions, bulletins, and newsletters he could get his hands on, and kept informed about the military characteristics of each type of carrier aircraft.

Spruance watched the operations aboard *Enterprise* when he could, and had Cdr. Earl Junghans, his air officer, close by to explain in detail what was going on. When the opportunity arose, Spruance "picked the brains" of any young aviator that crossed his path. One such was Lt. Charles R. Ware, a Naval Academy classmate of Oliver's and a division leader in *Enterprise*'s Scouting Group Six. When his SBD Dauntless was hit by antiaircraft fire and forced to ditch, Ware and his radioman were pulled "out of the drink" by *Northampton*. After Ware came aboard, changed into dry clothes, and ate some hot chow, Spruance cornered him in the wardroom to ask questions and discuss the operation. Evidently impressed by Spruance, Ware afterward asked Oliver, "How in the hell does that man know so much about naval aviation?"[15]

Important lessons learned from these early raids included the need to assign more fighter aircraft to the carrier air groups. A number of aircraft damaged by enemy fire had to ditch because they ran out of fuel; as a result, self-sealing fuel tanks were installed as quickly as possible. Likewise, the installation of Identification, Friend or Foe (IFF) equipment was deemed necessary, as the scout planes of VCS-5 were often mistaken for Japanese float planes and fired upon by their shipmates. Pilot fatigue from long flights and continuous action also became a serious concern, and the number of reserve pilots available was increased by 50 percent. While the raids were largely a nuisance to the Japanese, they provided the sailors and aviators of the task forces with valuable experience in combat operations and gave a much-needed boost to morale. Admiral Nimitz's commentary on the Marcus attack noted that while the military impact of the raid was minimal, it left a calling card on the doorstep of the Japanese empire. The next major raid would do more than that.[16]

TF 16 returned to Pearl Harbor on 10 March, and the ships of CRUDIV 5 spent the remainder of the month there undergoing repairs and refit, not least of which included repairs to *Northampton*'s radar array and the installation of additional antiaircraft guns. One of Spruance's personality quirks was his avoidance of confrontation and unpleasantness unless absolutely necessary. This was seldom an issue with his immediate staff or others who had worked closely with him in the past. They found Spruance warm and caring once they had gotten past his initial reserve.

But he did not establish such a rapport with Capt. William Chandler, the skipper of *Northampton*. Spruance used Oliver as his messenger to communicate his displeasure, such as during the Wake raid when the scout planes were late in launching. On the other hand, he had no reticence about dressing down non-service members who had finally pushed his usual tolerance to the limit. For several weeks during the refit in Pearl Harbor, Spruance had to share his cabin with yard workers, who drilled holes through the deckhead to mount some new 1.1-inch antiaircraft guns. After many days of observing their languid pace from his standing desk, Spruance finally had enough and vented his pent-up ire on one unfortunate worker. "I lost my temper and lit into him," he wrote to Margaret, adding with a hint of sarcasm, "I have never seen so many lazy, worthless bums drawing high wages assembled in one place—it was somewhat like the W.P.A., at least it was the same willing, enthusiastic spirit."[17]

The enforced inactivity while waiting for new orders gave Spruance time to catch up on his mail and letter-writing. He found out from Margaret that their daughter had developed tuberculosis and was in a sanitorium in Monrovia, California. Margaret had found a house and relocated there as well. Fortunately, young Margaret's prognosis was good, but it was one more thing on Spruance's mind. His son Edward and *Tambor* had returned to Pearl Harbor, and they were able to spend time together. And, of course, Spruance went on long hikes into the hills whenever he could coerce someone into joining him.

On 27 March, CRUDIV 5 put to sea for training and gunnery practice with their new antiaircraft guns. While they were at sea, Halsey and Browning flew to San Francisco for a secret conference. Bad weather delayed their return flight, but when Halsey landed on 7 April, he had some surprising news for Spruance: TF 16 was going to conduct a bombing raid on the Japanese Home Islands, specifically on Tokyo. When the task force sailed the next morning without the usual conference, it was evident that something big was in the offing. Once at sea, Spruance revealed their destination to his stunned staff. "I guess you fellows want to know where we're going," he said. "We are going to bomb Tokyo!" Shocked, the staff pressed him for details, incredulous that such a raid could be made with carrier aircraft. Spruance explained that Army B-25 bombers were coming out from San Francisco on the *Hornet*. "You'll see next morning," Spruance told them while cautioning them to keep it a secret for the time being.[18]

Everyone knew something was up when *Hornet*, commanded by Capt. Marc Mitscher, and TF 18 hove into view on 13 April. They saw sixteen ungainly olive-green twin-engine medium bombers crowding her flight deck, while her usual complement of carrier planes was stowed below on the hangar deck. The combined task forces, consisting of two carriers, four cruisers, eight destroyers, and two fleet oilers, were now at a point roughly 600 miles northwest of Midway. They then changed course to steam southwest toward Japan, following approximately the same route that the Kidō Butai had taken on their return to Japan after Pearl Harbor. Nimitz stationed two submarines off the coast of Japan, on the lookout for any movement of Japanese warships, and except for periods of bad weather Halsey kept scout planes airborne, with searches ranging 200 miles ahead of the line of advance. As usual, strict radio silence was maintained, leaving Nimitz, the brass in Washington, and the President anxious for news.

On 17 April the combined force refueled and continued west, but heavy seas and high winds kept the destroyers and the oilers well astern of the advancing TF 16. Early in the morning of 18 April, the force's radar began picking up the presence of small Japanese patrol boats dead ahead. Scout planes were launched. At 0740, another patrol boat was spotted, and it seemed likely that they had radioed a warning back to Tokyo. In accordance with the plan he had made with Lt. Col. James "Jimmy" Doolittle back in San Francisco, Halsey signaled *Hornet* to launch the bombing raid immediately.[19]

Salt Lake City took up a position astern of *Hornet* to serve as a plane guard, while *Northampton* took up station off her starboard bow. "I had a ringside seat," Spruance later recalled, "and felt much relieved when the last plane was in the air." At 0820, Doolittle flew the first bomber off the flight deck of *Hornet*, followed by the rest. All had departed by 0921, and the Task Forces came about shortly thereafter. They steamed east at high speed and arrived back in Pearl Harbor on 26 April.[20]

The Army bombers flew west just above the waves, arriving over Tokyo at noon. They dropped their loads of four 500-pound bombs but caused little damage and few casualties. The raid did catch the Imperial Navy completely by surprise. Warned that carriers were approaching, they thought the American carrier planes unlikely to be within range to launch an attack until the next day. The first hint that the raid had been a success was when Pearl Harbor picked up Japanese news broadcasts reporting that there had been an air raid on Tokyo and other cities.[21]

Spruance, however, saw the raid as an unnecessary risk of two precious carriers for minimal military benefit. "The raid was a spectacular operation, good for American morale; but unless it caused the Japanese to retain at home forces which they intended to send to the South Pacific, it did not impress as particularly valuable from a military point of view." What Spruance did not realize was the profound psychological effect the Doolittle Raid had on the Japanese psyche. Shamed by the idea that an enemy had succeeded in attacking the sacred homeland, possibly even endangering the emperor, the Imperial General Headquarters immediately put into effect a plan devised by Admiral Yamamoto for the neutralization of Hawaii, beginning with the seizure of Midway Atoll, codenamed Operation MI.[22]

Operation MI was the most complex plan yet devised by the Combined Fleet, requiring the commitment of all their available carriers and surface warships. First, Yamamoto planned to lure the remaining carriers of the Pacific Fleet into a decisive battle leading to their destruction, and an amphibious assault on Midway Atoll was deemed to be just the bait for such a trap. He also hoped that a simultaneous attack on the Aleutian Islands would split the American response and secure Japan's northern flank from another American assault coming out of the North Pacific. Time and tide dictated the timetable for the amphibious landing as there were only a few days in the first week of June when slack high water after dawn allowed the *daihatsu* landing craft to get over Midway's coral reefs. As Spruance found out later, these same forces of nature would also govern the timetables of his amphibious operations.

However, before Yamamoto could move north, he had already committed to first securing the empire's southern reaches by capturing Port Moresby in Australian New Guinea. On 30 April, less than a week after it had returned to Pearl Harbor, Nimitz ordered TF 16 to head south at flank speed to join Vice Admiral Fletcher's TF 17 in heading off the Japanese thrust. During the two-day Battle of Coral Sea beginning on 7 May,

Fletcher's force, combined with TF 11, engaged three Japanese carriers supporting the invasion force heading to Port Moresby. In the first-ever carrier-against-carrier engagement, the venerable *Lexington* suffered such heavy bomb damage that she had to be scuttled. *Yorktown* received a direct hit from a single 250-kg bomb and suffered several near misses, leaving her damaged and in need of immediate repair. Fletcher and TF 17 headed back to Pearl Harbor.[23]

The Japanese, however, had also taken heavy losses. The light carrier *Shōhō* was sunk while the fleet carrier *Shōkaku* had been so badly damaged by American dive bombers that she had to return to Japan for repairs. The third Japanese carrier, *Zuikaku*, was not hit but lost many aircraft and aircrews. More importantly, these two Japanese fleet carriers were sidelined for Yamamoto's planned Midway operation. The Battle of Coral Sea is often seen as a tactical victory for Japan, but without carriers to protect the landing forces the invasion of Port Moresby was called off. The failed operation marked the last significant advance of the Empire of Japan into the South Pacific.

Arriving too late to participate in the battle, TF 16 patrolled the area north of Efate in the New Hebrides to ensure the Japanese would not probe further west into the South Pacific. With *Yorktown* damaged and *Saratoga* still under repair at the Bremerton Navy Yard, *Enterprise* and *Hornet* were the only carriers immediately available for operations. In Spruance's opinion, Halsey's carriers should have been at Coral Sea on the more critical strategic mission to head off an invasion of Port Moresby. The outcome of that battle might have been very different if four American carriers had been present.[24]

On 9 May, Halsey received a dispatch from Nimitz informing him that it appeared that the enemy had postponed the attack on Port Moresby and was concentrating in the Bougainville area to occupy Nauru and Ocean Islands. The ever-aggressive Halsey prepared to sail due north along the East 170th meridian to attack the Japanese strike forces if they ventured west toward the Gilbert Islands.[25]

During this period, the Pacific Fleet's Combat Intelligence Office noted an increase in Japanese radio traffic, indicating perhaps that a major operation was impending. Cdr. Edwin T. Layton, a highly experienced naval intelligence officer who spoke Japanese fluently, led the office, assisted by Station Hypo, the Fleet Radio Unit run by Lt. Cdr. Joseph Rochefort, perhaps the most talented cryptographer in the U.S. Navy. Together they deduced that the Japanese were planning a major offensive to strike west, likely aimed at Midway Atoll with a diversionary seaplane attack on Oahu. A Japanese attack on the Aleutians was also indicated. Unknown to Halsey and the other task force commanders was Nimitz and Station Hypo's struggle with OP-20-G, the codebreaking unit of COMINCH, who had the ear of Admiral King and the naval intelligence chiefs in Washington. They believed that the Japanese were still planning an attack through the New Hebrides to take Fiji and New Caledonia to cut the sea line of communications with Australia. King issued orders to keep the carriers, and the orphan aircrews of *Lexington*, in the south to deal with such a threat.[26]

Nimitz, however, was convinced that the attack would be aimed at Midway. Layton and Rochefort had proven their decryption talents to him leading up to the Battle of Coral Sea, and he had greater faith in their interpretation of the radio intercepts than in Washington's. Unable to persuade COMINCH, Nimitz had to find a way to release TF 16 and bring it north. On 14 May, Halsey received a dispatch from CinCPac informing him, "It is not intended that you shall attack enemy island bases when returning this area. Consider it important that you not be sighted by the enemy." Despite this directive Nimitz sent out another dispatch to Halsey later that day marked "eyes only," directing him to ensure that the enemy *did* spot his force as part of a clever subterfuge.[27]

The next day, Halsey dutifully reported that TF 16 was being shadowed by "snoopers," most likely operating from the seaplane base on Tulagi. The presence of a powerful American carrier task force in the vicinity had the desired effect, intentional or otherwise, of dissuading the Japanese from proceeding with their planned occupation of Nauru and Ocean Islands, something they put off until August. It might also have given Yamamoto reason to accelerate the planned attack in the northern Pacific, thinking that the remaining American carriers were occupied well to the south. Nimitz decided that the threat in the south, if not fully contained, could be managed for the time being, and ordered his only available carriers north.

On 18 May, Halsey and TF 16 received a cable stating, "Expedite return to Hawaiian Area."[28]

There still remained disagreement between Station Hypo and the intelligence people in Washington as to the exact target of the planned attack. The radio intercepts had given the intended target the code letters "AF," which OP-20-G insisted meant that Johnston Atoll was the target. To trick the Japanese into clearly identifying the target and to silence the doubters five thousand miles away, Station Hypo devised an ingenious plan. With Nimitz's approval, they sent a message to Midway via a secure submarine cable instructing them to radio an urgent request back to Pearl Harbor to send fresh water as their water evaporator plant had failed. Midway dutifully sent the message back in "plain" language and using an older code known to the Japanese. When the Japanese listening post on Kwajalein sent a message back to headquarters informing them that "AF" was out of fresh water, the identity of the target became clear.[29]

Since the death of Isaac Kidd at Pearl Harbor, Spruance had been the second-ranking officer in Task Force 16, and he and Halsey maintained a close working relationship, as only two old friends could. Oliver had the opportunity to observe their interaction closely. "Having attended all pre-sailing conferences, I never detected anything but the highest mutual trust, confidence, respect, and esteem between these two outstanding men," Oliver recalled. "The two consulted frequently on the conduct of the war. Each had a clear understanding of the other's thinking. Spruance told me in general what they talked about and indicated that he was in agreement with Halsey's views. I recall specifically that the matter of transfer of command in battle in case of Halsey's casualty was resolved between them, particularly as to how Spruance was to fight the Force."[30]

On the return trip, Halsey had received a stream of intelligence reports that portended a major Japanese operation against Midway Atoll and the North Pacific. He shared these with Spruance, his second-in-command, and Spruance and his staff studied every scrap of information they received. As the intentions of the Japanese became apparent, Spruance wondered, "Why is the enemy mounting such a massive operation to capture Midway when the place just does not have that much strategic importance?" Adding to the mystery was the projected Japanese thrust into the Aleutians.

Several times, Spruance was heard to ask, "If we only knew what they were thinking." It was becoming evident that the Japanese were dividing their forces again and that there might be an opportunity to catch them by surprise. Spruance thought deeply about this developing strategic situation during the return to Pearl Harbor.[31]

Thus began a chain of events that would have a profound impact on both the course of the war in the Pacific and the career of Raymond Ames Spruance.

CHAPTER 5

THE BATTLE OF MIDWAY

AS SPRUANCE AND TF 16 headed north on 28 May for Point Luck, the cryptographers at Station Hypo and in Washington worked feverishly to refine the details of the coming attack. Much to the alarm of Station Hypo, on 27 May it appeared that the Japanese had revised their JN-25 code, and suddenly they could no longer read the Japanese radio traffic. "You might say that the curtain went down and we weren't reading anything in JN-25 for a period of possibly a month or so," Rochefort later recalled, which is how long it took his team to decipher the new code groups. However, they could continue to monitor what was being sent and from where, and this traffic analysis was still of great value. In the meantime, Rochefort had some of his men reevaluate the mass of material they had on hand that they could read. On 31 May, this effort determined that fighter pilots from *Zuikaku* had been transferred to the light carriers sailing with the Northern Striking Force heading for the Aleutians. Clearly, *Zuikaku* was incapable of flight operations for the time being, and there were likely only four carriers in the Midway Striking Force.[1]

In assessing Japanese carrier tactics, OP-29–42 mirrored an assumption common to American carrier tactics: that the four Japanese carriers were divided into two separate groups attacking in two separate phases, with one task group of two carriers standing in for the preliminary air bombardment and remaining in position for close air support of the landing forces, while the second carrier group stood off at some distance away acting as a screen to ward off American attacks. In actuality, Japanese doctrine dictated that the carriers of the Kidō Butai remain and operate together as a mutually supporting group.[2]

In Nimitz's plan, the Marines stationed on Midway would hold the atoll while the air forces there conducted air searches and, when the enemy force was located, "inflict maximum damage on the enemy, in particular carriers, battleships, and transports." Submarines would take up patrol positions to the northwest, directly in the projected path of the Japanese advance, with the same orders to "inflict maximum damage." An appendix to the plan instructed Spruance and TF 16 to take up a station west of Point Luck, latitude 32° N and longitude 173° W, to be "the cocked pistol" waiting to ambush the Kidō Butai, while Fletcher and TF 17 stood to the east of the same to provide scouting and act as a reserve. They were to meet at Point Luck in the forenoon of every day while on station to exchange communications by visual signals or by air. At all times, they were to maintain strict radio silence.[3]

As historian Jonathan Parshall has pointed out, Nimitz carefully specified the location of Point Luck to be 360 miles northeast of where the Kidō Butai was expected to be on 4 June. Nimitz believed that early during the first day of the battle, the patrolling submarines and the air forces on Midway would whittle down the Japanese with attritional attacks and fix their location, giving Fletcher time to gauge the size of the attacking forces and reposition his carriers to within the 175-mile striking range of his bombers for an attack on the second day of the battle.[4]

While the U.S. Navy believed that the attack on the Aleutians was mainly a diversion, it was the price demanded by the Imperial Japanese Army for agreeing to Yamamoto's Operation MI and redirecting Japan's main effort from the South Pacific. The Japanese Army wanted to occupy a piece of American territory not only as a demonstration of Japanese strength but also to prevent the Allies from using the area as a base from which to launch long-range bomber attacks or even an invasion of the northern Home Islands. To deal with this threat, Nimitz directed the creation of Task Force 8, commanded by Rear Adm. Robert A. Theobald, consisting of two heavy cruisers, three light cruisers, and four destroyers, and sent them north.[5]

Nimitz had taken the precaution of reinforcing the defenses on Midway well before there was a consensus that it would be the object of a major enemy operation. On 2 May he visited the island and conferred with the garrison commanders. As a result, additional Marine rifle companies, antiaircraft guns, and Stuart M3 light tanks were detached from Hawaii to augment the defenses. The Navy had thirty-one PBY Catalina seaplanes on Midway. These were the vital "eyes" of the Pacific Fleet. Nimitz also convinced the Army Air Corps to relocate to the atoll seventeen B-17E heavy bombers and four B-26 medium bombers modified to carry torpedoes. The Marine aviation units also received reinforcements so that by June, the fighter unit, VMF-221, consisted of twenty-one F2A-3 Brewster Buffaloes and seven F4F-3 Wildcats, and Squadron VMSB-241 consisted of seventeen SB2U-3 Vindicator and nineteen SBD Dauntless scout bombers. Six of the new TBF Avenger torpedo bombers from *Hornet*'s VT-8 reinforced these. These bombers would attack the Japanese assault forces, while the fighters would defend the island from aerial attack.[6]

At sea, Halsey's staff were getting acquainted with their new boss. Since Spruance arrived the previous September, Halsey had talked glowingly of his old friend, building him into "some sort of super-being." Nervous and tense, they asked Oliver all manner of questions about Spruance's likes and dislikes, habits, and quirks, but they seemed unconvinced by the answers. At their first meal together, most of the staff dined with Spruance in the Admiral's Cabin, and they sat staring at their plates, eating in icy silence. Spruance spoke up as the coffee was being served, saying, "Gentlemen, I want you to know that I do not have the slightest concern about any of you. If you were not good, Bill Halsey would not have had you." In a few words, the ice was broken, and they got off to a cordial start. However, the good feelings the staff enjoyed that evening did not survive the coming battle.[7]

As the task force steamed to Point Luck, Spruance spent most of his time in the Flag Shelter, which was high on *Enterprise*'s island, silently observing. Oddly, Oliver found him even more relaxed as the task force commander than he had been as the commander of CRUDIV 5. He allowed the staff to go about their jobs without interference, and unless a major decision was called for, he stayed out of their hair. However, he occasionally came down from the island to indulge in his usual practice of taking walks for exercise, and on the flight deck he found a lot more room than he usually had while at sea. There, he was joined by several amiable companions: Lt. Cdr. C. Wade McClusky, the *Enterprise*'s Air Group Commander, and Lt. Earl Gallaher, commander of Scouting Six, both of whom also enjoyed stretching their legs and having a chance to talk freely with the Admiral.[8]

Fletcher and TF 17 departed Pearl Harbor early on the morning of 30 May, with *Yorktown* having been adequately repaired for the task ahead. At CinCPac headquarters, Layton and his staff were busy maintaining the fiction that TF 16 and 17 were still in the South Pacific. Halsey and Fletcher had been instructed to maintain radio silence on their return trips to Pearl Harbor for the same reason. The seaplane tender *Tangier* was at Efate sending signals pretending to be a fleet carrier carrying out flight operations. *Salt Lake City*, known to the Japanese as part of CRUDIV 5, was on patrol in the Coral Sea, playing a similar role.[9]

On 2 June, TF 17 rendezvoused with Spruance and TF 16. Unknown to them, they had passed through a Japanese submarine picket line during their journey north—or what was supposed to be a picket line. Due to shoddy planning by his staff, Yamamoto's submarines operating out of their Kwajalein base were late in sailing and not yet in position. Like Nimitz, Yamamoto and Nagumo were counting on their submarines to warn them about an enemy force's approach and conduct attritional attacks. Like Nimitz, they would also be disappointed. To confirm the presence and number of American carriers at Pearl Harbor, a planned surprise air attack by Japanese seaplanes operating from French Frigate Shoals was planned, but scratched when American flying boats were found moored in the lagoon there. Nevertheless, when Yamamoto and Nagumo were informed of these failures, they did not alter their plans.[10]

The damage done to the Japanese carriers at Coral Sea and the inability of the Imperial Japanese Navy to replenish the air group on *Zuikaku* in time for it to rejoin the Kidō Butai helped to even the odds for the coming battle. While Nimitz hoped the odds were good enough to justify a "calculated risk," Nagumo was confident that the odds were entirely in his favor. He assumed that only one American carrier was available at Pearl Harbor, unaware that *Yorktown* was still afloat, and thought that TF 16 was still far to the south. Although the Marine aircraft on Midway were generally inferior to their Japanese counterparts, the airpower on Midway was still a force to be reckoned with. The atoll constituted an additional, unsinkable American aircraft carrier as long as the action was within range of these aircraft. This idea continued to haunt Nagumo's thoughts as the battle unfolded.

With the confirmation that *Zuikaku* was not with the Striking Force, Nimitz reassessed his tactical disposition and decided to move Fletcher and Spruance further west from Point Luck so that they could attack on the first day of the battle. The odds were being evened. Nimitz still believed that the Japanese were operating two separate carrier groups, and Spruance could surprise the first carrier group providing close air support to the Midway invasion. Combined with a "softening up" by the air forces on Midway, this gave Spruance an excellent chance of success. After dealing with the first two Japanese carriers, the two American commanders would then combine forces to find and destroy the hypothetical second group. As the officer in tactical command, Fletcher would determine the best course of action. However, the firm belief in two separate Japanese carrier groups became a fixation for the staff of TF 16, with serious ramifications on the command decisions made during the battle.[11]

On the evening of 2 June, the two task forces began their move west, and by midday of 3 June, they were 175 miles west of Point Luck and 260 miles north of Midway. Fletcher placed TF 16 ten miles southwest of his position and ordered Spruance to have it ready for immediate action when the enemy's carriers were sighted. Searches were flown from *Yorktown* to augment the long-range searches by the PBYs operating out of Midway, but heavy weather to the northwest was helping to conceal the approach of the Japanese fleet. At 0445, they received a dispatch from CinCPac informing them that Dutch Harbor on the island of Unalaska had been attacked by carrier planes, as predicted. Layton and the Station Hypo intelligence estimates were proving to be accurate.

Later that morning, a PBY from Midway spotted two "cargo ships," which later turned out to be minesweepers, about 470 miles southwest of Midway on a course heading for the atoll, the first sign of the coming Japanese offensive. A search later in the day reported seeing the "main body" some distance from the first sighting but on the same general heading. This caused some consternation at CinCPac: the "main body" of what? It was approaching Midway from a much different heading than had been indicated by the Layton-Rochefort analysis. The direction of approach was consistent with that of the Occupying Force coming from the west, but the fact that no carriers had yet been identified was worrying. Nimitz discounted that the ships sighted were from the Striking Force, but he nevertheless directed Midway to attack it.

At 1445, the B-17Es of the 431st Bombardment Squadron (Heavy) conducted a high-level bombing attack from 8,000 feet. The ships below could see the clusters of 600-pound bombs falling their way and had time to maneuver out of harm's way. No damage was done, but that did not stop Lt. Col. Walter C. Sweeney, USAAF, from reporting that they had scored five direct hits and several near misses.[12]

Early in the morning of 4 June, the first real damage was done when, at 0230, a flight of four PBYs conducted a night torpedo attack against the same convoy. The Catalinas strafed the transport ships, and the tanker *Akebono Maru* was hit, suffering some casualties; however, the convoy continued on. At 0420, Fletcher ordered seventeen SBDs and twelve TBDs to search and sent a Combat Air Patrol (CAP) of six F4F Wildcats into the air. As soon as these were airborne, the strike group, consisting of eight F4Fs, seventeen SBDs, and twelve TBDs, was spotted on the flight deck. However, *Yorktown*'s strike group was not designated as the first to attack. This honor was given to TF 16. Aboard *Hornet* and *Enterprise*, similar measures had been completed, and the fliers nervously waited for the word to take off, their aircraft fueled, armed, and engines warmed up. At Midway, the PBYs continued their searches, and the Army Air Force bombers and Marine aircraft were rearmed and made ready to sortie again.

Meanwhile, Admiral Nagumo and the Kidō Butai, still undetected, finally reached a position 240 miles northwest of Midway from which to begin their first air attacks. At 0445, thirty-six Type 99 Val dive-bombers and thirty-six Type 97 Kate torpedo bombers were launched and headed for Midway, escorted by thirty-two Zero fighters. At 0500, Nagumo's cruisers launched their float planes to search for any American surface forces lurking nearby. Japanese doctrine dictated that carrier aircraft be dedicated to offensive operations above all else, and air searches were

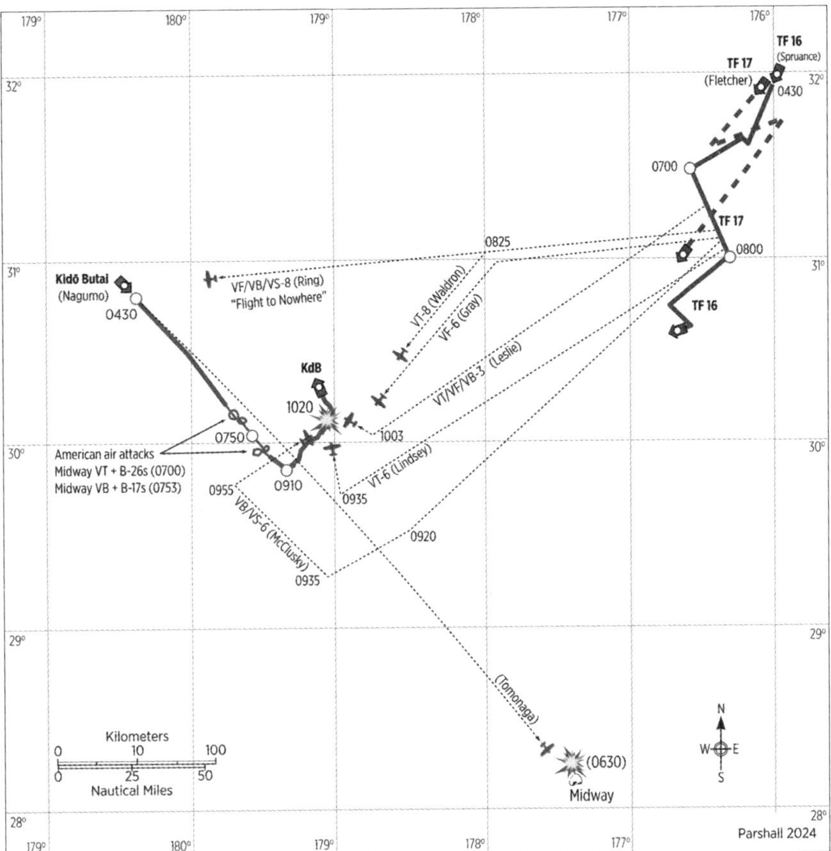

MAP 2. The Battle of Midway, 4 June 1942: The First Phase

mainly left to the escorting cruisers. Thus, Nagumo and his staff were hampered by a serious flaw in Japanese planning. They had launched their air search too late, with far too few aircraft to cover such a vast area. Instead, the Kidō Butai were spotted first, the cardinal sin of carrier warfare.[13]

At 0523, a PBY from Midway reported sighting a Japanese seaplane, which was followed a few minutes later by a report identifying two enemy carriers. This signal was sent to Midway and was also heard by Fletcher and Spruance, but the details of their location were garbled. Finally, at 0552, they received the message they had been waiting for, relayed in the clear: "Many planes heading Midway, bearing 310, distance 150." This conformed to Layton's intelligence estimates and seemed to align with the assumption of OP-29–42 that two enemy carriers were to be used for the preliminary air bombardment of Midway.[14]

Fletcher turned TF 17 to an eastward course to recover the search planes. At 0607, he ordered Spruance and TF 16, "Proceed southwesterly and attack enemy carriers as soon as definitely located. I will follow as soon as planes are recovered." TF 16 dutifully complied, coming about to a course of 240 degrees at twenty-five knots. At 0623, CinCPac rebroadcast the report that the enemy Strike Force, consisting of two carriers and battleships, was 180 miles bearing 320 degrees northwest of Midway, heading 135 degrees at twenty-five knots. This put them approximately 175 miles away from TF 16, at the range limit of the TBDs and F4F fighters.

When the report came in, the staff in the cramped Flag Shelter of *Enterprise* sprang into action after hours of tense waiting. Oliver, Browning, and Buracker "dived at the chart table and began a grabbing contest for the one pair of dividers" to plot the reported location of the enemy fleet. "For a moment it looked like someone was going to get stabbed," recalled Oliver. Spruance stood in the background and reached for a maneuvering board he had been carrying around for several days. Spruance asked for the report to be read back to him. Satisfied that it was authentic, he plotted the location of the Japanese fleet and TF 16, and "using his thumb and index finger as a pair of dividers, he measured the distance between the opposing forces. As he rolled up the maneuvering board and tossed it aside, he ordered, 'Launch the attack.'"[15]

Or so goes the dramatic recounting by Robert Oliver. In reality, the decision was more complex. To launch the planes, the carrier had to come about to a southeast heading to place the flight deck into the wind and maintain a speed of twenty-five knots. During the forty-five minutes it took to launch the entire strike force, the carriers would move away from the enemy, increasing the flight distance. In consultation with Browning, at 0638, Spruance ordered *Enterprise* to maintain an intercepting course heading of 240 degrees and a speed of twenty-five knots to close the distance first and then commence launching aircraft at 0700.[16]

Per American carrier doctrine, the scout bombers, which had greater fuel reserves, took off first, followed by the lighter fighters, and then the heavy, slow torpedo planes, which required a longer takeoff run and needed the extra deck space. Each section was supposed to circle the carrier until the entire attack force was in the air before they headed to the target. They then proceeded together, albeit separated by thousands of feet of altitude, as the torpedo planes stayed low while the dive bombers and fighters flew high. Ideally, when the enemy was sighted, they would split to launch their attacks from different directions, with the torpedo and bombing attacks occurring simultaneously to overwhelm the defenders. The TBD torpedo planes had to come in low and slow, maintaining a steady course to launch their "fish" successfully. This left them highly vulnerable to enemy fighters and antiaircraft fire. Far overhead, the SBD dive bombers would form up and, once over their target, roll into a nearly vertical dive that was almost impossible for the defenders to stop. The F4F fighters aimed to keep the enemy fighters off their comrades as best they could.

That was the ideal. Combat operations rarely unfold precisely as envisioned by peacetime doctrine. However flawed it might be, doctrine nevertheless provides a valuable base to modify and adapt using hard-won experience. The Japanese attacks on Midway were carried out with near-flawless professionalism based on their many years of training and fighting in the skies over China. By contrast, the American counterattacks were done piecemeal and, due to their inexperience, appeared amateurish, at least in the first exchange. Midway picked up the incoming Japanese air attack on radar, and by 0600, the mixed force of F2-A Brewster Buffaloes and F4F-3 Wildcats had scrambled and was in the air. These fighters managed to surprise the incoming bombers and destroyed several, but they were savaged by the experienced Zero pilots who were flying escort. Thirteen Buffaloes and two Wildcats were shot down, and the survivors were heavily damaged, leaving just two of the Wildcats airworthy.[17]

At 0620, the Japanese carrier planes hit Midway. The reinforced antiaircraft batteries put up an intense and accurate wall of fire, shooting down four Kate bombers and damaging many others. In all, of the 108 Japanese aircraft in the attack, 11 were destroyed and more than a third were damaged. The attack force nevertheless carried out their attacks with skill and determination. Many air base buildings and hangars were destroyed or damaged, but the runway remained mostly intact. More worrisome was the fact that the Marine defenders and their shore batteries were intact and combat-effective, ready to repel the Japanese invasion force. The raid's section leader, Lt. Tomonaga Joichi, conveyed this information to Nagumo with a recommendation that another strike be made before landing operations could safely begin.[18]

While the first wave of the Japanese attack was underway, Midway responded with counterattacks of its own. At 0710, the four B-26 bombers and the six TBF torpedo bombers from *Hornet*'s VT-8 staged the first attack against the Kidō Butai. However, the CAP from the Japanese carriers quickly overwhelmed the attackers. While several torpedoes were launched, none found their mark. Two B-26s and five TBFs were lost. The attack did, however, succeed in disrupting the Kidō Butai's formation as the carriers maneuvered in circles to avoid the torpedoes, thus retarding their progress along their southeasterly course. The fast and maneuverable B-26s managed to strafe the carriers, and one, piloted by Lt. Herbert Mayes, appeared to have attempted to crash dive into the island of the carrier *Akagi*, narrowly missing Nagumo and his staff. These attacks, along with the failure of the first strike to neutralize Midway, convinced Nagumo that the atoll and its air forces still posed a threat that had to be dealt with immediately. In direct violation of his orders from Yamamoto, at 0715 Nagumo ordered the Kidō Butai to prepare the aircraft held in reserve, fully half of the entire force, for a second attack on the atoll.[19]

As the Japanese attackers began their return flight to their carriers, a second wave of American planes from Midway, consisting of sixteen SBD Dauntlesses and eleven of the slower SB2 Vindicator dive bombers from Marine VMSB-241, began their attack runs. At nearly the same time, Lt. Col. Sweeney and his B-17E bombers, redirected from a second attack on the Occupying Force, appeared overhead at 0754 and began a high-level bombing attack on the carriers below. Once more, the carrier skippers adroitly maneuvered their ships to avoid the falling bombs while the Zero CAP smashed the incoming SBDs. The Marines flying these bombers had no training in dive bombing and resorted to glide bombing, leaving them highly vulnerable to attack from both the defending fighters and the ship's antiaircraft fire.

The slower Vindicators arrived about twenty minutes later. Neither flight had a fighter escort. The brave Marine pilots pressed home their attacks with tenacity, again to no effect, while their radioman-gunners held off the Zeros as best they could. Among those lost was Maj. Lofton R. Henderson, who was leading the squadron of SBDs, and for whom Henderson Field on Guadalcanal was later named. Nagumo's staff and the Japanese pilots watching below thought these Americans were braver than anticipated, but their tactics were deemed amateurish.[20]

While the ineffective air attacks against the carriers were going on, Lt. Cdr. William Brockman, commanding USS *Nautilus* (SS 168), was lining up a torpedo attack on *Kirishima*, one of the Kidō Butai's escorting fast battleships. At 0820, *Nautilus* fired two torpedoes but scored no hits. She immediately submerged and was attacked by the escorting destroyers as the Japanese fleet reformed and continued on its course. One of her tormentors, the destroyer *Arashi*, was left behind to deal with the submarine. After enduring over an hour's worth of repeated depth charge attacks, Brockman and his crew were relieved when *Arashi* abruptly quit and headed away at high speed to rejoin the carrier force.

While the American air and subsurface counterattacks did not do any damage, they inflicted crucial delays, causing the carrier fleet to disperse and maneuver. The reserve aircraft, waiting in the hangar decks below the flight deck, had been intended to strike at the American carriers when they were located and were armed with armor-piercing bombs and torpedoes. To attack Midway's ground defenses, these had to be replaced with general-purpose high explosive ordinance. This task was made more difficult as the carriers went through extreme turns and maneuvers to avoid the bombing and submarine attacks. CAP operations occupied the flight decks of the four carriers for quite some time, landing, refueling, and rearming the fighters. To complicate matters for Nagumo, at 0740, a scout plane from the cruiser *Tone* reported sighting an enemy force of "ten surface ships" to the east without specifying exactly what type of ships had been spotted. It was not until 0830 that he received confirmation that this force included at least one carrier.

On hearing this, Nagumo canceled his previous order. The rearming of the reserve aircraft for a ground attack was halted and re-rearming with anti-ship ordinance began. As there was no time to return the high-explosive bombs to their magazines, they were moved to the sides of the hangar deck as the Japanese ordinance men hurried about their jobs. At 0837, the aircraft from the first Midway strike began returning, and the flight decks had to remain clear to receive them. These delays prevented the Kidō Butai from getting the aircraft of the reserve force spotted on the flight deck, launched, and on their way to strike the American carriers. They would still be waiting below on the hangar deck when the dive bombers of *Enterprise* and *Yorktown* found the Japanese carriers.[21]

Meanwhile, back in the Flag Shelter of *Enterprise*, Spruance began to worry about the slow progress being made to get his planes on their way. As a "black shoe," Spruance left the details of carrier flight operations to Miles Browning and William Buracker of his staff and the carrier captains, George D. Murray of *Enterprise* and Marc Mitscher of *Hornet.* But as a tactician who had absorbed the lessons of the Fleet Problems well, Spruance understood the importance of finding and hitting the enemy carrier force with everything he had before they could do the same to him. He ordered Browning to send the entire air group and not keep anything in reserve. "I wanted to hit the Japanese carriers as early as possible with all of the air strength we had available," Spruance later explained. "I wanted to sink the ships we attacked, if possible, and not merely spread the damage we might inflict among a number of units, which could then get home, be repaired, and come out to fight again."[22]

The planes had started launching on time, but mechanical delays hindered the process. The SBDs of VS-6 and VB-6 under the command of Wade McClusky circled overhead, wasting fuel as they waited for the fighters of VF-6, led by Lt. James S. Gray, and the torpedo bombers of VT-6, led by Lt. Cdr. Eugene E. Lindsey, to launch. Lt. Gilven M. Slonim, Spruance's Japanese intelligence expert, came up to the Flag Shelter to inform him of the 0740 message sent in clear by the *Tone* scout that had identified the presence of TF 16, alerting the Japanese commander that there was an American force somewhere on his flank. This spurred Spruance to action, and at 0745, he sent a visual signal to McClusky: "Proceed on mission assigned." Once at cruising altitude, McClusky, considering the time that had elapsed, steered his section on a new course heading of 226 degrees to intercept the Japanese carriers. As the dive bombers headed west, the fighter and torpedo bombers were launched and cleared by 0806. Lindsey's group, now nearly half an hour behind, nevertheless kept to the original heading, and flying at a lower altitude, lost sight of McClusky, who had disappeared among the scattered clouds. After the final planes had left, *Enterprise* came about and returned to her previous course, heading southwest.[23]

If Spruance's relative inexperience with the nuts and bolts of air operations had any detrimental effect, it was that he placed too much trust in Halsey's air operations staff. Browning had ordered the air groups to "delay departure" until all sections were airborne. It was up to him to tell the air group commanders of both carriers which course to follow to find the enemy and give them the course heading and speed of "Point Option," the location where they could expect to find TF 16 when they returned. Browning performed poorly at both tasks, with near disastrous consequences. His only instruction regarding the location of the enemy was that the carrier captains, Murray and Mitscher, should direct their air groups to use standard search methods along a course heading of 240 degrees, toward the estimated location of the Kidō Butai based on its last known course and speed.

Each of the three American carriers had its own command culture and conducted operations somewhat differently based on their previous experience and training. The air group and crew of *Yorktown* had the most combat experience of the three, as their performance demonstrated. They had successfully engaged the more experienced Japanese pilots at Coral Sea and weathered repeated attacks. On the other hand, while *Enterprise* also had many months of combat experience conducting bombing missions against the various Japanese island outposts, her air group had yet to meet their counterparts in aerial combat. Finally, while *Hornet* had been in commission since October 1941, her air group and crew had the least combat experience, having only the Doolittle Raid under their belts.

Hornet had followed the motions of the flagship and began her launch operations at 0700 as well. Her air group commander, Cdr. Stanhope C. Ring, had organized the launch of the strike group in accordance with the standard "delayed departure" doctrine so that the dive bombers, torpedo bombers, and fighters could proceed to the target as one group. Marc Mitscher then gave Ring a heading that took *Hornet*'s strike group nearly due west, placing them far north of where Spruance and Browning had estimated the Kidō Butai would be at 0920. Mitscher, the senior aviator in either task force, possibly thought he knew better than the "black shoes" about fighting a carrier battle. Without informing the flagship and lacking any actual intelligence, Mitscher decided on his own initiative to strike the hypothetical second Japanese carrier group, which he evidently believed to be following in the wake of the two carriers that had already been sighted. At a stroke, a third of Fletcher's strike capacity had been sent on a "flight to nowhere."[24]

As TF 16 completed their launch, Fletcher in TF 17 decided to delay his launch as their northern search position left them many miles behind Spruance and so further from the Japanese. Fletcher ordered *Yorktown* to come about to follow TF 16 and close the distance with the Japanese carriers. After an hour and a half of steaming to the southwest, with *Yorktown's* strike group armed and spotted on the flight deck, at 0838 Fletcher ordered her to change course to the southeast to bring her head into the wind to begin his launch. Most of his strike group had been transferred from the damaged *Saratoga* to compensate for *Yorktown*'s losses at Coral Sea. Like Spruance, he was spurred on by reports that a Japanese floatplane was hovering around the periphery of the task force. Unlike Spruance, he decided to hold back about a quarter of his strike capability in case the unlocated, hypothetical second Japanese carrier group should materialize. At this point he estimated that TF 17 was about 160 miles distant from the Japanese. *Yorktown*, more experienced in combat flight operations, had her strike group in the air by 0914 and headed southwest as a single body, as per doctrine. By now, the distance had closed to roughly 150 miles, well within the fuel range of the torpedo bombers and F4F fighters. Fletcher sent a TBS message to Spruance informing him that TF 17 had launched three-quarters of its strength and turned to a Point Option course of 225 degrees at twenty-five knots.[25]

The Americans were now searching for the Japanese in five distinct, poorly coordinated groups, each flying on different headings. Operating under strict radio silence, they were not supposed to communicate with each other or their home carriers until they found the Japanese. By now, McClusky and the SBDs of *Enterprise* were nearing the point where he expected to find the Japanese. Lindsey with VT-6 was to his north. Neither had spotted the enemy. *Yorktown*'s coordinated strike group was behind them on the same heading. Far to the north, Ring and his SBDs of VB/VS-8 were still flying west, accompanied by the fighters of VF-8. Earlier at 0825, Cdr. John C. Waldron, leading *Hornet*'s VT-8 torpedo bombers, had broken radio silence to tell Ring they were on the wrong heading to find the known Japanese carriers and that he was changing course. Furious, Ring ordered him to follow, but ignoring a direct order, Waldron winged over to a new heading to the southwest. He was joined by the fighters of Lt. Gray's VF-6, who had mistaken Waldron's group for their torpedo bombers.[26]

Meanwhile, Nagumo was having problems of his own. The land-based air attacks disrupted his carrier formation and delayed air operations. Until he had received the 0830 report, he and his staff persisted in the belief that the American carriers were still back in Pearl Harbor. Based on the recommendation of his senior staff, he decided to wait to launch an attack until the aircraft available from all four carriers could be dispatched in a single, concentrated force protected by a fighter escort. The performance of the U.S. Navy had not impressed them up to this point and engendered a fearless overconfidence. In the words of Cdr. Fuchida Mitsuo, they felt that "there was little to fear from the enemy's offensive tactics." The last of the first strike aircraft had landed by 0917, and Nagumo ordered the Kidō Butai to come about to a new heading of 070 degrees, at thirty knots, heading northeast toward the American forces.[27]

Time, however, was running out for Nagumo. Minutes later Cdr. Waldron and his fifteen torpedo bombers of VT-8 found his ships. The Kidō Butai had now stretched out into a rough box formation with *Soryū* and *Hiryū* in line abreast, followed at some distance by *Kaga* and *Akagi*. Upon spotting the incoming torpedo bombers, the Japanese fleet turned west, and the combined CAP of the fleet fell upon the Americans. Coming in low and slow, without fighter cover, they were sitting ducks for the expert Zero pilots and were quickly annihilated. The only survivor was Ens. George H. Gay, who managed to crawl out of his sinking TBD and hide under his seat cushion to avoid detection in the middle of the enemy fleet.

The torpedo bombers of Lt. Lindsey's VT-6 were next, arriving at around 0940 from the south. He split his division into two sections of seven planes each and concentrated on *Kaga*, the carrier closest to his approach, coming in from either side. Once more, the Zeros fell on the lumbering TBDs, as the skipper of *Kaga* skillfully maneuvered his huge ship to avoid the few torpedoes that VT-6 managed to launch. Another piecemeal attack had been broken up, but again at the cost of precious time. With Zeros launching, then returning to rearm and refuel, there was no time to spot and launch a counterstrike, but if the Americans kept attacking in the same haphazard fashion, the Japanese had little cause for concern. However, things were about to take a dramatic turn for the worse for the Kidō Butai.

The course changes the Japanese fleet had undergone for the previous two hours had rendered McClusky's estimation of their location useless. After overflying the point where he believed the Kidō Butai should be, at 0935 he turned his force northwest on a reciprocal course, thinking that perhaps the Japanese carriers had retired after retrieving their first strike. After flying another twenty minutes along this heading, he had to consider ending his search as his planes were running dangerously low on fuel for the return trip. There then occurred one of those lucky flukes of warfare, for far below he spotted the long wake of the destroyer *Arashi*, heading at high speed to rejoin the Japanese fleet following her attack on *Nautilus*. McClusky made the brave decision to forget their fuel situation and follow the destroyer, hoping to finish the mission on which so much counted. At 1002, he broke radio silence to tell Spruance the news: "This is McClusky. Have sighted the enemy." Back on *Enterprise,* the Flag Shelter broke into a cheer. They had been waiting anxiously for news of the attack. "I can't express the immense relief we felt in the *Enterprise*," Buracker later recalled, "to get Wade McClusky's long-delayed 'Tally-Ho.'"[28]

As McClusky, hidden in the clouds and as yet unseen, approached the Japanese carrier formation from the southwest, the *Yorktown* air group also arrived, coming from the southeast. At 1007 the twelve torpedo bombers of VT-3, led by Lt. Cdr. Lance E. Massey, began their attack run aimed at the *Hiryū*, the closest target, at an altitude of 2,500 feet, escorted by six Wildcats led by Lt. Cdr. John "Jimmy" Thach, stationed to their rear and some 2,000 feet higher. They were met by a Japanese CAP of nearly forty Zeros, spread out at the north end of the carrier's box formation, who quickly swarmed Thach and his flight. Greatly outnumbered but undaunted, Thach, for the first time, initiated the maneuver that became known as the "Thach Weave": pairs of Wildcats alternating position so that if an enemy were on the tail of one, the two would weave and cross paths to get a snapshot at the bandit from the side. Thach and his wingmen kept the Zeros busy for the next twenty minutes while VT-3 lumbered toward its target.

Far above them, the seventeen Dauntless dive bombers of VB-3, led by Lt. Cdr. Maxwell Leslie, were swinging around to the north to coordinate their attack with Massey's. When VT-3 began its approach, the carriers, which had been on a northeast heading, now turned eight points west, putting them on a northwest heading to put their sterns toward the attackers to minimize their exposure to torpedoes. This made *Soryū* the northernmost carrier and the one now directly in front of VB-3. They found the carrier coming about to a new heading to the east to launch planes, placing the entire length of her deck along their approach path. At 1020, they began their attack.[29]

At that exact moment, McClusky began his own attack. Below him were the carriers of Nagumo's Carrier Division 1. *Kaga*, to the west, was nearest, while to the east and further away was *Akagi*. The lookouts aboard these ships had been preoccupied with watching the action to the northeast when one suddenly spotted the Dauntlesses coming through the clouds from a new and unexpected direction. It was too late for the Japanese CAP, concentrated as they were far to the north, to respond. Alerted to the danger, Nagumo ordered the division to get more Zeros into the air, but they were still being spotted and launched when the fatal attacks began. McClusky, a former fighter pilot, chose to lead his first group, consisting of his section and Gallaher's eighteen SBDs of VS-6, to attack *Kaga* first, in violation of standard doctrine, which required the leading group to go for the farther target. Behind him was Lt. Cdr. Richard Best and his fifteen SBDs of VB-6 who, following doctrine, were also attacking *Kaga*.

Luckily, Best realized what was happening at the last moment, pulled out of his dive, and broke off to lead his section to the right to attack *Akagi*.[30]

The two carriers maneuvered violently to disrupt the aim of the incoming dive bombers. The antiaircraft gunnery officers below tried in vain to obtain a firing solution on the steep diving targets. The previous months' carrier raids paid their true dividends as that valuable experience helped *Enterprise*'s dive bomber pilots find and hit their targets with professional skill. Gallaher's planes of VS-6, carrying 500-pound bombs, scored at least four direct hits and numerous damaging near misses on *Kaga*. One of the first hits was to her bridge, killing her captain, Okada Jisaku, and his staff. One of the Dauntlesses of VB-6, which was carrying 1,000-pound bombs, put one in the middle of her flight deck. Aboard *Akagi* Nagumo and his staff watched in horror as *Kaga* was racked by explosions and engulfed in flame. Their turn was next.

Best had only his and the two other bombers that had followed him to deal with *Akagi*, which was further away to the east. They had lost some altitude but were not opposed by the Zeros, nor was there any antiaircraft fire aimed their way until they were over the target. Once more, the Japanese did not see the Dauntlesses until they were almost overhead. Captain Aoki Taijiro put his ship into a maximum starboard turn, but instead of presenting a smaller target, he only managed to present his ship full on the beam to the three incoming dive bombers. At 1026, Best and his wingmen, flying in a V formation, pushed over and dived down on the carrier. Best, in the middle of the V, put his 1,000-pound bomb into the *Akagi*'s central elevator. His wingmen scored near misses on either side; the one on Best's right clipped the edge of the flight deck and damaged *Akagi*'s rudder.

The slow TBDs of Massey's VT-3 to the north were still approaching *Hiryū* as Leslie and his planes pushed over to hit *Soryū*. Due to an electrical malfunction, four of the bombers dropped their 1,000-pound bombs prematurely, leaving only thirteen bombs armed and ready. Three of these were neatly placed along *Soryū*'s flight deck. One pierced through into her lower hangar deck, destroying her engine uptakes, putting her engines offline, and leaving her dead in the water; the others landed in the hangar decks. The Zeros attempting to launch on her flight deck were shattered and scattered like chaff in the wind.

The flight decks of the Japanese carriers, like their American counterparts, were not armored and were easily pierced by the falling bombs which exploded on the hangar decks below among the tightly packed and fully armed strike aircraft. The resulting conflagration of vaporized fuel and high explosives created multiple fires too intense for the poorly trained and badly equipped Japanese damage control parties to extinguish. All three carriers hit that morning were burning beyond any salvation, *Soryū* so fiercely that she was abandoned within twenty minutes. *Kaga* and *Akagi* were scuttled early the next day. Nagumo was forced to escape his burning flagship by climbing down a rope to a waiting boat that took him to the cruiser *Nagara*.[31]

Nagumo's fourth carrier, *Hiryū*, was the only one to escape damage that morning. Massey's TBDs closed in valiantly, but as with all of the torpedo attacks that day, they failed. *Hiryu*'s skipper, Captain Kaku Tomeo, once more skillfully evaded the five torpedoes that VT-3 managed to launch. Meanwhile, the Japanese CAP and antiaircraft fire brought down Massey and ten of his planes.

Rear Admiral Abe Hiroaki, the commander of the escort cruiser division, was now in temporary command of the Kidō Butai as Nagumo transferred his flag. At 1045, he received a concrete sighting report of American cruisers and destroyers some 130 miles from Midway. Abe relayed this information to Admiral Yamamoto aboard *Yamato,* some six hundred miles to the north, and a few minutes later sent another message to the commander of the Combined Fleet, informing him of the loss of the three carriers. Abe told Yamamoto that he intended to engage the American carriers with *Hiryū*, and receiving no countermand, ordered the Carrier Division 2 commander, Rear Admiral Yamaguchi, to attack. At 1054, Captain Kaku turned *Hiryū* east into the wind and launched his available strike group, which consisted of eighteen Type 99 Val dive bombers and six Zeros, under the command of Lieutenant Kobayashi Michio. The American carriers were estimated to be just ninety miles away. *Hiryū* resumed her base course of 030 degrees to further close the distance.[32]

Meanwhile, the remains of the various American strike groups began the return trip to their home carriers. Cdr. Stanhope Ring and his *Hornet* air group had ventured far to the west. Having found nothing and running low on fuel, they turned around and headed back long before their *Enterprise* and *Yorktown* comrades had begun their attacks. The fighters of VF-8 were unable to locate *Hornet* and ditched, as did some of the SBDs of VB-8, although eleven of these made it safely to Midway. Only Ring and the fifteen SBDs of Lt. Cdr. Walter Rodee's VS-8 managed to return to *Hornet*, the last arriving around 1145.[33]

Enterprise's air group was particularly hard hit. As with the other air groups, her torpedo squadron ceased to exist as an effective force when only three serviceable TBDs made it back. After the air group had left earlier that morning, *Enterprise* was forced to maneuver to launch her CAP, placing her far from where the original Point Option course had predicted. As a result, many of the SBDs ran out of fuel and were forced to ditch, a predicament for which they blamed Miles Browning. Most of these pilots were rescued by PBY patrols, but not all were so fortunate. Lt. Charles Ware of VS-6, Oliver's classmate whom *Northampton* had pulled from the sea during the Marcus Raid, was lost along with his entire section during the return trip.[34]

Even though the Japanese had suffered a terrific blow, Nagumo reorganized the surface ships of the Kidō Butai, consisting of two battleships, two heavy cruisers, and destroyers, around *Hiryū* and headed northeast. Captain Kaku ordered the remaining ten torpedo planes made ready for another strike. The scouts from his cruisers were still actively searching for the Americans, and at 1100, one of them reported a sighting of three American carriers and escort cruisers. Although aware that he might be putting his head in a noose by attacking with a single carrier, Nagumo also knew that he had savaged the American torpedo planes. With these gone, Nagumo, a battleship admiral at heart, perhaps felt his surface ships had less to fear from the bombers. He might yet salvage a victory if he could engage the Americans with his still formidable force.

Aboard *Yorktown*, the reserve planes of VS-5 were spotted on the flight deck and ready to go. Fletcher, aware that he had been sighted, ordered them into the air to search to the north and northwest to look for the hypothetical second Japanese carrier group. Their departure also cleared the deck for landing operations. *Yorktown* was recovering her planes when, at 1135, her radar picked up a contact twenty-five miles away, the incoming

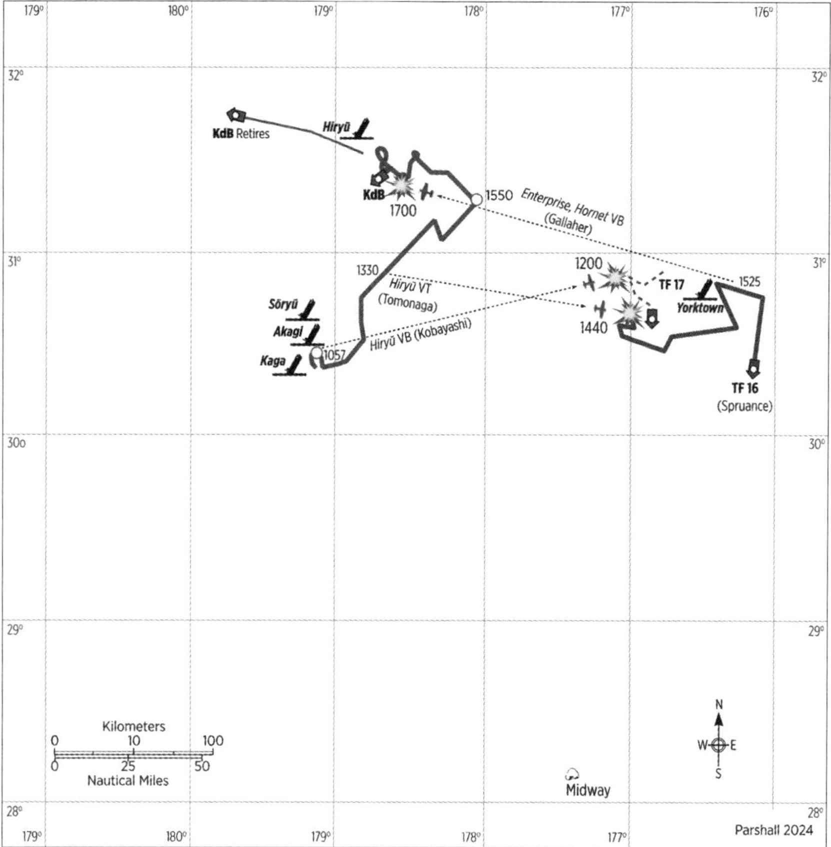

MAP 3. The Battle of Midway, 4 June 1942: Counterstrikes

attack from *Hiryū*. Fletcher immediately launched his remaining CAP and directed any available aircraft still in the air to assist.[35]

The movements of the two American task forces during the morning of 4 June ended with Fletcher and TF 17 being further west than Spruance and TF 16. As a result, it was Fletcher that Lieutenant Kobayashi and his Type 99 dive bombers found first at 1200. The American CAP decimated the incoming attack, but seven of the attackers fought their way through and dived on *Yorktown*, dropping their 250-kg semi-armor piercing bombs. Their results mirrored those that *Soryū* had earlier endured: three hits on the flight deck, including one that penetrated *Yorktown*'s engine uptakes, putting her engines out of commission and leaving her dead in the water, and two near misses. Kobayashi managed to transmit a report of their success at 1211 before disappearing. Only five of his attack force returned.[36]

While *Yorktown* took hits similar to *Soryū*, she did not immediately suffer the same fate. Fortunately for Fletcher and the crew of *Yorktown*, the damage-control measures of the U.S. Navy were far superior to Japan's. In addition, *Yorktown*'s radar had provided an advanced warning that the Japanese never had. Watertight bulkheads were closed, the fuel supply lines were purged and filled with carbon dioxide, and any loose ordnance was struck below into the magazines. American damage-control training was extended to the entire crew, not just to a few engineering officers as in the Japanese navy, and they were much better equipped with portable firefighting apparatus. Plus, they had been through this experience once before, at the Battle of Coral Sea. As a result, the fires were brought under control, and work quickly began to repair the flight deck. After inspecting the damage, Fletcher departed the stricken carrier just after 1238, transferred his flag to the cruiser USS *Astoria* (CA 34), and ordered that *Yorktown* be taken under tow. However, by 1335, her engineers had managed to get her underway again under her own power, to cheers all around.[37]

Spruance and TF 16 were just over the horizon, and the first indication of trouble was the thick plumes of black smoke rising from the northwest. Spruance detached the cruisers USS *Vincennes* (CA 44), USS *Pensacola* (CA 24), and several destroyers from his screen to assist TF 17. Six F4F fighters from VF-6 were also sent. As this drama unfolded, Spruance and Fletcher were unaware that a second strike from *Hiryu* had launched at 1331 and was on its way. At 1430, the Japanese strike force commander, Lieutenant Tomonaga, spotted what appeared to be an undamaged carrier some thirty-five miles distant. Braving the CAP and a furious antiaircraft barrage, Tomonaga's flight launched four torpedoes, two of which struck *Yorktown* on her port side.

Unlike the American torpedoes of the early war, the Japanese Type 91 aerial torpedo was deadly. The two struck amidships, close together, and blasted a huge hole below the waterline, flooding the port-side engineering spaces and knocking out all power, including the standby emergency generators, leaving the ship totally dark. *Yorktown* began to take on a steep list to her port side, so much so that her captain Elliott Buckmaster feared she might capsize at any moment. As the list approached 30 degrees, and without power to counter-flood or conduct damage control, Buckmaster issued the order to abandon ship. At 1455, Fletcher directed the escort destroyers to remove her crew and radioed CinCPac shortly thereafter with a doleful message: "*Yorktown* apparently sinking—have no idea location carriers attacking Task Force 17."[38]

This came as an unwelcome surprise to Spruance. He had sent a message to Nimitz forty minutes earlier stating that the "Air groups of Task Forces 16 and 17 attacked carriers of enemy force consisting probably of four CV, two BB, four CA and six DD. All four CV believed badly damaged." Spruance had relied on the reports of the returning pilots for his information, but by now he ought to have been wary of aviators' often exaggerated claims. The first strike on *Yorktown* at noon might have been launched by an undamaged Japanese carrier just before the attacks in the morning, but this second strike could only have come from an intact carrier.

But at least one aviator had a different story. Dick Best told historian John Lundstrom many years later that the senior aviation staff—that is, Browning—had never asked him or any other pilot to report on what they had seen. "Two hours earlier, I reported (to Browning) in Spruance's hearing that three Japanese carriers would not operate any aircraft that day but that a fourth to the north of the three was untouched. At no time after I left the flag bridge did anyone ask if I had any info on the fourth carrier." In Best's opinion, this was indicative of a mutual antipathy: "The staff had the same arrogance about the aviator's knowledge as the fliers had about the flying savvy of the senior aviators."[39]

Such a communication breakdown could be easily laid at Browning's feet. He was gruff and abrasive with his subordinates, and they resented him for it. Gallaher recalled, "As for Miles Browning . . . I very much disliked him as a man, but I did consider him to be an excellent tactician and the most capable person available at the time he was selected . . . by Admiral Halsey." Another aviator, Cdr. Walter F. Boone, the *Enterprise*'s executive officer, opined that Browning "possessed a very active and imaginative mind, but lacked sound judgement to go with it. . . . His value . . . depended upon having a superior who was sufficiently experienced in air operations to sort out his good ideas from the bad. . . . As a non-aviator, Spruance was handicapped by having an aviator of Browning's type . . . to advise him on air operations." After the first strike on *Yorktown*, a second wave of scout bombers should have been launched to confirm the earlier results; instead, it took several hours and the crippling of a carrier before such action was taken.[40]

Spruance and Browning might be excused on the basis that the grievous losses suffered by *Enterprise*'s air group left them little to strike back with. At 1200, *Enterprise* had nearly a full complement of fighters but only seven SBDs in Gallaher's VS-6 and four in Best's VB-6, and a mere three torpedo bombers. *Hornet* had Rodee's fifteen SBDs plus the eleven that had yet to return from Midway. Spruance was reluctant to send such a meager force until he had more information about the location of the fourth carrier. At 1445, one of the scouts from VS-5 that Fletcher had launched before noon reported "one carrier, two battleships, three heavy cruisers, four destroyers," bearing 278 degrees and 110 miles from TF 16. Spruance ordered both carriers to begin launching at 1530.[41]

By this time, the much-reduced air group from *Enterprise* was augmented by the now orphaned SBDs of *Yorktown*'s VS-3, for a grand total of twenty-four bombers with four F4Fs for escort. Gallaher replaced McClusky, who had been wounded during the morning strike, as the air group commander. Gallaher's plan was for his ten *Enterprise* bombers to attack the carrier while VS-3 attacked the escort battleships. They spotted *Hiryū* to their north at 1700. Gallaher led his planes a bit further west and north to attack her coming out of the sun from an altitude of 13,000 feet. At the last moment, Lt. Dewitt Shumway, leading VS-3, decided to ignore the battleships and join Gallaher, which was in keeping with American carrier attack doctrine.

Once more, the Japanese lack of radar allowed the Americans to catch them by surprise. As Gallaher pushed over into a steep dive, Captain Kaku put his carrier into a tight turn to port to throw off the aim of dive bombers. Gallaher's 1,000-pound bomb missed, as did the next two, but Dick Best and his section were able to maneuver at the last moment, scoring four hits on *Hiryū* forward of her island, including one that blasted her forward elevator onto the bridge.[42]

Bad luck continued to dog the air group of *Hornet*, as they were late in launching due to a communications issue. When they reached the scene of the action twenty minutes later, *Hiryū*, while still underway and making thirty knots, was already engulfed in flames. They chose to attack the escorting cruisers *Tone* and *Chikuma* instead, but they came away with only a few near misses, as the cruisers maneuvered their way from under the attacks. *Hornet*'s air group had failed to make a single hit on an enemy ship on 4 June. As a coda to the events of the day, Colonel Sweeney and a flight of six B-17Es from Midway arrived around 1740, joined by a second flight of six B-17Es from Barking Sands Airfield on Kauai flying at the relatively low altitude of 3,600 feet. Once more, the big four-engine bombers looked impressive, but they all missed their intended targets.[43]

As the American attackers turned around for their flight back to TF 16, Spruance called Fletcher on the TBS at 1811 to report on the success of the attack. Spruance told Fletcher that he was about thirty miles east of his position and intended to steam west to recover his planes. "Have you any instructions for me?," asked Spruance, to which Fletcher replied, "Negative. Will conform to your movements." This, in effect, made Spruance the officer in tactical command of the combined task forces. As Spruance turned TF 16 to the southeast to recover aircraft, Fletcher mirrored the movement and returned the loaned cruisers to TF 16.[44]

Fletcher was still the senior officer and could have easily transferred his flag into *Enterprise* or *Hornet*, remained in overall command, and delegated the *Yorktown* salvage effort to his cruiser division commander. Over the years, Fletcher's detractors have faulted him for turning over his command to a junior. He may have been overtired from months at sea and the loss of his flagship. To his defenders, such as John Lundstrom, his decision to transfer command to Spruance was the selfless act of a man of high integrity. Fletcher bowed out with the satisfaction of knowing that on his watch four Japanese carriers had been sunk, and the main objectives of OP-29–42 had been accomplished. He left the final sweeping up to Spruance. It was Spruance's battle to lose from now on. Spruance was grateful for the opportunity, as he told Emmet Forrestel, his first biographer: "He was my senior, and I did not know what he wanted to do himself or wanted me to do. His reply was a message that I have always appreciated."[45]

At the close of the day of 4 June, Spruance still had much to consider. As far as he knew, a Japanese invasion convoy was still on its way, and the two battleships and two cruisers that escorted the Japanese carriers were still a threat to be reckoned with. He also knew the Japanese were well-trained for night surface actions. What he did not know, however, was that Yamamoto had ordered the battleships and cruisers that accompanied the Midway Occupation Force to head east at full speed to join Nagumo and for the cruisers of the Support Force to bombard Midway.

On Spruance's orders, TF 16 was organized into a cruising formation and at 1915 headed due east, a course they maintained until midnight, heading away from the Japanese. Early on 5 June, they put about, steaming back toward Midway to attack at daybreak in case the invasion went ahead. This decision infuriated Miles Browning, who insisted on continuing along a westerly heading and using their air superiority to finish off the remains of the Kidō Butai. Spruance, however, was still under orders from Nimitz to preserve the carriers above all else. Engaging the Japanese at night with fliers not trained for night operations and facing battleships with carriers defended by "tin-can" treaty cruisers was not something that Spruance was going to do.

It was not until 0600 on the morning of 5 June that Spruance had some solid information about the Japanese fleet, but he was still unsure if these ships portended an invasion or not. Plus, he received reports from PBYs flying out of Midway about another possible carrier. The carrier *Akagi* had been scuttled by torpedoes fired by her escort destroyers late on 4 June. *Soryū* and *Kaga* met the same fate early in the night, but *Hiryū* was still afloat and drifting along. She was sighted early on 5 June and reported as not burning, which added to the confusion. That report was amended early in the afternoon to "smoking badly and going at a slow speed," but by that time she had already been scuttled by a Japanese torpedo. She sank at 0912 on 5 June. The fourth carrier was now indeed a phantom.[46]

Robert Oliver joined Spruance for breakfast in the wardroom that morning. He found his boss relaxed and in high spirits. When Oliver got up to leave, Spruance told him to sit with him for a while, saying, "They don't need us up there. Besides, you and I had a busy day yesterday and it won't hurt us to relax for a while." They discussed the events of the previous day, and Spruance explained how, in his view, the battle was typical of a major action. "You went in with a good plan and hoped it would work. Then the fog of war sets in and you are never quite sure of what is going on but you must have faith." He allowed that luck played a role in their success, and his only regret was that they had lost so many brave men.[47]

At 0630, a PBY noticed an oil slick being left in the wake of the cruiser *Mikuma*, which had collided in the night with her sister *Mogami*. *Mogami*'s bow had been badly damaged, and both were now proceeding at reduced speed. Midway reported the position of what they identified as "battleships" and promptly launched attacks with its available dive bombers. Facing the combined antiaircraft fire of both cruisers, several bombers were shot down, and no hits were scored. This was followed by yet another fruitless attack by the Army B-17Es, which dropped their 500-pound bombs from 20,000 feet, completely missing their targets.

Spruance and his staff were still concerned about the crippled carrier they had heard about and decided to let the shore-based air of Midway deal with the "battleships." By midday, it was concluded that the crippled carrier was still out there, some 240 miles from the last contact. It also appeared that the threatened invasion would not occur that day, as there had not been any preparatory bombardment by the Japanese. With the carriers free to move west, Browning drafted an attack plan calling for the launch of the combined task force's remaining SBD Dauntlesses, loaded with 1000-pound bombs. Taking into account the movements of the carriers turning into the wind to launch, the distance to the target once the air group was in the air and organized would be closer to 275 miles, on the very edge of the Dauntlesses' range.

This plan triggered pushback by the pilots, who were already sore with Browning due to the Point Option miscalculation. They pleaded with McClusky. Had Browning considered the fact that these planes now had self-sealing tanks, which reduced their fuel capacity? That the added weight of armor and the 1,000-pound bomb increased fuel consumption? They were being ordered on a mission that would end with them ditching in the sea. McClusky, although due to his wound not slated for this attack, led a delegation that included Gallaher and Captain Murray up to the Flag Bridge to protest. A furious row ensued. Spruance, who was standing by, heard the arguments and agreed with McClusky. "I will do what you pilots want," he told them. Browning, furious at this "mutiny," reportedly threw his hat to the deck, stomped on it, and went to his cabin in a rage.[48]

The 1,000-pound bombs that Browning had ordered were exchanged for 500-pound bombs, but the task meant that the launch was delayed until 1512, when a total of thirty-two SBDs were launched, setting off at 1530 to search for the reported carrier. Part of the group formed a scouting line at low altitude, while the rest flew at 18,000 feet. After nearly three hours of searching, the *Enterprise* group came across the Japanese destroyer *Tanikaze* searching for survivors from *Hiryu* and attacked. Her skipper put her through a series of high-speed S-turns and maneuvered from under the dive bombers' attacks. The plucky destroyer had been attacked by a total of sixty-four dive bombers and lived to fight another day.[49]

Dusk was quickly turning to night, and none of the pilots in either strike group had experience in night carrier landings. Fearing the loss of yet more pilots and aircraft in the dark, Spruance ordered both of his carriers to turn on their thirty-six searchlights and deck lights, a highly unorthodox move in waters known to harbor enemy submarines. However, Spruance later recalled, "A carrier without its air group is a disarmed ship, a liability, not an asset. The time to consider the risk of turning on the lights for a night recovery is before launching the attack. . . . If the tactical situation is such that you are not willing to do what is required to get the planes back safely, you have no business launching the attack in the first place." All of the returning Dauntlesses found the carriers and made their first night landing safely, except for one that ran out of fuel just before landing, but whose crew was quickly recovered. Spruance was irritated to find out that this was one of six bombers from *Hornet* that had flown with 1,000-pound bombs, against his orders.[50]

Spruance ordered TF 16 to reduce speed to fifteen knots to conserve fuel after all the planes had been recovered. He was still concerned about running into a powerful Japanese surface force in the night. Unknown to him, Yamamoto had regrouped the remains of Nagumo's Kidō Butai and Kurita's Support Force and ordered a retirement to the west. The Occupying Force and its troop transports were ordered to stand by. Yamamoto still hoped that a rash American commander would continue to pursue the battered Kidō Butai and fall into a trap. Indeed, Spruance recalled years later that Yamamoto had tried to trick him into doing so by having one of his battleships send out a fake, uncoded distress call. Spruance, however, was too wily to fall for such an obvious ruse.[51]

The early morning of 6 June found TF 16 some 350 miles northwest of Midway. At 0500, planes were dispatched 200 miles west in search of the phantom Japanese carrier and her escorts. At 0645, one of the SBDs spotted "one battleship, one cruiser, and three destroyers" heading west at ten knots, located 138 miles southwest of TF 16. Somehow, the message was garbled into "one carrier and five destroyers," which got Spruance's attention. He ordered the CRUDIV 5 to launch their scout planes at 0745 and increased the task force speed to twenty-five knots, heading southwest. For a change, *Hornet* was first to launch, beginning at 0800. Mitscher sent up twenty-five SBDs, armed with a mix of 500 and 1000-pound bombs, under Commander Ring. After the strike had departed, the scouts that had been sent out earlier landed and corrected the report: there was no carrier after all.[52]

Guided by reports from the SOC float planes, Ring found *Mogami, Mikuma,* and their two escorting destroyers at 0930, still heading west at the best speed the stricken *Mogami* could make. For the loss of two SBDs, Ring's group made just two hits, both on *Mogami.* As the *Hornet*'s group was returning, *Enterprise* got thirty-one SBDs into the air, along with her three remaining torpedo planes. Before they left, Spruance gathered the pilots and the group commander, Lt. Wallace Short, and told them, "Now listen carefully. I want to put that cruiser [*Mogami*] down, and the surest way to do it is to put some torpedoes into her. I want the bombers to silence their guns before you make your run. But if there is one single gun firing out there under no circumstances are you to attack. Turn around and bring your torpedoes home. I am not going to lose another torpedo plane, do you understand?" They nodded their affirmation and climbed into their waiting planes.[53]

Short and his SBDs found the Japanese cruisers just after noon and attacked from high altitude under a hail of antiaircraft fire from their prey below. The three torpedo planes slowly approached at low altitude, watching for the outcome. The cruisers maneuvered as best they could, but *Mogami* received two more hits. Her sister *Mikuma* suffered worse, receiving five direct hits, including one that struck amidships, setting off her loaded torpedo tubes. The warheads of the deadly Long Lance Type 93 torpedoes exploded with devastating effect. The previously undamaged cruiser was now a flaming wreck. Though badly damaged, *Mogami* managed to put up antiaircraft fire, and in obedience to Spruance's orders, the torpedo planes turned about and headed for home, joined by Short and his group. None of *Enterprise*'s planes were hit on this run.[54]

As the cruisers had yet to be "put down," another strike was ordered. At 1445, a second wave of SBDs from *Hornet* arrived to find *Mikuma* in a sinking condition with *Mogami* and the destroyers attempting to take off survivors. *Mogami* was hit again, as was one of the destroyers. When apprised of the attack and informed that *Mikuma* was doomed, Yamamoto ordered the Main Force to head south to meet *Mogami*, hoping that the Americans would follow the stricken cruisers into a trap.[55]

Again, however, Spruance was not to be taken in so easily. TF 16 was now well west of Midway, and as night fell, Spruance was determined to place his ships beyond the 700-mile range of the land-based aircraft on Wake Island. Spruance recalled later, "I was faced with the possibility of running into that big Japanese force at night, short on fuel, and outgunned. I had no intention of running into that force. I had a feeling, perhaps an intuition, that we had pushed our luck as far to the westward as was good for us."[56]

At 1956, Spruance radioed a report to Nimitz that a cruiser had been hit by three bombs and three attacks had been made on a "BB," and that she was left gutted and abandoned. Earlier, planes from *Enterprise* had flown out to observe *Mikuma* and take photographs. She was indeed a gutted wreck. The photos showed her surviving crew huddled on the fantail. There was no sign of the phantom carrier, and Spruance reported that he believed she had sunk. Spruance had fifty-four fighters, sixty-four SBDs, and three TBDs remaining, and as TF 16 was low on fuel, he was proceeding east to meet the oiler USS *Cimarron* (AO 22) to refuel. As *Enterprise* headed east for the night, Spruance and his staff took the opportunity to shave, shower, and change clothes for the first time in three days. Halsey had instilled in his staff the idea that it was unlucky to shave during a battle, a custom to which Spruance conformed. Now they gathered in the wardroom for hot food and well-deserved relaxation.[57]

That same evening, Yamamoto and his staff on *Yamato* were not enjoying anything that resembled relaxation. After fleeing the last American strike, one of the escort destroyers returned and confirmed that *Mikuma* had sunk. The Combined Fleet came about to refuel and then resumed its course heading southwards to meet the retreating *Mogami* and perhaps catch an intemperate American commander by surprise. But search planes sent out early on the morning of 7 June found only open water and no sign of the Americans. There was some good news from the north, as Operation AL had successfully landed troops on the Kiska and Attu Islands without meeting any resistance. But better news was to come.[58] Early on 6 June, Captain Buckmaster and a salvage crew boarded *Yorktown*, which had stayed afloat for a day and a half after her abandonment, and prepared for her to be towed back to Pearl Harbor. Work was ongoing to restore engine power when, at 1330, the Japanese submarine *I-168* managed to evade the tight cordon of escorting destroyers and fired four torpedoes, two of which hit *Yorktown* on her starboard side. Once more, Buckmaster and his crew were forced to abandon ship. At dawn on the morning of 7 June, *Yorktown* rolled over on her port side and slowly sank, with all her battle flags still flying.

After witnessing this profoundly sad sight, Fletcher and the rest of TF 17 were directed to rendezvous with *Saratoga* on the afternoon of 8 June. She had arrived in Pearl Harbor on 6 June for refueling and left that afternoon. At the same time, Nimitz dispatched the oiler USS *Guadalupe* (AO 32) to meet TF 16 and *Cimarron* at 0930 on 8 June at a point latitude 32° N, longitude 178° W, to conduct refueling and transfer much-needed aviation gasoline (avgas) to the carriers. Spruance sent one of his staff officers in *Cimarron* back to Pearl Harbor with a detailed account of the battle, amplifying the very few reports that had been made by radio during the battle. Later that day, Spruance received orders directing him north to Point Blow, some 425 miles southwest of Dutch Harbor, to reinforce TF 8. There, he would come under the command of his classmate

Fuzzy Theobald with orders to interdict the Japanese operations in the Aleutians.

At the time, due to the prevailing fog and rain, Theobald and thus CinCPac were unaware that the landings at Kiska and Attu had already occurred and that the Japanese Northern Strike Force had already withdrawn south beyond the range of air patrols flying out of Dutch Harbor. Spruance dreaded having to operate in such conditions: the only thing worse than carrier operations at night was carrier operations in heavy fog with zero visibility. Several days later, it appeared that the Japanese operation in the Aleutians was no longer a significant threat, and on 12 June, Nimitz canceled his previous orders, directing Spruance and TF 16 to return to Pearl Harbor, much to Spruance's delight. Unknown to either man, that same day the Northern Strike Force had been reinforced with the fleet carrier *Zuikaku*, the light carrier *Zuihō*, and the battleships *Hiei* and *Kongō* in the hope that the carriers of TF 16 would rush to the defense of the Alaskan islands. With the order to return, Spruance may have escaped another deadly trap that would have made the victory at Midway a very hollow one indeed.[59]

During the return of TF 16 to Pearl Harbor, Spruance stretched his legs with Gallaher on the flight deck of *Enterprise* when they were joined by Wade McClusky, who was holding a press release. "Admiral, you had better count to ten before you read this," said McClusky. It was a copy of the "The Washington Merry-Go-Round," a syndicated column written by Drew Pearson and Robert S. Allen, which claimed that the bombers of the Army Air Corps had won the Battle of Midway, not the Navy's "battleships." Seemingly unaware of the role of carrier-based air power, Pearson and Allen had no idea what they were talking about. Spruance's reaction was to use some extremely salty language, a very rare occasion for him. "It was the only time I ever heard the Admiral use strong language," recalled Gallaher.[60]

TF 16 entered Pearl Harbor on the afternoon of Saturday, 13 June. Fletcher and TF 17 had returned some hours earlier. Unlike the fanfare that met them in February, there were no cheers and sailors manning the rails to greet them. It was rather anticlimactic, matching the air of uncertainty about what exactly had happened during the previous week.

After *Enterprise* had berthed, Spruance took his barge across the harbor to report to Nimitz at the Submarine Base. Giving his subordinate commanders a few days to compose their Action Reports, he forwarded these to Nimitz in a letter dated 16 June, along with his specific insights and recommendations.

In his report, Spruance noted the importance of getting the first strike in a carrier duel, the vulnerability of carriers to fire, and the need for air groups to be highly trained and operate as whole units. Spruance went on to state that the Navy's aerial torpedo attacks were "fatally inadequate" due to the slowness of the TBD and the "lack of punch" and slow speed of the current torpedoes. Such attacks against ships defended by CAP had to be protected by friendly fighters. However, this was problematic as the F4F Wildcat was inferior to the Zero and lacked the necessary range and endurance. Spruance recommended that the TBD be replaced as soon as possible by the new TBF Avengers. Unfortunately, the hidden flaws of American torpedoes were not fully recognized for another year. On a more positive note, Spruance commended the handling of the *Enterprise* and *Hornet* and pointed out that "the advantages of operating at least two carriers together were manifest." Indeed, a case for three carriers operating within flying distance was demonstrated when *Yorktown*'s air group was used to make up for losses in the other two.

Spruance's papers contain two versions of this report, Serial 0144 and 0144-A. The first is a draft with pencil notes, which he concludes with the statement, "As a matter of historical record, the HORNET report contains a number of inaccuracies. The ENTERPRISE report is considered accurate and should be relied upon for reference." In the second version, this is toned down to say, "Where discrepancies exist between the HORNET and ENTERPRISE reports, the ENTERPRISE report should be taken as more accurate." A possible reason for the difference is that the second report was routed "via Commander, Task Force Seventeen," that is, through Fletcher, who may have directed the change.[61]

An explanation for this is that Marc Mitscher appears to have significantly fudged his after-action report regarding his (mis)direction of *Hornet*'s air group. He claimed that the *Hornet* air group had followed the southwest course given by Browning, but failing to find the Japanese carriers at the point predicted, they turned south instead of north as McClusky had done, and thus missed hitting the Japanese on the morning of 4 June. Spruance undoubtedly discussed this strange fabrication with Nimitz, and as a result, Mitscher was reassigned to training duties. He was recalled to take over the fast carriers under Spruance in early 1944, thanks to the influence of Adm. John Towers. Mitscher's talent and dedication as commander of TF 58 eventually restored Spruance's trust in him.[62]

Midway showed that aviation experts such as Miles Browning and Marc Mitscher could make mistakes as easily as any "black shoe." These experienced aviators had the flying time and the coveted gold wings that Spruance did not, but it is fair to point out that much of their aviation experience was based on older aircraft types. Spruance was wise to heed the advice of the younger men, such as Wade McClusky and W. E. Gallaher, who were flying the newer aircraft and were aware of their strengths and weaknesses.

Spruance was criticized for not pursuing the Japanese fleet on 4 June, even many years after the war. An early analysis of the battle by the Naval War College also faulted him, and it appeared that Adm. Ernest J. King agreed. Many of Spruance's staff officers were furious with his decision to retire east at the end of the day on 4 June, seeing his caution as typical of a "black shoe" admiral who did not understand aviation tactics. They regretted that their beloved "Uncle Bill" was not in command. One of these opined later that Spruance's lack of aviation experience made him "ultra-conservative" and that "Spruance threw away the opportunity for a truly tremendous victory by retiring; from then on Browning couldn't stand him." However, it is fair to ask what Halsey might have done differently, given Nimitz's directive to preserve the carriers as vital strategic assets. Would he have charged west in pursuit of the "cripples" on the evening and night of 4 June, perhaps with fatal consequences? As will be seen, Spruance's decisions were the correct ones.[63]

CHAPTER 6

CINCPAC CHIEF OF STAFF, 1942

SPRUANCE'S COMMAND OF TF 16 was meant to be temporary, as Nimitz had already drafted his orders before the Battle of Midway to relieve Milo Draemel as the CinCPac Chief of Staff. On 17 June, Spruance received his official orders, relieving him of command of CRUDIV 5 and instructing him to report for duty as the "CINCPAC Duty Chief of Staff and Aide" the next day. He spent the next several weeks working with Draemel to familiarize himself with the new job.[1]

In addition to his chief of staff duties, Spruance advised Nimitz on the strategy necessary to carry out the directives being sent from Admiral King. Nimitz and Spruance had been acquaintances prior to the war, and Nimitz was well aware of Spruance's long association with the Naval War College and his reputation as a naval strategist. One staff member recalled that Nimitz brought Spruance on board "to bring to the staff some first-hand knowledge of what planning was necessary to prosecute the war." Nimitz and Spruance quickly developed a deep and lasting personal friendship, along with a mutual understanding that helped them devise a winning strategy for the war in the Pacific.[2]

Once Nimitz and Spruance had worked out a concept, the CinCPac War Plans staff drafted an operations plan for Spruance to review, with the final decision-making to be done by Nimitz. Capt. Lloyd Wiltse, who was already Nimitz's assistant chief of staff when Spruance arrived, recalled that Spruance was "an excellent administrator and a superb creative planner. . . . He was a quiet and reserved personality. However, his humanizing ability and leadership generated down through his staff and through the Fleet later. . . . He was a leader and not a driver. Admiral Nimitz had great confidence in him . . . (and) allowed great freedom in his planning as he did all members of his staff, however there no doubt that he referred all matters of importance to Nimitz (who) held a tight string on everything."[3]

At Nimitz's invitation, Spruance moved out of the house he and his wife Margaret had been renting into Nimitz's own four-bedroom house in the officers' compound on Makalapa Hill. A routine of hard work, punctuated by periods of relaxation, soon set in. Every day, Nimitz and Spruance walked down to the new headquarters building, a reinforced-concrete two-story structure nicknamed "the Cement Pot." Nimitz and Spruance had offices on the main floor, while the staff, who were expected to be at their desks by 0800, occupied the lower level. At 0845, fifteen or so key officers convened in Nimitz's office to discuss the events of the previous day and the dispatches that had arrived overnight. Spruance had a larger version of his usual standing desk in his office but no chairs, ensuring that visitors would not get too comfortable; instead, they had to state their business and leave. Spruance was not one for idle chit-chat, but as he preferred being on his feet, he felt free to move around the headquarters and discuss matters with the staff when necessary. He hated writing lengthy memoranda and liked to think on his feet and "work the problem" verbally with the staff.

Around noon, Nimitz and Spruance usually had lunch with Wiltse and the staff, and afterward, they engaged in recreation such as long walks and swimming, which Nimitz loved almost as much as Spruance. It was important for Nimitz and Spruance to be able to relax and blow off a little steam, especially during this period of the war when the continuous pressure from COMINCH was high, and the news from the South Pacific was often bad. As soon as he arrived, Nimitz introduced Spruance to the game of throwing horseshoes. As Spruance later recalled, "That game was never in my line. He could always beat me with either hand." Nor did Spruance partake in Nimitz's daily pistol target practice. But when it came to swimming, it was Spruance who beat Nimitz. Wiltse recalled that before Spruance had arrived, Nimitz would invite a new staffer or a guest for a swim along Kailua Beach on the north shore of Oahu. Nimitz, an excellent swimmer, invariably outlasted them. But when the invitation was extended to Spruance, "to our surprise, we saw Admiral Nimitz walking back to his towel with Admiral Spruance still continuing his swim."[4]

After lunch, the staff returned to work until 1700 or 1730, which was cocktail hour in the Nimitz quarters. While Nimitz enjoyed a strong bourbon Old Fashioned, Spruance preferred to stick with fruit juice; if he had a drink, he nursed it throughout the evening. Eventually, Spruance became a dab hand at mixing elaborate rum cocktails for others. After a fine dinner, which for Spruance meant a salad and some of the wonderful varieties of local fresh fish, he and Nimitz relaxed in the company of their housemate Capt. Elphege Alfred M. Gendreau, MC, the Fleet Surgeon, while they listened to classical music. Thanks to Nimitz, Spruance developed a lifelong taste for classical music.[5]

While the Americans were settling in to the new routine of the war, Yamamoto had relocated his headquarters and the major elements of the Combined Fleet to Truk, the massive fleet anchorage from which they could readily move warships and aircraft into and out of Rabaul to support operations in the south. Japanese offensive operations in the South Pacific had been put on hold for Yamamoto's Operation MI, but now the Imperial General Headquarters was anxious to continue their occupation of New Guinea. However, serious divisions remained among Japanese planners about their next primary strategic goal. Although Midway was seen as a setback, it could still be overcome. Some, such as Yamamoto's Chief of Staff Vice Admiral Ugaki Matome, advocated a renewed naval thrust into the Indian Ocean and a move to attack India. The Imperial Army, however, was still bogged down with operations in China and reported they would not be ready for such an undertaking for another year. Ugaki fretted that Japan was missing opportunities that would not come again, as the Combined Fleet was already feeling the pinch of low fuel reserves.[6]

King, however, was not going to wait for the next Japanese move to act, and when the dust had settled after Midway, he directed Nimitz to initiate offensive operations. On 2 July, CinCPac received a directive from King and the Joint Chiefs of Staff that kept them occupied well into the following year. It set out three general tasks to be completed. Task One called for the seizure and occupation of Santa Cruz Island, Tulagi Island, and "adjacent positions," that is, Guadalcanal; Task Two called for the seizure and occupation of the rest of the Solomon Islands and the northeast coast of New Guinea; and Task Three the seizure and occupation of the major Japanese base at Rabaul. Task One was the responsibility of Nimitz as CINCPOA, the Commander in Chief of the Pacific Ocean Area, while Tasks Two and Three would be the responsibility of General Douglas MacArthur as COMSOWESPACFOR, the rather unwieldy acronym for "Commander, South West Pacific Force," operating from his headquarters in Brisbane, Australia.[7]

The Solomon Islands campaign began in response to the Japanese seizure of the Royal Australian Air Force (RAAF) seaplane base at Tulagi during the Battle of Coral Sea. The fact that the Japanese had started to construct an airfield on Guadalcanal was not discovered until later. King had been eyeing the area since the beginning of the war, and in early 1942 he directed Rear Adm. Richmond Kelly Turner, Spruance's old shipmate from the Naval War College and the chief of the War Plans Division in Washington, to start planning an operation in the South Pacific aimed at securing the Santa Cruz Islands.[8]

In June King decided that since Turner was behind the planning of what became known as Operation Watchtower, he should personally lead the amphibious operations in the South Pacific, under the command of Vice Adm. Robert L. Ghormley, who had just returned from London to be Nimitz's Commander, South Pacific Forces. Turner still had a cloud hanging over his head due to his poor handling of intelligence prior to the Japanese attack on Pearl Harbor, and King, who greatly valued Turner's ability, wanted him out of Washington both to deflect closer scrutiny of the affair by Congress and to give Turner a chance to rehabilitate his reputation.[9]

Turner gathered his staff in late June to begin planning, and within a few days he presented a draft of his operations plan to Nimitz and King at their meeting in San Francisco on 5 July 1942. Turner and his staff then followed Nimitz back to Pearl Harbor, where they closely coordinated with the CinCPac staff, including Spruance, before departing on 8 July for Auckland, New Zealand, to join Ghormley. Ghormley then issued Operation Plan 1–42 for Watchtower, with D(og)-Day set for 7 August 1942. There was precious little time to waste; that Turner and his staff could create a credible operations plan from scratch in such a short time could be attributed to Turner's experience at the Naval War College.[10]

While the U.S. Navy had an amphibious doctrine and was acquiring specialized equipment and ships, it lacked actual experience in conducting landing operations under combat conditions. Nor were there any senior Navy officers trained in amphibious operations. Turner was the closest thing available. This was critical, as the Navy's amphibious doctrine required that the senior officer in overall charge of landing operations must be a Navy flag officer, while the Marine Fleet Force commander in charge of the landing force would be his subordinate.[11]

Landing operations on Cactus, the codename for Guadalcanal, commenced on 7 August without any opposition from Japanese surface naval forces. The transports and cargo vessels anchored in their designated areas and began unloading the landing craft. When the 1st Marine Division landed on Guadalcanal they encountered light opposition, as the Japanese force there mainly consisted of engineering units sent to build an airfield. During the initial naval bombardment, these troops quickly retreated into the surrounding jungle, abandoning their equipment and supplies. The Marines soon put these to good use, completing the runway and making it operational by 18 August. They named it Henderson Field for the Marine aviator who died at Midway.

The Guadalcanal landings may have caught the Japanese by surprise, but they reacted quickly. On the night of 8–9 August, Vice Admiral Mikawa Gunichi, commander of the Imperial Navy's Eighth Fleet, led a strike force of seven cruisers from Rabaul against the larger Allied naval force protecting the landing, sinking four cruisers and damaging another in what became known as the Battle of Savo Island.

Holding Guadalcanal was a near-run thing for Ghormley and the Marines. Over the next five months, the U.S. Navy and the Imperial Japanese Navy engaged in seven sea fights in and around the Solomon Islands. The Marines, and later the U.S. Army, endured six months of ground combat until the Japanese withdrew from the island on 7 February 1943. The campaign drove home a lesson that the U.S. Navy would not deviate from in the future: the absolute necessity of obtaining air superiority and sea control within the immediate theater of operations.[12]

In early September, Nimitz left Spruance to oversee operations in Pearl Harbor while he traveled to San Francisco to meet with King for one of their bimonthly conferences. There, they were joined by Bill Halsey, who had recovered from his extreme dermatitis. They discussed the costly battles of the previous month and the lessons that might be learned from them. Eventually, the discussion turned to the idea of replacing Ghormley, as it was becoming increasingly apparent that he could no longer withstand the physical strain. Nimitz told King he would check on Ghormley's condition and report back.[13]

On 11 September, Bill Halsey returned to Pearl Harbor with Nimitz, who invited him to lodge in his house with his old friend Ray Spruance. Halsey attended the daily conferences and messed with Nimitz and Spruance, where they could discuss the war effort freely and frankly. Halsey was slated to take back TF 16, and as the senior aviation officer, the position of COMAIRPAC, the staff officer in charge of coordination and logistics for the air operations in the Pacific Ocean Area. He did not retain the latter job for long, as he was soon replaced by Vice Adm. John H. Towers. In another personnel shuffle, King had reassigned Towers, whom he disliked, to CinCPac to get him out of Washington. Halsey was not sad to be rid of the staff job, much preferring an active sea command.

Vice Admiral Towers was the heart and soul of naval aviation. A true aviation pioneer, he was Naval Aviator No. 3, and with Marc Mitscher, had flown the Curtiss NC flying boats in the Navy's trans-Atlantic crossing in 1919. Throughout his career, Towers saw naval aviation as the key to sea power and strongly advocated that an experienced naval aviator should hold any command that involved carriers. He had advocated for more aviation captains and admirals and had testified about this matter before the House Naval Affairs Committee in 1940, while Nimitz, as chief of the Bureau of Navigation, opposed the idea, perhaps shortsightedly. Congress approved Towers' request. As a result, Nimitz was decidedly cool to Towers and maintained a strictly formal relationship with him. As far as Nimitz was concerned, Towers would be flying a desk while under his command.[14]

Nimitz, however, was beginning to worry about the situation in the South Pacific in general, and Ghormley's performance in particular, and decided it was time to travel south and make his own assessment. He arrived at Nouméa on 28 September, where he met with Ghormley, Kelly Turner, and Maj. Gen. Richard K. Sutherland, MacArthur's Chief of Staff, who had traveled from Brisbane. Also present was Army Air Forces Chief of Staff Lt. Gen. Hap Arnold, who was on his inspection tour of the South Pacific. Nimitz found a spirit of defeatism and near desperation. Ghormley was haggard, in pain from abscessed teeth, and beset by a literal sea of woes. He told Nimitz and the others that to hold Guadalcanal, he needed more aircraft. Arnold replied that aircraft were already available in the theatre, although due to logistical snarls they were not being employed, and that in light of the demands in Europe, no more could be expected. Sutherland conveyed MacArthur's problems with turning back the Japanese on New Guinea. Earlier in August, MacArthur had requested, through Gen. George Marshall, that Nimitz release both amphibious troops and transports for the job to his command. Nimitz, however, stood firm in the belief that the Solomons campaign was "vital to future offensive operations." Besides, there simply were no extra trained amphibious troops or ships to spare.[15]

Nimitz traveled to Henderson Field two days later, where he met with Marine General Alexander Vandegrift, commander of the 1st Marine Division, to assess the situation firsthand, a step Ghormley had never taken. He toured the defenses and the field hospital, finding the Marines hard-pressed but cheerful and confident that they could hold out as long as they could be supplied with replacements for the lost men and aircraft.

Nimitz returned to Pearl Harbor on 5 October, disturbed by what he had seen. Some days later, better news reached CinCPac headquarters when it was reported that Rear Adm. Norman Scott had turned back an attempt by a force of Japanese cruisers to bombard Henderson Field on the night of 11–12 October in what would be called the Battle of Cape Esperance. Their joy was to be short-lived, however. While Scott could claim a minor tactical success, the Slot still belonged to the Japanese Imperial Navy at night, and he had not prevented the landing of a large convoy of Imperial Army reinforcements.

On the night of 14 October, the Japanese battleships *Kongō* and *Haruna* returned unopposed and lobbed nearly one thousand high-explosive 14-inch shells on Henderson Field, severely damaging the airfield in what the Marines called "The Bombardment." Two nights later, they were followed by additional attacks by IJN cruisers. Meanwhile, at Truk, the

Combined Fleet had assembled a five-carrier task force and was preparing to move it southwest into the open waters north of the Solomons. Here, Yamamoto hoped to engage and destroy the American carriers that his intelligence staff said were in the area, partly to atone for his loss at Midway but mainly to support a planned major offensive by the Imperial Army to capture Henderson Field. The Japanese, like the Americans, saw controlling Guadalcanal as the key to victory in the South Pacific.[16]

Nimitz wanted his chief of staff's opinion on the situation. On 14 October, Spruance and Vice Adm. William Calhoun, the fleet's logistics chief, left Pearl Harbor for an inspection trip of the Espiritu Santo and the Solomon Islands, arriving at Nouméa on 18 October. They were joined by Halsey, who was on his way south to assume command of TF 16. While they were en route, "The Bombardment" occurred, and in view of the ongoing nightly attacks, Nimitz ordered Spruance not to travel to Guadalcanal.

The CinCPac staff were becoming greatly alarmed at the deteriorating situation on Cactus. The CinCPac Running Summary for 15 October noted, "It now appears we are unable to control the sea area in the Guadalcanal area. . . . The situation is not hopeless, but it is certainly critical." At their regular staff meeting, they urged Nimitz to relieve Ghormley, but he refused. Several days later, they approached Nimitz at his quarters one evening and made their case again. Halsey was on his way, and this was the perfect time to replace Ghormley with a known fighter. This time Nimitz acquiesced, and after consulting with King, on 16 October he sent Ghormley and Halsey an eyes-only cable informing them of his decision.[17]

Upon his arrival in Nouméa, Halsey was handed a sealed envelope containing Nimitz's orders. It was tough for Halsey to face his old friend Ghormley, but they both knew it was for the best. Once the orders were officially read, the news spread quickly. Halsey's reputation as a dogged fighter reinvigorated the command and gave them new hope. On hearing the news, one Marine officer on Guadalcanal said, "One minute we were too limp with malaria to crawl out of our foxholes; the next we were running around whooping like kids."[18]

Spruance and Calhoun went across the harbor to meet with Kelly Turner aboard his flagship USS *McCawley* (APA 4), where they went over the situation in the South Pacific in general and at Cactus in particular. Turner confirmed Nimitz's prohibition about traveling to Guadalcanal as the position there was still too precarious. After Turner's usual cocktail hour, they had dinner and spent the night aboard the flagship. Ghormley joined Spruance and Calhoun aboard the waiting Coronado on the morning of 21 October for the return flight.[19]

While Spruance and the rest flew back to Pearl Harbor, Halsey set about making changes. The *Enterprise* and *Hornet* task forces were merged into one, TF 61, under the command of Rear Adm. Thomas C. Kinkaid. Acting on his own authority, Halsey canceled the occupation of the Santa Cruz Islands so that the troops scheduled to land there could be used to reinforce Guadalcanal, countermanding the JCS directive of 2 July to "take and hold" the islands, something Ghormley and Turner had been reluctant to do. There was little time to act, as the Japanese were on the move. Aware from radio traffic analysis that the Combined Fleet was in motion, Nimitz requested, through COMINCH, that the British Admiralty conduct an operation against the Malay Barrier to divert some of Japan's attention to the west. Unfortunately, the Royal Navy was in no position to help.[20]

Yamamoto moved his carriers south to conduct coordinated air attacks against Henderson Field, but to little effect. A slugfest ensued on 26 October between Kinkaid's TF 61 and the Combined Fleet's First Carrier Division in what became known as the Battle of the Santa Cruz Islands. Kinkaid lost *Hornet* to a combination aerial bomb and torpedo attack, and *Enterprise* was heavily damaged, forcing him to withdraw. It was a tactical victory for the Japanese, as none of their carriers were sunk; however, two, *Zuihō* and *Shōkaku*, were so severely damaged that they had to withdraw to the Home Islands for repair. Worse still, the battle had cost the Japanese heavily in terms of aircraft and aircrew, to the extent that the carrier *Zuikaku* had to return to Truk for replacements. While the Japanese now had temporary control of the seas around Guadalcanal, the failure of the Imperial Army to overrun Henderson Field made it a hollow victory indeed.

Yamamoto was not ready to call it quits, however. He still had his surface battleships and cruisers with which to fight. Twice more, on the nights of 13 and 14–15 November, he sent a mixed force of destroyers, cruisers, and the battleships *Hiei* and *Kirishima* at night down the Slot to bombard Henderson Field in the First and Second Naval Battles of Guadalcanal.

In the first battle, the American commanders, Rear Adm. Daniel J. Callahan and Rear Adm. Norman Scott, were willing to put their lives on the line, knowing that their best hope to stop the superior IJN force with their cruisers and destroyers was, in the words of Lord Nelson, to "engage the enemy more closely." This meant engaging the battleships at such close range that their 8-inch guns might do some damage. They succeeded in the chaotic melee that ensued, turning the *Hiei* into a smoking wreck, but at a terrible cost: both Callahan and Scott were killed, and one heavy cruiser, two light cruisers, and four destroyers were sunk.[21]

The Japanese commander, Admiral Abe Hiroaki, had won a tactical victory but had expended so much ammunition that he decided he could not commence the bombardment mission and withdrew to avoid being caught in the daylight by aircraft from Henderson Field and *Enterprise.* The transport convoy that he had been escorting was less fortunate, as they were ripped to pieces the morning of the 14th by those very planes as they attempted to land men and supplies.

On the night of 14 November Yamamoto sent his surviving ships, refueled and resupplied and augmented by two heavy cruisers, back down the Slot one more time to clear the area of American surface forces, destroy Henderson Field, and complete the resupply and reinforcement mission. In response, Halsey assembled a scratch force by stripping *Enterprise* of her fast battleship escorts USS *South Dakota* (BB 57) and USS *Washington* (BB 56), accompanied by four destroyers, none of whom had worked together before. In command was Rear Adm. Willis "Ching" Lee, the U.S. Navy's foremost gunnery expert. In another close-quarters night combat, the Japanese wiped out the escorting American destroyers and damaged *South Dakota.* Lee in *Washington*, undetected by the Japanese, used his radar to maneuver within point-blank range and opened fire on *Kirishima*, leaving her a flaming ruin. Lee maneuvered *Washington* away from the battle scene with the remaining Japanese cruisers in pursuit, allowing *South Dakota* to escape. Lee had succeeded in overcoming the IJN's superiority in night fighting by a combination of aggressive action and a crew well-trained in the use of radar and gunnery.[22]

Early on 15 November, the remaining Japanese ships retired back up the Slot to Rabaul as *Kirishima* capsized and sank. The four transports that followed the Japanese fleet beached themselves at Tassaforonga, a planned expedient to quickly unload men and supplies without a port. However, they were quickly discovered and destroyed by Marine artillery and the Cactus Air Force, denying the beleaguered Imperial Army much-needed food and supplies and dooming any chances for a renewed offensive. The Naval Battles of Guadalcanal were the high point of the Japanese Imperial Navy. Afterward, they were unable to inflict such grievous casualties on the U.S. Navy in a surface fleet encounter.

The first six months of Spruance's time as Nimitz's chief of staff had seen the forces under their command take a beating and rebound to come out on top. Things were often tense at CinCPac headquarters when fragmentary reports came in from subordinate commanders about ship losses and setbacks without getting a sense of the bigger picture. However, things changed in early December with the relief of the 1st Marine Division by fresh troops from the 2nd Marine and 25th Infantry Divisions. A lack of supply forced the Imperial Army to retreat into the jungles of northern Guadalcanal, where they suffered from disease and starvation. The repeated failures of the Imperial Navy to neutralize Henderson Field and protect the transports carrying reinforcements and supplies convinced the Imperial General Headquarters of the futility of their efforts. On 31 December, with the emperor's blessing, they ordered that the Guadalcanal be evacuated. This defeat, coupled with the failure of their campaign to take Port Moresby, ended any further advancement of the Imperial Army into the South Pacific.

In late November, after a staff meeting, Spruance asked Layton into his office to discuss the latest intelligence briefing, as he often did. This morning, however, was different. Spruance wondered if there was any new intelligence from decoded messages or POW interviews that shed some light on the Japanese intentions on the night of 4 June during the Battle of Midway. It seemed to Layton that Spruance was unusually "keyed up" when discussing the matter. Spruance explained that he was upset by the recent Naval War College analysis of the battle, which faulted him for retiring eastward in the night instead of westward, where he might have been in a better position to attack the retiring Japanese fleet on the morning of 5 June. The report had come through Nimitz with a strong endorsement by Admiral King, which explained Spruance's uncharacteristic agitation. Layton told Spruance he would dig into the matter. A few days later, he produced a captured Japanese map of the track of the Combined Fleet during the battle and a notebook of deciphered message traffic between Yamamoto, Nagumo, and Kurita. These documents clearly showed that the Japanese were planning a night action to destroy any force that was in pursuit. Spruance reviewed the information point by point and made notes for his rebuttal. He asked Layton to show the information to Nimitz, who was pleased that Spruance's decision had been vindicated. A grateful Spruance told Layton, "The weight of a score of years has been lifted from my shoulders."[23]

In December Nimitz ordered Spruance to go to the Presidio in San Francisco to meet with Gen. John L. DeWitt, the Army commander of the Western Defensive Command, to discuss the situation in the Aleutians and to initiate joint planning for recapturing Attu and Kiska, after which time he was to go on leave. Since the Japanese seized these islands in June, there had been little in the way of offensive action against them other than an occasional air raid by the Army Air Force and submarine patrols to interdict Japanese supply ships. Even in the summer, air and sea operations were hampered by bad weather and frequent heavy fog, so the Japanese forces remained.

After conferring with General DeWitt, Spruance flew south to San Diego and traveled on to Monrovia, California, in the foothills of the San Gabriel Mountains, for Christmas with his family. It was the first time he had seen his wife Margaret since February. He was concerned about the health of their daughter, who was staying at the nearby Pottenger Sanitorium for treatment of her tuberculosis. His wife recalled that when he first came home, he looked quite tired, but after enjoying long hikes into the hills, he was his old self again. Spruance, as usual, avoided publicity, but at Margaret's urging, he attended a luncheon that had been arranged by the town's mayor where, in his dress uniform, he explained the Battle of Midway and how the war was progressing, much to the delight of those in attendance. After three short days, he bid his family a very reluctant farewell and returned to to San Francisco for the long flight back to Honolulu.[24]

Looking back, Spruance was profoundly grateful to be working for Nimitz as his chief of staff. "The better I got to know him," Spruance recalled, "the more I came to admire his intelligence, his open-mindedness, and his approachability for any who had new or different ideas, and above all, his utter fearlessness and courage in pushing the war."[25]

CHAPTER 7

CINCPAC CHIEF OF STAFF

Planning the Trident, 1943

WHEN SPRUANCE ARRIVED back in Pearl Harbor early in the new year, things were much the same as when he had left. The *Arizona* still lay shattered at her moorings, slowly being explored to salvage useful material and recover the remains of her crew when possible. The USS *Oklahoma* (BB 37) was still capsized but was being prepared for righting, refloating, and then salvage, her damage being too great to repair. Conspicuous in their absence were the aircraft carriers. The remaining fleet carriers, *Enterprise* and *Saratoga*, were with Halsey in the South Pacific conducting flight training, as were four new escort carriers of the *Bogue* class. Both big carriers needed refit and repair after their battles in the Solomons. At one point the previous October, Halsey had been desperate for carriers, requesting that the British send one from their Eastern Fleet. However, it would not be until May that HMS *Victorious* could be spared.[1]

Indeed, the main strength of the Pacific Fleet was not at Pearl Harbor but at Nouméa, New Caledonia. Rear Adm. Willis Lee was there aboard his flagship *Washington*, in company with the other fast battleships of his TF 64, USS *Indiana* (BB 58) and USS *North Carolina* (BB 55), for resupply and training. While there, a team of Navy scientists led by Lt. (jg) James Van Allen came aboard with a supply of the new super-secret "VT" (Variable Timing) proximity fuzes for testing, which were highly successful, much to Lee's delight. As the name implies, these were designed to explode and destroy an enemy aircraft without having to impact it, using miniaturized radar. As the mission of the fast battleships was to screen the all-important carriers from both surface *and* air attack, this technology, as will be seen, was vital to their success.[2]

Despite their losses at Midway and in the South Pacific, the Japanese Combined Fleet still boasted four fleet carriers. These were believed to be at Truk and possibly en route south to Rabaul, although their exact whereabouts were not known as the IJN cipher had recently changed again. In terms of offensive capability, the Japanese were still a force to be reckoned with, and while all signs pointed to renewed efforts in the Solomons, another attack on the Hawaiian Islands could not be ruled out. A COMINCH analysis concluded that the Japanese had shifted to a "strategic defensive" in the Solomons-New Guinea area by reinforcing existing bases and building new airfields, freeing up their mobile forces for action elsewhere.[3]

On the other side of the globe, Adm. Ernest J. King was in Casablanca, Morocco, to discuss the next phases of the war with President Roosevelt, Prime Minister Churchill, and the Allied Combined Chiefs of Staff. The Casablanca Conference, from 14 January to 24 January 1943, took place at the site of the Torch landings of the previous November. Throughout the conference, King remained adamant, indeed implacable, in his determination to begin an offensive against Japan in the Pacific in 1943. After days of discussion, cocktail parties, and charm offensives by both Roosevelt and Churchill, it was agreed that knocking Italy out of the war and defeating Germany remained the top priorities. King, however, was pleased that the conference statement authorized "operations, after the capture of Rabaul, against the Marshalls and Carolines" in 1943, subject to certain conditions. In theory, the war in the Pacific remained subordinate to the prosecution of the war in Europe, and as it was primarily an American affair with minimal British contribution, the British would have little to say about it, as King preferred.[4]

Although King and the U.S. Navy had wrangled approval for the Central Pacific drive from the Combined Chiefs, there yet remained perhaps their most challenging foe to convince: the Supreme Commander of the Southwest Pacific and Field Marshal of the Philippine Army, Gen. Douglas MacArthur. MacArthur was confident that his strategy to leapfrog along the northern coast of New Guinea, capture Rabaul, and then move to the Philippines was the best path to Japan, and he wanted the necessary resources devoted to that end. It was an argument destined to continue well into the following year, with significant implications for the war.

While the President and King were traveling east, Secretary of the Navy Frank Knox was headed west to meet with Nimitz and MacArthur in Hawaii. To prepare for the meeting, Nimitz had Spruance and the staff prepare a detailed "Estimate of the Situation—Solomon Islands" that, in Naval War College fashion, laid out the status of assigned objectives, the strength of the existing friendly forces, the estimated enemy strength and capabilities, and an analysis of the Joint Chiefs' directive of 2 July to complete the conquest of the Solomons and capture Rabaul. Its recommendations for immediate action included building air bases in the Lower Solomons and moving north to capture the Japanese airbase at Munda Point. More aggressive moves further north into Bougainville were not deemed feasible with the forces available.[5]

While the CinCPac staff was working on their estimate, on 13 January MacArthur sent his appreciation of the situation as a five-part "utmost secret" dispatch "for Nimitz and Halsey only." MacArthur reiterated his plan to capture Rabaul as the best course of action, and wrote that such an operation "must now be regarded as a major campaign which might well become the decisive action in the Pacific Zone of the war." However, after describing the deficiencies in his available forces, he stated that he was unable to conduct such a major offensive action at present. In the final part of his message, MacArthur said that he preferred an "exchange of views" between himself and Nimitz rather than a conference, leaving the detailed planning to their senior staff. He was unwilling to leave his headquarters; if Nimitz wanted to meet with him, he would have to travel to Brisbane.[6]

Nimitz doubtless shared this gem with Knox, and they decided to skip MacArthur altogether and instead confer with Halsey at his headquarters in Nouméa. They agreed to further develop Cactus as a major base and assault Munda Point, with the aim of striking concentrations of Japanese air and surface units whenever possible. Task One was complete, and now Halsey advocated for a move toward the next objective in the Solomon Islands chain, the occupation of Rendova in the New Georgia Islands. Rear Adm. Turner first wanted to establish a small advance base in the

Russell Islands to provide air support for the move north and received the green light to proceed from CinCPac on 28 January 1943.[7]

The growing disagreement between Nimitz and MacArthur on the future strategy for the Pacific War was now reaching an impasse and required resolution at a higher level of command. MacArthur wanted to methodically assemble all the forces he thought necessary before beginning the assault on Rabaul. There was no question about what King wanted to do. If MacArthur was unable to use his ships in the immediate future, he wanted them employed on the offensive in the Northern and Central Pacific.

With this in mind, King asked Nimitz and Halsey to weigh in on the viability of operations against the Ellice and Gilbert Islands to draw Japanese forces away from the Solomons-New Guinea area, providing MacArthur with some breathing room and cover to the lines of communication into the South Pacific. Nimitz flatly stated that while he fully supported such an operation, "until present balance has been upset by the further destruction of enemy's naval and air forces and by growth of our own believe our experience in capture of Guadalcanal indicates operations proposed . . . not now feasible." After some back and forth with Nimitz and Halsey, on 13 February King directed Nimitz to prepare a plan of operations in the Pacific Ocean Area for the next four months, including a move into the Ellice, Gilberts, and Marshall Island areas, in preparation for their upcoming conference in San Francisco slated for 20 February.[8]

In preparation for the meeting, Spruance and the CinCPac War Plans staff updated their previous Estimate of the Situation and prepared a memo on simultaneous attacks in the Solomon Islands and the Central Pacific. Their plan called for Halsey to attack Munda in New Georgia with the 1st Marine Division, while in the Central Pacific, Tarawa and Makin in the Gilbert Islands would be seized, along with the recapture of Wake Island. A target date of 15 May 1943 was set for this operation. However, to carry off these attacks simultaneously, practically every ship in the Pacific theater would be needed, and some rather optimistic assumptions were made about the availability of transports and landing craft for these attacks. It was projected that the new fast carrier *Essex* might be available by that date, as well as the long-promised HMS *Victorious*. However, even then, it was estimated the Japanese would still have greater numbers of cruisers and destroyers available to counterattack. The plan's downfall was that the estimated number of Army troops and Marines required for such a large, combined operation were not available in the Pacific theater, a situation that was unlikely to change by the target date. Furthermore, while the Gilberts might be taken, holding them from a determined counterattack appeared doubtful. For these reasons, the memo concluded that the operation was unfeasible.[9]

This study served as the catalyst for Spruance to seriously consider taking the Gilberts as a necessary preliminary step toward King's long-stated goal of seizing the Marshall Islands. A major problem with moving into the Marshalls was the lack of useful intelligence about the islands, as the Japanese had long closed the area off to outsiders. Spruance had been in the Marshall Islands with TF 16 during the previous year's raid and had been frustrated at the time by the lack of actionable aerial photo reconnaissance. He felt that the bombardment at the time was ineffective, shooting blindly into the islands' interior in the hope of hitting something. Only aerial photography's multiple overhead and oblique views could give an accurate idea of the scope and size of the defenses. The problem was that the Marshalls lay beyond the range of the available reconnaissance aircraft. Submarines might provide some information, but only from a periscope at sea level, and they could not give any information inside the shallow lagoons of the atolls.

The Gilbert and Ellice Islands were British colonies outside the Japanese Mandates, some 875 miles southwest of the Marshall Islands. The Japanese had attacked and seized the Gilberts on 8 December 1941. In August 1942, Makin Atoll in the Gilberts had been the subject of an attack by two companies from the 2nd Marine Raider Battalion. The Raiders, led by Lt. Col. Evans F. Carlson, were transported to the island by the submarines *Nautilus* and USS *Argonaut* (SS 166), and on 17 August, they landed by rubber boats and attacked the small Japanese garrison there. Their purpose was to divert attention from the ongoing operations in the Lower Solomon Islands, but the raid had the unintended consequence of alerting the Japanese to the fact that the Gilberts were poorly defended. Shortly thereafter, they began to reinforce and fortify them, establishing an air base on Betio Island in the Tarawa Atoll and a seaplane base on Makin. From here, the Japanese could send their own long-range reconnaissance snoopers to keep an eye on the Allied lines of communication with the South Pacific.

Spruance proposed establishing several air bases in the northern Ellice Islands, approximately 700 miles south of the Gilberts, for the express purpose of conducting air attacks and photoreconnaissance missions over Tarawa and Makin, ultimately leading to the capture of these islands. Once advance bases in the Gilberts had been established, the process could be repeated for taking the Marshalls. One wag likened this to "performing a tonsillectomy through the rectum." Despite those optics, Spruance's "clear and forceful" logic convinced Nimitz that this series of operations was the only sure way to seize the Marshall Islands.[10]

Before such moves could be made, a substantial buildup of naval, air, and ground forces in the Pacific Theater was required. In the meantime, planning was needed, and to that end, the Joint Chiefs of Staff invited MacArthur, Halsey, Nimitz, and their respective staff to join them in Washington for a Pacific Military Conference to resolve the next moves. Spruance was designated the CinCPac representative, accompanied by Lt. Gen. Delos C. Emmons, the military governor of Hawaii, and Capt. Forrest P. Sherman. MacArthur sent his chief of staff Major Gen. Richard J. Sutherland, USA, while Halsey sent his chief of staff Capt. Miles Browning and the Southwest Pacific Army commander Gen. Millard F. Harmon, USA.

Spruance and the others departed Honolulu on 7 March on a Pan Am flight, landing in San Francisco the next day, and after a brief rest continued on to Washington, arriving on 9 March. Spruance and Sherman spent the next several days conferring with King and his planning staff, during which they discussed the desirability of seizing the Gilberts as a necessary move preparatory to an assault on the Marshall Islands. While there, Spruance also met with his old friend, Capt. Charles J. "Carl" Moore, who chafed at being stuck on the Joint War Plans Staff, asked Spruance to help get him assigned to the Pacific.[11]

The conference opened on 12 March with the presentation by General Sutherland of MacArthur's long-anticipated plan for the capture of

Rabaul, codenamed Elkton. He detailed a five-phase plan, as yet undated, to move north along the New Guinea coast and the Bismarck Archipelago, encircling Rabaul with air bases before launching an all-out assault on the heavily fortified base. The requirements set forth for military, naval, and air support staggered the Army's Washington planners. Trained divisions were in short supply, as were landing craft and attack shipping. Providing MacArthur with the requested quantity of available and projected aircraft, the Washington team argued, would seriously weaken the combined bombing campaign over Germany, and the request was therefore unacceptable.[12]

After several days of discussion and debate, the conference was reconvened with the Joint Chiefs present on Sunday, 21 March 1943. Spruance laid out the CinCPac case. With the Japanese retreat from Guadalcanal, "the situation has radically changed" as the Combined Fleet had regained freedom of movement. Until Rabaul was threatened, no operation in the Pacific Area would likely draw the Japanese into another attritional campaign. Additionally, the situation was complicated by the fact that due to changes in the Japanese naval code, the U.S. Navy did not know the exact disposition of the Japanese fleet. As a precaution, a portion of the naval forces in the South Pacific therefore should be returned to Hawaii to protect Pearl Harbor.

Spruance stated that the Japanese should be cleared out of the Aleutians as their small presence was tying down "considerable" naval assets needed elsewhere. He noted that Japanese positions in the Central Pacific were mutually supporting and that any operation in the Gilberts and Marshall Islands required sufficient carrier air support to smother attacks from adjoining areas. Such operations would be "unprofitable if we were not prepared for continuous progress," he said, restating Nimitz's often repeated reply to King's frequent prompting for more offensive action that unless adequate forces were available, a major thrust into the Japanese defensive cordon was inadvisable.

Admiral King then weighed in on the same theme. If the Japanese were no longer tied down in the Solomons, the lack of a significant Allied operation gave them the freedom to attack anywhere in the Central and North Pacific. The Pacific Fleet needed to maintain the initiative and "beat the Japs to it." The JCS needed to look at the Pacific theater as a whole and consider "whether we can allow a concentration of our forces in the South Pacific to remain idle or whether we can operate them in such a way to pin down a Japanese fleet which can otherwise roam free." This rationale became the origin of the basic strategy for the remainder of the war: parallel, reciprocal operations in the South and Central Pacific to keep the Japanese uncertain about where the next blow would land.[13]

The Joint Chiefs considered the arguments and then decided that their directive of 2 July 1942 was to be replaced with a new one with realistically obtainable goals and that Task Three, the reduction of Rabaul, should be postponed until a future date. This was codified in their directive of 28 March, which told MacArthur to establish supporting airbases in the Coral Sea and to continue moves to develop a lodgment in Bougainville and prepare for the seizure of the Bismarck archipelago, an operation now renamed Cartwheel. Although not explicitly mentioned, they also agreed to Spruance's proposition to settle the Aleutians issue as soon as conditions warranted, thereby freeing up troops and ships that could be used more profitably elsewhere.[14]

On his way back to Hawaii, Spruance stopped in San Diego on 26 March to visit with Major Gen. Holland M. Smith, USMC, to observe the ongoing amphibious training at Camp Elliott and to reacquaint himself with the beefy, bespectacled Smith, whom he had first met back in Puerto Rico during FLEX 7. Despite first appearances, Smith was a dogged and determined Marine who had well earned the nickname "Howlin' Mad" for his intolerance of sloppiness and inattention and, most especially, for the ire he directed at anyone who belittled his beloved Marine Corps. Smith was responsible for making prewar amphibious doctrine a reality. Spruance was impressed by Smith's depth of knowledge and commitment and later recommended him to Nimitz as their Marine Landing Forces commander. Spruance also took the opportunity to briefly visit his wife and daughter in Monrovia before departing for Pearl Harbor, arriving back on 29 March.[15]

In the wake of the severe losses suffered during the night actions in the Solomons, King established the Tactical Analysis Section at COMINCH headquarters in December 1942. Their job was to compile the after-action reports of the commanders involved in those battles and provide analyses to glean lessons learned and make recommendations for improvements. The result was the issuance of the *Secret Information Bulletins of Battle Experience* series. The typical format of these bulletins included a narrative of the subject battles with maps and excerpts from the reports made by the various commanders and ship captains, with their recommendations for improvements in equipment, tactics, and operations. Among the earliest to reach CinCPac was Bulletin No. 2, "Battle Experience: Solomon Island Actions, August and September 1942," issued on 16 March 1943. Several important conclusions were drawn from the report of August carrier action made by Rear Adm. Thomas C. Kinkaid, the TF 16 commander.

First, it was found that having the fast battleship *North Carolina* as part of the formation proved extremely valuable thanks to its large radar-controlled antiaircraft battery and ability to keep station with the carrier even during extreme evasive maneuvers. The only downside was that the group was limited by *North Carolina*'s maximum speed of twenty-seven knots. Not only did the fast battleship bring down a number of attackers, but she was also such a tempting target that many of the attackers went for her instead of *Enterprise*. The circular cruising formation was "considered to be excellent defense against aircraft." Second, there was a need for "a serious reconsideration" of current doctrine on the use of carriers. Kinkaid believed that three or more carriers in a Task Force was feasible and desirable and that they should operate in closer proximity to each other to provide mutual support; "the advantages of such a concentration of air power would offset the disadvantages."[16]

The often confused night actions came in for criticism in the bulletins covering the Battle of Cape Esperance and the Naval Battles of Guadalcanal. In both actions, destroyers were used as part of the battle line and not in the night search and attack formations described in the current doctrine. While there were valid reasons for this, it nevertheless brought to the fore the need for a common doctrine that could be readily accessed and understood by all.[17]

With these criticisms in mind, Nimitz set another task for Spruance in early April: form a board of experienced officers to review the Pacific Fleet's tactical doctrine. The result was *Current Tactical Orders and Doctrine*,

U.S. Pacific Fleet, more commonly known as PAC-10. The final version was issued on 10 July 1943. The board, consisting of two senior surface officers and one aviation officer, looked at the current doctrinal publications, after-action reports, *Battle Experience* bulletins, and interviews with commanders to synthesize a new "syllabus" of tactical orders for use by the fleet, with an emphasis on optimal, compact formations suited for combat in the islands of the Pacific. Each formation in the syllabus was given a coded alpha-numeric designation so that upon receipt, every commander knew how to act without the need for lengthy written orders except in extraordinary circumstances. Task force commanders no longer had to prepare detailed instructions before action, and ships could move freely between formations or combine into a new task force with minimal coordination.[18]

It was at this time that Admiral Nimitz discussed with Spruance the issue of who might command the Central Pacific campaign that they had been proposing for months now. One morning in the spring of 1943, as Spruance and Nimitz were walking to the CinCPac headquarters, Nimitz suddenly told him, "There are going to be some changes in the high command of the Fleet. I would like to let you go, but unfortunately for you I need you here." Nonplussed, Spruance replied, "Well, the war is the important thing. I personally would like to have another crack at the (Japanese), but if you want me here, this is where I should be," and thought no more of the matter. However, the next morning on their walk to the office, Nimitz said, "I have been thinking this over during the night. Spruance, you are lucky; I have decided to let you go after all."[19]

While Spruance, telling this story later, did not mention the emotions that passed through his mind upon hearing this, he must have been elated. He was now going to sea once more, in operational charge of the largest naval force ever assembled. Spruance's tightly controlled personality did not permit him a yelp of joy, but the sparkle in his eyes told Nimitz all he needed to know. Spruance then said, "Sir, I would like to get Admiral Kelly Turner from Admiral Halsey if I can steal him," to which he added, "I want Major General Holland Smith for the Marines."[20]

To provide Spruance with a rank befitting his new assignment, Nimitz recommended that he be promoted to vice admiral. Secretary Knox, in a letter dated 29 May, informed Spruance that President Roosevelt, with the advice and consent of the Senate, had appointed him to the temporary rank of vice admiral, dated to 15 May 1943. Admiral King, as CNO, had also approved Spruance's promotion before it was submitted to the president, and given the date, this must have occurred sometime after his last conference with Nimitz. The CinCPac Running Summary noted on 18 May that Rear Adm. Charles H. "Soc" McMorris, the victor of Komandorski, would relieve Spruance as Nimitz's next chief of staff.[21]

Soon after, Spruance contacted Carl Moore and asked if he wanted to be his chief of staff, an offer that Moore quickly accepted. Spruance gave Moore the task of assembling a staff, and Moore immediately asked Lt. (jg) Charles F. Barber, a Harvard-trained Naval Reserve officer who was also on the War Plans staff, if he would like to get out of Washington as well and serve as Spruance's flag secretary. Barber jumped at the chance to be part of the great offensive.[22]

The CinCPac Running Summary for May 1943 describes the South and Central Pacific areas as "generally quiet," with the enemy on a "strategic defensive" posture. However, things were finally starting to take shape in the north as the campaign to drive the Japanese from the Aleutians began on 11 May. Delayed by bad weather, Operation Landcrab, the third major amphibious landing of the Pacific war, saw elements of the 7th Infantry Division land largely unopposed on Attu Island. The Japanese commander, Colonel Yamasaki Yasuyo, had decided to defend Attu from the island's rugged interior rather than at the beach. This was indeed fortunate as the landing operation, which took five days in all, was confused, slow, and poorly organized in many respects. While the embarkation of troops onto the landing craft and the ship-to-shore movement went as planned, there was severe congestion on the beach as shore parties were pulled away to support combat operations. Ships had been poorly loaded or loaded with materiel unnecessary for a combat assault. There were not enough landing craft, and the rough surf conditions on the rocky beach easily damaged what there was. Inadequate winter clothing for Navy personnel on the beach required them to use Army-issued clothing, adding to the general confusion. An opposed landing might have resulted in a catastrophe.[23]

Holland Smith had been training these troops for this operation all spring in California and was anxious to see how they were getting on. He was present when, on 30 May, the defenders, many starving, launched a desperate banzai attack aimed at capturing supplies and an artillery position. They succeeded in overrunning the defensive perimeter and penetrating deep into the rear echelon, resulting in intense, bloody hand-to-hand combat as the remaining Japanese fought to the death. Smith recalled, "That mad charge through the fog made a profound impression and alerted me to the ever-present danger of just such a final desperate attack during my operations in the Central Pacific."[24]

The experience of Attu provided many valuable lessons for Spruance and the staff at CinCPac for planning future amphibious operations, including the importance of beach reconnaissance, combat loading, designated shore parties, and the need for clear lines of communication between the Navy's amphibious and gunnery support forces and the Army's landing forces. Intelligence failures had also underestimated the number of Japanese troops.

In late May, King presented his proposed strategy for the defeat of Japan to the Combined Chiefs. He gave a brief description of War Plan Orange, in which the seizure of the Marianas and the destruction of the Japanese fleet "were of primary importance." In the Pacific "unremitting pressure" had been maintained, the Japanese advance had been halted, and Allied forces were now in a position to attack. The defeat of Japan would require a combination of naval blockade and aerial bombing. An invasion of Japan was deemed feasible only after Japan's armed forces and economy had been sufficiently weakened. King outlined the objectives for 1943–44:

1. Conduct of air operations in and from China;
2. Operations in Burma to augment supplies to China;
3. Ejection of the Japanese from the Aleutians;
4. Seizure of the Marshall and Caroline Islands;
5. Seizure of the Solomons-Bismarck Archipelago and Japanese-held New Guinea.

These recommendations were approved by the Combined Chiefs when they met the next day.[25]

King believed the best path to the Chinese mainland was through the Central Pacific, and now he had the green light to proceed with his long-envisioned plan. The British agreed, in principle, to reopen the Burma Road through a ground offensive in Burma and to naval operations in the Strait of Malacca to cut Japan off from her oil supply. The decision to postpone the invasion of northern Europe until late spring 1944 was a major boon to King's plans. After Operation Husky (the invasion of Sicily), he had the first claim on the shipping and landing craft he needed for the Central Pacific drive. By late summer, the fast carrier task forces required for such an operation would finally be available. The pieces for a major offensive in the fall of 1943 were falling into place.

King met Nimitz in San Francisco on 30 May to discuss the planned Central Pacific offensive, confirm Spruance's elevation to command the effort, and review and approve the assignment of flag officers to the operation, including Turner and Smith. While there, Holland Smith and General DeWitt briefed them on the Attu operation. Smith relayed his general satisfaction with the landings on 11 May, but he was unhappy with the lack of aggressiveness on the part of the Army troops who had repeatedly allowed the Japanese to fall back and regroup.[26]

On 31 May 1943, Spruance witnessed *Essex*, the first of its class of new fast carriers, enter Pearl Harbor. Before the end of August she would be joined by her sisters, the reincarnated USS *Lexington* (CV 16) and *Yorktown*. Together with the light carriers USS *Independence* (CVL 22), USS *Princeton* (CVL 23), and USS *Belleau Wood* (CVL 24), these ships became the basis for the fast-carrier task forces Spruance needed for the planned drive into the Central Pacific.

In June, the momentum for planning the assault on the Gilberts began to build. Halsey reported that bombers operating out of the South Pacific had carried out bombing and photo-recon missions on Nauru, Jaluit, Milli, and Tarawa. In late July, the Joint Chiefs of Staff directed Nimitz to "capture, occupy, defend, and develop bases in the Gilbert Group and NAURU" and then "undertake the preparation of outline plans for follow-up operations to capture, occupy, defend, and develop bases in the MARSHALLS about 1 January 1944."[27]

Turner left Halsey's command on 15 July and reported to Pearl Harbor to meet with Spruance and Nimitz before taking some weeks of well-earned leave stateside. Carl Moore arrived in Pearl Harbor on 30 July, but before he left Washington, he had arranged for the nucleus of the new staff to be transferred to Spruance's command. These men included Capt. Emmet P. Forrestel, the Operations Officer; Capt. Burton B. Briggs, the Logistics Officer; and Cdr. Russell S. Smith, the Gunnery Officer. Cdr. Justus R. Armstrong, the Communications Officer, was already in Pearl Harbor, being reassigned from the CinCPac staff. Charles Barber was the first to arrive, reaching Pearl Harbor on 1 August. After settling in, he began scrounging furniture and equipment to set up their offices on the floor below those of Nimitz and the CinCPac staff in the "Cement Pot" on Makalapa Hill.[28]

On 5 August, Moore officially reported for duty to Spruance as his chief of staff, receiving a warm welcome from both Nimitz and his old friend. For the first several weeks, Moore stayed in the same house Nimitz and Spruance shared. Moore wrote to his wife, "I am most pleasantly situated here. Messmates are delightful, surroundings most pleasant and comfortable. Most pleasing is the satisfaction and confidence that Raymond has in me and his apparent pleasure in having me on hand. I hope I can fulfill his expectations."[29]

Almost immediately, Spruance took him on an eight-mile hike into the hills above Makalapa. Moore enjoyed their intense conversation but found the coerced physical activity to be both a challenge and an annoyance. He wrote to his wife, "Raymond is up to his old tricks already. . . . (His) object in life is to improve my health. The others say he is sadistic about it. If he can get me burned to a crisp or crippled from walking, he'll be completely happy. Then he will guard me and nurse me back to health."

Spruance was not one to openly display his emotions or be garrulous; this was his way of showing affection for his old friend. Thereafter, Moore and Barber were often coerced into Spruance's daily health regimen of hikes into the hills, punctuated by frequent swims off Kailua Beach. Barber was an excellent swimmer and was appointed lookout for jellyfish. Nimitz assigned him to be Spruance's "bodyguard" to ensure his fleet commander would not be sidelined by some unfortunate accident.

Barber later recounted that they did not talk shop during their walks, but Spruance quizzed him on his hobbies, interests, and books he had read. Spruance wanted to get to know his staff, but his innate shyness, seen as reticence by those who did not know him well, sometimes prevented him from developing close personal relationships with officers that he did not find sympatico. If Spruance was not effusive in his praise, neither was he harshly critical but always very supportive. Like King and Nimitz, Spruance preferred to keep his staff as small as possible, of a size that could be accommodated easily in the flag quarters of his new flagship, the heavy cruiser USS *Indianapolis* (CA 35), another "treaty cruiser." Spruance preferred a cruiser as it was fast enough to keep pace with the carriers and could join the shore bombardment groups if desired. Many of his staff recalled later that there were no petty jealousies, no infighting or jockeying for favor with the chief, but that they all worked together in harmony. This was much the same atmosphere as Spruance had established as Nimitz's chief of staff. As Barber recalled, "He said little, but there was no nitpicking, no pushing."[30]

Spruance and his staff had less than four months to plan for what became known as Operation Galvanic, set to be the largest amphibious operation ever conducted by the U.S. Navy, which would make landfall against a very hostile shore. There was much work to be done.

CHAPTER 8

PLANNING OPERATION GALVANIC

VICE ADM. RAYMOND A. SPRUANCE was relieved of his duty as Nimitz's chief of staff and officially assumed command of the Central Pacific Force on 5 August 1943. There were some, such as Vice Adm. John H. Towers, who believed that an aviator, ideally himself, should have that billet. Unfortunately for Towers' aspirations, he had run afoul of both King and Nimitz. Nor could Towers go to sea as the commander of the Fast Carrier Forces, as he was senior to Spruance in rank. If Towers could not have the job, he wanted his protégé Marc Mitscher to have it. Spruance, however, had not yet overcome his lack of confidence in Mitscher after his performance at Midway. Nimitz agreed, and assigned the job to Charles A. "Baldy" Pownall, the aviator with the next highest seniority in the Pacific. The often openly hostile attitude of the naval aviator clique continued to present problems for both Nimitz and Spruance as the aviators opposed having a black-shoe admiral in command of the carrier forces.[1]

Carl Moore was frustrated that the staff office was still in disarray and found it hard to get to work. That soon changed as Nimitz ordered him to accompany Spruance on a tour of the South Pacific battlefields. They left Pearl Harbor on 9 August aboard a PB2Y Coronado; after stops on Canton Island and in Fiji, they arrived at Nouméa on 12 August and reported to the headquarters of Admiral Halsey to discuss his plans for continuing the Solomons campaign. Munda Point had just been captured, and Army engineers were busy reconstructing the airfield there. The invasion of Vella Lavella was scheduled for 15 August and planning for the Bougainville campaign as part of Operation Cartwheel was underway. Keeping the Japanese occupied with "unremitting pressure" in the South Pacific was vital to the success of the upcoming push into the Central Pacific.

Their next stop was Wellington, New Zealand, to meet with Major Gen. Julian C. Smith, whose 2nd Marine Division had been tapped for the assault on Betio. The division was there to rest and recuperate after their fighting on Guadalcanal. Although Smith was aware of Galvanic, he and his staff had nothing specific on the objective, Tarawa Atoll. Many of his men were replacements who needed additional training; indeed, the entire division had no experience with amphibious landings. To remedy this, Spruance and Moore flew to Espiritu Santo to confer with Rear Adm. Harry W. Hill and arranged for transports to embark the division for landing rehearsals as Hill's battleships conducted shore bombardment training.

In company with a Seabee engineer, they flew to Nuka Fetau, one of several coral islands in the northern Ellice group slated for airfield construction. Airfield construction was also underway on Baker Island. These islands were the closest American outposts to Tarawa and bombers flying from here had the dual role of providing the much-needed photoreconnaissance and softening up the objective before the landings.

During their trip, Spruance found time to walk for exercise whenever his feet were on the ground. He dragged Moore along with him, whether up and down the hills of Wellington or across the coral reefs of Nuka Fetau. Moore recalled, "Spruance had feet like sole leather and he could go walking over any coral. . . . It would nearly kill me, trying to walk on it." Moore ended up sitting in waist-deep water to put his shoes back on. Walking over the reef gave them both a small taste of what the Marines would experience landing at Betio Island.[2]

They returned to Pearl Harbor, arriving on 22 August, but not without incident. As the big Coronado flying boat made its landing approach, the pilot, Lieutenant Pearson, noticed that the pontoon on the port-side wing had not folded down. He radioed ahead to report the problem, and Admiral Towers came out on his gig and stood by with life preservers. The quick-thinking Pearson had a number of the flight crew exit a hatch on the top of the aircraft as it landed to move out on the starboard wing to hold that pontoon down, and the plane landed safely. Had the port wing hit the water, even at a relatively low speed, the big plane might have cartwheeled and been badly wrecked.[3]

Shortly after his return Spruance had a more pleasant experience when First Lady Eleanor Roosevelt joined the Nimitz mess on 25 August. The First Lady was on a Red Cross inspection tour of the Pacific, despite her husband's wishes to the contrary. Spruance found her a most amenable dinner companion, writing to Margaret, "She is very simple, charming, and has a delightful sense of humor. Whatever one thinks of the possibility of achieving her ideals, she certainly has them and has a deep faith in the underlying goodness in the ordinary human being. She is certainly a very fine person."[4]

Kelly Turner had returned from leave and reported to Spruance earlier that day to assume his new duties as commander of the Fifth Amphibious Force. He brought his staff, including Capt. Paul S. Theiss, whom he "stole" from his replacement Admiral Wilkinson, to be his chief of staff. Theiss had probably more practical experience in amphibious operations than any other staff officer at CinCPac headquarters, and his even temperament and attention to detail were useful adjuncts to Turner's sometimes hot-headed brilliance.[5]

Coinciding with the push into the Central Pacific was the maturation of the Fast Carrier Force. Aviators like Towers had long dreamed of the day when aviation supplanted the "gun club" and their battleships as the primary weapon of naval warfare. The destruction of the Pacific Battle Force on 7 December 1941 pushed the U.S. Navy toward that goal, but the desperate battles of 1942 had left the carrier forces almost as badly depleted. By August 1943, however, the vision of a Fast Carrier Force was at hand as the new *Essex*-class and *Independence*-class carriers arrived at Pearl Harbor. That summer, Tower's aviation planners, using the doctrine laid out in PAC-10, adapted the standard circular formation into a new carrier-centered formation, the task group, which became the basic tactical unit for all future carrier operations.

A task group comprised one or more fleet carriers (CV) of the *Essex* class, along with several light carriers, several fast battleships of the *North Carolina* class or newer, cruisers, antiaircraft cruisers, and destroyers arranged in a circular cruising formation. These task groups could operate independently or combine to form a powerful task force. The surface warships' function in the formation was to use their formidable antiaircraft batteries to knock down attacking aircraft and to be available to engage enemy surface forces if the occasion should arise. The new ships, and those recently overhauled, were now provided with as many 5-inch/38 dual-purpose guns, 40-mm Bofors quad-mount guns, and 20-mm Oerlikon cannons as could be fitted, and equipped with improved gunsights, range finding, and air search radar. The bigger guns fired the new top-secret "VT" proximity fuzed shells. Altogether, these developments made aerial attacks on the new formations particularly deadly for Japanese aircrews.

The first test of the new Fast Carrier Force came when Pownall was ordered to attack Marcus Island with TF 15, composed of the carriers *Essex*, *Yorktown*, and *Independence*, the battleship *Indiana*, two light cruisers, and ten destroyers. Approaching from the northwest on 31 August they picked up a returning Japanese patrol plane on radar and followed it back to its base. In the early morning dark, the carriers began launching and caught the defenders unprepared. The new F6F Hellcats strafed the airfield, followed by five bomber sorties destroying aircraft and facilities. The planes landed and were refueled and rearmed without incident. Except for the loss of three aircraft, the mission was a success. Submarines were staged nearby to rescue downed pilots, an innovation suggested by Pownall that was used for all future operations.[6]

Spruance's team began to take shape. On 2 September his classmate and good friend Vice Adm. John H. "Johnny" Hoover arrived at Pearl Harbor. Hoover had succeeded Spruance as commander of the Tenth Naval District and oversaw the completion of the airfield and naval facilities that Spruance had started at San Juan. This experience made him perhaps the most knowledgeable non-Civil Engineer Corps officer when it came to the construction of airfields in adverse conditions. Maj. Gen. Holland M. Smith, USMC, Commander, Landing Forces, arrived on 5 September, bringing his staff. Turner met him at the airport and greeted him warmly. Smith wrote later that while their relationship was often "stormy," he nevertheless admired Turner for his drive: "Kelly Turner is aggressive, a mass of energy, and a relentless task master. The punctilious exterior hides a terrific determination. He can be plain onery. He wasn't called 'Terrible Turner' without reason." Although Smith and Turner did not always see eye to eye, they made a formidable team. Spruance recalled,

"Between them they turned in a magnificent job, of which I have always been proud."[7]

Smith would command not only his Marines but also the soldiers of the 27th Infantry Division, the previously unknown "division to be named," who were now assigned to his Fifth Amphibious Corps. It was unprecedented that a Marine should command Army troops in the field; Lt. Gen. Robert C. Richardson, who had succeeded Emmons as the commander of the U.S. Army Hawaii Department and the military governor of Hawaii, was not pleased and complained to the War Department. Richardson requested clarification of command authority, but the Joint Chiefs sidestepped the issue, and the somewhat ambiguous relationship between Nimitz and Richardson as the senior Army officer in Hawaii remained to fester.[8]

Holland Smith not only had the Army trying to curtail his command authority; he also had to deal with some Navy prejudice as well. On 12 September, Spruance received a memo from Kelly Turner suggesting that the training of landing forces should be under his supervision, an idea to which Smith objected vehemently. If Smith was to command these troops during the landing and combat phase of the operation, he rightly considered it his prerogative to oversee their training, the very thing he had been doing for the past year. Spruance agreed, and the matter was settled. Later, when the draft of the CinCPac operation orders for Galvanic were distributed, Smith was astonished to see that he was to remain behind at Pearl Harbor while the Navy directed the landing operations at Tarawa and Makin. "Howling Mad" Smith lived up to his nickname that day as he loudly protested to Spruance. Spruance was dumbfounded and immediately ordered that Smith sail with the Task Force as his handpicked commander of the Fifth Amphibious Force. These events only deepened Smith's distrust of anyone, except perhaps Spruance, who did not wear the Eagle, Globe, and Anchor.[9]

The combination of Turner and Smith started getting on Moore's nerves. In these early days of their relationship, each (and particularly Smith) complained to Moore about the other. Moore, perhaps showing his Navy partisanship, found Smith an annoying whiner: "He loved to talk and he loved to complain, and he would sit on my desk and growl about

Turner. 'All I want to do is kill some Japs. Just give me a rifle. I don't want to be a commanding general. . . . I want to fight the Japs.'" Turner, for his part, complained about "that blankety-blank Smith."[10]

Rear Adm. Harry W. Hill was the last senior commander to arrive, reporting on 24 September. He had been selected by Nimitz and approved by King to assist Kelly Turner as commander of Amphibious Group Two. Spruance selected as subordinates men whom he not only liked and trusted, but also who, he believed, were the best for the big jobs ahead. He recalled later, in his usual self-deprecating way, that "looking at myself objectively, I think I am a good judge of men, and I know that I tend to be lazy about many things, so I do not try to do anything that I can pass down the line to someone more competent than I am to do it."[11]

Spruance's team had only a few months to finalize the detailed operational planning before the scheduled start of Galvanic. The JCS provided the outline plan in July, and the CinCPac planning staff began more detailed planning in coordination with the Army, assigning specific ships, transports, Marine and Army ground forces, and logistics support. Nimitz had reorganized his headquarters in early September to improve joint operations with the Army. His Pacific Fleet staff now worked in parallel with a Joint Staff that included Army officers, who coordinated with General Richardson's staff.[12]

Once the CinCPac War Plans staff drafted the operation plan for Galvanic, Nimitz sent it on to Spruance for further action. As Spruance's staff occupied the same building, a great deal of coordination, negotiation, and revision was done in face-to-face meetings, streamlining the process. Charles Barber recalled that much of the work was done orally and little was put down in writing until later. Yeomen, enlisted service members specializing in clerical work, typed the drafts; then Barber reviewed them for accuracy and passed the work on to Moore.[13]

During normal "business" hours, Moore was often interrupted by important visitors, such as Admiral Halsey, or was forced to mediate between Turner and Smith. Spruance preferred to avoid such confrontations, leaving that to Moore. On one such occasion, a dispute arose regarding when the control of the amphibious troops should be transferred from the senior naval officer commanding the Joint Expeditionary Force to the authority of the Marine or Army general in command of the Landing Force. Smith demanded that this be clearly defined. Moore had gone to Spruance for guidance, but Spruance seemed unconcerned, telling him not to worry so much: "They'll do exactly what I want them to do. I know them both so well and they know me, and they'll be alright." Moore acknowledged that that might be the case, but the issue was how their subordinates might deal with the ambiguity. A clear chain of command was needed. Moore drafted a policy establishing that once the Landing Force's commander was ashore and in full control of the situation, he would inform the Joint Expeditionary Force's commander, who would then relinquish control, which would be communicated down the line. It succeeded so well that it was used for the remainder of the war.[14]

Logistics was vitally important and presented a potential bottleneck for the coming offensive. Inadequate shipping, poorly organized logistics, and the lack of aircraft and ships had greatly constrained operations in the South Pacific. Logistics in the Southwest Pacific were handled through MacArthur's command, and shipping sent south often stayed there and was not returned. Throughout the spring and summer of 1943 Vice Adm. William L. Calhoun, the commander of the Service Force, Pacific Fleet, reorganized and expanded the bases at Nouméa and Espiritu Santo, constructing extensive fuel oil tank farms, large warehouses, food refrigeration, hospitals, and recreation facilities. Ship repair units, units for ordinance and aircraft overhaul, and floating dry docks arrived, in huge contrast to the chaotic conditions that had bedeviled Ghormley a year earlier. Calhoun would have to coordinate logistics on a grander scale in the coming months. The coral islands of the Central Pacific lacked the land mass to build the large bases found in the South Pacific, and the fleet would have to bring its resources with it as it advanced west in the form of the new mobile service squadrons.[15]

Spruance asked Rear Adm. Charles A. Lockwood, commander of the submarines of the Pacific Fleet, to prepare the submarine defense of the operation. Lockwood responded with a memo dated 26 August in which he stated that up to ten submarines could be used in the operation, with four stationed in the Marshalls, five south and east of Truk, and the *Nautilus* reprising her role to carry Marine raiders, this time to seize

Abemama. The submarines would report any movement of the Combined Fleet, shadow it if it sortied, and then attack if possible. Allied aircraft would be ordered not to attack submarines north of a line drawn between the Gilberts and Marshalls to minimize confusion as to friend or foe.[16]

As initially conceived, Galvanic had the additional objective of seizing the island of Nauru, where the Japanese had built a substantial air base. Nauru is a sea mount of phosphoric rock rising several hundred feet out of the ocean, ringed with a coral reef, but with narrow beaches and no lagoon. Prewar strip mining had left numerous defiles and caves perfectly suitable for fortification. Holland Smith and his staff recommended that Nauru be bypassed as it would be too difficult to capture both it and an unspecified target in the Gilberts with the forces and transport ships allocated for the operation. Furthermore, Nauru was 380 miles from Tarawa, the main objective, which greatly complicated the task of the covering forces to defend both areas.[17]

Smith was also concerned about the unit designated to conduct the assault, the 27th Infantry Division. The combat-tested 2nd Marine Division was assigned to the main objective, Betio Island in the Tarawa Atoll, known to be heavily fortified and likely to be "a tough nut to crack." The 27th Infantry had been training hard but were nonetheless green and inexperienced. Most of the original enlisted guardsmen had transferred out due to age, hardship, or promotion, while many of the original National Guard officers remained. Some had received additional training in advanced warfare and amphibious operations, but their outlook was based on Army infantry doctrine that stressed slow, methodical combined arms attack. In contrast, Marine amphibious doctrine valued rapid action by light infantry who could not count on artillery and armor support in the initial assault. Smith was sure that sending such an inexperienced unit to attack a heavily defended island was a recipe for disaster.

On 10 September the CinCPac staff handed Spruance the outline plan for the next major assault, the seizure of the Marshall Islands, known as Operation Flintlock. Initially, Nimitz proposed taking Kwajalein, Wotje, and Maloelap simultaneously, but the Joint Chiefs rejected the proposal due to the lack of troops available in theater. Next, he proposed taking Kwajalein alone, bypassing the other active Japanese bases. Turner and

Spruance objected as the entire fleet and transports would have to transit through an area covered by Japanese land-based air forces. They preferred taking Wotje or Maloelap first, and attempted to pressure Soc McMorris into agreeing with their assessment to get Nimitz to change his plans. McMorris disagreed, believing that the Fast Carrier Force could deal with the adjacent Japanese air bases, and refused to submit to their pressure. Spruance, however, was not to be dissuaded when convinced he was right. He and his staff looked at alternatives and decided that Ujae Atoll, located just 125 miles due west of Kwajalein, made a good place to establish an advance base to support the main assault.[18]

Before the COMINCH conference at Pearl Harbor, Spruance and Turner approached Nimitz about dropping Nauru from Galvanic. As Nauru was explicitly mentioned in the JCS order of 20 July, Nimitz was unwilling to request a change until they conferred with King, who was due to arrive on 25 September. Spruance asked Smith to detail his objections in writing, which he did. During the meeting, Spruance passed Smith's letter to Nimitz, who read it and passed it on to King. King read it, turned to Spruance, and asked, "What do you propose to take instead of Nauru?" Spruance replied, "Makin." Spruance then proceeded to lay out Smith's arguments. King gave Spruance "the old fish eye," but in the end agreed to ask the JCS to approve the requested change, which he did the next day.[19]

As Spruance had previously arranged to meet with the Army commanders to discuss this change, on the morning of the second day of the conference he sent Moore as his representative with the directive to present their case for the seizure of Ujae Atoll. As this was a last-minute brainstorm, Spruance did not have an opportunity to discuss it with Nimitz first, and when Moore presented the idea, Nimitz, normally unperturbable, was furious that his subordinates were attempting to introduce a new element into what he considered to be a settled matter. According to Moore, King chortled at Nimitz's distress in seeing his carefully orchestrated presentation upset, saying, "I thought there was something going on around here." Nimitz ended the discussion by stating, "The thing is settled. We know what we're going to do, we're not going to take Ujae!" Spruance later went to Nimitz to smooth things over, but the question of Kwajalein was one he would revisit after Galvanic.[20]

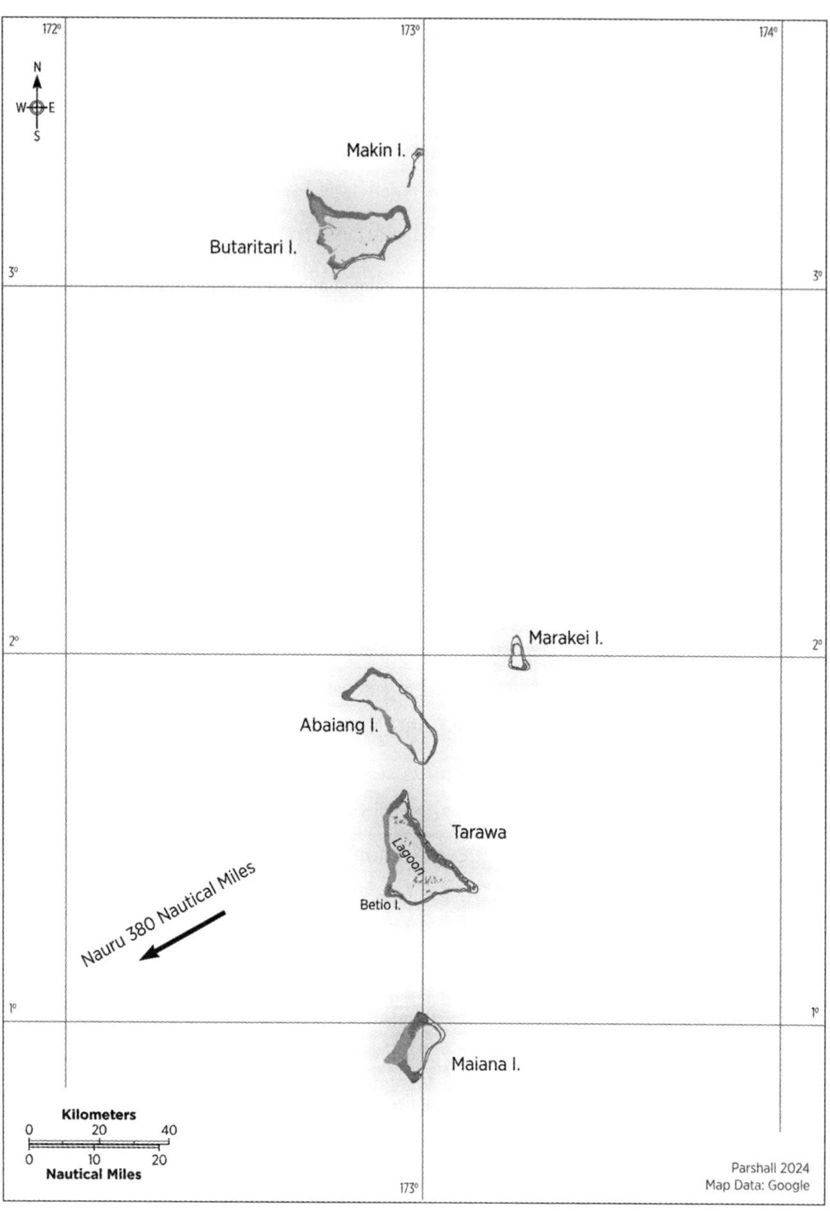

MAP 4. The Gilbert Islands

Pownall and the Fast Carrier Force conducted raids against Makin and Tarawa on 18–19 September. The carriers and their escorts gained experience sailing in the new formations, and the hundreds of sorties flown by the aviators under combat conditions were the capstone of their months of training on the West Coast. While the Japanese air cover over the islands was meager, there was plenty of antiaircraft fire, and the defenders expended ammunition they could not replenish before the assault. Fresh aerial photography enabled the cartographers to update their extensive mapping of the island's defenses.[21]

During this period the Combined Fleet was not idle. In May 1943 Vice Admiral Koga Mineichi succeeded Admiral Yamamoto Isoroku as the commander of Japanese naval forces in the Pacific after the latter's death in April of that year. Koga reported to Truk that summer with a new staff in train, but it was not until August that they had worked out a plan to entice the U.S. fleet into a decisive battle (*kantai kessen*). The Imperial Japanese Navy had long been aware of the U.S. Navy's strategy to use the Mandate Islands as stepping stones to the Japanese Home Islands. Admiral Koga, recognizing Japan's dwindling strength and rapidly increasing American power, was convinced that the Imperial Japanese Navy had to successfully bring off a decisive victory against the Americans in 1943 or the war would inevitably be lost.[22]

Koga's strategy was outlined in two complementary, interrelated operation orders, both issued on 15 August 1943: Combined Fleet Ultra Secret Operation Order 41, "Outline for Z Operations," and Operation Order 42, "Outline for the Establishment of Interception (Yōgeki) Zones." It should be noted that the Japanese word *yōgeki* can also be translated as "ambush" or "counterattack." Plan Z did not contain operational specifics for just one area, but was written so that it could be readily adapted in response to an American attack anywhere within the vast Japanese defensive perimeter. A total of nine interlocking interception zones, running from the Kurile Islands in the north, across the Central Pacific, to the New Guinea in the south, would be "forged into a ring of steel" and arranged in depth in three succeeding layers. In each zone, there were strong advance bases located within mutual air support distance from each other, typically 300 nautical miles.[23]

One of the main functions of the interception zones was to establish air and sea patrols within the reconnaissance perimeters to provide an early warning of any large-scale American incursion and then keep such forces under constant observation. Through the strategy of "interceptive operations," or Z Operations, submarine attacks and air strikes would be launched from the advanced bases to weaken American strength in carriers and capital ships. The Combined Fleet, based in the heart of this "ring of steel" at Truk, would be held in readiness to attack at the propitious moment. Once the order to attack was given, the basic policy for Z Operations was that "enemy carriers will be neutralized by our massed air strength and after gaining air superiority, our main attack will be directed against the transport group. If the situation permits, the enemy fleet will be attacked. Depending on the situation the transport group will be attacked first."[24] The advance bases were to resist the assault forces as long as possible until the Combined Fleet could respond. According to the operations order issued by the IJN 6th Base Force, garrisons were to defend their bases "to the death, rallying the full defensive strength when the enemy lands, and endeavoring to destroy him on the water's edge."[25]

Alerted by radio intercepts to the presence of American carriers operating in the Gilberts, Koga sortied the Combined Fleet from Truk on 18 September, reaching Eniwetok in the Marshalls on 20 September. Pownall, however, was by now on his way back to Pearl Harbor, unaware of how close he might have been to a major action. The outcome of such an encounter of Koga's veterans against the still green Fast Carrier Force may have been in doubt when one considers the CinCPac Running Summary for 13 September which, noting the significant build-up of forces at Truk, stated, "Our sources of information may not be able to report the departure or destination of this force in time to take effective counter action. . . . The Central Pacific Force must be trained as a team before it can meet the main enemy fleet with reasonable assurance of success."[26]

The Imperial General Headquarters in Tokyo, taking into account the recent Allied advances in New Guinea and the Solomons, the British build-up for an offensive in Burma, and the carrier and bomber attacks in the Central Pacific, reconsidered its general strategy. In a conference held on 30 September in the presence of the emperor, Admiral Nagano presented Directive Number 280, which stipulated the importance of defeating any Allied advance into the Bismarck Archipelago and holding Rabaul as a joint Army-Navy imperative. The Imperial Army specified holding Burma at all costs, while the Navy added a new inner defense zone, running north from the Philippines through the Carolines and the Marianas, with the Kuriles now as the northern terminus as the Aleutians had been abandoned in August. This was the line that the Allies could not be permitted to breach and was seen as the theater where the decisive battle would and must occur.[27]

The Fast Carrier Force, now designated Task Force 14, struck again on 5 October, this time at Wake Island, part of Nimitz's larger strategy to keep Koga guessing. TF 14, under the command of Rear Adm. Alfred E. Montgomery, consisted of all six of the new carriers, plus escorts. Montgomery arranged the carriers into three task groups, which gave the task force experience in maneuvering together or independently. This time, they found that the target was better defended by heavy antiaircraft fire and fighters. Thirty Zeroes met the TBF Avengers and SBD Dauntlesses on their bombing runs, but the new F6F Hellcats soon proved their superiority over the old nemesis. The raid was not without cost as twelve aircraft were lost; fortunately, the submarine USS *Skate* (SS 305) was on station to rescue six of the downed pilots. After destroying the radar and radio installations, the task force withdrew the next day. Montgomery's chief of staff, Capt. Herbert S. Duckworth, recalled this operation's importance as "virtually all the techniques of ship handling for a multi-carrier force which were later used successfully had their origins in this operation."[28]

Koga reacted the same way as before, ordering a large portion of the Combined Fleet to move from Truk to the Eniwetok base on 16 October. Air searches in the vicinity of Wake found no sign of the Americans, who were long gone, and they returned to Truk. The Japanese saw these carrier raids without any attempt at landing troops as diversionary and concluded the real blow was about to fall in the South Pacific. Koga sent his cruisers and the bulk of his carrier aircraft to reinforce Rabaul to meet this perceived threat. As will be seen, this move had significant ramifications for the Galvanic operation.[29]

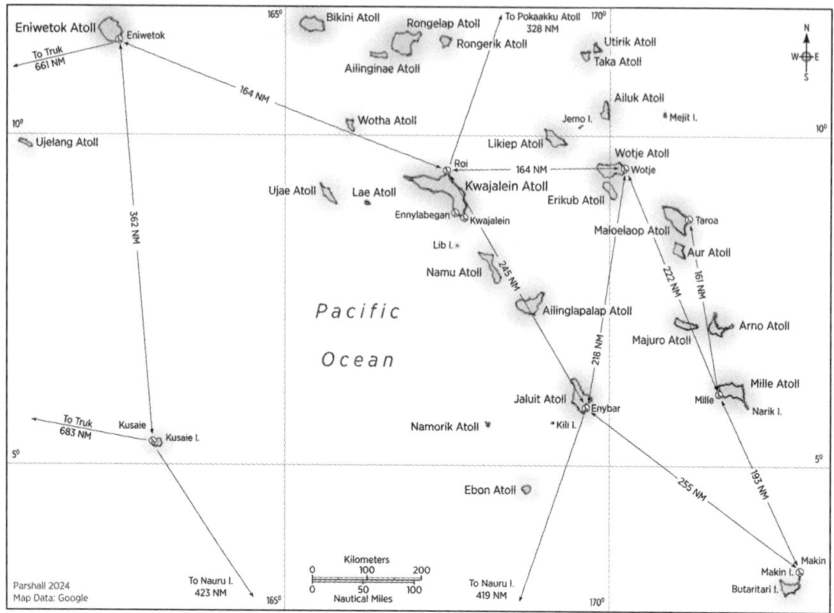

MAP 5. The Marshall Islands

The stage was now set. Nimitz issued his Operations Plan No. 14-43 to Spruance as Commander, Central Pacific Force on 5 October 1943, with D(og)-Day set for 19 November 1943. The main objective of Operation Galvanic was Tarawa Atoll, along with Makin Island as previously agreed upon. The Abemama Atoll would also be taken as a fleet anchorage and supply base, and air bases established on all three. Japanese airfields on Nauru and the Marshall Islands would be subjected to heavy aerial bombardment to "vigorously deny" them to enemy use.[30]

The Central Pacific Force consisted of three main elements: the Fifth Fleet, directly under Spruance's command, consisting of all the carrier groups, battleships, and their escorts and supporting warships; the Assault Force commanded by Turner, consisting of all transports, attack cargo ships, landing ships, and amphibious vessels; and the Fifth Amphibious Corps, consisting of the 2nd Marine Division and the 27th Infantry Division, commanded by Holland Smith.

Spruance, his commanders, and their respective staff now had less than a month to finalize the orders for the operation, often working from

0800 to midnight. Moore complained to his wife that he was working long hours while Spruance was not. Typically, after dinner Moore returned to the office to continue working while Spruance kept to his usual routine of relaxing and retiring early. Spruance valued a good night's sleep but felt a little guilty that he did so while his staff worked. He wrote to Margaret, "My staff has been working up to midnight every night, and I have been working during the day but refuse to go on the night shift. Their labors are almost over now, I hope." Spruance greatly valued his chief of staff. In the same letter to his wife, he wrote, "There's a lot to do in a short time, and Carl is so conscientious that I don't like to walk out and leave him plugging away at his desk. . . . [I]t is certainly fortunate that I have someone like Carl to put the ideas in orderly form on paper and to marshal the mass of details involved and get things in orderly shape."

Spruance and Moore made a great team as their strengths played off one another, Moore being the stickler for detail and Spruance having the ability to see the big picture and synthesize a mass of information to arrive at an optimal solution. Spruance did not like expressing his thoughts in writing but preferred to work via discussion, which was part of his successful relationship with Nimitz. It also explains why so little documentation of his interaction with Nimitz exists. As Spruance explained to Margaret, "Carl likes to commit his thoughts to paper, which is something I never do if I can help it. Details and writing get me bogged down immediately. I hate to write, get my best results by talking to people and thinking out loud, but I get bogged down as soon as I have to assemble my ideas on paper. I can do so if necessary, but I have to go off alone, be completely undisturbed, and labor excessively."[31]

The final version of the operation plan was ready by 29 October, and for the next several days Moore, Charles Barber, and their yeomen made final revisions and began compiling hundreds of pages of orders, appendices, and maps into a single document, one that eventually weighed in at three pounds. As three hundred copies were required, Barber called upon one hundred men from the CinCPac Headquarters Marine detachment for assistance, creating an assembly line to mimeograph, collate, and staple the final document, which was then packaged and sent out to the various commands. They finally wrapped up their task at 0500 on 31 October.

On 5 November Spruance and his staff relocated into *Indianapolis*. He took the opportunity to write to Margaret, telling her that it was so much like *Northampton* that he felt very much at home. He and his staff messed together, and due to space constraints during the day his cabin was used for "utilitarian purposes, such as dispatches, charts, and conferences." Spruance praised the work that Carl Moore and his staff were doing for him and told her, in his typical understated way, that "this is the last letter you will receive from me in some weeks—probably until about Christmas time—as I shall be too occupied with other matters to do any writing."[32]

CHAPTER 9

THE TRIDENT STRIKES

Operation Galvanic

THE PRIMARY OBJECTIVE of Operation Galvanic was the capture of the Japanese airfield located on Betio Island in the Tarawa Atoll. Betio, situated on the southwest end of the atoll, adjacent to the mouth of the 20-mile-wide lagoon, is a low-lying coral island, some 2.3 miles in total length, shaped like a bird lying on its back. With its head on the west end, some 850 yards in width, the "body" tapers down to just 20 yards in width at its tail on the extreme east end. The bird's back faces the open ocean, and from its "breast" an 800-yard-long pier juts out into the lagoon.[1]

Seizing coral islands and atolls within the Japanese defensive perimeter was far more dangerous and difficult than previous operations in the Solomon Islands. The small size of the target islands offered few opportunities for landing on a beach without opposition and little room for maneuver once ashore. Offshore, the supporting naval task forces were at risk of attack by Japanese aircraft and submarines. Successful landing operations and the follow-on assault therefore called for speed and efficiency to minimize the time such forces were exposed to counterattack.

On 2 October, Julian Smith and his staff arrived in Pearl Harbor to meet with Spruance, Holland Smith, and Turner to discuss the 2nd Marine Division's plans for the assault on Betio. Using the vast amount of recently collected aerial photography and the comprehensive collection of photographs of Tarawa taken by *Nautilus*, the Marines had created detailed mapping and a scale model of the defenses on Betio, showing the location of the 8-inch Vickers shore batteries at the ends of the island, the dual-purpose antiboat and antiaircraft guns, the heavy machine-gun emplacements, and the concrete blockhouses.[2]

The reconnaissance also revealed dozens of smaller concrete and steel pillboxes, coconut-log dugouts equipped with 7.7-mm machine guns, and an unknown number of rifle pits on the island's lagoon and ocean sides. A coconut-log seawall, located twenty feet from the beach's edge and about five feet tall, surrounded most of the island. As the Japanese expected an assault would most likely come from the ocean side, this area was more fortified, ringed with barbed wire, and heavily mined. The aerial photos indicated that concrete and wire barriers were located on that side of the island, designed to funnel landing craft into fields of fire. Marine intelligence estimated that more than 4,700 troops were defending the island, including 2,100 men of the tough 3rd Special Base and 7th Special Naval Landing Forces, as well as construction engineers, air force personnel, and Korean laborers.[3]

The Marines' plan called for an intensive and prolonged preliminary air and naval bombardment before the landing and the seizure of Bairiki, the small island to the east of Betio, to be used as a base for supporting artillery. Spruance and Holland Smith rejected the idea of seizing Bairiki prior to the main landings, as this would undoubtedly alert the defenders on Betio. A prolonged bombardment was also ruled on the basis that time was of the essence and that the entire operation had to be complete before the Combined Fleet had time to sortie. The supporting naval force needed to be freed from protecting the landing forces to meet such a counterattack, and therefore they allotted only three hours to the preliminary bombardment.

Julian Smith wanted the 2nd and 6th Regiments, totaling six battalions, to conduct the assault, but Holland Smith decided that the assault force would consist of just the 2nd Regiment, reinforced with a battalion from the 8th Regiment. The other two battalions of the 8th Regiment were to be held as a divisional reserve. Holland Smith kept a battalion in reserve for the Fifth Corps, to be used at either Betio or Makin as he saw fit. Julian Smith objected strongly, as this reduced his strength to a mere 2:1 superiority over the defenders, far less than the landing operations doctrine called for. He put his objections in writing to Holland Smith, who accepted responsibility.[4]

The island had coral reefs on either side, so timing the landings to coincide with optimum tide conditions was critical, especially on the lagoon side

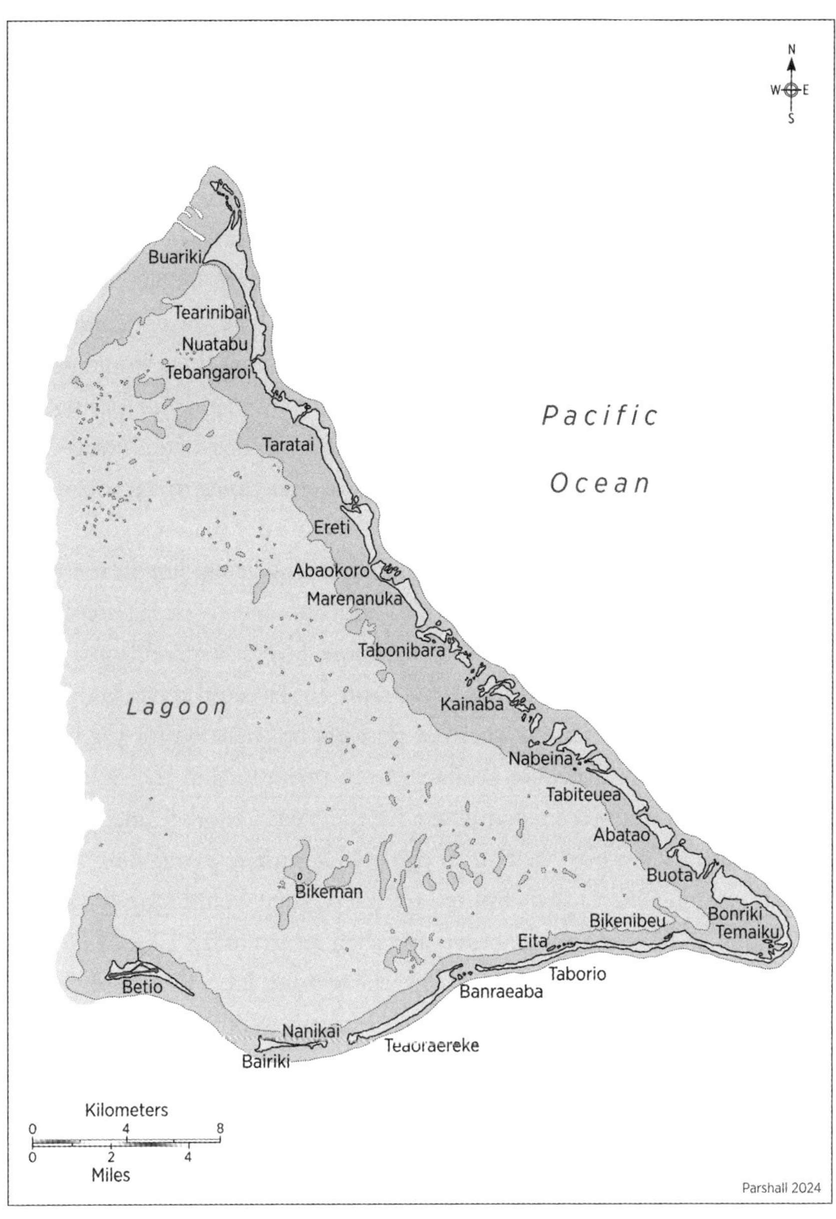

MAP 6. Tarawa Atoll

where the coral formed a wide shelf extending hundreds of yards into the sea. British officials and officers of the Royal Australian Navy and the Royal New Zealand Navy familiar with the island were called to Pearl Harbor to consult with the planners. Late November was the time of the third quarter lunar neap tide, and the morning of 20 November was the best time for a rising tide to coincide with the H-Hour, when the first wave was to hit the beach. As a result, the original landing date was delayed by one day. There was, however, disagreement among the old hands about the possibility of a "dodging tide," where the depth might vary enough that there would not be enough water to float a Higgins boat over the coral reef. In preparing the tidal tables for the operation, the planners hedged their bets: "Neap tides are variable and occasionally ebb and flow several times in 24 hours, but variations from the heights given should not be greater than one foot."[5]

The possibility that the LCVPs might become grounded on the coral reef remained a calculated risk. Nimitz and Spruance were insistent that the operation could not be delayed for more favorable conditions. Holland Smith knew that the tracked Alligator LVTs could traverse the reef and insisted that as many of these as possible be collected for use by the first wave. Seventy-five were available from operations in the Solomons, although these were somewhat worse for the wear. Another one hundred were awaiting transport in San Diego and Smith reserved half for the Makin assault. Due to their limited numbers, they would have to unload their cargo of Marines on the beach and then return to the Line of Departure to load the subsequent waves from the waiting LCVPs. In the worst-case scenario, after unloading at the beach, they would then return to any Higgins boats left stranded on the reef to transfer men to the shore.[6]

A vast armada of unprecedented naval strength was now set to converge from seven directions and descend upon the Gilberts on or about 20 November 1943. To achieve tactical surprise, they sailed under strict radio silence. Task Force 52, the Northern Force, led by Rear Adm. Kelly Turner aboard *Pennsylvania*, departed Pearl Harbor on 10 November, heading for Makin Atoll to land elements of the 27th Infantry Division. Task Force 53, the Southern Force, commanded by Rear Adm. Harry W. Hill, would launch the amphibious assault on Tarawa Atoll, supported by three battleships, four cruisers, and six destroyers for fire support and

TABLE 1. Operation Galvanic Task Groups

			SHIP TYPE								
COMMANDER	**TASK FORCE**	**TASK FORCE GROUP**	**FAST CARRIERS**	**LIGHT CARRIERS**	**ESCORT CARRIERS**	**FAST BATTLESHIPS**	**VETERAN BATTLESHIPS**	**CRUISERS**	**LIGHT & ANTIAIRCRAFT CRUISERS**	**DESTROYERS & ESCORTS**	**TRANSPORTS & SUPPORT**
Turner	**TF 52**	**Northern Attack Force**									
Loomis	52.1	Transport Group								4	6
Griffin	52.2	Fire Support Group					4	4		6	
Mullinnix	52.3	Air Support Group			3					4	1
Hill	**TF 53**	**Southern Attack Force**									
Knowles	53.1	Transport Group								7	17
Pierce	53.2	Minesweeper Group									2
Kingman	53.4	Fire Support Group					3	2	2	9	
Ragsdale	53.6	Air Support Group			5					5	
Pownall	**TF 50**	**Fast Carrier Force**									
Pownall	50.1	Carrier Interceptor	2	1		2				6	
Radford	50.2	Northern Carrier Group	1	2		3				6	
Montgomery	50.3	Southern Carrier Group	2	1				3	1	5	
Sherman	50.4	Relief Carrier Group	1	1					2	4	
Totals, Operation GALVANIC			6	5	8	5	7	9	5	56	26
								Total Ships:			127

Source: VADM E. P. Forrestel, USN (Ret.), *Admiral Raymond A. Spruance, USN, A Study in Command*, Appendix III & IV, 251–54.

five escort carriers for close air support. They departed Wellington on 1 November, sailing to Efate to rehearse landing operations. Conducting an amphibious rehearsal in the South Pacific also helped confuse the enemy regarding the intended target.

Rear Adm. Charles A. Pownall's Task Force 50, the Fast Carrier Force, consisted of four task groups with four separate missions. TG 50.1, the Carrier Interceptor Group led by Pownall, departed Pearl Harbor on

10 November, heading for the Marshall Islands to suppress or destroy Japanese air strike capability on Wotje, Milli, and Jaluit. TG 50.2, the Northern Carrier Group under Rear Adm. Arthur W. Radford, would support the Makin assault and remain on station between Makin and Tarawa. TG 50.3, the Southern Carrier Group under Rear Adm. Alfred E. Montgomery, was coming from the south to provide screening and air support for the Tarawa operation. Finally, TG 50.4, under Rear Adm. Frederick Sherman, was tasked with attacking Nauru to eliminate Japanese air strength there and then head northeast to join the other carrier groups in the Gilberts. In all, the Fast Carrier Force had at its disposal six fast carriers, five light carriers, five fast battleships, and five cruisers, plus their screening destroyers, should the Combined Fleet decide to sortie from Truk.[7]

Task Force 57, the Defense Forces and Shore Based Air under Admiral Hoover, would take Abemama, develop it into an airbase and anchorage, and provide construction troops for repairing the airfield on Betio and building a new airfield on Makin as soon as possible. Hoover had at his disposal nearly four hundred land-based Army and Navy aircraft. Beginning on 13 November, they launched daily bombing raids against the Japanese bases in the Gilberts and Marshalls, flying from the recently built airfields on Baker Island and the Ellice and Samoan Islands.

The possibility that the Combined Fleet might respond in force to the operation was still a concern. Spruance's "General Instructions for Flag Officers, Central Pacific Force, for Galvanic" is worth quoting here:

> If a major portion of the Jap Fleet were to attempt to interfere with Galvanic, it is obvious that the defeat of the enemy Fleet would at once become paramount. . . . The destruction of a considerable portion of the Japanese naval strength would go far towards winning the war. . . . [W]e must be prepared at all times during Galvanic for a fleet engagement. . . . The possibility of an enemy attack in force on the Makin area with little or no warning necessitates that on and after D-day the carrier task groups operating there with the new battleships in their screen must remain in as close tactical supporting distance of the Northern Attack Force as the nature of their air operations and their fuel situation permits. In such a

> position they will be able, also, to provide very effective fighter protection against enemy air attacks coming from the Marshalls against our ships at Makin.[8]

While the "defeat of the enemy Fleet" was important, for Spruance the operation's main objective was the occupation of the islands. As will be seen, in this and future operations, he placed the success of the amphibious assault above all else. The carrier commanders were, however, less than pleased about being required to stay "in close tactical distance" of the landing forces, as it might leave them too easily found by enemy "snoopers" and vulnerable to attack.

Spruance and his staff sailed with Turner's group on 10 November. They adopted a circular sailing formation with the transports in the center, flanked by the heavy cruisers and surrounded on all points by screening destroyers. The formation zig-zagged during daylight hours but maintained a steady course at night. Frequent gunnery and antiaircraft drills kept all hands busy during the voyage. Aboard *Indianapolis,* Spruance and his staff monitored American and Japanese radio traffic but maintained radio silence. Any necessary communication between ships was conducted either by short-range TBS or blinker light, a form of visual communication in which Spruance's flag lieutenant E. H. McKissick, formerly an enlisted signalman, was an expert. Spruance's staff stood four-hour watches and recorded the movement of the formation in the Flag Log.[9]

On 19 November, the formation met Hill's TF 53 coming north from Efate. *Indianapolis* departed TF 52 as Turner sailed for Makin, joining Hill to add her guns to the Fire Support Group for the Tarawa operation. For tactical purposes, the flagship remained under Hill's control throughout the operation, with Spruance and his staff along for the ride. This suited Spruance, who wanted to be in proximity to monitor the operation closely but had no intention of interfering with his subordinate commanders unless absolutely necessary. If the Combined Fleet should sortie and attempt to attack, he would detach *Indianapolis* and join Pownall's task group to direct the counterattack.

Complementary operations were already well underway in the South Pacific to land troops on Bougainville and attack Rabaul as part of

Operation Cartwheel. The 3rd Marine Division landed at Empress Augusta Bay on 1 November. Admiral Koga dispatched a force of destroyers and cruisers to disrupt the landing and perhaps replicate the IJN's success at Savo Island. Instead, these were severely mauled by Halsey's TF 39 during the Battle of Empress Augusta Bay. Koga then sent a force of his heavy cruisers from Truk to reinforce Rabaul, intending to counterattack. Sherman's carriers, then part of Halsey's TF 38, attacked these ships at Rabaul on 5 November and badly damaged four, which were subsequently withdrawn to Truk.

As Spruance departed Pearl Harbor on 10 November, Sherman's carriers were joined by Montgomery's TG 50.3 to conduct a second raid on Rabaul, sinking a destroyer and a cruiser in Simpson Harbor. The Japanese retaliatory counterstrike against the American carriers was a disaster, resulting in the loss of thirty-five aircraft and their trained aircrews without damaging a single carrier, thus proving the value of the new fast carrier battle formation and its dense screen of antiaircraft fire. The failure of the counterstrike, the damage to his precious cruisers, and the loss of his carrier aircraft defending Rabaul seriously limited Koga's ability to respond to Galvanic. Without adequate air cover and cruisers to screen his carriers, Koga decided to keep the Combined Fleet at Truk. The defenders of the Gilberts were on their own.[10]

The success of the Rabaul raids confirmed that the best way to ensure the success of an amphibious operation was at the strategic level: by maintaining an "unrelenting pressure" on the Japanese through parallel operations in the South and Central Pacific that severely limited their ability to predict where the next blow would fall and react in time with sufficient force to counterattack.

Without any opposition from the Combined Fleet, Pownall's TG 50.1 was free to move between the Gilberts and the southern Marshall islands, striking the airfields on Mili and the seaplane base on Jaluit on 19 November. He continued to strike Mili throughout the operation, ensuring that the bombers there did not threaten the landings on Makin and Tarawa and denying the airbase to air reinforcements arriving from Truk. With its new fast carrier strike groups, the U.S. Navy could now achieve and retain air and sea control within a chosen area of operation.

The transports of TF 53 arrived offshore of Betio in their designated staging area at 0400 on 20 November and began the process of transferring the Marines of the first wave into the landing craft. The Landing Ship Tank (LST) disgorged the tracked Alligators, which then rendezvoused with the LCVPs at the Line of Departure to make the transfer. A searchlight on Betio blinked out a coded challenge, and when there was no reply, at 0507 the Japanese shore batteries opened up on the invasion fleet. These were quickly silenced by the big guns of the old veterans of the Pearl Harbor attack, *Maryland* and USS *Tennessee* (BB 43), along with fire from the accompanying heavy cruisers, including the flagship *Indianapolis*. After the first few salvos there was a tremendous explosion on the southwest end of Betio when a 16-inch shell landed in the shared magazine of the 8-inch Vickers guns. Many smaller antiboat and dual-purpose guns held their fire for fear of revealing their positions.[11]

Due to communication problems, the carrier aircraft began bombing and strafing at 0610, thirty minutes late, triggering a ripple effect of cumulative delays. At 0622 the first phase of the naval bombardment began, smothering the island with intense shelling. At 0745, the Fire Support Group moved inshore and began their second phase of systematic bombardment of the shore defenses, using radar fire control to acquire targets hidden by the huge clouds of smoke and dust that now blanketed the island.[12]

The time designated for the first wave to land, H-Hour, was originally 0830, but the LVTs had to fight a westerly set in the open sea before they entered the lagoon, which unexpectedly slowed their progress. Consequently, Hill revised the H-Hour to 0900. The "worst-case" tidal scenario had also occurred, and while the tracked LVTs made it over the reef, the LCVPs could not, and men were forced to debark into chest-high water and wade the five to eight hundred yards to their respective target beaches under heavy fire from the defenders.

Hill lifted the bombardment at 0854, and the final, but ineffective, strafing run was complete by 0900. This left another fifteen to twenty minutes before the LVTs hit the beaches, enough time for the remaining defenders to recover their wits and shift from the less hard-hit areas on the ocean side into the heavily reinforced gun emplacements, pillboxes, and small arms positions on the lagoon side. Most of these survived the intense bombardment due to their ingenious construction of coconut logs and reinforced concrete, covered by many feet of coral sand. As a result, the Marines were met with a murderous fire that killed many men and knocked out a number of the lightly protected LVTs.

Despite the volume of fire, the first wave made it ashore largely intact, landing, from left to right, on Red 3, east of the pier, Red 2 on the west side, and Red 1 on the right. Many of the LVTs they came in on were damaged or sank as their bullet-riddled hulls filled with water on the return trip. Others ran out of fuel or fell victim to mechanical faults, so the plan to use them to ferry troops from the stranded LCVPs largely failed. The succeeding waves had fewer and fewer LVTs as these were disabled or destroyed, and most of the Marines who landed on Betio the first day were required to wade to the beach from LCVPs and suffered heavy casualties as a result. The fire was so intense that elements of the fourth wave that were supposed to land on Red 1 went around to the south side of Betio, designated Green Beach, and landed there. This proved providential, as they could provide flanking fire for the other beaches and secured one of the few areas where tanks could be landed on the second day of the assault.

The tactical radio sets carried by the Marines were soon found to be highly susceptible to damage from shock and were not waterproof, resulting in loss of command and control. The commander of the 2nd Marine Regiment, Col. David M. Shoup, struggled to make it ashore but managed to do so by 1200, setting up his command post against the back wall of a still occupied concrete bunker fifty yards from the pier. Using field telephones and runners and with one of the few working radios, Shoup began to bring the assault under some resemblance of command and control. The Marines who made it ashore managed to hang on, huddled against the protective seawall until rallied by their commanders to go over the wall and take out the gun positions that were killing their comrades wading in from the reef. Thus, they were able to make some small gains that first day. They were also fortunate that the intense bombardment had blown away the concealing camouflage and destroyed Japanese communications. The Japanese commander, Rear Admiral Shibazaki Keiji, and his staff were killed outside of their command bunker, reportedly by a

5-inch shell from one of the destroyers in the lagoon. As a result, the Japanese defense was poorly coordinated, and each position was effectively on its own. Without command and control, the defenders failed to launch an effective counterattack on the first night, when it could have caused the most damage.[13]

Julian Smith anxiously watched the landings from *Maryland*, but he was only getting sporadic reports, and none were good. At 1331, he told Holland Smith, who was directing the operation at Makin, that "the issue is in doubt," and requested the release of the Fifth Corps reserve to him. Meanwhile, the 2nd Marines commander threw all his divisional reserves into the assault. By sunset, more than 5,000 Marines had landed.

The struggle to land reinforcements and supplies improved the next day, aided by changed tidal conditions that allowed the landing craft to reach the beach. The beaches on the island's west end were secured, and the regiments held in corps reserve now landed and began clearing the west end of the runway and attacking the fortifications on the south shore. The attackers required high explosives, flamethrowers, and direct tank artillery fire to neutralize the heavily reinforced blockhouses, pillboxes, and gun emplacements.

The Marines moved from the west end to the east end and linked up with their comrades on the Red Beaches, supported by naval call-fire and bombing by the carrier planes of TG 50.3. The relentless application of firepower and the tenacity of the Marines was having its effect, as defenders were methodically killed in their bunkers. No quarter was asked, and none was given, except to a small fraction of the Korean laborers who had no interest in dying for the emperor. At 1603, war correspondent Robert Sherrod noted that jeeps towing 37-mm guns were moving down the pier, saying, "If a sign of certain victory were needed, this is it: the jeeps have arrived."[14]

In desperation, Japanese troops on the east end of the island rallied for a series of mass banzai charges during the night of the second day, lasting into the early morning of the third day, D+3, attacking a line held by elements of the 2nd Battalion, 8th Regiment. The Marines expected such an attack and readied their defense with heavy machine guns and artillery. Deserting their bunkers for open ground, the Japanese were cut down by the dozens, but their numbers were so great that, at times, the Marines had a difficult time coping with the onslaught. In the end, more than six hundred Japanese were killed; the irony is that they could have extracted a higher price in American lives had they held their defensive positions instead. Lt. Col. Evans F. Carlson, who with his raiders had attacked Makin the year before, remarked, "This was not only worse than Guadalcanal, it was the damnedest fighting I've seen in thirty years of this business."[15]

By 1330 that day, Betio was declared secure, but there were still many smaller islands on the east side of the atoll to clear. Five days later, Julian Smith reported that the "remaining forces on Tarawa were wiped out." The concrete runway, which was spared bombardment on purpose, was largely intact, and the Seabees were already at work making repairs. The first F6F fighter landed at noon on 23 November. In all, 18,000 Marines and Navy corpsmen had landed on Tarawa, although they suffered heavy casualties, including 1,099 either killed in action or who died of their wounds later. Of the 4,700 Japanese defenders, most were killed, leaving only 17 Japanese and 129 Korean laborers to be taken prisoner.[16]

Turner and TF 52 landed the 165th Regimental Combat Team of the 27th Infantry Division on Makin Island beginning at 0830 on 20 November. Makin's defenses were not as numerous or as formidable as Betio's, and the garrison of some 800 men was a tenth of the size of the attacking U.S. Army units. The prelanding naval and air bombardments went as planned, and the troops landed without much opposition. Nevertheless, owing to the inexperience and the excess of caution shown by the green troops of the 27th Infantry, the island was not declared secure until D+3, the same date as Betio. The initial landing operations were also much slower than anticipated due to the presence of coral rock, which hampered the use of LSTs. The unloading of supplies was delayed by the narrow beach, which only permitted six landing craft at a time to land. This series of delays would have tragic consequences.[17]

Although Admiral Koga was unwilling to commit the Combined Fleet, he did send submarines to the area, and early on the morning of 24 November, one of these managed to evade the destroyer screen and torpedo the escort carrier USS *Liscome Bay* (CVE 56), which was supporting the Army landings on Makin. The escort carrier, lacking antitorpedo bulges, exploded and sank with the loss of more than 640 of her crew, including TG 52.3 commander Rear Adm. Henry M. Mullinnix. Clearly, the delay in operations prevented a timely release of the assault force. Even though *Liscome Bay* was not part of a fast carrier group, Towers and the aviation admirals held her loss, and the death of Mullinnix, against Spruance and those black-shoe admirals who (they believed) did not fully appreciate the power of the fast carrier groups and who should not be allowed to tie them down to amphibious operations.[18]

Abemama Atoll was captured on D+1 by a company of Marines who debarked from the submarine *Nautilus* in rubber boats. The small contingent of Japanese defenders offered some resistance, but after shelling from the submarine and the 5-inch guns from the destroyer USS *Gansevoort* (DD 608), they committed suicide rather than surrender. By 25 November, the atoll was in American hands, and the assault phase of Galvanic was effectively over. Marines continued to mop up and secure the outer islands of Tarawa and the other atolls until 1 December 1943. Three days later, Hoover's group assumed control of the atoll and began transforming it into the planned advance base.[19]

In his report on the operation to Nimitz, Spruance noted, "This operation was our first amphibious assault against strongly defended enemy atolls. The distance of the area from our bases and the size and complexity of the required forces (comprising some 116 combatant vessels and 75 auxiliaries) posed problems of unusual difficulty. This operation is considered to have been highly successful. Island bases essential to our advance across the Pacific were captured from the enemy with the complete loss of all his defending forces."[20]

Spruance praised the performance of the 2nd Marine Division as the highlight of the operation. "Nothing in the record of the Marine Corps can exceed the heroism displayed at Tarawa by the officers and men of the Second Marine Division and the naval units that accompanied them in their landing." Spruance wrote, "Of the lessons learned during the Gilbert Operation, the chief and most expensive ones were from the assault and capture of Betio island," singling out the failure of the bombardment to neutralize the Japanese defenses, determining the best type of landing craft to cross a fringing reef, and the tactics and equipment of the landing force. “Matters such as these,” he wrote, “must be studied and discussed thoroughly by the best qualified personnel before sound conclusions can be reached.”[21]

The application of naval gunfire, aerial bombardment, and strafing were discussed at length during the aftermath of the operation. Turner urged the use of large-caliber AP (armor piercing) projectiles as the best means of penetrating the reinforced structures and well-protected gun emplacements and suggested an allocation of armor-piercing projectiles for future bombardments. He further elaborated on the technical details, stating that the angle of fall of the projectiles was not steep enough to provide the best plunging fire and that powder loads should be reduced to lower velocities to avoid skips and ricochets. These issues needed to be carefully studied using live fire practice against mock-ups of the type of structures encountered on Betio.[22]

Perhaps Turner’s most essential and emphatic recommendation was that the preparatory bombardment should not last mere hours but should be inflicted on the defenders for days in advance. This applied to both naval gunfire and aerial bombardment. He wrote, “Far more attention should be paid to the destruction of enemy defenses before landings are attempted. Preliminary air attacks should start weeks in advance of the assault. . . . [R]eplenishment of supplies should be denied by air. The assault should be preceded by several days (not hours) by deliberate bombardment and day and night air attacks. Defenders should be given no rest day or night for at least a week prior to the landing.”[23]

Regarding the best type of landing craft to use, Turner called for the expanded use of the new and improved amphibious tractors that were becoming available. The new LVT-2 Buffalo and LVT(A)-1 had increased armor protection, and some were equipped with 37-mm gun turrets or 75-mm howitzers. However, Turner was disappointed by their low speed and called for ramps at the stern to avoid troops having to unload over the gunwales, which exposed them to enemy fire.[24]

Admiral Chester Nimitz concluded with a response to the criticism that the Tarawa assault was too costly in human lives, saying, “It is unfortunate that the limited time and area in which they occurred have made them seem disproportionately large.” Compared to operations that achieved comparable results but spread their casualties over many months, the losses on Tarawa were not "unreasonably great. The personnel loss on the LISCOME BAY was over 70% of that incurred in the landings yet has to be accepted as the fortune of war. It is because our assaulting troops paid for what they gained on the spot instead of little by little that the price may seem large."[25]

In his memoir *Coral and Brass,* Holland Smith bitterly criticized the choice of Tarawa Atoll. While acknowledging that many valuable lessons were learned there, Smith blamed the Marine casualties on the JCS for targeting what he called "the most completely defended island I have ever seen." Smith concluded that "Tarawa was a mistake." When asked about Smith's comment many years later, Spruance, ever the soul of discretion, responded that while he had immense respect and admiration for the Marine, he would defend the choice: "I think I know about the basic strategy of the Central Pacific better than he does, just as he knows more about amphibious landings and subsequent operations on shore. His memory may not always be too accurate, however. . . . Smith is devoted in his loyalty to the Marine Corps, and very sensitive to anything he might think reflect adversely to it."[26]

Spruance and his staff landed on Betio on 27 November, joining Admiral Nimitz and his staff for a tour of inspection. This was the first time that he had seen and smelled wholesale death, as unburied Japanese bodies still littered the island. The planners of the operation now saw firsthand the fruit of their work. Looking at how the heavily reinforced structures withstood the most intense bombardment that the U.S. Navy had ever delivered and seeing that it took the utter annihilation of the defenders to finally secure the island, they gained a better sense of the immensity of the tasks ahead.[27]

After visiting Makin and Abemama on 4 December, Spruance went aboard *Indianapolis* and sailed back to Pearl Harbor, arriving by 11 December 1943. Immediately upon arrival, he met with Kelly Turner and Holland Smith to discuss the upcoming Operation Flintlock. Since returning, Nimitz had twice suggested that Spruance take leave to visit his family, but he found the press of business too great. As he wrote to Margaret, "Admiral Nimitz wanted me to go to the coast before the Gilberts operation, but there was too much to do, right up to the last the minute. . . . [T]he same situation holds true. You know that I am never so happy as with you, but so many men's lives depend on how well I am able to do my job now, so the war must take first place. The Japs started this war and they are going to have to say when they want to stop it—on our terms."[28]

CHAPTER 10

THE TRIDENT STRIKES AGAIN

Operations Flintlock and Catchpole

WHILE SPRUANCE AND HIS STAFF were deep into the planning for Galvanic, the Joint Chiefs of Staff issued a directive to CinCPac on 1 September 1943 ordering the "secure control" of the Marshall Islands and specifying the seizure of Wake Island, Eniwetok Atoll, and Kusaie Atoll by 1 January 1944. On 22 October, this was followed by a request from King for "broad recommendations concerning sequence, timing, and nature of Pacific operations" for 1944. Nimitz replied three days later that the next operation, codenamed Flintlock, would seize the Marshall Islands, including Eniwetok, but not until early February 1944. King concurred with the overall plan but rejected Nimitz's proposed date. After some negotiation, they set D-Day for 17 January 1944.[1]

Nimitz met with Spruance and his staff to discuss Flintlock on 14 December 1943. Spruance took the opportunity to revisit the discussion about Kwajalein from the previous September. Before this meeting, Nimitz had conferred with Rear Adm. Forrest Sherman, his new Deputy Chief of Staff for Planning, who convinced Nimitz that Hoover's land-based air forces in the Gilberts could handle the remaining Japanese bases in the Marshalls and the fast carrier groups could deal with any air threats from Truk and the Marianas. From decrypts of Japanese radio traffic, Edwin Layton informed Nimitz that, in the wake of the Gilberts operation, Koga was moving troops and artillery from Kwajalein to reinforce Mili, Wotje, Maloelap, and Jaluit—the very outer islands in the Marshall group that Spruance wanted to attack. Nimitz, however, told Spruance, Turner, and Smith in no uncertain terms that Kwajalein Atoll "was the enemy's weakest point and they won't expect us." It would remain the main objective, and if they didn't like it, Nimitz could replace them with commanders who would do as ordered. Spruance and his staff backed down.[2]

Spruance, however, was not yet done. Acting on Carl Moore's advice, he suggested that Majuro Atoll, located southeast of Kwajalein, should be taken and developed into a supporting base and fleet anchorage. It would provide a base for protecting the lines of communication with Kwajalein. When Layton told them that the atoll was practically undefended, Nimitz agreed.[3]

Nimitz issued his Operation Order 16–43C, Flintlock (revised) on 15 December 1943, with Kwajalein and Roi Islands in the Kwajalein Atoll as the main objectives. Moore headed up the final planning process, which began immediately. The planning, coordination, and execution of Flintlock were made much more manageable since most of the forces and ships that would comprise Task Force 50 were still available from Gilbert's operation and were located at Pearl Harbor. More importantly, most of the same personnel were involved in the new operation, and these men were now amphibious warfare veterans who knew their jobs well and had learned some hard lessons at Tarawa.

Kwajalein Atoll is located just over 500 miles northwest of Makin Island. It contains nearly thirty coral islands and tiny islets arranged in a rough crescent shape, with the open side facing the southwest, and has one of the largest lagoons in the world. Kwajalein Island, the largest land mass, anchors the extreme southeast corner of the crescent, and Ebadon Island the northwest corner, with over sixty miles between them. At the top on the north edge of the atoll is Roi Island, which is actually two islands, Roi and Namur, connected by a causeway, located 40 miles from Kwajalein Island. Since the Japanese had thought that Wotje and Maloelap were the likely targets for the next American attack, they did not have time to fortify Kwajalein Atoll as they had done at Tarawa. However, they managed to send Imperial Army reinforcements and aircraft to the Marshalls in late December 1943. By the time the U.S. operation began in early 1944 there were approximately 8,000 troops and aviation personnel divided between the islands of Kwajalein.[4]

The Japanese built their major air base on Roi-Namur. The twin islands had better defensive fortifications than Kwajalein but nowhere near the

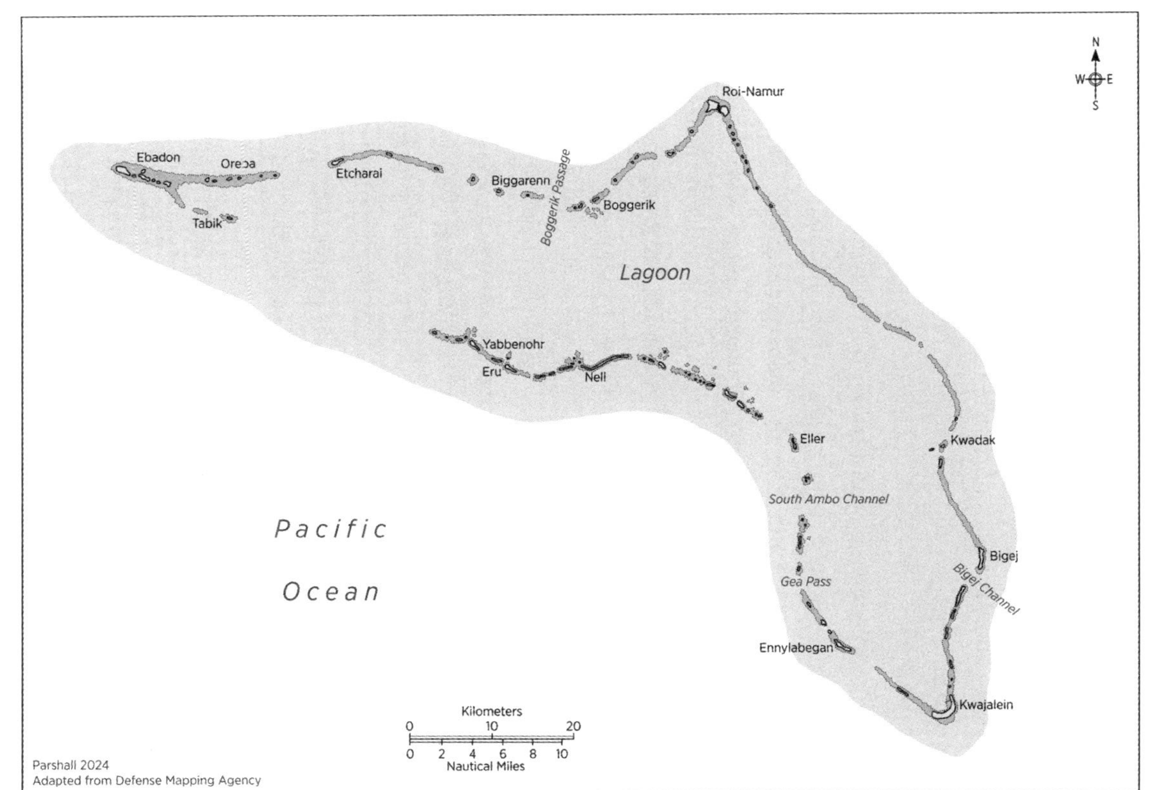

MAP 7. Kwajalein Atoll

standard of those found on Betio. According to the information gathered from the extensive photo reconnaissance of the target islands, there were relatively few heavy machine guns located in open emplacements, concrete pillboxes, and blockhouses, and little in the way of artillery. Most of the defenses faced the ocean side of the islands, as the defenders did not expect to be attacked from inside the lagoon. In keeping with the current Japanese tactical doctrine of stopping the invaders at the water's edge, there were multiple concentric lines of trenches and rifle pits along the beaches where it was intended to stop the landing forces, but little in the way of defense in depth.[5]

Spruance's staff worked feverishly over the holidays and had their draft operations plan ready by 6 January. As before, Moore, ever the perfectionist, led the effort, combining the plans prepared by Turner's Fifth Amphibious Force and Smith's Expeditionary Troops with those of the naval task groups. Spruance and his staff quickly realized there was not enough time to organize and equip all the units involved, and they persuaded Nimitz and King to agree on a revised D-Day of 31 January 1944.[6]

While usually not one to celebrate Christmas, Spruance took the opportunity to socialize, attend parties, and even receive some presents, including a khaki web belt from Nimitz. As always, he was grateful for Moore's efforts. A few days later he wrote to Margaret, "Our work here is almost wound up. . . . I tried to get Carl to declare a holiday for himself and the staff, but he refused on the ground that there was too much pressure of work. In a few days, I hope to send many of my people over to the Damon House to get some restful rest. They are a fine, hardworking crowd of men, and all pull together like a good team."[7]

As before, Spruance was in overall command of TF 50. Roi Island would be attacked by the Northern Attack Force, TF 53, commanded by Rear Adm. Richard L. Conolly, consisting of the untested 4th Marine Division, coming from training in San Diego. Kwajalein Island was the objective of the Southern Attack Force, TF 52, commanded by Turner, with Army troops from the 7th Infantry Division, veterans of the Aleutians campaign, making the assault. Finally, Rear Admiral Hill and TF 51.2, consisting of the 2nd Battalion of the 106th Infantry Regiment, plus a company of Marines, were tasked with capturing Majuro Atoll.

The Fast Carrier Force, redesignated TF 58, was now commanded by Rear Adm. Marc Mitscher, who had relieved Pownall. After Tarawa had been secured, Pownall had taken his TG 50.1 to raid Kwajalein on 4 December but failed to stay in the area long enough for a second strike to destroy all of the Japanese shipping and aircraft on the atoll. Towers and the aviation clique in Pearl Harbor thought that Pownall was not aggressive enough, and after this episode, Nimitz agreed. During their bimonthly conference in San Francisco in early January 1944, Nimitz suggested relieving Pownall, and King concurred. They also decided to reorganize the CinCPac/POA command structure, making John Towers the Deputy CinCPac. Almost immediately, Towers and Forrest Sherman decided that Rear Adm. Marc A. Mitscher would replace Pownall, without consulting Spruance. Spruance liked Pownall and thought he had done a fine job, but Nimitz did not countermand the decision despite his protests. Nimitz knew that Towers had powerful friends, including Undersecretary of the Navy James Forrestal, and saw Pownall's relief as a way to keep the peace between the aviation and battleship admirals.[8]

Spruance accepted his boss' decision without complaint and in the spirit of a team player, but his doubts about Mitscher remained for the time being. TF 58 consisted of four task groups with six fleet carriers, six light carriers, eight fast battleships, six cruisers, and forty-four destroyers divided between them. The task force was responsible for suppressing any remaining Japanese air strength in the Marshall Islands and dealing with any reinforcements that might arrive from the Japanese bases elsewhere in the Central Pacific. The force's fast battleships under Willis Lee would also provide the battle line if the Combined Fleet chose to sortie from Truk, although this appeared unlikely.

Long-range USAAF bombers flying from the Ellice Islands and Tarawa had begun bombing raids into the Marshalls in December. Medium bombers and fighter-bombers operating from the new air bases in the Gilberts hit Milli, Wotje, Maloelap, Jaluit, Roi, and Kwajalein daily during January. These neutralization attacks were further augmented when TF 58 began its attacks on D-2. Piers, seaplane ramps, hangars, workshops, barracks, storehouses, fuel tanks, and most unreinforced structures within the target area were destroyed or rendered useless. By the end of the month, there were practically no Japanese aircraft, surface warships, or cargo transport to be seen in the Marshall Islands.[9]

Spruance departed Pearl Harbor aboard *Indianapolis* on 19 January 1944, arriving at Tarawa a few days later, where he conferred with Hoover about the land-based air support for the operation. Spruance marveled at the changes to Tarawa since he was last there and was highly impressed by the work the Seabees had done with the same types of heavy earth-moving equipment he had used back in San Juan. The Japanese, on the other hand, as he told his wife, "have to rely on hand labor, which they are probably much better at than we are. They can build a lot of things, such as dugouts, which require hand labor very well, but when it comes to building roads and airfields they are totally outclassed."[10]

Leaving the Gilberts on 26 January, Spruance joined Task Group 58.2, commanded by Rear Admiral Montgomery, en route to Kwajalein. Also aboard was Baldy Pownall, now an observer and aviation advisor for Spruance. The Northern and Southern Attack Forces departed Pearl Harbor for Kwajalein on 23 January 1944. Each of the attack forces was allocated a transport group with a dozen transports, LSTs, and other landing ships, a fire support group of veteran battleships with escorting cruisers and destroyers, an air support group with three escort carriers and twenty-two destroyers, plus additional minesweepers, salvage ships, and hydrologic vessels.

On D-2, 29 January 1944, the fire support groups, TG 52.8 and TG 53.5—consisting altogether of seven battleships, five heavy cruisers, three light cruisers, and eighty destroyers, separated from their attack forces and together with the eight fast battleships of TF 58—began the naval gunfire bombardment of the islands of the Kwajalein Atoll, concentrating on Roi-Namur and Kwajalein Island. This continued for three days, lasting until the morning of D+1. Unlike the Gilberts operation, their targets were located in the same atoll, allowing them to concentrate their firepower. The air bombardment from the twelve carriers, eight escort carriers, and the land-based air support flying out of the Gilberts delivered an unprecedented volume of fire.

During the night of D-1, the transports of the attack forces, having approached the Marshalls from the west, threaded their way between the

TABLE 2. Operation Flintlock Task Groups

COMMANDER	TASK FORCE	TASK FORCE GROUP	SHIP TYPE								
			FAST CARRIERS	LIGHT CARRIERS	ESCORT CARRIERS	FAST BATTLESHIPS	VETERAN BATTLESHIPS	CRUISERS	LIGHT & ANTIAIRCRAFT CRUISERS	DESTROYERS & ESCORTS	TRANSPORTS & SUPPORT
Knowles	52.5	Transport Group									27
Coleman	52.6	Control Group								8	5
Giffen	52.8	Fire Support Group					4	3		11	12
Davison	52.9	Air Support Group			3					4	
Sims	52.10	Minesweeping & Hydologic									9
Curtis	52.11	Salvage									3
Conolly	**TF 53**	**Northern Attack Force**									
Buchanan	53.10	Transport Group								12	42
Pierce	53.3	Minesweeper Group									8
Oldendorf	53.5	Fire Support Group					3	2	3	9	9
Ragsdale	53.6	Air Support Group			3					3	
Foss	53.12	Salvage									3
Mitscher	**TF 58**	**Fast Carrier Force**									
Reeves	58.1	Carrier Task Group 1	2	1		3			1	9	
Montgomery	58.2	Carrier Task Group 2	2	1		3			1	9	
Sherman	58.3	Carrier Task Group 3	1	2		2		1		9	
Ginder	58.4	Carrier Task Group 4	1	2				2	1	8	
Small	50.1	Neutralization Grp.						3		6	
Loomis	51.1	Reserve Force (Eniwetok)								7	9
Hill	51.2	Majuro Attack Force			2			1		5	4
Totals, FLINTLOCK, CATCHPOLE			6	6	8	8	7	12	6	100	131
								Total Ships:			284

Source: VADM E. P. Forrestel, USN (Ret.), *Admiral Raymond A. Spruance, USN, A Study in Command*, Appendix V, 255–56.

small atolls north of Wotje and, giving that atoll a wide berth, swung south to Kwajalein. After the approaches had been swept for mines, they entered the lagoon and split, with the Northern Attack Force heading to Roi-Namur and the Southern Attack Force to Kwajalein. Advance reconnaissance teams were sent ahead under the cover of darkness to scout the reefs and the proposed landing approaches for mines and obstacles, but none were found. There was nothing to stop the Marines' landing craft and the Army's DUKWs.[11]

Landing operations in both sectors were carried out in a similar fashion. Heavy bombardment from the surface ships commenced again at daybreak and continued as the transports were unloaded and the new and improved LVT-2 and LVT(A)-1 amphibious tractors moved to the Line of Departure. The larger Landing Craft Infantry (LCI), equipped with 4.5-inch barrage rockets, moved within range of the beaches and provided fire directly on the landing areas. When the landing craft were about 3,000 yards out, the final air strikes would occur, followed by strafing timed to occur minutes before the first troops hit the beach.

On 31 January, the Northern and Southern Attack Forces began operations by seizing the smaller, lightly defended islands of the atoll adjacent to their primary objectives. These small islands provided positions to site field artillery to support the landing operations. The first landing on territory that belonged to Japan before the war started occurred at 0952 when the men of Company B, 25th Marines, landed on the islet of Ennuebing just southwest of Roi-Namur. They found this and the other small islands lightly defended and quickly secured them by noon that first day. Elements of the 7th U.S. Infantry enjoyed similar success in the southern half of the atoll, establishing artillery positions on the small islands flanking Kwajalein. At the same time on Majuro, the Marines found only a handful of Japanese, who disappeared into the scrubland without a fight.[12]

On D+1, the Northern Attack Force commenced its shore bombardment at 0710. At 1150, the gunfire lifted as the first wave of men of the 4th Marine Division hit the beaches of Roi and Namur and found the remaining defenders dazed and completely disorganized, incapable of mounting any coherent defense. The rocket bombardment from the LCI gunboats that supported the first waves had put the final touches on the utter destruction of the Japanese defensive trench system along the beaches. Altogether, the results of nearly three days of intense aerial and naval bombardment had shattered the ability of the Japanese to defend the islands effectively. This treatment came to be known as the "Spruance haircut."[13]

Medium tanks were unloaded, and the Marines began moving inland. Individual tanks and small units took the initiative and surged forward with such speed that they quickly moved beyond their assigned initial objectives, causing some confusion with their company and regimental commanders. Roi, covered mostly by runways, was relatively easy to clear, whereas the ruined buildings and base facilities on Namur provided some cover for the defenders. Roi was secured by 1802 that day and Namur by 1418 on D+2.

At 0930 on D+1, the 7th Infantry landed on the southern and western end of Kwajalein and found the same thing the Marines had seen in the north. After a massive bombardment, no defensive positions remained, and the few surviving defenders moved into the extensive scrub beyond the beaches to snipe and harass the invaders. The Army units secured their beach area and then moved cautiously inland. A total of six infantry battalions, forty-four medium tanks, eighteen light tanks, and five self-propelled guns had landed that first day. They halted at 1700, having taken the southern half of the airfield and dug in for the night. The northern half of Kwajalein was more densely developed, and some buildings and blockhouses were still standing, providing cover for the remaining Japanese forces.[14]

The next day, the GIs began to advance slowly, with the lead elements bypassing many strong points, leaving them to be mopped up by other units moving up from the rear. This policy expedited the forward progress but often left scattered pockets of defenders still alive and active, especially at night. Japanese snipers were always a threat, and at night the nervous soldiers fired at any noise or movement, which caused several unfortunate friendly fire incidents. It took another three days for the Army to secure the island, but caution had kept their casualties to a minimum.

An intelligence bonanza in the form of charts and hydrographic information was recovered from the shattered Fourth Fleet headquarters building on Kwajalein. The information provided detailed information on Eniwetok, Truk, the Carolinas, and the Marianas that was not previously available. Charts of Kwajalein Atoll were translated, copied, and dispersed to the fleet while operations were still underway.[15]

On 2 February, D+2, Spruance and *Indianapolis* left Montgomery's TG 58.2 and entered the lagoon at Kwajalein. There, he met Undersecretary Forrestal aboard *Tennessee*, and they went ashore on Roi-Namur to inspect the battlefield, accompanied by Pownall, Holland Smith, Conolly, and Vice Admiral Morrell, who had come out from Washington with Forrestal. Forrestal was most impressed with the rapid success of the operation. Nimitz arrived on 6 February to inspect Kwajalein and to confer with Spruance, Turner, and Smith on the next steps. At this time, the Central Pacific Force was redesignated the Fifth Fleet.

There remained one more objective in the Marshall Islands: Eniwetok Atoll. Spruance had previously suggested to Nimitz that Eniwetok be taken immediately following Kwajalein and before the scheduled transfer of the Fifth Fleet to Halsey's command for the planned assault on Kavieng as part of MacArthur's Operation Cartwheel. Now that the capture of Kwajalein had happened faster than anticipated, Nimitz asked Spruance if he thought taking Eniwetok was feasible. Spruance immediately conferred with Turner and Holland Smith, and the answer came back in the affirmative.[16]

Holland Smith had already devised a plan for the assault, and the 10,000 fresh troops held in reserve for Kwajalein were still embarked on the ships of TG 51.1. Nimitz authorized the assault in conformance with his outline plan for Operation Catchpole, which he had issued back on 18 January 1944. The original date for Catchpole was set for May, but thanks to the early completion of Flintlock, a new D-Day for this operation was set for 17 February, barely two weeks after Kwajalein had been secured.[17]

On 6 February, the Marine and Army troops that had assaulted Kwajalein embarked on the transports to return to Pearl Harbor for rest and recuperation. Rear Admiral Hoover and TF 57 set about repairing and expanding the runways on the captured islands. Majuro Atoll was quickly transformed into a major fleet anchorage, providing a haven for ships to refuel, resupply, and effect repairs without having to return to Pearl Harbor but while remaining safe from Japanese submarine attacks. The remaining Japanese-held islands in the Marshalls—Wotje, Milli, Jaluit, and Maloelap—would be bypassed and allowed "to wither on the vine,"

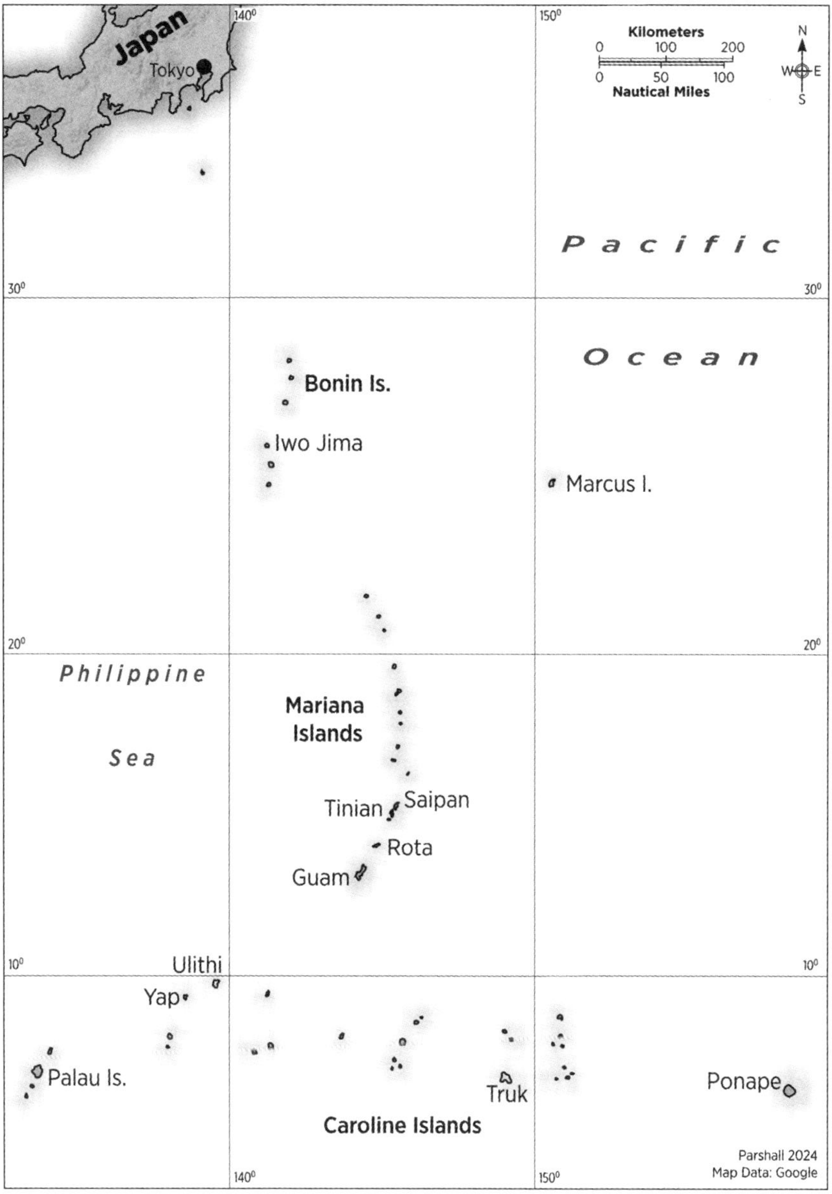

MAP 8. Western Micronesia

providing an opportunity for live, albeit dangerous, training for bomber pilots and naval gunnery.[18]

Before Catchpole got underway, Spruance took TF 58 west for another mission: Operation Hailstone, the neutralization of the Japanese base at Truk in the Caroline Islands. The original plan called for Hailstone to be implemented as a prelude to MacArthur's Operation Cartwheel, but before Catchpole. Flintlock had been so successful that the timetable was flipped, as Spruance had suggested, and Truk would be attacked the same day as the start of Catchpole. Neutralizing the Japanese forces at Truk would ensure that the Eniwetok operation would not be subject to attack from that direction. A reconnaissance overflight by Marine B-24s on 4 February indicated three battleships, two carriers, six heavy cruisers, twenty-five light cruisers and destroyers, and a large amount of shipping in the lagoon. The Combined Fleet, up to this point, had seemed incapable or unwilling to sortie to defend the Marshalls. For the attack on Eniwetok, only one of the TF 58 carrier groups, Rear Adm. Samuel P. Ginder's TG 58.4, was designated to support the amphibious assault, while Mitscher's other three task groups and the fast battleships attacked Truk.[19]

Task Force 58 regrouped and refueled in Majuro lagoon, where Spruance met them on 8 February. The next day, he and his staff moved aboard *New Jersey* to prepare for Hailstone. In addition to *New Jersey*, Spruance took *Iowa*, the cruisers USS *Minneapolis* (CA 36) and USS *New Orleans* (CA 32), and four destroyers from Sherman's TG 58.3 to form TG 50.9. Together with the three remaining carrier groups, he reformed TF 50 as the Truk Strike Group. Spruance was in overall tactical command of the force but let Mitscher operate TF 58 independently. If it looked like the Combined Fleet would come out, then the remaining six fast battleships would join Spruance's group to form a battle line. Coincidentally, that same day, 9 February, Spruance learned that he had been promoted to admiral and Kelly Turner to vice admiral.[20]

If Spruance harbored any thoughts of catching the Combined Fleet and engaging them in a classic battle-line duel, these were dashed when the bulk of that fleet sailed for Palau on 1 February. From their radio traffic analysis, the Japanese had sensed a major operation was headed their way. The photo reconnaissance mission of 4 February was the deciding factor for them to abandon Truk. Admiral Koga, deciding that discretion was the greater part of valor, especially when his available carrier strength was no match for that of TF 58, sailed from Truk lagoon aboard the superbattleship *Musashi* on 10 February in company with a light cruiser and four destroyers, bound for Yokosuka.[21]

TF 50 left Majuro on 13 February for Truk, some 1,300 miles distant, proceeding north of Eniwetok and, after refueling, approaching Truk from the northeast. When the reconnaissance photos from 4 February were examined more closely, it became evident that only one battleship and some cruisers remained at Truk, and radio intelligence reports continued to indicate that the Combined Fleet was likely at sea but nowhere near Truk. The birds had flown the coop, but the Truk strike proceeded anyway, hoping to catch and destroy the remaining ships before they evacuated.[22]

Spruance received another bit of unwelcome news on 15 February. While walking on the foredeck of *New Jersey* with his flag secretary Charles Barber, he was handed a copy of the Running Summary for the day with a report from Halsey that New Zealand troops had landed on Green Island. This was the second time Barber had seen his boss truly upset—not with Halsey, but with MacArthur, whom Spruance suspected acted in his own interests, ignoring the bigger picture. Green Island is a coral atoll located between Bougainville and the Bismarck Archipelago, just 120 miles due east of Rabaul. Spruance thought this operation might prompt the Japanese to counterattack, necessitating the cancellation of Hailstone, a shift south, and leaving the Eniwetok operation dangerously exposed. As it turned out, the atoll was quickly overrun, and the reaction from Rabaul was limited to a few bomber raids, but a deviation from previously agreed plans was surely one way to get under Spruance's skin. "That's typical MacArthur," he told Barber.[23]

TF 50 was not detected as it approached Truk, and early on the morning of 17 February a fighter sweep destroyed most of the Japanese aircraft on the ground. Those Zeros that managed to get airborne were quickly dispatched by the F6F Hellcats, leaving Truk with little more than a few handfuls of non-radar-assisted antiaircraft guns for its defense. The succeeding waves of dive and torpedo bombers attacked the remaining ships in the lagoon, sinking seventeen merchant ships, six oilers, and several auxiliaries. The few warships present got underway quickly and made for the open sea. Repeated attacks by the carrier planes sank the auxiliary cruiser *Akagi Maru* and damaged the light cruiser *Katori* and the destroyer *Maikaze*, leaving both dead in the water. Another destroyer, *Nowaki*, was not hit. Mitscher called off his carrier planes, leaving the cripples for TG 50.9.

By now, Spruance had detached his TG 50.9 from the carriers and commenced a counterclockwise maneuver around the atoll to intercept the escaping ships. He placed his units in a rather unusual column formation, with the battleships *Iowa* and *New Jersey* in the van, followed by his two heavy cruisers, *Minneapolis* and *New Orleans*, and the four destroyers bringing up the rear. Carl Moore objected to this formation and recommended that they adopt the standard circular formation for antiaircraft defense. Aware that the Japanese airpower on Truk had been eliminated, Spruance replied testily, "We're not out here fighting aircraft, we're out here fighting surface vessels. I want to remain in column."[24]

Spruance ordered the cruisers to dispatch the crippled *Katori* and the secondary batteries of the battleships to deal with the destroyers. This gave the crews some much-needed surface battle practice, which may also explain his choice of formation. While the two cruisers were battle-scarred veterans of the Solomons campaign, this would be the first taste of combat for the two new battleships. *Katori* went down fighting, her guns still firing as she sank, as did the destroyer *Maikaze*. Before she sank, Moore saw flashes on the deck of the destroyer, indicating that she had fired a salvo of deadly Long Lance torpedoes, one of which passed between *Iowa* and *New Jersey*. When informed of this, Spruance turned to Barber, standing nearby, and remarked laconically, "Well, that would have been embarrassing!"[25]

The undamaged *Nowaki* retreated at full speed away from the action, disappearing over the horizon. Using a combination of radar range-finding and spotting from carrier planes, *New Jersey* fired on *Nowaki* with her 16-inch main guns at a range of more than 34,000 yards, achieving a straddle but no hits. *Nowaki* escaped with little more than shell splinter damage. In a bizarre coda, Spruance ordered *New Jersey* to sink what appeared to be an abandoned Japanese trawler that passed within 200 yards of the ship. The 5-inch secondary batteries hit the little ship, which exploded in a terrific ball of fire. It was apparently carrying munitions to Truk, but the crew was nowhere to be seen.[26]

Historians have criticized Spruance's parade around Truk as needlessly putting his task group in harm's way. Thomas Buell believed Spruance acted on a "whim," living out the fantasy of a "black shoe" admiral pining for a major surface action. In fact, Spruance was well aware from intelligence reports that the Combined Fleet had fled, and this was confirmed by the attacks on the morning of 17 February. While Spruance never fully explained his motivation, much more likely than a "whim" is that he wanted to provide a training opportunity for the inexperienced crews of the new battleships under combat conditions. He knew that such experience would pay dividends if they were ever to take on the superbattleships of the Combined Fleet. Moore later opined that Spruance was acting out some revenge for Pearl Harbor, demonstrating to the Japanese that they were powerless to defend their primary base of operations. As Moore wrote in a memo that Spruance passed on to Nimitz, it also showed that Truk was no longer of value to the Japanese and could be safely bypassed, avoiding another costly amphibious operation.[27]

The shooting over, Spruance then passed tactical command to Rear Adm. Robert C. Giffen aboard *Minneapolis*, who immediately ordered TG 50.9 to assume a circular formation, which it maintained as it completed a circuit of Truk, joining Sherman's TG 58.3. Spruance left TF 58 a day later and returned to Kwajalein in *New Jersey* with a destroyer escort, arriving there on 20 February. There, he hoisted his four-star pennant from the foretruck of *New Jersey*. He wrote to Margaret, "The day before yesterday (21 February) I found time to have my medical examination for promotion, and when it was successfully over, I put on my four stars. I told the doctor this was the last time I would ever have to bother the Medical Corps for an examination for promotion. Getting this rank was something beyond my utmost expectation."[28]

OPERATION CATCHPOLE

Eniwetok Atoll is located at the northern and most westerly end of the Marshall Island group, 660 miles from Truk and half that distance from Kwajalein. The atoll was similar to Kwajalein in that it had a better-fortified air base at its northern end on Engebi Island and the larger, less developed Eniwetok Island at the lagoon's south end. Based on later body counts, the atoll was found to have been defended by 3,400 men, primarily Imperial Army troops.[29]

"Better" fortified was a relative term, as the Japanese had neglected to provide much in the way of defenses until alerted by the Kwajalein operation. Afterward, they attempted to build reinforced concrete structures as quickly as possible, but with little success. There was an older well-built trench system to defend the ocean side of Engebi, which included underground dugouts built of coconut logs that were well camouflaged and proved difficult for the invading ground forces to locate. Realizing now that the Americans would likely land from inside the lagoon, the defenders hastily built a trench system to cover that side, but with time running out, it was neither deep nor well-constructed.[30]

By now, the procedure for assaulting a coral atoll was well established and was repeated at Eniwetok. Daily bombing runs were underway, and TG 58.4 arrived on D-2 to begin its aerial and naval gunfire bombardment. On D-Day, 17 February, an impressive array of assault transports, supporting destroyers, and battleships navigated the narrow lagoon entrance in a long column, as cooly as if entering a home port. Artillery positions were soon established on adjacent islands. In the north, Engebi was assaulted by the Marines of the 22nd Regiment, and elements of the U.S. Army 106th Regimental Combat Team attacked Eniwetok in the south. On D+2, after two hours of intense bombardment, LVTs and LCIs loaded with Marines left the Line of Departure at 0815, landing on Engebi at the assigned time. They found conditions similar to those at Kwajalein and encountered no meaningful opposition on the beach. Moving inland, they met scattered opposition from the hidden dugouts. Strong points were bypassed, the airstrip was overrun, and at 1400, the island was declared secure. Mopping-up operations using flamethrowers and high explosives continued through the next day.[31]

On the same day, elements of the 106th Regimental Combat Team landed on the northern lagoon side of Eniwetok, meeting little opposition on the beach but running into problems as they moved inland. The naval bombardment here had been less intense, as it was thought that the island was only lightly defended and that the assault troops would have little difficulty. However, this proved not to be the case, as a large group of Japanese troops intended to reinforce Kwajalein had been left on Eniwetok due to a lack of transport, thereby bolstering the defense. Once again, the Army was cautious and moved slowly. Meeting this unexpectedly heavy resistance, the regimental commander requested that the Marine reserve—the 3rd Battalion, 22nd Marines—be landed to assist. In the end, it took three days to complete the conquest of Eniwetok.

Casualties for the Marshall Islands operations amounted to 863 men killed and another 2,312 wounded, fewer than had been the case for Galvanic and even more remarkable when considering the scope of the conquests, covering three major atolls. The shore bombardments of the early operations had misled planners as to the character, volume, and duration of naval gunfire and aerial bombardment required to reduce well-engineered defenses, such as those found on Betio. Instead of hours of bombardment, Kwajalein and Eniwetok had been subjected to days of unrelenting firepower that shattered both the physical defenses and morale of the men who remained alive after its onslaught. As a result, casualties in these operations were among the lowest of any in the Pacific War.[32]

After Hailstone, Mitscher and TF 58 proceeded to the Marianas and carried out raids on Saipan, Tinian, and Guam with impunity for several days, bombing the air bases there, destroying 168 aircraft, and obtaining much-needed photo reconnaissance. Waiting submarines sank 45,000 tons of shipping seeking to escape the onslaught. The task force returned to Majuro on 27 February and spent the next several weeks in the protected anchorage, enjoying some well-earned rest and relaxation on the still pristine islands of the atoll.

Service Squadron 10 had been established on Majuro to provide logistical support and had facilities for minor repairs. By March floating drydocks, repair ships, and huge stocks of fresh and frozen food, fuel, and ammunition were in place. Henceforth, the task groups would no longer have to return to Pearl Harbor for provisions or repairs unless they were severely damaged. Spruance directed the carriers and battleships to conduct aerial and shore bombardments against the bypassed islands as live training exercises to ensure they did not lose their combat edge.[33]

On 14 March, Spruance flew back to Pearl Harbor for a conference with Admiral Nimitz to discuss Operation Forager, the assault on the Marianas. Nimitz had just returned from a conference in Washington with President Roosevelt, King, and the Joint Chiefs, and they decided to continue alternating offensives in the South and Central Pacific. TF 58 would go south to support MacArthur's operation to take Hollandia in mid-April, followed by the occupation of Saipan, Tinian, and Guam beginning in mid-June. The JCS issued their detailed directive on 12 March, which also included the cancellation of the Kavieng operation, the capture of Palau in September, and a landing on Mindanao in the Philippines in November, as preparation for an advance to Formosa in February 1945.[34]

When Spruance returned to Majuro, he turned over the detailed preparation of the Forager operation orders to Moore. He intended to take TF 58 on a raid of Palau to deny the Japanese the use of the base in advance of the planned Hollandia operation. Palau is 1,200 miles west of Truk and was well inside the Japanese inner defense perimeter. Retaining *New Jersey* as his flagship, Spruance and TF 58 set out from Majuro on 22 March, sailing along the equator far south of Truk on a western course, maintaining radio silence to obtain tactical surprise, intending to strike on 1 April. When a Japanese snooper spotted the task force on 26 March, however, Spruance ordered the force to head directly for Palau at best speed and advanced the strike date to 30 March.[35]

Japanese intelligence units were monitoring American radio traffic and based on their analysis warned that a carrier strike in the western Pacific appeared to be imminent. A reconnaissance flight over Palau on 28 March alerted Koga once more that the Americans were on their way, and this time Palau was the likely target. He ordered the Combined Fleet to sea the next day to await orders. Unfortunately for Koga, his flagship *Musashi* was struck by a torpedo fired from USS *Tunny* (SS 282), forcing the superbattleship to retire to Kure for repairs.[36]

Mitscher's carrier planes struck on 30 March and, over the next two days, claimed the destruction of 150 aircraft on the ground and in the air. Several attempts by Japanese bombers flying from Palau and Guam to hit the carriers were easily rebuffed, with heavy losses. American carrier planes sank more than 100,000 tons of shipping and, in a first, managed to lay mines across the three outlet channels of Palau lagoon, cutting off the base's ability to respond to MacArthur's Hollandia operation.

Koga became so alarmed at the prospect of a landing that he decided to move immediately with his staff to the base at Davao, located at the southern end of Mindanao. Denied the protection of *Musashi*, they boarded two Kawanishi flying boats to take them south. Off the coast of the Philippines, they ran into violent tropical storms. Koga's own plane disappeared, and he was never seen again. The plane carrying his chief of staff, Admiral Fukudome Shigeru, crashed off the coast of Cebu. Fukudome survived but was captured by Filipino guerrillas, who also recovered his briefcase containing key documents, including Koga's decisive-battle plan, the Z Operation Plan. Through a remarkable series of events, these eventually made their way to the Allied Translator and Interpreter Section (ATIS) in Brisbane, and then on to Edwin Layton at Pearl Harbor. As will be seen, these plans would play a significant role in the events that became known as the Battle of the Philippine Sea.[37]

TF 58 returned to Majuro on 6 April for rest and resupply, and Spruance transferred his flag back to *Indianapolis* shortly thereafter. A week later, when TF 58 headed south to Hollandia, Spruance returned to Pearl Harbor, arriving there on 14 April. He and his staff then moved ashore to continue the planning for Operation Forager.

Finally taking Nimitz's advice, Spruance took a week's leave to see his two Margarets in Monrovia. Wanting to avoid any publicity or fuss, he arrived unannounced on Mother's Day, but he was a bit perturbed to find them gone, having left nothing to eat in the house. His wife thought he looked tired, but he soon recovered after some restful nights and long walks in the hills. He flew back to Hawaii at the end of the week, arriving on 22 May. A few days later, he wrote Margaret a letter with the usual gossip, including the fact that Carl Moore was to be relieved and that their son Edward was due to travel to Portsmouth, New Hampshire, to take delivery of USS *Lionfish* (SS 298), his first command. Spruance admitted that he was "down" after their too brief visit and missed them both. He also warned Margaret that "my letters will be irregular and infrequent from now on," which Margaret knew meant that he was about to embark on another major operation.[38]

Admiral King was not easily impressed or inclined to lavish praise on his subordinates, but the Marshalls operation did elicit from him what can only be considered high praise. His biographer writes that King was "well pleased not only with Spruance's excellent planning but with the almost perfect timing of his forces in the execution of those plans. He considered the operation a noteworthy example of the results that may be expected when good staff work is implemented by efficient fleet operations under superior leadership."[39]

Rear Adm. Raymond A. Spruance, USN, wearing his favorite cap with a left-facing eagle. Taken in 1943 when he was the CinCPac chief of staff. *NH 124463*

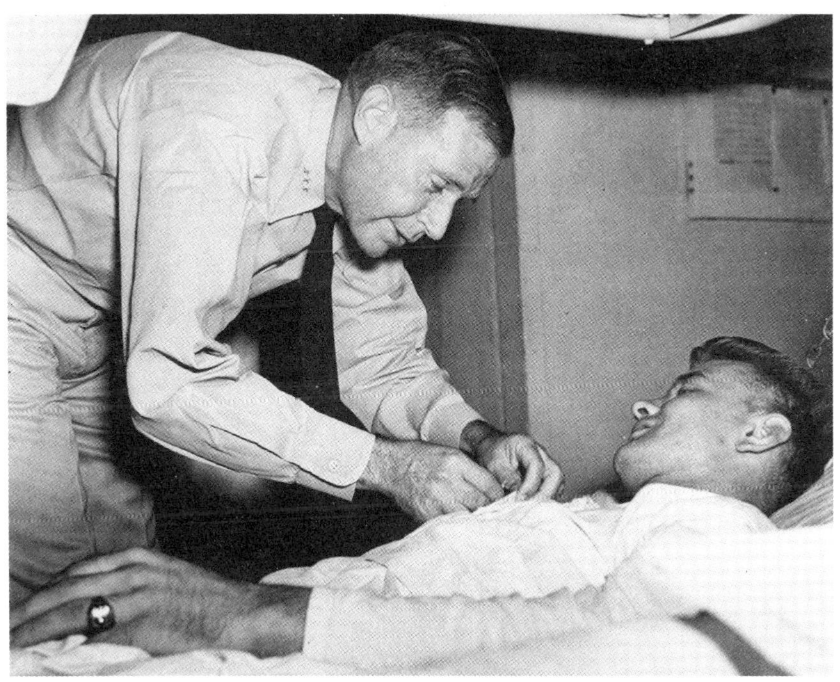

Spruance presents the Purple Heart to Cpl. John K. Galuszka, USMC, on a hospital ship at Pearl Harbor, 17 December 1943. Corporal Galuszka had been wounded during the Gilberts Operation. *80-G-203817*

Nimitz, King, and Spruance confer aboard USS *Indianapolis* (CA 35) on 18 July 1944, just after the conquest of the Marianas. *80-G-287121*

Spruance (*fifth from left, front row*) and staff on the foredeck of *Indianapolis*, 18 July 1944. Capt. Charles J. Moore is to Spruance's left and Capt. Emmet P. Forrestel is to his right. Lt. Cdr. Charles F. Barber, USNR, is smiling on the far left, second row. *NH 53233*

Spruance and Lt. Gen. Holland M. Smith, USMC, attend flag-raising ceremonies at Smith's headquarters, Charan Kanoa, Saipan, marking the end of organized Japanese resistance on the island, 10 July 1944. *80-G-287225*

Commo. Worral A. Carter, Spruance, and Nimitz walk the deck of *New Mexico* at Okinawa, May 1945. *80-G-321072*

New Mexico (BB 40) hit by kamikaze, 12 May 1945. *80-G-328653*

Bill Halsey relieves Spruance aboard *New Mexico* at Okinawa, 27 May 1945. *80-G-322429*

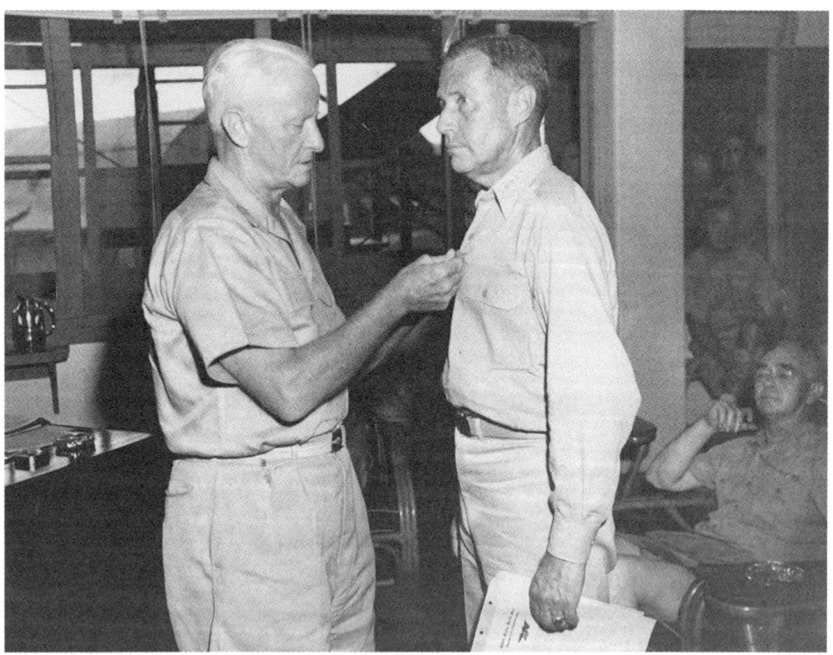

Fleet Admiral Nimitz pins the Navy Cross on Spruance at CinCPac Adv. HQ on Guam, 1 June 1945. A relaxed Kelly Turner looks on. *80-G-329473*

Adm. Raymond A. Spruance relieves Fleet Adm. Chester W. Nimitz (*left*) as commander in chief, Pacific Fleet, at 1130 (Hawaii Standard Time) aboard *Menhaden* (SS 377) at Pearl Harbor Sub Base, 24 November 1945. At right are Vice Adm. J. H. Newton, Vice Adm. Charles H. McMorris, Rear Adm. D. C. Ramsey, and Cdr. James Loo. Nimitz and Spruance signed this copy of the photo. *NH 49706*

Ambassador Spruance confers with president-elect Ramon Magsaysay of the Philippines and Vice President Richard M. Nixon in Manila, November 1953.
NH 4486.1

CHAPTER 11

THE MARIANAS AND THE BATTLE OF THE PHILIPPINE SEA

IN EARLY 1943, the Allies declared at Casablanca that only the unconditional surrender of the Axis powers was acceptable. However, nearly eighteen months later, the "end game" for the ultimate defeat of Japan was still uncertain. As a means to coerce Japan to surrender, the U.S. Army's airpower advocates wanted bomber bases within range of the Home Islands to conduct a strategic bombing campaign against Japan similar to that which they were using against Nazi Germany. Adm. Ernest J. King and the sea power advocates, meanwhile, saw a naval blockade as the best means to force a Japanese surrender. A study by the Strategic Section of the War Department in early 1944 concluded that an invasion of Japan was also required. Air bombardment, blockade, and eventual invasion required advance bases that could not be acquired by carrier attacks alone; joint Army-Navy amphibious operations were needed to put boots on the ground.[1]

Nimitz and Spruance saw the seizure of bases inside Japan's defensive perimeter as essential to this process. The problem they faced in 1944 was that while the Combined Fleet was still formidable, Japanese commanders continually avoided being drawn into battle with the Pacific Fleet unless they believed they could first obtain a clear advantage. While Operation Forager was not conceived as a means to bring on a decisive fleet action, like the earlier operation plans it contained a codicil that if the opportunity presented itself, "all combatant types" should be employed "to oppose the full strength of the enemy fleet." If Forager finally brought the Combined Fleet out to fight a battle they could not refuse, all the better.[2]

The operation plan for Forager was broadly similar to that of Flintlock but on a much larger scale, involving three Marine divisions and one reinforced Army division. Vice Adm. Richmond Kelly Turner was again in command of the Northern Attack Force, now tasked with capturing Saipan and Tinian Islands, with D-Day set for 15 June. The recently promoted Lt. Gen. Holland Smith remained in command of the landing forces, which consisted of his tried-and-true 2nd and 4th Marine Divisions and the 27th U.S. Infantry Division.

On 25 May, the final addenda and updates to the Forager operations plan were made and distributed to all commands. Spruance, Moore, and the Fifth Fleet staff then moved back aboard *Indianapolis*. The next day, they left Pearl Harbor and shaped a course for Kwajalein, where they met the Southern Attack Force, commanded by Rear Adm. Richard Conolly, which had already arrived from Tulagi with the 3rd Marine Division embarked. They were tasked with capturing Guam, with a tentative landing date of 18 June.

The assembled fleet moved to Eniwetok on 6 June to join Turner, Smith, and the Northern Attack Force. Spruance and his commanders went ashore to confer on the upcoming operation. At dinner that evening, they heard a radio address to the nation by President Roosevelt concerning the invasion of Europe—the long-anticipated Operation Overlord, which would soon dominate the attention of the American public. Among their messmates that evening was Adm. John S. McCain, Sr., who was along as the aviation observer. In awe of the vast armada that had been assembled in the lagoon, McCain remarked to Spruance that "every commander must be a gambler," thinking perhaps of the quip attributed to Vice Adm. John Towers that Spruance "would use a sledgehammer to drive a tack." Spruance told McCain that if this were so, he wanted to be one of the professional variety: "I wanted all the odds I could get stacked in my favor."[3]

Meanwhile, Vice Adm. Marc Mitscher and TF 58 left the anchorage at Majuro to begin the air operations to hit the target islands and suppress Japanese air forces in the north Central Pacific. TF 58 was organized as before into four fast carrier task groups, but with one additional *Essex*-class fleet carrier, for a total of seven, and two additional light carriers, for a total of eight. The seven fast battleships were detached from the task groups and organized into a single battle line, commanded by Vice Admiral Lee, allowing them to be better positioned to respond to the heavy battleships of the Combined Fleet should they come out to fight.

While at Eniwetok on 8 June, Spruance received a twenty-two-page, mimeographed copy of a top-secret document flown out from Pearl Harbor. This was a copy of Koga's Plan Z, the plan for decisive battle against the American fleet. As previously related, it had been recovered from the briefcase of Admiral Fukudome, translated by MacArthur's intelligence team in Brisbane, and then sent to Pearl Harbor. Edwin Layton modified the translation to incorporate naval terminology, and Nimitz immediately passed it on to Spruance. Mitscher received a copy by airdrop aboard his flagship *Lexington* while underway. The principal American commanders now had in their hands the product of one of the most critical intelligence coups of the war.[4]

Officially known as "Combined Fleet Secret Operation Plan No.73, Plan for Z Operations," Plan Z might be considered a Japanese version of Nimitz's plan for the Battle of Midway. This was unsurprising as the Japanese now found themselves in a similar position: on the defensive and confronting a superior force as it attempted an amphibious operation against a strategic base. Plan Z did not contain operational specifics for just one area but was written to be readily adapted to an American attack anywhere within the vast Japanese defensive perimeter. The forces specified in Koga's original plan consisted of three main elements: the Base Air Battle Force, consisting of the strike aircraft of the First Air Fleet located on the island bases of the Central Pacific; the Surface Battle Force, being the carriers and battleships of the Combined Fleet; and the Advance Expeditionary Unit which, despite how its name rendered into English, was not an invasion force but the submarines available for the operation.

The submarines of the Advance Expeditionary Force would be placed in a picket line across the Pacific Fleet's projected line of advance west. Once located, the subs would concentrate to attack and weaken the American forces, emphasizing hitting the troop convoys. It was vital that reconnaissance aircraft from the Base Air Battle Force locate the American intruders and keep them under constant observation for at least a day before the Surface Battle Force arrived. On the day of battle, the air units were to "smash the carriers first, to retain control of the air and then turn to attack, disorganize, and annihilate the transport convoy. Circumstances may require that the convoy should be attacked at the same time as the carriers, or should receive the brunt of the attack."

Working in close cooperation with the Base Air Battle Force, when the Surface Battle Force arrived it would divide into carrier and surface battleship formations. The plan specified that "the carrier nucleus will try as far as possible to operate outside the limits of the area of the enemy bases. They will attack the enemy striking force on the flank and annihilate them within the limits of the area of our bases." Meanwhile, the surface battle line "will make the transport convoy their primary objective and will deliver a sudden attack near the vital areas we hold." If they found the landings already in progress, they would destroy them "at the water's edge." It should be noted that the word "base" used here refers to both land and ship bases, that is, carriers and capital ships with scout planes.[5]

The plan provided some general guidance for the forces involved. If the land-based air forces found the enemy's carriers and transport convoy at the same time, they were to "aim the full attack at the transport convoy." The carrier forces would attack the American carriers within the range of friendly land-based air, but after the initial attack, "quickly withdraw from the enemy . . . unless all types of the enemy's forces are positively ascertained or it is attacking in pursuit." The battleship surface force "will cooperate in an air attack. They will advance at high speed from their waiting positions . . . however the battle will generally be a night engagement, but if the situation is such that we have complete air superiority they will cooperate with the airplanes in a daytime engagement."[6]

Ideally, elements of the Combined Fleet would withdraw to lure the American carriers into an ambush on their flanks by the carriers of the Mobile Force. In accordance with Japanese surface action doctrine, the battleships and cruisers would take advantage of their excellent night fighting tactics and avoid American air attacks by attacking under the cover of darkness. The document also included a list of the air, surface, and submarine forces available for the Z Operation, along with their locations and current assignments. It provided a detailed estimate of current strength when the document was written in early March and the anticipated month-to-month increases through the end of May. Receipt of this document gave Spruance an unprecedented look at the intent and capabilities of the force he was about to face. Its emphasis on attacking troop transports worried Spruance and profoundly influenced the decisions he made in preparation to meet that force. But as he would discover, the Japanese now had other ideas. Plan Z was about to undergo radical changes to emerge as the A Operation plan.

In early May, Admiral Toyoda Soemu replaced the vanished Koga as the commander of the Combined Fleet. On 3 May 1944, he issued Combined Fleet Ultra Secret Operation Order 76, "Outline for A Operation," and rescinded Operation Order 73. Based on extensive tabletop war gaming by his staff, the new plan differed from Koga's in several important ways. First, it was focused on fighting a decisive battle in a specific geographic location, either Palau or the Western Caroline Islands. Second, it relied heavily on air attacks for the decisive battle: "The greater part of the Base Air Force and the full strength of the Task Force will be concentrated in the battle area. The enemy will be lured into this area and decisive battle with full strength will be opened at a favorable opportunity. The enemy task force will be destroyed for the most part in a day assault."

Importantly, these air strikes would be made "with large forces operating beyond the range of enemy carrier-based airplanes." Third, it called for *tatsumaki*, "whirlwind" raiding operations made by submarines and amphibious tanks attacking the captured bases in the Marshalls, principally the Majuro anchorage, to weaken the enemy task force before the decisive battle. Lastly, and somewhat optimistically, it called for the pursuit and destruction of any crippled enemy ships. Attacks on the transport convoy would occur only after the enemy task force had been defeated.[7]

Highlighting its emphasis on air operations, Operation Order 76 went into great detail, listing the air units available to the Base Air Force and specifying the daily patrol patterns to be used for reconnaissance. A major shortcoming of Toyoda's plan, like Koga's before it, was that it relied on the ability of Japanese reconnaissance to provide a timely warning of any incursion into the interception zone and then remain in "constant contact." Other than requiring that the carrier-based airplanes maintain close cooperation and coordination with the land-based air forces, there is no specific mention in Order 76 of "shuttle operations" where carrier planes were launched at the extreme limit of their range to attack the American carriers, and then land on the base airfields to refuel and rearm. This was an innovation made by the First Mobile Fleet commander, Vice Admiral Ozawa Jisaburo, and his staff.[8]

Compared to Plan Z, Toyoda's plan was far more oriented toward offense, seeking to lure the Americans into a battleground of his choosing with land and sea-based air forces ready to pounce. Unfortunately for Toyoda, Spruance's moves in the Central Pacific alternated with those of Halsey and MacArthur in the South Pacific, forcing him to react and denying him a chance to regain the initiative. As a result, his plans for the A Operation would have to be revised on the fly to meet changed conditions.[9]

Toyoda had another major problem: the lack of fuel stocks in the Japanese Home Islands and the shortage of oilers and tankers to carry that fuel limited his ability to maneuver. The aggressive patrols of Vice Adm. Charles Lockwood's submarines had done a superb job in whittling down Japan's merchant shipping and sinking many of her hard-to-replace tankers. At least six of the Combined Fleet's oilers lay at the bottom of Truk's lagoon. Toyoda was forced to send his fleet and the handful of fleet oilers that he could muster directly to the source, the oil fields of Borneo.

Another issue was that the Japanese were still rebuilding their land- and carrier-based air forces. Replacement aircraft, often updated versions of the same types that had been in production for many years, were being produced at a steady rate, but there was a dearth of trained pilots. The First Air Fleet had been created the year before to provide a land-based naval air force specifically for the decisive-battle concept. It was built around a cadre of highly experienced pilots who would train new aviators in the use of the newest high-performance aircraft, but the training times were cut short to get pilots into the front-line units. The shortage of all types of fuel also hindered training efforts, as there was not enough fuel for carriers to conduct training at sea, leaving Japanese carrier pilots with significantly less training than their American counterparts. This disparity was so pronounced that carrier landing accidents became a constant concern.[10]

On 9 June, *Indianapolis* was at sea again and met TF 58 northwest of Eniwetok to refuel. That same day Japanese snoopers found the Majuro anchorage largely empty, tipping off Toyoda that the Americans were again on the move in the Central Pacific. But were they conducting another hit-and-run raid or an amphibious operation? The Combined Fleet was concentrated in the southwest Pacific to respond to MacArthur's operation to capture Biak Island off the northwest coast of Dutch New Guinea. The Imperial Headquarters considered this a base of major strategic value and sent troops and aircraft to reinforce the garrison and thwart the operation. Toyoda intended to send Admiral Ugaki and the superbattleships *Yamato* and *Musashi* to smash the landings. He had also shifted many aircraft from the First Air Fleet defending the Marianas south to support the operation.[11]

Knowing the importance of land-based air forces to Plan Z and aware of intelligence reports that the Japanese were sending air reinforcements south through the Marianas, Spruance directed Mitscher to begin systematic air attacks on the islands one day earlier than planned, on 11 June. TF 58 began by launching a fighter sweep over Rota and Guam from a position approximately 190 miles east of the islands. For the remainder of that day and the four days that followed, carrier planes bombed and strafed the airfields and defensive works on Rota, Guam, Tinian, Saipan, and Pagan Islands. They also updated the photo-reconnaissance intelligence to pinpoint the locations of pillboxes, beach obstacles, and artillery emplacements.[12]

The fighters that rose to meet Mitscher's Hellcats were flown by mostly inexperienced pilots without combat experience. They attacked as individuals, lacking coordination and teamwork. As a result, they were red meat for the highly trained and experienced flyers of TF 58, who claimed a total of 150 planes destroyed in the air or on the ground, the bulk of the First Air Fleet's strength.[13]

While Mitscher's planes knocked out one leg of Toyoda's plan, the submarine component of the A Operation also met an early demise. In late May, the Imperial Headquarters had directed Vice Admiral Takagi Takeo, the commander of the Sixth Submarine Fleet, to deploy his submarines in several picket lines north of the Admiralty Islands across the projected line of advance for the next major American carrier operation. Messages sent to the subs on the picket line were intercepted and decoded, providing their location to Halsey's antisubmarine forces. As a result, the picket lines were rolled up using the latest antisubmarine techniques drawn from the U-boat war in the North Atlantic. In an incredible demonstration of skill and efficiency, USS *England* (DE 635) bagged five Japanese submarines in almost as many days, from 19–26 May, with a sixth sunk on 31 May. All told, of the twenty-five Japanese submarines deployed during the Marianas campaign, seventeen were sunk. Only a handful of subs were available to attack the Fifth Fleet, and none of them managed to score a kill. Another leg of the A Operation had been knocked away.[14]

On 13 June, the fast battleships of TF 58.7 began the shore bombardment of Saipan, targeting shore batteries, coastal positions, antiaircraft guns, and known artillery emplacements while also providing cover for the minesweepers clearing the avenues leading to the landing beaches. There was no question now in Toyoda's mind that an American amphibious operation in the Marianas was imminent. Later that day, as Ugaki and his ships were readying to attack the Biak landing, he received an emergency dispatch telling him to "stand by for Operation A," followed by another telling him to prepare to sortie to the Marianas. At 2200 Ugaki's force, consisting of the two superbattleships and the cruisers *Myōkō* and *Haguro*, escorted by nine destroyers and one light cruiser, left the anchorage at Halmahera and sped north at 20 knots.[15]

The main body of the First Mobile Fleet was at the anchorage of Tawi-Tawi in the southern Philippines when the order to commence the A Operation was received. Commanded by Vice Admiral Ozawa Jisaburō, it consisted primarily of three carrier divisions and their escorts. Carrier Division 1 comprised the three best carriers in the fleet, the recently commissioned *Taihō* and the Pearl Harbor veterans and sister ships *Shōkaku* and *Zuikaku*. Carrier Division 2 contained the carriers *Junyō* and *Hiyō* and the light carrier *Ryūhō*, escorted by the battleship *Nagato*, the cruiser *Mogami,* and ten destroyers. Carrier Division 3 consisted of the light carriers *Chiyoda*, *Zuihō*, and *Chitose*. The battleships *Haruna* and *Kongō*, four heavy cruisers, and nineteen destroyers acting as escorts completed the force.

Upon receiving the order to commence, Ozawa had the same battle ensign that Admiral Tōgō flew at Tsushima raised on the topmast of his flagship *Taihō* and issued the same general instructions that Tōgō had given his men: "The Fate of the Empire rests on this one battle. Every man is expected to do his utmost." They departed Tawi-Tawi at 1000 on 13 June and headed northeast across the Sulu Sea toward the central Philippines. Fortunately, Lockwood's submarines were well placed to make observations and provide critical intelligence. The submarine USS *Redfin* (SS 272) reported sighting four battleships and six carriers, along with escorts departing the roadstead. Early on 14 June USS *Haddo* (SS 255) reported that the Tawi-Tawi anchorage was completely empty.[16]

Based on these reports, Edwin Layton told Nimitz that he believed that Toyoda had initiated Plan Z, unaware that the Japanese were now sailing under a new set of orders. Spruance then notified his forces: "Estimate separated enemy forces may assemble and be within striking distance Marianas on 17 June." Now that the Japanese were on the move, Spruance ordered TG 58.1 and 58.4 to proceed to Iwo Jima to begin several days of bombing to neutralize the airfields there but to be ready to be recalled if required. TG 58.2 and 58.3 continued air strikes on the Marianas. Early on 14 June the seven veteran battleships of Turner's two fire support task groups, joined by six cruisers, including *Indianapolis*, relieved the fast battleships from bombardment duty. The same day, the underwater demolition teams reported that the reef at Saipan was flat and clear of mines and obstacles, with enough water depth for landing craft and DUKWs to operate freely.[17]

At 0835 on the morning of 15 June, Turner's Northern Attack Force began its landings on the southwest coast of Saipan, south of Garapan, the largest town on the island. The 2nd Marine Division landed on the Red and Green beaches north of Susupe Point, while the 4th Marine Division landed to their right on the Blue and Yellow beaches south of the point. The 27th Infantry was held in reserve and did not land that day. Initial resistance appeared light, but the Marines soon met heavy fire directed from the high ground of Mount Tapotchau as they hit the beaches in their LVT(2) tractors. Despite heavy casualties, the Marines pushed ashore and established a secure beachhead, reaching their initial

TABLE 3. Operation Forager Task Groups

COMMANDER	TASK FORCE	TASK FORCE GROUP	SHIP TYPE								
			FAST CARRIERS	LIGHT CARRIERS	ESCORT CARRIERS	FAST BATTLESHIPS	VETERAN BATTLESHIPS	CRUISERS	LIGHT & ANTIAIRCRAFT CRUISERS	DESTROYERS & ESCORTS	TRANSPORTS & SUPPORT
Blandy	51.1	Joint Exp. Reserve								12	25
Turner	**TF 52**	**Northern Attack Force**								15	95
Oldendorf	52.17	Fire Support Group 1					4	2	3	19	
Ainsworth	52.1	Fire Support Group 2					3	4	2	11	3
Bogan	52.14	Carrier Support Group 1			4					6	
Sallada	52.11	Carrier Support Group 1			3					6	
Moore	52.13	Minesweeping & Hydologic								8	19
Peck	52.7	Service & Salvage Group									17
Conolly	**TF 53**	**Southern Attack Force**									
Connolly	53.10	Attack Groups								26	122
Reifsnider	53.2	Minesweeper Group									
Ainsworth	53.5	Fire Support Group (same as 52.1)									
Ragsdale	53.6	Southern Carrier Support Group			5					7	
Knowles	53.19	Corps Reserve Group								8	12
Carter	53.12	Fueling, Service, Salvage Group			4					21	48
Mitscher	**TF 58**	**Fast Carrier Force**									
Clark	58.1	Carrier Task Group 1	2	2				3	2	14	
Montgomery	58.2	Carrier Task Group 2	2	2					3	12	
Sherman	58.3	Carrier Task Group 3	2	2				1	4	13	
Harrill	58.4	Carrier Task Group 4	1	2				1	3	14	
Lee	58.7	Battleline				7		4		13	
Totals, Forager			7	8	16	7	7	15	17	205	341
							Total Ships:				623

Source: VADM E. P. Forrestel, USN (Ret.), *Admiral Raymond A. Spruance, USN, A Study in Command*, Appendix VI and VII, 257–60.

objectives and landing 20,000 troops, artillery, and medium tanks by nightfall.[18]

Meanwhile, two Japanese fleets were heading toward the Marianas. As Ozawa's force passed through the San Bernardino Strait and entered the Philippine Sea, it was spotted on the evening of 15 June by the submarine USS *Flying Fish* (SS 229), steaming on a nearly due east heading. This sighting was later confirmed by coast watchers in the Philippines. Just before midnight, Ugaki's force was spotted by the submarine USS *Seahorse* (SS 304) some 200 miles east of Surigao Island heading north by east. At 1000 the next day, Ugaki met the 1st Supply Force coming from Davao and then rendezvoused with Ozawa at 1700. The combined forces then continued to head east to regroup and refuel on 17 June, managing to stay beyond the reach of the PBY search planes operating out of the Marshalls.[19]

On the morning of 16 June, Spruance came aboard the command ship USS *Rocky Mount* (AGC 3) to meet with Turner and Smith to discuss what changes in the ongoing operation were needed in light of the impending fleet action and the Plan Z intelligence he had received. Turner agreed to transfer seven cruisers and eighteen destroyers from the fire support groups to TF 58, retaining his seven veteran battleships and his remaining cruisers and destroyers to maintain call fire support during daylight and act as a blocking force during the night in case the Japanese surface units managed to make an end run around TF 58 to attack the transports, as Plan Z suggested. The three divisions of escort carriers would continue to provide air support for the assault troops and conduct CAP for themselves and the remaining ships around Saipan. Based on Spruance's explanation of Plan Z, Turner was also concerned that the Japanese intended to reinforce the air bases on Rota and Guam to launch air attacks against his transports. Per his orders, the transport unloading continued through the next day, and any ship not needed withdrew eastward until recalled. The Southern Attack Force remained on station some 200 miles east of Guam, and the landing slated for 18 June was postponed to a date to be determined.[20]

Smith had already landed his reserves and had amassed 30,000 tons of supplies on Saipan. The 27th Infantry had started landing that day, and except for the 106th RCT, which was kept in reserve, they were ashore by the next day. Smith was confident that his troops could hold out for several days even as combat operations continued. As the conference concluded, Smith asked Spruance if he thought the Japanese would turn tail and run at the last minute. "No," Spruance replied, "not now. They are out after big game. If they had wanted an easy victory they would have disposed of the relatively small force covering MacArthur's operation at Biak. But the attack on the Marianas is too great a challenge for the Japanese navy to ignore." Spruance returned to *Indianapolis* and sailed to rejoin TF 58.[21]

Mitscher relayed his recommendations for reorganizing TF 58 for the coming battle to Spruance: "After the initial air attack fails, or before if it becomes feasible, recommend Task Group 58.1 (which included his flagship *Lexington*) take station 50 miles to north-northwest of Task Group 58.3 in order to hit Japs from northern flank and to cut them off from escaping to the north." Spruance approved Mitscher's suggestions, which sought to repeat their tactics at Midway. There was only one problem: unlike at Midway, Spruance and Mitscher did not have any actionable intelligence on where the enemy would appear on the day of battle.[22]

Early in the day of 17 June the submarine USS *Cavalla* (SS 244), on her maiden war patrol, observed a large oiler with escorts some 800 miles west of Guam heading south by east, apparently to meet the Japanese fleet for a refueling rendezvous. The task groups raiding Iwo Jima were recalled, and Spruance ordered TF 58 to regroup and refuel. Aircraft losses were made up by taking replacements from the escort carriers. At 1445, Spruance issued the following battle plan: "Our air will first knock out enemy's CVs as operating carriers, then will attack enemy battleships and cruisers, to slow or disable them. TG 58.7 [the Battleline] will destroy enemy fleet either by fleet action if enemy elects to fight or by sinking slowed or crippled ships if enemy retreats. Action against the retreating enemy must be pushed vigorously by all hands to ensure the complete destruction of his fleet."[23]

Spruance then followed this with a directive to Mitscher and Lee: "Desire you to proceed at your discretion, selecting dispositions and movements best calculated to meet the enemy under most advantageous conditions. I shall issue general directives when necessary and leave details to you and Admiral Lee." Not long after, Spruance received a dispatch from Nimitz: "On the eve of a possible fleet action, you and the officers and men under your command have the confidence of the naval service and the country. We count on you to make the victory decisive."[24]

Cavalla kept shadowing the Japanese oiler and observed a portion of Ozawa's force at a position some 590 miles west of Guam late on 17 June but was unable to make a report until early the next day. She reported at least one carrier and several battleships or cruisers, apparently zig-zagging but heading east. The lack of a definitive estimate of the enemy's strength was a major concern to Spruance and his chief of staff, Carl Moore. *Cavalla* might have only seen the force that had exited the San Bernardino Strait. They could not be sure that there wasn't another Japanese force somewhere southwest of the Marianas. Radar-equipped long-range Martin Mariner PBM seaplanes had been flown in from Eniwetok to Saipan, and these were ordered to conduct night air searches out to 600 miles southwest and west.[25]

Mitscher and his staff plotted the *Cavalla* reports and concluded that the Japanese would be within range of his search planes sometime that afternoon. Assuming the Japanese would maintain their reported speed, the fleets would likely meet that night. He sent Willis Lee a dispatch: "Do you desire night engagement? It may be we can make air contact late this afternoon and attack tonight. Otherwise, we should retire to the eastward for tonight." Lee responded, "Do not, repeat, do not believe we should seek night engagement. Possible advantages of radar more than offset by difficulties of communications and lack of training in fleet tactics at night. Would press pursuit of damaged or fleeing enemy, however, at any time." Lee had succeeded brilliantly at the night action of the Second Battle of Guadalcanal, but he was fully aware of the danger that a melee at night might entail and wisely decided to avoid the risk.[26]

Spruance was also in a conundrum. His training at the Naval War College had taught him to base his plans on the enemy's capabilities, not on a belief in what they intended to do. Yet Plan Z had provided him with information on both counts. It was dangerous for a commander to attempt to predict an enemy's intent, especially that of an adversary trained in a very different military culture. Spruance knew that Japanese doctrine permitted them to divide their forces if a tactical advantage could be obtained. They had done so at Tsushima in 1905, as well as at Coral Sea and Midway. Spruance believed the Japanese had the capability and the intent to divide their forces to engage his carriers from a safe distance while sending another force to attack the transports. For Spruance, the Fifth Fleet's primary objective was the seizure of the Mariana Islands. The destruction of the Japanese fleet would be pursued only when such was consistent with the primary objective. With this in mind, he sent out the following general directive to TF 58 on the morning of 18 June:

> Task Force 58 must cover Saipan and all forces engaged in that operation. I still feel that the main enemy attack will come from the westward, but it might be diverted to come in from the southwestward. Diversionary attacks may come in from either flank, or reinforcements might come from the Empire. Consider that we can best cover Saipan by advancing to the westward during daylight, and retiring to the eastward at night, so as to reduce possibility of enemy passing us in darkness. Your air operations will naturally restrict distance which you can make westward during day, and by a necessity to conserve fuel. We should however remain in air supporting condition at Saipan until information of enemy requires other action. Consider seeking night action undesirable initially, in view of superior strength of all types. Earliest possible strike on enemy carriers is necessary.[27]

Mitscher and his staff were not happy with this directive, but complied. Mitscher placed his task groups west of Saipan in a north-south line of bearing, 12 miles distant from each other, with Task Groups 58.1 and 58.2 on either side of TG 58.3 and Mitscher's flagship *Lexington*. He ordered Lee and TG 58.7, along with TG 58.4 serving as CAP for the battle line, to a position 15 miles west. Owing to the need to turn eastwards into the wind for air operations, TF 58 made little progress westwards during the day on 18 June, covering just 112 miles. At 2030 that evening TF 58 came about on an easterly heading in accordance with Spruance's directive.

As TF 58 steamed east, Spruance and Mitscher received a dispatch about a radio direction finding that Pearl Harbor had picked up. At 0830, the commander of the Mobile Fleet broke radio silence on a call to his subordinate commanders, which located him at latitude 13° N, longitude

136° E, roughly 500 miles west of Guam, and 355 miles west-southwest of TF 58. At 2325, Mitscher sent a message referencing this report to Spruance and recommending that TF 58 should come about at 0130 to a new course, heading due west, to be in a position to launch strikes at 0500.

Spruance and his staff considered the proposal for an hour. Gil Slonim and Chuck Barber plotted the Japanese position based on the best available information and showed it to Spruance. There still was no confirmation that only one force was headed their way—just the opposite, or so they thought. *Indianapolis* had intercepted a transmission from ComSubPac to the submarine USS *Stingray* (SS 186). Based on the location of the sub, 435 miles southwest of Saipan and 60 miles south of the track of the Mobile Fleet, this was interpreted to mean that *Stingray* may have made contact with a second Japanese force but that the Japanese were jamming their report.

Spruance responded to Mitscher: "Change proposed in your TBS message does not appear advisable. Believe indication given by *Stingray* more accurate than that contained in CinCPac dispatch. If that is so, continuation as at present seems preferable. End run by other fast ones remains a possibility and must not be overlooked." A report received not long after from the submarine USS *Finback* (SS 230), in a position not far from the direction finding fix, reported seeing searchlights turned on. It seemed to Spruance that the Japanese were deliberately revealing their position, playing the same tricks they had attempted at Midway to lure him into a trap.[28]

It turned out later that *Stingray* had not reported a sighting of the Japanese fleet and that one of the carriers of the Mobile Fleet had, in fact, turned on its searchlights to recover a reconnaissance plane. At 0115 on 19 June, one of the PBM search planes reported sighting thirty enemy ships, located 520 miles west of Guam heading east, which correlated closely with the direction-finding report. This report, however, did not reach Spruance and TF 58 until 0914 that morning. This eight-hour delay had serious repercussions, as that information might have convinced Spruance that just one force was heading his way; he might then have heeded Mitscher's advice to put TF 58 in a better position to launch strikes against the Japanese carriers.

On the other hand, spotting bombers on the carrier decks to make such a strike reduced the number of fighters available to meet an incoming Japanese attack. Due to the shorter range of the Navy's bombers, a carrier strike required placing TF 58 closer to the enemy and perhaps open to the sort of flanking attack mentioned in Plan Z. Furthermore, in previous carrier-on-carrier battles the Navy had suffered grievous losses and it is possible that some of the TF 58 carriers might have faced a similar fate. Considering these factors, Spruance made a carefully reasoned decision based on the information he had at hand. He would neither shy away from battle nor place his fleet and the landings on Saipan in needless jeopardy. Aware that Nimitz expected a decisive outcome, Spruance nevertheless did not intend to gamble unless the odds were heavily stacked in his favor.[29]

In the early hours of 19 June, Ozawa's Mobile Fleet assumed its attack dispositions. In the lead was the Van Force led by Vice Admiral Kurita Takeo, consisting of Ugaki's Battleship Division 1 with *Yamato* and *Musashi*, Battleship Division 3 with the battlecruisers *Kongō* and *Haruna*, four heavy cruisers, and one light cruiser leading nine destroyers. They provided escort for Carrier Division 3 with its three light carriers carrying sixty-one AM6 Zeros, nineteen B5N Kates, and nine of the new B6N Jill torpedo bombers. At 0530, the two Mobile Fleet carrier divisions were some 120 miles behind the Van Force, steaming along parallel courses heading northeast, with Carrier Division 1 on the right and Carrier Division 2 fifteen miles away on the left.

At that same time TF 58, some 340 miles northeast of the Van Force, came about and turned into the wind to launch search, antisubmarine, and combat air patrols, after which it changed course to west-southwest. Mindful of Plan Z's reliance on land-based air forces, Spruance requested Mitscher to conduct bombing raids of Rota and Guam to damage the runways and suppress the land-based air operations there, provided the dawn search failed to locate Ozawa's forces. Mitscher reported that after the strikes made in the previous week, he had only armor-piercing bombs left in his magazines, but he would carry out fighter sweeps of the islands.[30]

While the search to the west turned up empty, the fighters over Guam encountered considerable opposition, including planes arriving from Truk and Yap as reinforcements. From the time the Hellcats arrived over Guam at 0720 until they were recalled three hours later, they were involved in almost constant air combat. Thirty-three Hellcats, mostly from Clark's TG 58.1, accounted for thirty Zeros and five bombers without a loss. Just before 1000 the air search radar of TF 58 began to pick up bogeys approaching from the west, and the recall code "Hey, Rube!" was broadcast. While the remaining land-based aircraft continued to attempt to enter the fray, they had been effectively neutralized as a threat.[31]

Ozawa had an excellent idea of where the American carriers were located. The land-based air reconnaissance, thanks to the activities of TF 58, had been unable to provide the continuous observation called for in Plan Z, but an air search launched from his carriers on 18 June had located one of Mitscher's task groups at a position estimated to be 160 miles west of Saipan. During that evening and night, Ozawa maneuvered his forces to keep them well beyond the reach of the American carriers and ordered his fleet to prepare to initiate air strikes at dawn. Mitscher did not enjoy being placed between a hostile carrier force somewhere to the west beyond the reach of his strike aircraft and a lee shore containing hostile air bases, but his aviators proved to be up to the challenge. His carrier operations required him to turn south-eastwards into the wind frequently, meaning that no progress west was made that day to close the distance with Ozawa.

As they had done at Midway, the Japanese relied heavily on the scout planes of their surface forces to be the fleet's main source of reconnaissance. At 0340, the Van Force launched a dozen float planes to search the seas to the east. An hour and a half later, additional searchers were launched from the light carriers. Three hours later the first group reported back: "Enemy force including carriers sighted, number of carriers unknown. Position 14 deg. -40'N, 143 deg. -10'E, sailing SW." They had seen TG 58.4 just after its initial launch of the day. Soon after, Carrier Division 3 launched its first strike, Raid 1, consisting of sixteen Zero fighters, forty-five Zeros carrying bombs, and eight Jill torpedo bombers, in the direction of TF 58.[32]

At 1000, this first raid appeared on the air search radar screens of Lee's battleships, and ten minutes later Mitscher ordered TF 58 to prepare to launch all available fighters. At 1023, TF 58 swung southeast into the wind and began launching. Some 70 miles distant, the incoming Japanese planes regrouped at 20,000 feet, giving TF 58 enough time to get most of its fighters in the air, positioned and stacked at different altitudes. The fighter directors in the Combat Information Centers of the carriers could see the direction and altitude from which the raiders were approaching and vectored their planes to meet them best, hitting them at 60 miles out.

The Japanese bombers were flying in textbook formation, but when attacked they broke ranks and dispersed individually in different directions, leaving them vulnerable. The Zero fighters fought as individuals, not as sections or pairs, preferring aerobatics to teamwork. Most of the intruders fell to the initial interception, but some made it as far as Lee's battle line, arranged in a standard PAC-10 circular formation. Here they were met by a wall of V-T fuzed antiaircraft fire. At 1049, a single Japanese bomber managed to score a hit on *South Dakota*, causing minor damage to the ship but killing seventeen men. None of the raiders made it through to the carriers beyond. In less than thirty minutes after the order to launch was given, more than forty of Carrier Division 3's planes were shot down.[33]

At 0807, Ozawa ordered the Mobile Fleet to turn southeast to launch the next series of raids and keep his carriers beyond the strike range of the American carriers. At 0856, Raid 2, consisting of forty-eight Zero fighters, fifty-three D4Y Judy bombers, and twenty-seven B6N Jill torpedo bombers, was launched from Carrier Division 1. Minutes later, the submarine USS *Albacore* (SS 216), one of many ordered by Lockwood to converge on the Marianas, launched a spread of torpedoes on *Taihō*, one of which hit her on the starboard side, just ahead of the island. The blast ruptured an aviation fuel storage tank and jammed the forward elevator between the flight deck and hangar deck. Ozawa was not initially concerned. It would take more than one torpedo to stop this newest and greatest carrier of the Mobile Force. He ordered the elevator opening to be planked over so that flight operations could resume.[34]

A harbinger of things to come, as Raid 2 flew northeast it passed over the Van Force, and having failed to identify themselves properly, they came under friendly fire from the nervous antiaircraft gunners below, losing two aircraft and damaging another eight so badly that they had to abort the mission. The remainder of the raid flew on, was intercepted at 1139 in almost the same position as the first raid, and met a similar fate. Mitscher kept his CAP rotating to refuel and rearm so they were ready to tackle the incoming raiders in much the same style as they had done an hour earlier. Seventy were destroyed in this interception. Approximately twenty

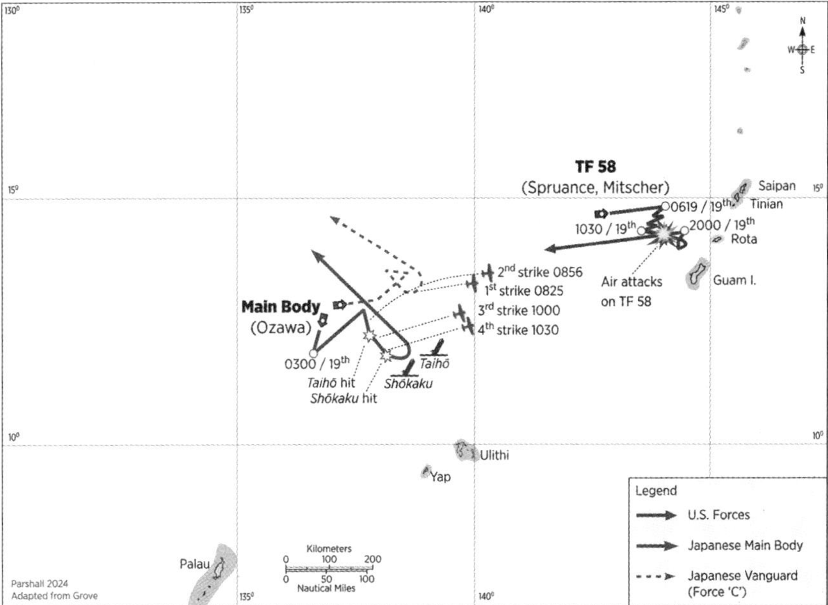

MAP 9. The Battle of the Philippine Sea, 19 June 1944

slipped past to attack the battle line, where they met intense antiaircraft fire from below and Hellcats from above. *Indianapolis* was credited with getting one of these. Six Judys were deflected south and managed to make it through to attack TG 58.2 but scored no hits. One survivor landed on Guam, another on Rota. Ozawa's dream of shuttle bombing had just met reality.[35]

Two more raids, both from Carrier Division 2, were launched that day, but they fared no better. The forty-seven planes of Raid 3 launched at 1000, and based on an erroneous search contact report flew far to the northwest. When no American ships were found at the designated position, most of the raiders decided to return to their carriers; however, twenty headed southeast, where they eventually found TG 58.3. Their attack was intercepted at 1300, but it was not pressed home with any enthusiasm. Seven were shot down as the rest broke off and fled.

Raid 4 was more of the same. Eighty-two planes were launched at 1030, including some from *Taihō*, which had resumed flight operations and headed nearly due west but in the direction of another erroneous position report. Upon reaching the designated position and finding nothing, some planes returned to the carriers, while most headed north to Rota or the Orote airbase on Guam. The aircraft headed for Rota were soon spotted by the carriers of TG 58.2. Four B6N Jills attempted to glide bomb the carriers USS *Wasp* (CV 18) and USS *Bunker Hill* (CV 17), causing some casualties but no damage to the latter. Of the forty-nine planes attempting to land on Guam, thirty were shot down, and the remaining nineteen that did land were so damaged as to render them beyond repair.[36]

With the major raids at an end, Mitscher could redirect his strike aircraft to attack the airfields on Guam and Rota, accompanied by fighter sweeps to mop up any remaining Japanese planes attempting to land or oppose the bombing. The antiaircraft fire over Orote was intense, and at least four Hellcats and one bomber were shot down. By sundown at 1845 on 19 June the Japanese had lost about 315 planes, against American losses of 23 shot down and 6 lost operationally. This phenomenal success was rewarded with the epithet "The Great Marianas Turkey Shoot," perhaps making it sound too easy. Turkeys, after all, typically do not shoot back. American air casualties included twenty pilots and seven aircrew killed, together with four officers and twenty-seven enlisted sailors on the three ships that suffered near misses. The Japanese casualty figures by the end of the day would be far, far worse.

After the last sorties had left the decks of *Taihō,* her crew attempted to mitigate the effects of her ruptured aviation fuel system, which was causing fuel vapor to collect in the forward elevator well. With only three months in commission, *Taihō*'s damage control personnel were inexperienced and poorly trained. Their efforts to ventilate the ship by opening hatches and watertight doors only served to spread the deadly fumes throughout the ship. Nearby, the submarine *Cavalla* had been shadowing Carrier Division 1, and *Shōkaku* was now in her sights. As the carrier was recovering and refueling aircraft from Raid 2, at 1120 she was hit with at least three torpedoes fired by *Cavalla*, one of which struck her starboard-side forward aviation fuel storage tank, which erupted into a massive fireball. *Shōkaku*'s damage control personnel, in contrast to *Taihō*, were among the best in the Imperial Navy, but the damage was too extensive and vital machinery spaces had flooded, cutting power to her fire pumps and ventilation fans.

Dead in the water, the damage from the torpedo strike was causing her to take on water and settle by the bow.

At 1408 *Shōkaku* suffered a cataclysmic explosion when an aerial bomb touched off the vapors from aviation fuel and volatile bunker oil. Her hangar decks were now a raging inferno, and her forward flight deck was awash. When the sea flooded the forward elevator, her stern rose far out of the water. Crewmen who had collected on her fantail now tumbled down the steeply tilted flightdeck to their deaths through the open aft elevator into the flaming hangar spaces below. Within minutes she corkscrewed and plunged into the deep, taking with her nearly 1,300 men, many of whom were Japan's most experienced naval aviators.[37]

Taihō was about to experience a similar fate. At 1430, a spark somewhere onboard ignited the volatile vapors that had saturated the ship. Her armored flight deck was seen to heave and buckle, and the sides of her enclosed hangar deck blew out. The ship was totally engulfed in flame as she fell out of the formation and began to settle. Ozawa, who had just witnessed the horror of *Shōkaku*'s sinking, was now the victim. He wanted to go down with his flagship, but his staff prevailed upon him to live to fight another day, so he transferred his flag to the cruiser *Haguro*. Beyond saving, *Taihō* continued to burn for another two hours before she was rent by another horrendous explosion at 1628 p.m. She rolled onto her port side and sank minutes later, taking 650 men with her.[38]

Late that afternoon Spruance sent a dispatch to Mitscher, saying, "Desire to attack enemy tomorrow if we know his position with sufficient accuracy. If our patrol planes give us required information tonight, no searches should be necessary. If not we must continue searches tomorrow to insure adequate protection for Saipan. Point Option should be advanced westward as much as air operations permit." Due to their maneuvers during the battle, the men and ships of TF 58 found themselves far south and east of the position they had started from that morning. Unknown to Spruance and Mitscher, at 1800 Ozawa ordered a general withdrawal to the northwest. The Americans had not made contact with the Japanese fleet sincc *Cavalla* had struck *Shōkaku* earlier that day. Indeed, it was unknown whether the two carriers that the subs had reported hitting had actually sunk. After TF 58 had recovered all of her aircraft, at 2000 Mitscher ordered the fleet to come about on a course heading of 260 degrees true, at a speed of 23 knots, which Mitscher hoped would allow him to catch the enemy, which was heading northwesterly but slowed by cripples. TG 58.4 was left behind to refuel and keep Guam and Rota suppressed.[39]

Despite Spruance's assumption that Mitscher would launch patrol planes that night, none were, a decision for which Mitscher has been criticized. There were radar-equipped night fighters in every task group suited for this purpose. In Mitscher's defense, historian Clark G. Reynolds points out that the night fighters were not trained for long-range reconnaissance and were held back in defense against a possible nighttime torpedo plane attack, a tactic certainly favored by the Japanese. Clark's assertion, however, is belied by the fact that from 0230 to 0730 that same morning, *Enterprise*'s VT-10 had carried out a night search with radar-equipped Avengers out to a range of 325 miles. It had just missed Ozawa's force by 40 miles. The nearest units of the Mobile Fleet were within that range at midnight on 19 June. If the Mobile Fleet had been found that night, an attack at dawn on 20 June might have produced decisive results. Mitscher's failure to launch a search that night and into the early hours of 20 June is difficult to understand.[40]

Monitoring the battle back at Pearl Harbor, Nimitz was clearly disappointed that the Japanese fleet had not yet been found and destroyed. John Towers and the aviators at CinCPac headquarters, furious that Spruance had ordered TF 58 to cover Saipan, went so far as to demand that Nimitz overrule Spruance's decision, something that Nimitz flatly refused to do. In a message to Spruance dated 19 June, Nimitz nevertheless expressed his disappointment, telling him, "We share with you a feeling that I know you must have—that of frustration in our failure to bring our carrier superiority to bear on the Japanese fleet during the last few days. . . . It now appears that the Jap fleet is retiring for replenishment. . . . If they come back, I hope you will be able to bring them to action."[41]

The exact location and tactical disposition of the Japanese fleet was still unknown. The Van Force had never been spotted. Situated far ahead of Ozawa's main body and under independent command, it could still have posed a threat during the night of 19 June, either in a flanking attack on TF 58 or a direct attack against Rear Adm. Jesse Oldendorf's blocking force of veteran battleships defending Saipan. Plan Z had foreseen the possibility of using the surface forces in a night action, but none had been ordered. Fortunately for Spruance, the sinking of *Taihō* and Ozawa's dazed and hurried transfer into a ship lacking the communications equipment necessary to direct a fleet action had left the Japanese without effective leadership for much of the battle. As Ugaki lamented in his diary, "It was extremely unfortunate that the flagship of the supreme commander was shifted twice at the most critical time of war. At a time like this I thought it might be better to transfer the command temporarily to the next number while changing the flag." If Ozawa had turned over his command as Jack Fletcher had done at Midway, the battle might have gone much differently.[42]

TF 58 renewed its search efforts at daybreak on 20 June but found no sign of Ozawa's fleet. There was speculation in Pearl Harbor, as referenced in Nimitz's letter, that they were heading for Davao in the Philippines. Spruance thought otherwise. At 0755 he told Mitscher: "Damaged *Zuikaku* may still be afloat. If so, believe she will most likely be heading N.W. Desire to push our searches today as far westward as possible. If no contacts with enemy fleet result, consider it indication that fleet is withdrawing and further pursuit after today is unprofitable. If you concur retire tonight towards Saipan. *Zuikaku* must be sunk if we can reach her. Advise." Here, Spruance assumed that the "*Shōkaku*-class" carrier reported being hit by *Cavalla* was her sister. He was hoping that even if Ozawa's main body continued to retreat that TF 58 could catch and destroy those ships left behind to protect any cripples.[43]

Spruance had been up with his staff since the night of 17 June, on the bridge or in the Flag Plot, paying close attention to information as it came in and conferring with Moore or Slonim. During the previous operations when there was little chance that the Combined Fleet would come out, he had mostly stayed in the background, allowing events to unfold in accordance with carefully laid plans. Now he was fully involved and attentive, facing an intelligent foe. Deep in thought, he walked the decks saying little and, if possible, more reticent than usual. As always, he showed no emotion, never shouted or became excited. When decisions were needed, he had already anticipated the problem and had a solution in mind. Moore found Spruance to be uncharacteristically brusque and even rude during this time. Clearly, much was on his mind.[44]

On the evening of 19 June, Ozawa, still aboard the cruiser *Haguro*, was largely unaware of how bad his tactical situation would become when he lost the cover of darkness. The survivors of Raid 1 had made the wildly inaccurate claim that they had sunk at least four American carriers and left another six burning. True, he had lost two carriers, but with American losses that much greater, Ozawa reasoned that he could salvage a victory if he had help from the rest of the Combined Fleet. Ozawa ordered his forces to refuel and regroup, intending to launch an attack on the remaining American task force the next day. From Combined Fleet headquarters came a message promising salvation. A rescue force was going to sail immediately from the Empire to join forces with him on 21 June. Together, they would attack the enemy task force "in cooperation with the Base Air Force" and send in the surface ships to destroy the landing forces at Saipan.[45]

Apparently, Toyoda was as deluded by the erroneous claims of victory as Ozawa. Neither was aware that the "Base Air Force" no longer existed as such and that no American ships had actually been sunk. When Ozawa shifted his flag aboard *Zuikaku* at noon the next day, the reality of his situation hit him. Just one hundred planes had returned to the remaining carriers. The land-based air forces were a shadow of their former strength. Without adequate air cover there was no recourse but to retire northwest as quickly as possible.

The daytime searches made by TF 58 were fruitless. At 1420, Spruance told Mitscher that he wanted to continue the pursuit of the enemy to the northwest if anything turned up that afternoon. Fortunately, at 1542 a search plane reported that it had spotted the Japanese fleet in several groups heading west at a slow speed, apparently in the process of refueling, at a position estimated to be 220 miles northwest. Mitscher advised Spruance that he intended to hit them with everything he had, and at 1624 the first strike was launched. Additional search plane reports identified the Japanese heading west in three groups. The southernmost and closest group was reported to have two carriers, two oilers, and destroyer escorts. As the strike was launching, however, the spotting report was corrected to place this closest group 60 miles further west than previously reported, and the largest group, containing another carrier and a number of battleships,

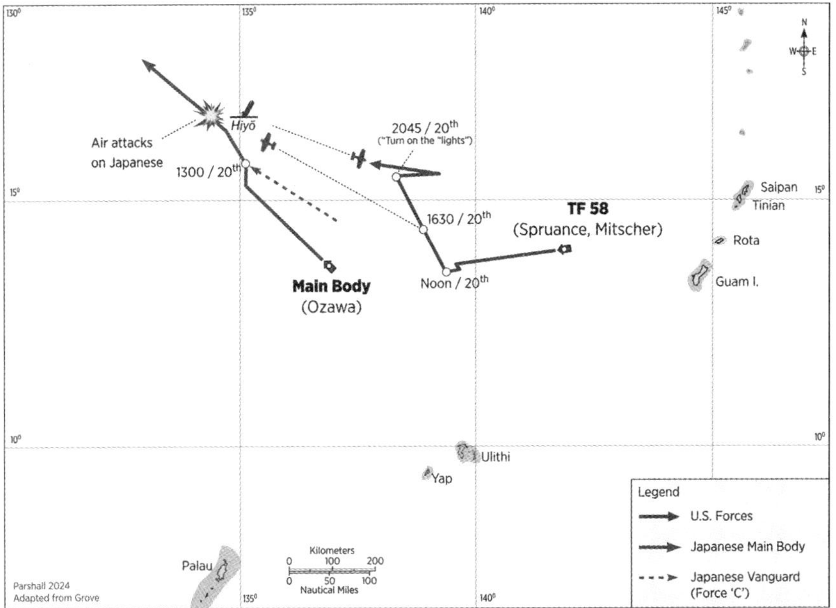

MAP 10. The Battle of the Philippine Sea, 20 June 1944

was 60 miles beyond that. Mitscher knew that even the closest group, at 280 miles distant, was at the extreme range of his strike aircraft, and that they would be returning to the carriers at night. Many would likely have to ditch in the darkness.[46]

A full "deckload," consisting of eighty-five Hellcats, twenty-six SBD Dauntless and fifty-one SB2C Helldiver divebombers, and fifty-four TBF Avenger torpedo bombers, flew west into the setting sun. At 1840, they encountered the oiler group well astern of the faster capital ships. Some dive bombers, already low on fuel, peeled off to attack, while the rest flew on to hit the carriers, which were their main objectives. The Japanese put up an intense wall of antiaircraft fire, but in the short twenty minutes that the attack lasted two oilers were left dead in the water ablaze, the light carrier *Hiyō* was torpedoed and sinking, the flight decks of the carriers *Zuikaku* and *Chiyoda* were wrecked and on fire, and the battleship *Haruna* was damaged. The Hellcats took on the seventy-five planes that Ozawa sent up as interceptors, claiming afterwards to have shot down forty. They strafed the ships below before heading back east into the gathering gloom.

Ozawa, however, was not ready to give up the fight. At 1900, he ordered Kurita to take the Van Force along with several heavy cruisers to mount a night attack on TF 58. They headed east for two hours until Ozawa or his staff realized that they would never reach the Americans under the cover of darkness, and Kurita was recalled. Of a similar mind, Mitscher asked Spruance for permission to send Lee and TG 58.7 west to attack the Japanese while TF 58 was busy recovering aircraft. This took many hours and caused him to put his carriers on an eastward course, away from Ozawa. He hoped Lee could mop up any cripples left behind or be in a position at daybreak to engage the retreating Japanese fleet. Spruance vetoed the idea for much the same reasons as the Japanese had done, realizing that the enemy was too far away and that the battle line would be open to air attack after daybreak. He also believed that the Japanese were still capable of making a surface attack at night, as indeed Ozawa had ordered. "Consider Task Force 58 should be kept tactically concentrated tonight," he replied, "and make best practicable speed towards the enemy so as to keep them in air striking distance." One can only speculate what might have happened if *Yamato* and *Musashi* had met the American fast battleships in a nighttime battle line duel.[47]

Of the 216 aircraft launched by TF 58, approximately 20 were shot down during the attack. As the rest returned from the west, the air search radar picked them up and Mitscher ordered, with Spruance's approval, that the carriers turn on their landing and searchlights and fire star shells to guide the returning pilots home, as they had done at Midway. Eighty planes were lost to ditching or deck accidents in the dark. Spruance ordered Dumbo air rescue searches, and with the assistance of destroyers and submarines, when all was said and done, all but sixteen pilots and thirty-three crewmen were recovered.

At dawn on 21 June another deckload strike was launched, but with orders to return once they reached the limit of their fuel reserves if nothing was sighted. A long-range search plane found the Japanese retreating at their best speed, some 360 miles distant. Spruance in *Indianapolis* joined the battle line and ordered Lee to proceed west in search of cripples. Five Japanese carriers were known to have been hit, but none were seen to sink. It was possible they were still out there, but when TG 58.7 reached the site of the previous day's strike, they found only nine American aviators in the water awaiting rescue. Ozawa was now some 400 miles to the west, beyond their reach. Spruance ordered the battle line to rejoin TF 58.

The final tally in what came to be known as the Battle of the Philippine Sea was 476 Japanese carrier- and land-based aircraft lost along with their aircrews, three aircraft carriers sunk, two oilers scuttled and lost, plus damage to other ships. An aircraft carrier without aircraft, as Spruance said, is a liability. Japanese naval aviation was dealt a blow from which it never recovered. By any measure, it was a decisive victory.[48]

There were many aviators who felt otherwise. In their opinion, Spruance had missed "the chance of the century" and failed to eradicate a major portion of the Combined Fleet. Spruance himself was deeply disappointed that he had not done so. He had, however, made decisions based on his interpretation of the information at hand, with the overriding purpose of protecting the landing forces at Saipan. As he explained in his report to Nimitz, Spruance had believed that once the Japanese had mobilized and entered the Philippine Sea, it meant "they (had) decided to risk everything in a determined attack on us while we were engaged in an early and critical part of a large amphibious operation. . . . I was wrong. . . . Their attitude about risking their fleet has not changed. . . . They intended to use their fleet to exploit any advantage that their carrier air might gain. They had no intention of throwing everything at us by coming into Saipan at high speed to fight it out."

Making a clear reference to the Z Plan, he continued, "With the information we had of their most recent plans, all of which fitted well with what we know of their previous operations, I felt it was necessary to remain with Task Force 58 in air supporting distance of Saipan until we knew definitely the location of the major portion of the Japanese fleet. We could not afford to be drawn off to the westward by a diversion created by a portion of their fleet, while the rest of it was enabled to go around one of our flanks and hit our transports and cargo ships at Saipan or in the areas to the eastward of Saipan."[49]

Spruance expressed his frustration about the battle in a letter to his wife. "Our experience with the Japanese fleet was disappointing," he wrote. "I never thought they would come out until they actually started. When they did start, I thought I was wrong and they would come boiling in on us with everything they had. Instead of that, they tried a very long range carrier-based air attack . . . (which) failed to inflict little appreciable damage; and they lost all the planes and all the pilots they sent against us."[50]

Spruance could be faulted for relying too heavily on the intelligence that had fallen into his lap and for not crediting the Japanese command with the ability to change plans on short order. The failure of the Combined Fleet to sortie during previous operations made him skeptical that they would do so in response to the Marianas landings, but once they had mobilized Spruance came to believe that Koga's Decisive Battle plan was about to unfold. He did not reckon on the Japanese keeping their fleet undivided and beyond the reach of American carrier-based air superiority.

That said, Vice Admiral Ugaki Matome did not doubt that he and his countrymen had suffered a major defeat. "It will be extremely difficult to recover from this disaster and rise again," he wrote in his diary. "When I think of the prospect of a victory fading out gradually, it's only natural that my heart becomes as gloomy as the rainy season sky." On the bridge of *Yamato,* he composed a five-line *tanka*:

Utterly awakened from the dream of victory,
Found the sky rainy and gloomy.
Rainy clouds will not clear up,
My heart is the same
When the time for battle's up.[51]

CHAPTER 12

OPERATION FORAGER COMPLETED

WHILE SPRUANCE AND TF 58 were consummating one of the greatest victories in the history of the United States Navy, back on Saipan the Marines and soldiers were also enjoying success, but at a much higher cost. Saipan is an island of forty-six square miles, many times larger than the coral atolls that the Marines had assaulted previously. Its terrain was also very different, with high, rocky hills running down the island's spine, rent by deep ravines, and riddled with caves that offered excellent defensive ground. Six miles across at its widest point and twelve miles in length, the island's center is dominated by Mount Tapotchau, whose summit is 1,554 feet above sea level. The Japanese had intended to heavily fortify the beaches, but the predation of American submarines on their supply convoys prevented the necessary cement and reinforcing steel from reaching the defenders. Instead, they utilized the limestone caves inland and constructed a well-concealed defense in depth, which turned out to be a much harder nut to crack.[1]

Despite the fearful losses from convoy sinkings, a significant number of Japanese troops had reached the island by June, although they had lost much of their equipment. There were now more than 25,000 Imperial Army troops, supported by heavy artillery and a tank regiment, under the command of General Saitō Yoshitsugu. Admiral Nagumo Chūichi, Spruance's old foe at Midway, commanded the Fourth Fleet, a primarily administrative command that included the 6,600-man naval garrison. Unlike Ozawa's forces, the men under Saitō and Nagumo had nowhere to run. In a culture that considered surrender to be deeply shameful, they had no choice but to inflict as many casualties on their enemies as possible before embracing an honorable death.[2]

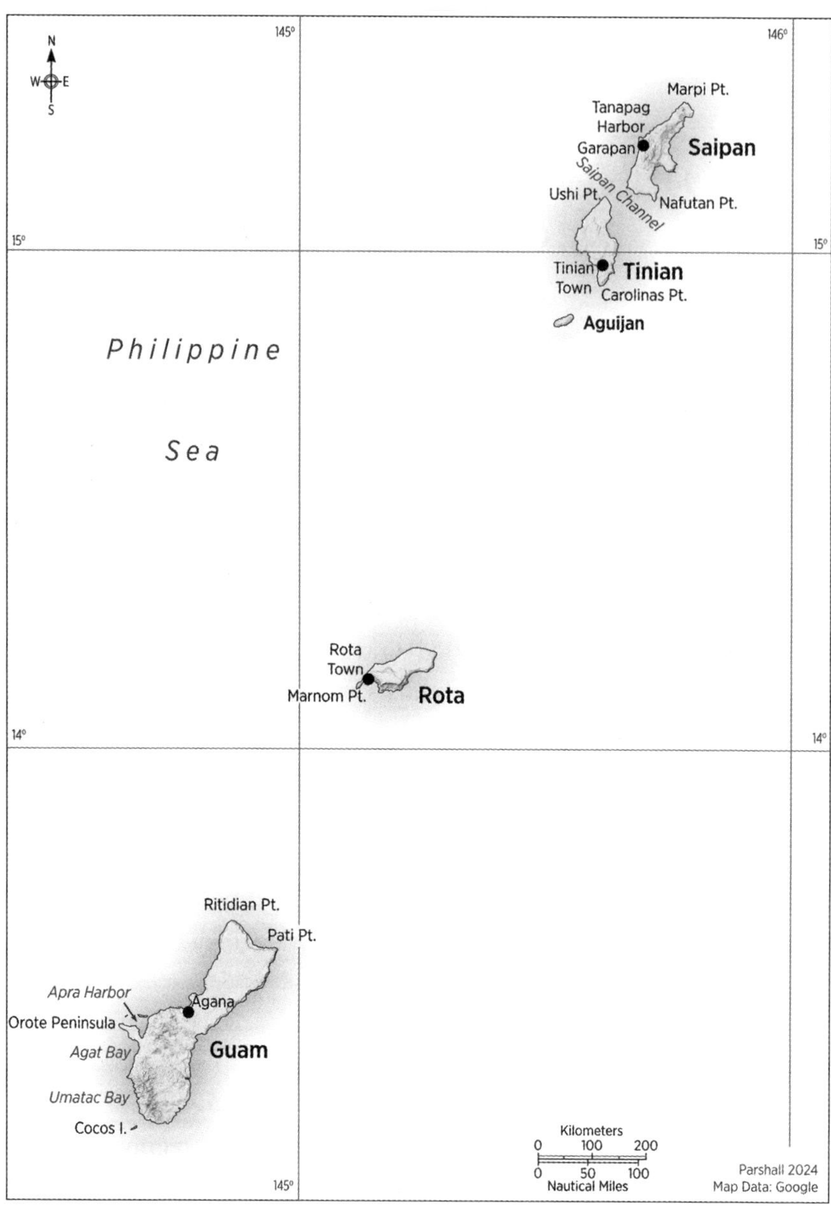

MAP 11. The Mariana Islands

By 22 June, the Marines and soldiers had taken most of southern Saipan, including Aslito Airfield, which now was home to three squadrons of Army P-47 Thunderbolts. The 2nd Marine Division had held off vicious counterattacks and occupied the western foothills of Mount Tapotchau. The 4th Marine Division had moved across the island to the east coast and pushed north to the eastern side of Tapotchau. Here, Saitō had established his main line of resistance, stretching across the island from Garapan to Magicienne Bay.

Holland Smith's plan for attack on 23 June called for all three divisions to advance north, with the line of attack pivoting on the 2nd Marines on the left flank. In the center, two regiments of the 27th Infantry passed through the Marine lines at dawn and attacked the southern flanks of Tapotchau through a deep valley dubbed "Death Valley" and over the steep "Purple Heart Ridge" that formed the boundary with the 4th Marine Division. This area earned its nicknames due to its rugged terrain, thick vegetation, and concealed positions. The 4th Marine Division continued their push north along the east side of Tapotchau. The 2nd Battalion of the 105th Infantry was tasked with cleaning out a pocket of Japanese troops at Nafutan Point on the extreme southwest of the island.

By noon that day, the two Marine divisions were on their way to meeting their objectives. The 2nd Marine Division moved up to Garapan, and the 4th Marine Division advanced on the east up the slopes of Tapotchau, but confused orders caused the 27th Infantry units to start late. Meeting determined resistance from a well-entrenched and hidden enemy, they had not advanced far, leaving the flanks of the adjacent divisions exposed to enemy counterattacks and causing the Marines to halt their advance.[3]

Holland Smith was displeased with this turn of events. He was already predisposed to look askance at the 27th Infantry after their lackluster performances on Makin and Eniwetok. Smith thought the unit suffered from "militia-itis" and was more show than go. The division was commanded by Maj. Gen. Ralph C. Smith, USA, a soldier Holland Smith liked and respected but who was too reluctant to discipline his subordinate commanders. Unfortunately, things did not go well on the morning of 24 June; the Army's attacks stalled once more in the face of fierce fire, and the flanking Marine divisions had to halt their operations. Holland Smith had

had enough. He went to Kelly Turner and demanded that Ralph Smith be relieved.

Turner agreed, and they both went aboard *Indianapolis* to discuss the matter with Spruance. Holland Smith explained his reasons and told Spruance that Gen. Sanford Jarmon, USA, was available as a temporary replacement until a new commander could be sent in from Pearl Harbor. Jarmon had promised Holland Smith that he would get the 27th on the move and restore some offensive spirit. Spruance agreed and had Moore draft a dispatch addressed to Holland Smith which stated, "You are authorized and directed to replace Major General Smith, commander of the 27th Army Division, by Major General Sanford Jarmon, in order that the offensive on Saipan may proceed in accordance with the plans and orders of the commander of the Troops and Landing Forces."[4]

Ralph Smith accordingly departed Saipan and reported to his boss Lt. Gen. Richardson at Fort Shafter, Hawaii, beginning a chain of events that would lead to serious interservice acrimony. While Spruance took full responsibility for the dismissal, the full fury of the U.S. Army was about to come down on Holland Smith in what became known as the "Smith v. Smith" affair. Meanwhile, the Marines and soldiers continued their offensive against Saito's defensive line across the slopes of Mount Tapotchau. By 25 June, the 2nd Marine Division had reached the mountain's summit, and the 4th Division had cleared Kagman Peninsula. The 27th Infantry continued to press forward under Jarmon's direction; he relieved the colonel commanding the 106th Infantry Regiment, finally clearing "Death Valley" and "Purple Heart Ridge" by 29 June.[5]

Progress was slow, and the attackers bypassed stubborn strong points, leaving them to be mopped up by the reserve troops moving up from the rear. On the southern shore of Saipan, the XXIV Corps Artillery, a combination of five regiments of Marine artillery and eight regiments of Army artillery, totaling ninety-six 105-mm and sixty 155-mm "Long Tom" guns, pounded the Japanese positions before the Marines and soldiers pushed off. Sherman medium tanks and half-tracks, mounting 75-mm guns, provided mobile firepower, and M3 Stuart tanks modified with flamethrowers were employed to burn out caves and pillboxes. Much of the island's agriculture was devoted to sugar cane plantations, and flamethrowers were also used to burn the cane fields to deny cover to Japanese snipers and infiltrators. The Army's P-47s provided on-call fire support, as did the dive bombers of TG 52's escort carriers. As always, the veteran battleships of the fire support groups stood just offshore to bombard enemy concentrations and fixed positions.

Spruance came ashore on 25 June to confer with Holland Smith regarding the operation's progress and to view the areas already secured. They decided to send TF 53 and the Southern Attack Force, who had been at sea for more than a month, back to Eniwetok for rest and resupply. They also requested that the 77th Infantry Division be sent from Hawaii to act as a reserve for the pending invasion of Guam, reasoning that they would likely encounter similar resistance there as they were experiencing on Saipan. The Guam invasion date was now set for 21 July, with the invasion of Tinian to begin three days later.[6]

Saito's troops, without hope of reinforcement or resupply, died in place or in mass attacks. They had been told that the Combined Fleet was coming to their rescue, but by now they knew that no help was coming. By 3 July, Mount Tapotchau and central Saipan were completely in American hands, and the remaining Japanese began withdrawing to their last-stand positions on the north of the island, unable to resist American firepower. In a testimony to the effectiveness of that firepower, General Saitō complained in a dispatch to Tokyo that "if there were just no naval gunfire, we feel we could fight it out with the enemy in a decisive battle."[7]

Spruance came ashore again on Friday, 2 July. He took the opportunity to take a jeep ride, under heavy Marine escort, up Mount Tapotchau. From there, with the aid of field glasses, he could see the battle unfold to the north in all its aspects: the air and naval bombardment, the artillery shells passing overhead, the movement of men and tanks pressing their attack forward, and more troops coming up from the rear in trucks. Holland Smith would not permit Spruance to get any closer to the fighting. "All of which is understandable," he wrote Margaret, "but prevents me from satisfying my curiosity as I would like to. This operation has been slow and very tough on the troops. The Marines have done magnificent fighting, as usual, and without them we would never have been able to do the job." In the same letter, he noted the almost complete destruction of the buildings on Saipan and the ever-present stench of the unburied bodies of the Japanese. He described the wretched state of the civilians who were being given food and medical attention but did not mention that many chose suicide rather than seek American protection.[8]

The Japanese were forced to fight from concealed defensive positions during the day and conduct largely uncoordinated small-unit counterattacks at night. However, star-shell illumination and artillery support made these attacks suicidal. The campaign for the island culminated with the largest *Hokusai* (banzai) charge of the war, in which more than 4,000 Japanese troops, including some armed civilians, made a futile attack on the night of 7 July. The attack swamped the 105th Infantry Regiment, which stood its ground and bravely poured fire into the human wave that plowed over them and into the command posts, supporting artillery emplacements, and supply dumps in the rear before it was abated. Nearly all of the attackers, some wielding bamboo poles with bayonets affixed, died in the effort. Following this bloodbath, General Saitō committed suicide, as did Admiral Nagumo. On 9 July, the island was declared secure.[9]

General Richardson flew in from Hawaii on 12 July to "investigate" Ralph Smith's dismissal. Ignoring protocol, he bypassed both Spruance and Turner, went directly to Holland Smith, and admonished him for the dismissal, telling him that the Marines were no better than "a bunch of beach runners" who had no business commanding Army troops at corps level. Spruance had extracted a promise from Holland Smith to hold his tongue. Kelly Turner, however, was not one to be stifled, and he turned his terrible temper on Richardson, excoriating him for the breach of protocol.[10]

When Richardson complained to Spruance about his treatment, Spruance tried to placate him, telling him that Kelly Turner was just being Kelly Turner and not to worry about it. This hardly satisfied Richardson, who, when he returned to Pearl Harbor, went straight to Nimitz to express his extreme displeasure. A serious breach in Army-Navy relations was in the offing. Nimitz tossed this hot potato to Washington, where it was finally settled between Admiral King and General Marshall, who together agreed to sweep it under the rug. While Nimitz was not pleased with Holland Smith for initiating the imbroglio, he greatly valued his service and promoted Smith to commander of the Fleet Marine Force, Pacific.

To placate Marshall and the Army, it was agreed that henceforth, Marines would not command Army troops in the field.[11]

On the heels of Richardson's visit, Nimitz and King flew into Saipan on 17 July to inspect the conquest and discuss future operations. They were met at Aslito Airfield by Spruance, Turner, and Holland Smith. This was King's first opportunity to view the fruits of the campaign he had lobbied for so long and hard. A pleased King pulled Spruance aside and told him that he had done the correct thing to cover Saipan during the Battle of the Philippine Sea, as there was another Japanese fleet in the Inland Sea that could have attacked the transports. That night, Nimitz and King joined Spruance, Turner, and Smith for dinner aboard *Indianapolis*. Carl Moore recalled that the dinner was somewhat spoiled by a plague of large black flies from Saipan—their presence was bad enough, but the realization of where they had been previously may have made the food rather unappetizing.[12]

During his time on Saipan, King asked Spruance for his thoughts on the next objective after the Marianas. Spruance knew that King had long favored seizing Formosa, but he answered, "Okinawa." King asked if he thought it could be taken, and Spruance said he thought it could, but due to the proximity to Japan and the land-based air forces there, the fast carriers would have to remain on station during the assault, which would require them to be replenished at sea. Nothing was settled at this meeting, and the strategy for closing in on the Home Islands remained in flux for some time to come.[13]

In the near term, Spruance was more concerned about completing Operation Forager, turning his attention to Guam and Tinian. Guam was the largest land mass yet assaulted by the Fifth Fleet. It had been an American territory since being acquired from Spain in 1898, and the indigenous Chamorro people were looking forward to their liberation from Japanese occupation. The geography of Guam is broadly similar to that of Saipan, but the island is more than twice the size at 212 square miles, with a high, jagged limestone ridge running down the west side of the southern half. The island's northern half is a limestone plateau characterized by high cliffs that drop into the sea. The southwest side of the island is dominated by the Orote Peninsula and Apra Harbor, on either side of which are located the best beaches for large-scale landings, fringed by shallow reefs.

The Japanese defenders were well aware of the most likely landing sites and heavily defended these areas and the Orote Peninsula, which linked them. Guam had little in the way of defensive fortifications until the American successes in the Gilberts and Marshalls awakened the Imperial High Command to the need to seriously bolster the defenses of the Marianas. The Fifth Fleet had been bombarding the island since mid-June. Most identifiable defensive works and shore batteries had been eliminated to a depth of approximately two miles behind the beaches. But in the hills beyond the immediate bombardment zone, the Japanese had carefully concealed field artillery and mortars zeroed in on the landing sites, which could not be seen except when revealed by muzzle flash. The concentrated bombardment on the west side of the island had served to confirm the likely landing zones, and the postponement of the original landing gave the Japanese an additional five weeks to dig in even deeper.[14]

More than 18,500 Japanese troops were on the island, a mix of Imperial Army regiments recently relocated from Manchuria, an Imperial Navy garrison, and aviation support troops. The size of the island complicated the Japanese defense strategy. Most troops were located within striking distance of the landing areas, leaving much of the island sparsely defended, especially along the rugged southern and eastern coasts. Lieutenant General Takashina Takeshi, the Imperial Army commander, planned to launch a counterattack to push the Marines off the beaches at the first opportunity.[15]

The Southern Attack Force carrying the 3rd Marine Division was recalled from Eniwetok and began landing on the beaches north and south of the Orote Peninsula on W-Day, 21 July, leaving the Line of Departure at 0800. As the LVTs approached, they came under heavy fire, and a number were lost; however, the landings continued according to schedule. The Marines moved inland almost immediately and had taken the high ground beyond by midday with the help of tanks and call-fire from Conolly's destroyers. Despite taking heavy casualties, the 3rd Marine Division was several thousand yards inshore by nightfall.

For the next several days, the Marines continued to push inshore and resist sporadic Japanese infiltration and small-unit counterattacks during the night along their entire front line. Supplies were unloaded around the clock, and call-fire support from ships and aircraft neutralized gun emplacements as they were identified. South of Orote, the 77th Infantry was ashore by the afternoon of 23 June, and they were in a position to relieve the 4th Marine Regiment, who had moved out to support the 22nd Marine Regiment movement over Orote, which was accomplished by 25 June.

General Takashina had gathered his remaining forces and launched a general counterattack at 2330 on 25 June all along the front, heavily concentrated on the left flank of the 3rd Marine Division's perimeter, intending to roll up the American defenders. The Marines responded with incredible tenacity and the application of all available firepower. Conolly's cruisers and destroyers provided star-shell illumination of the battlefield at night and naval call-fires at all times. Marine machine guns, mortars, and howitzers blasted the attackers and mowed them down in fearsome numbers.

By dawn of the next day, it was clear that the counterattack had failed. The Marines estimated that they had killed 3,200 Japanese troops, including some 300 that had infiltrated behind their lines. General Obata Hideyoshi, the senior Japanese officer on Guam, reported to Tokyo that they had suffered 80 percent casualties, with 95 percent of senior officers killed and 90 percent of weapons and equipment lost. It was decided to conduct a withdrawal toward the north end of the island, with the goal of causing as many American casualties as possible before they met their inevitable fate.[16]

By 31 July, the Americans had captured Agana, the principal city, and secured the entire southern half of the island. The Japanese had moved most of the Chamorros into concentration camps on the south end of the island; these were liberated, and the people were fed and given temporary housing. More escaped the combat zone and found their way south, providing details of the enemy's dispositions. Some Chamorros were enlisted into provisional police units to locate and assist in the elimination of Japanese stragglers. Spruance was impressed by the Chamorro people, terming them "good looking" in marked contrast to the ragged civilians he had seen on Saipan.[17]

After a short rest, the American offensive continued north, with the 3rd Marine Division on the west and the 77th Division on the east. They used the scant north-south road network for logistics and spread out along branching, narrow trails, employing armored units in advance to do reconnaissance and clear roadblocks. Opposition to the advance was sporadic, usually at road junctions in the jungle. Whenever a concentration of enemy forces was encountered, air and naval call-fire hit the area, followed by tank-infantry team assaults. The remaining Japanese troops, running out of food and ammunition, continued to fight until they had been pushed into the extreme northwest corner of the island, where they were relentlessly pounded by air and naval bombardment. By 10 August, the last organized resistance had been quashed, and Guam had been declared secure. General Obata committed suicide the next day. More than 10,000 Japanese bodies were counted, and many more were lost in sealed caves or bunkers. As many as 7,500 melted away into the jungle, where they were subject to disease and starvation and hunted down as training exercises.[18]

While the Marines on Guam were expanding their beachheads in the face of heavy fire, the invasion of Tinian was planned to avoid heavy casualties. Tinian is approximately twelve miles long and five miles wide, fringed with high coral cliffs that provided little in the way of beach areas suitable as potential landing sites. Because it is only three miles from the southern coast of Saipan, bypassing the island was never considered an option. Being relatively flat compared to the other islands in the Marianas, Tinian's military value lay in being an ideal site for airfields, a fact not lost on the Imperial Navy, which had built three large aerodromes with a fourth under construction. The U.S. Army Air Force valued Tinian for the same reasons, seeing it as an ideal location to launch its B-29 bombing campaign against Japan.[19]

Although no definitive plans had been drawn up for the assault on Tinian before the arrival of the Fifth Fleet, it had always been the idea that the troops of the Northern Landing Force would move there next after securing Saipan. In the weeks preceding the landings on Tinian, Holland Smith's planners had acquired a substantial collection of aerial reconnaissance photos and Japanese documents found on Saipan, which provided the locations of most of the defensive positions. The Japanese still clung to the idea of repulsing the American landings at the most likely beach and had configured their defenses accordingly.

The "most likely beach" on Tinian was a stretch of sandy beach on the island's southwest side, south of Tinian Town, the largest settlement and the only harbor. Here was where the Japanese Army commander, Colonel Ogata Kiyochi of the 50th Infantry Regiment, expected the landing to occur and where most of the defenders' guns were sited. His troops, numbering approximately 3,800, had recently transferred from Manchukuo and were considered well-trained. Another 1,400 men were Imperial Navy troops and coastal gunners under the command of Captain Oie Goichi of the Imperial Navy. Including air defense troops, ground support staff, construction personnel, and a company of light tanks, the Japanese could count on about 7,100 personnel for the defense of Tinian.[20]

Asiga Bay on the east coast was another possible landing beach, and the two tiny beaches on the northwest coast were the third and least likely options for a major assault. Ogata sited his troops accordingly, maintaining a battalion and some tanks as a mobile reserve in the south but only a single infantry company at the northwest beaches. Lacking the rugged hills and deep defiles found on Saipan, the terrain of Tinian consisted of a series of sugar cane fields and small farms connected by a good road network. One Marine historian described it as "almost perfect tank country." Unfortunately for the Japanese tankers, their Type 95 Ha-go light tank was no match for the Marines' M4 Sherman.[21]

The landing date, J-Day, was set for 24 July; yet the issue of which beach to land on remained a major concern for the planners. The beaches south of Tinian Town, designated Orange, Red, Blue, and Green, were excellent landing sites and, therefore, heavily defended, and the Japanese were well prepared to meet the assaulting forces on the beach. Seeking to create the element of surprise, the planners explored alternatives. Accordingly, they sent Underwater Demolition Teams (UDTs) to scout the beach at Asiga Bay, Yellow Beach, and the two northwest beaches, designated White 1 and 2.

Yellow Beach was only 125 yards wide, with a pounding surf. It was heavily mined, ringed by pillboxes, and had a steep exit avenue that looked difficult to traverse. The White beaches, while extremely narrow and having an area suitable for LVTs of only about 60 yards in width, had the advantage of a shallow reef shelf much better suited for LSTs and DUKWs, and the ground behind the beach gave excellent access to the island's interior. The ledges on either side of the two beaches were only six to ten feet above the waterline and could be accessed fairly readily by Marines on foot, leaving the beach exits open for LVT(A)s and tanks. Best of all, the defenses here were sparse, with few mines.[22]

Holland Smith and Rear Adm. Harry Hill suggested the White beaches to Admiral Turner as the best alternative to obtain tactical surprise. The Japanese were not expecting an attack here, and the landing beaches were near the two largest airfields. The short distance from Saipan allowed the assaulting LSTs to sail directly from Tanapag Harbor on Saipan to the invasion beaches in a rare shore-to-shore movement. Logistics could be handled by loading DUKWs and landing craft at Saipan and, after the short crossing, driving them over the reef and off the beach into designated dump sites. Finally, and perhaps as important as any other factor, the island's northern half was within range of the XXIV Corps artillery. They began firing missions on northern Tinian shortly after Saipan was secured and picked up the tempo as J-Day approached. Their Long Tom 155-mm guns had a range of fourteen miles, enough to cover the entire island of Tinian.[23]

Despite these advantages, Turner remained adamantly opposed to the White beaches, believing that the wide beaches around Tinian Town were better suited to land two divisions at once and preferring the harbor there as a better place for unloading supplies. Admiral Hill appealed to Spruance, who liked the boldness of the plan but was loath to overrule his friend Turner out of hand. In Spruance fashion, he called the staff together, and a conference was held on 12 July to go over the planning in detail, correctly surmising that cooler heads would prevail removed from the dynamics of the Kelly Turner-Holland Smith relationship. Calling upon the most junior officers first, Spruance heard the opinions of his staff, all of whom favored the White beaches. Seeing how things stood and satisfied that the logistics could be handled efficiently, Turner acquiesced, much to Spruance's relief.[24]

In the days preceding J-Day, the 4th Marine Division embarked on their LVTs and carried out an invasion in reverse as they left the landing beaches on Saipan and loaded into the waiting LSTs. Meanwhile, their comrades of the 2nd Marine Division were loaded into transports for a diversionary "landing" at the Tinian Town beaches. Ten of the LVTs destined for the White beaches were equipped with an ingenious landing ramp known as the "doodlebug," built by the Seabees from steel scrap found on Saipan. When the LVTs stopped at the base of the ledge, they dropped the "doodlebug" ramp into place to provide a means for men and machines to drive up over the ledges adjoining the beaches, thus significantly widening the landing zones.[25]

As part of the deception plan, the bombardment of the White beaches in the days preceding the landings was only cursory. At 0530, USS *California* (BB 44), resurrected from the mud of Pearl Harbor, and the heavy cruiser USS *Louisville* (CA 28) opened fire on the White beaches. The massed artillery on Saipan also began firing on designated targets in the north of the island, and dense smoke was laid along the slopes of Mount Lasso, a 590-foot hill located near the center of the island where Colonel Ogata had set up his headquarters. With Spruance aboard, *Indianapolis* arrived from Guam and joined the bombardment group. At 0600, the LVTs carrying the men of the 4th Marine Division began to be disgorged from the LSTs offshore and headed for the real Line of Departure. At 0747, the first wave of armored LVT(A)s hit the beaches, supported by LCM(I)s firing rockets. The Marines continued to land the rest of that morning, meeting some resistance but successfully pushing out into open ground. By 1630 that day, 15,600 Marines, along with their tanks, artillery, and supplies, had landed and were dug in for the night with defensive fields of machine gun and artillery fire. There they waited for the inevitable counterattack. They did not have long to wait.[26]

Once again, the overwhelming superiority of American firepower compelled the Japanese to adopt defensive tactics that had become routine: fighting from concealed positions during daylight hours and, under cover of darkness, using infiltration to exploit any gaps in the American lines, followed by mass attacks. As the 2nd Marine Division landed on the morning of 25 July, the regiments of the 4th Marine Division moved north from the beachhead and secured the northern airfields, after which they turned south. The 2nd Marine Division advanced down the island's western side, with the 4th Marine Division moving in parallel on their left. Using the tactics they had learned on Saipan, the Marine assaults were preceded by intense naval and artillery bombardment, and followed by concerted attacks using tank-infantry teams. Strongpoints were singled out for naval call-fire and air strikes that used the new jellied gasoline napalm bombs for the first time. By 28 July, all of the Marines' 105-mm guns had relocated to Tinian and began direct-fire support of the advancing troops. A Japanese POW later complained, "You couldn't drop a stick without bringing down artillery."[27]

After overrunning Mount Lasso, the Marines, mounted on tanks and in halftracks, began such a rapid advance that their artillery regiments had to relocate continuously to stay within range. By J+6, 30 July, they had overrun most of Tinian, including Tinian Town and the fourth airfield. The surviving Japanese took refuge on the limestone ridge at the extreme south of the island. It took the Marines several more days to root out the stubborn defenders. The island was declared secure on 1 August, but for the next week scattered pockets of Japanese troops staged mass suicide attacks against the Marines, preferring death in combat to surrender. On 10 August, Spruance relieved the Marines and handed the island over to the garrison command.

On the same day that Guam was declared secure, Admiral Nimitz and Rear Adm. Forrest Sherman arrived to inspect the island and meet with Spruance and his staff. Nimitz intended to move his headquarters to Guam for the remainder of the war, and he directed Spruance to begin rebuilding the air base on Orote and enlarging the harbor at Apra. Nimitz told Spruance that on 26 August, the Fifth Fleet was scheduled to be turned over to Halsey and become the Third Fleet. Nimitz also wanted Spruance's opinion of Operation Stalemate, the plan for seizing Palau, Yap, and Ulithi, which would be assigned to Halsey. After some discussion, Spruance and Moore told Nimitz that Yap should be bypassed, as it offered little strategic benefit once Palau was in hand.[28]

Sherman told Spruance and Moore that he was in the middle of preparing plans for Operation Causeway, the invasion of Formosa, an operation that was dear to Admiral King. Nimitz told Spruance that Causeway would be his operation, with Kelly Turner in charge of the Joint Expeditionary Force once more, but with Lt. Gen. Simon Bolivar Buckner, USA, now in charge of the Expeditionary Force, replacing Holland Smith. Sherman and Nimitz thought Causeway would be impossible until Luzon in the

Philippines had been secured, which would eliminate a source of Japanese land-based air power and provide a base from which to invade Formosa.[29]

For the next several weeks, Spruance remained in the Marianas to oversee the conversion of Saipan, Guam, and Tinian into major bases of operation. The Seabees were hard at work enlarging the runways at Orote and Tinian, the latter to accommodate the USAAF's B-29 Superfortress bombers. Apra Harbor acquired a new breakwall that greatly expanded the anchorage there. On 25 August, Spruance welcomed Johnny Hoover, who was to move his base of operations to Guam as commander of the Forward Area, Central Pacific, overseeing the land-based air forces there. The next day, Spruance turned over the Fifth Fleet to his old friend Bill Halsey, and with that, it became the Third Fleet again. Mitscher's TF 58 became TF 38 and moved south to support Operation Stalemate. Shortly thereafter, *Indianapolis* weighed anchor and shaped a course back to Pearl Harbor.

The cost of the campaign was high. Based on the after-action reports, more than 60,000 Japanese were buried by U.S. troops, but this data needs to be taken with a grain of salt as the counts included not only trained Japanese naval and army troops but also garrison support troops, aviation ground crew, stranded pilots, civilian contract laborers, conscripted Korean laborers, and male civilians forced to fight. The figures for the Japanese also, however, do not include the many uncounted dead who were "buried" in fortifications and caves sealed by bombardment and ground combat operations.[30]

The invasion of Tinian Island in the Marianas was perhaps the Fifth Fleet's greatest amphibious success story, with a killed-in-action (KIA) ratio of over 20:1 against a relative troop superiority of nearly 5:1. Holland Smith, in his memoir, summed up the Tinian operation: "In war, as in every other phase of activity, there are enterprises so skillfully conceived and successfully executed that they become models of their kind. Our capture of Tinian, southern sister island of Saipan, belongs in this category. If such a tactical superlative can be used to describe a military maneuver, where the result brilliantly consummated the planning and performance, Tinian was the perfect amphibious operation in the Pacific War."[31]

The Japanese were also learning lessons from these campaigns. The tactic of massed attacks by night was seen to be wasteful of men; one Japanese

TABLE 4. Amphibious Forces and Casualties

OPERATION		MARINES		ARMY		TOTAL	JAPANESE		KIA RATIO	US VS JAPAN TROOP RATIO
							BURIED	POW		
Tarawa[1]	Deployed	15,545				15,545		146		
	KIA		990			990	4,690		4.7	3.2
	WIA		2,296			2,296				
	MIA									
Kwajalein[2]	Deployed	26,928		26,538		53,466		265		
	KIA		339		174	513	8,410		16.4	6.2
	WIA		617		829	1,446	See note 4			
	MIA									
Eniwetok[2]	Deployed	4,509		5,670		10,179		48		
	KIA		254		96	350	3,000		8.6	3.3
	WIA		555		311	866	See note 4			
	MIA									
Saipan[3]	Deployed	48,388		22,646		71,034		1,810		
	KIA		2,116		924	3,040	25,941		8.5	2.6
	WIA		10,419		2,633	13,052	See note 5			
	MIA		247		116	363				
Guam[3]	Deployed	37,292		19,245		56,537		86		
	KIA		973		192	1,165	16,679		14.3	3.4
	WIA		4,506		757	5,263	See note 5			
	MIA		443		48	491				
Tinian[3]	Deployed	35,606				35,606		404		
	KIA		286		4	290	6,850		23.6	4.9
	WIA		1,498		17	1,515	See note 5			
	MIA		23		1	24				

1. Battle for Tarawa, Hist. Section, HQUSMC, 1947, appendix B and C. Army data; see note 4.

2. Report of Flintlock Operation, Encl.(E), appx. 1 table 1; Encl. (C); USMC Personnel Department Figures. KIA includes MIA, presumed dead.

3. Report of Capture of the Marianas, Encl.(A), Annex (3).

4. Marshall Islands Japanese Defenses and Battle Damage, 8. U.S. Army W. D. Mission Report, 1 March 1944.

5. *Battle Experience: Supporting Operations for the Capture of the Marianas Islands*, 74–75, COMINCH, 21 December 1944.

commander commented that "in the execution of our night attacks, we must give further study to the coordinated use of our strength . . . but the chief consideration is the fact that . . . a night attack by the bulk of the defending force might defeat its purpose and help the enemy in securing his landing."[32]

In these campaigns, the Japanese still clung to the strategy of stopping the Marines at the beach, which left them highly vulnerable to American firepower. In response, the Japanese adopted tactics that involved conserving their troops for a defense in depth, relying on deep, nearly impenetrable man-made and natural fortifications that yielded only to the most determined and bloody assaults. The fighting in the islands of the Marianas provided a foretaste of what was to come at Peleliu, Iwo Jima, and Okinawa.

The loss of the Marianas came as a great shock to the Japanese at every level of society. For years, the popular press had boasted of nothing but victories, yet somehow, the Americans had acquired bases just 1,500 miles from Tokyo. As a result, the government of General Tōjō Hideki fell when a furious Emperor Hirohito withdrew his support. Looking back at the loss of the Marianas, Admiral Ugaki closed his diary entry for August 1944 with a doleful two-line poem:

Gone is the sun, and the mountain
Of the clouds loses its color.[33]

CHAPTER 13

OPERATION DETACHMENT

The Capture of Iwo Jima

SPRUANCE ARRIVED at Pearl Harbor on 1 September and immediately decamped into the house on Makalapa Hill that Halsey had just vacated. He met with Nimitz the next day to discuss Operation Causeway, the invasion of Formosa. When Spruance reiterated his dislike for the idea of taking Formosa, Nimitz asked, "What would you rather do?" Spruance replied, "I would prefer taking Iwo Jima and Okinawa." "Well," said Nimitz, "it's going to be Formosa."[1]

Nimitz knew that Causeway was an idée fixe for Admiral King, and there was little chance in arguing for another target. From a strictly logical military standpoint, Causeway had merit. King opposed MacArthur's insistence on retaking all of the Philippine archipelago, beginning with Mindanao and then moving northwards to Luzon and the capital of Manila, on the basis that it would take far too long. From a strategic standpoint, moving from the Central Pacific to Formosa was a more effective means of cutting Japan's lines of communication with Southeast Asia and establishing a link with the Nationalist Chinese. What King had not counted on was the influence of politics.

President Roosevelt arrived in Pearl Harbor on 28 July, shortly after he had been nominated for a fourth term, to confer with his two top Pacific Theater commanders, Nimitz and MacArthur, about the future conduct of the war. As expected, MacArthur strongly pushed for the recapture of the Philippines, making a point of reminding the president that the optics of allowing an American territory with thousands of American prisoners of war to languish under Japanese occupation would look bad in an election year. Roosevelt agreed in principle, and MacArthur returned to Brisbane, confident that he had made his point.[2]

Nimitz, however, was disturbed by the seeming lack of coordination between his command and MacArthur's and the lack of any official direction from the Joint Chiefs of Staff. On 23 August, he had sent a dispatch to King stating, "The lack of direction as to operations subsequent to STALEMATE is proving to be a serious handicap to sound decisions on current problems. . . . [I]n order that the pressure and momentum of our operations in the Pacific may be maintained I urge that a directive be issued now for the CAUSEWAY operation."[3]

Given the lack of a firm directive, Nimitz told Spruance to take several weeks' leave and come back refreshed to tackle the issue. Before he departed, Spruance officially welcomed Rear Adm. Arthur C. Davis as his new chief of staff. Davis had come aboard *Indianapolis* before they departed Saipan to familiarize himself with the job. By the arrangement that King had worked out to placate the aviation clique, senior black-shoe commanders like Spruance had to have an aviator as their chief of staff, and Davis qualified. Furthermore, four-star admirals were supposed to have a rear admiral as their chief of staff. As Carl Moore remained a captain, despite efforts made by Spruance and Nimitz to promote him, he would have to go. Spruance wrote to Margaret, "I will miss Carl a great deal, but Art Davis is a very fine officer whom I like very much. Having had Carl for the past year to write up our plans makes it easier for another man, not so experienced at that end of the game, to tackle the job, perhaps."[4]

As Spruance flew home on 9 September, Nimitz and MacArthur finally received the directive from the Joint Chiefs that Nimitz had requested. MacArthur was now directed to occupy the Leyte-Surigao area, and Nimitz was directed to provide the necessary fleet support and assault shipping to make it happen. MacArthur was to provide plans for the seizure of Luzon with a target date of 20 February 1945, and Nimitz was directed to have plans ready for the occupation of Formosa with a target date of 1 March 1945. The decision on which operation came first was still to be determined.[5]

A flurry of dispatches between Halsey, Nimitz, and MacArthur ensued. Late in the afternoon of 12 September, Nimitz received several dispatches from Halsey. Based on his intelligence, Halsey reported that there appeared to be no Japanese on Leyte and overall, the central Philippines was lightly defended. He recommended that the Stalemate operations, the capture of the Palau Islands, be abandoned and Leyte seized immediately. Later that day, Nimitz replied that the Palau operation was too far advanced to be abandoned and was needed to secure the western flank of operations in the Philippines. Still, he was willing to redirect the forces intended for Yap, which were already combat-loaded and ready to sail, and asked for MacArthur's opinion. MacArthur concurred with abandoning the Yap operation but disputed the assertion that Leyte was undefended. His intelligence indicated that Luzon was being heavily reinforced, and several Japanese divisions were headed for Leyte. Nevertheless, with the addition of the troops that Nimitz offered, MacArthur stated that his forces were "available for immediate action."[6]

The dispatch traffic between Halsey and Nimitz reached King, Leahy, and Marshall during the Second Quebec Conference. With this information in hand, the Combined Chiefs approved the JCS directives on the afternoon of 13 September. The next day, a pleased King followed this up, approving the redirection of the forces intended for Yap and telling Nimitz and Halsey that the early seizure of Leyte was "HIGHLY to be desired." The next day, the JCS authorized MacArthur to execute the Leyte operation with a target date of 20 October.[7]

Operation Stalemate II, the invasion of Peleliu, began on schedule on 15 September but turned out to be much tougher than anticipated. Instead of the three days predicted by Marine planners, it took three months to secure the island. The 1st Marine Division led the assault and was badly mauled by the unexpected ferocity of the well-concealed and deeply dug-in defenders. It was a harbinger of things to come, as here, unlike in previous operations, heavy naval and air bombardment had not neutralized the defenders. To root out the deeply entrenched enemy required up-close infantry fighting with grenades, flamethrowers, and bazookas. Here, there were no banzai attacks to simplify the killing; the Japanese defenders sought to take as many Americans with them in death as they could. The island was mostly in American hands by 30 September, when the Marines were relieved by the 81st Infantry Division. Still, it took another two months of brutal fighting to wipe out the last pockets of organized resistance.[8]

Things went better on Ulithi. Here, elements of the 81st Infantry Division seized the atoll on 23 September without opposition, and the Seabees and Army engineers immediately set to work, turning it into a major logistics hub with one of the largest lagoon anchorages in the Pacific. It eventually became the largest American naval base during the Pacific War.

Spruance had arrived in Monrovia on 10 September, where he found himself temporarily thrust into civilian life, experiencing what the average American family had to deal with during the war with gas and food rationing. Maintaining the family car was a perennial problem for Margaret, and Spruance had to be resourceful and pull a few strings to obtain a decent set of tires for it. But he was heartened by the progress of his daughter's tuberculosis treatments, and he managed to take several long walks in the San Gabriel hills. His two weeks in Monrovia passed quickly, ending when he received a notification from Nimitz to meet him in San Francisco for a high-level meeting with King to hammer out the next moves for the Pacific Ocean Area.[9]

Forrest Sherman had just returned from MacArthur's headquarters, where he met with General Sutherland and his staff to discuss the coming invasion of Leyte. While there, he also saw the draft plans for Operation Musketeer, the invasion of Luzon. Even before the first troops landed on the beaches of Leyte, MacArthur was already proposing to the Joint Chiefs that he be allowed to proceed directly with the invasion of Luzon, estimating that he could secure central Luzon and Manila by February 1945. On his return, Sherman met with Nimitz, and they concluded that there were not enough Army divisions and service troops in the Pacific to take both Luzon and Formosa within the March timeframe set by the JCS. On the other hand, they had enough Marines to capture Iwo Jima and enough Seabees to build runways there without Army participation.[10]

Spruance and his wife Margaret arrived at the St. Francis Hotel on 29 September. Always pinching pennies, they were glad to learn that their three-day jaunt would be all expenses paid. Spruance was scheduled to meet with King and Nimitz in the Federal Building downtown. Sherman showed the draft plan to Spruance before the conference. It recommended taking Iwo Jima starting on 20 January and then moving on to Okinawa with a start date of 1 March. "Read it carefully and tell me what you think of it," he asked. Spruance read the plan and handed it back, telling Sherman, "I wouldn't change a thing." After some back and forth, King was convinced. King was well aware that MacArthur's plan for Luzon would likely take precedence over Formosa now that Leyte was set for invasion. Margaret Spruance later recalled that once the meeting was over, her husband and Admiral Nimitz were ebullient, and together with Nimitz's wife, Catherine, they had a fine time in San Francisco. Admiral King also relaxed and joined in some friendly gambling and, doubtless, some drinking as well.[11]

Spruance returned to Pearl Harbor with Nimitz and Sherman on 3 October. They were greeted by a dispatch from the Joint Chiefs ordering MacArthur to seize and occupy Luzon with a target date of 20 December, with full fleet support from Nimitz. For his part, Nimitz was ordered to occupy "one or more positions in Napo Shoto" with a target date of 20 January and "one or more positions in Nansei Shoto" by 1 March 1945. The former is the Japanese name for the island chain that includes Iwo Jima and the Bonin Islands, and the latter is the name for the Ryukyu Islands. Things began to move quickly now. Less than a week later, Causeway was deferred, and planning for Operation Detachment, the invasion of Iwo Jima, was ordered with Spruance in overall command. Plans were to be ready by 25 October. Shortly thereafter came the preliminary warning order for Operation Iceberg, the invasion of Okinawa, with the same command structure as Causeway.[12]

As Spruance and his staff worked on the plans for Detachment, the largest naval battle in history was unfolding to the south. While Spruance was not directly involved in what became known as the Battle of Leyte Gulf, it is worth taking a brief look at that battle to put Spruance's decisions off the Marianas in perspective. While his good friend Bill Halsey orchestrated a brilliant campaign in the South Pacific and achieved a great victory, he also unwittingly placed his fate in the hands of his opponent.

Nimitz's orders to Halsey were clear: "In case the opportunity for destruction of major portion of enemy fleet is offered or can be created, such destruction becomes the primary task." Spruance had received a copy of the operations plan and told Carl Moore that he disagreed with this provision. He was sure that it had been added at the insistence of Towers and the aviators back at Pearl Harbor, who had faulted him for retiring east at the Philippine Sea.[13]

When it became clear that the Americans intended to invade Leyte, on 18 October, Admiral Toyoda transmitted the order to launch Sho-1, his plan for the decisive battle to defend the Philippines. The Sho, or "Victory" plan, was another, but bolder, even desperate, permutation of Plan Z. The Philippine archipelago and its surrounding seas gave Toyoda a far greater scope of operation than had the Marianas. He divided his available ships into three forces, each moving to attack from different directions. Toyoda intended to use the geography of the archipelago to his advantage to enable him to break up the concentrated power of the American forces and defeat them in detail. This time, the transport and supporting forces at the landing beaches were explicitly designated as the main targets.[14]

The Northern Force led by Admiral Ozawa, consisting mainly of the surviving carriers that had run from Spruance in June, approached the Philippines from the north, hoping to lure Halsey and his Third Fleet away and leave the landing forces at Leyte undefended. The Japanese knew from American press reports that Spruance had been criticized for not destroying all of Ozawa's carriers at the Battle of the Philippine Sea. They also knew Halsey's reputation for aggression and counted on him to take the bait. The Center Force, commanded by Admiral Kurita, was the largest and strongest surface fleet ever deployed by the Imperial Navy, consisting of the superbattleships *Yamato* and *Musashi,* accompanied by two fast battleships, ten heavy cruisers, and destroyer escorts. They left the anchorage at Brunei, transited the Sibuyan Sea, and exited the San Bernardino Strait to attack the U.S. Seventh Fleet and the transports in Leyte Gulf. The Southern Force, consisting of the battleships *Fusō* and *Yamashiro*, approached Leyte from the south through the Surigao Strait, and together with the Center Force, they would catch the landing force in Leyte Gulf in a pincer attack.

Early on the morning of 25 October, the Southern Force was detected moving into the Surigao Straits and ambushed by Rear Adm. Jesse Oldendorf's TF 77.2, which annihilated it with long-range fire. A few hours later, Kurita's Center Force exited the San Bernardino Strait and turned south, bearing down on Rear Adm. Clifton Sprague's TG 77.4.3, the Northern Task Group of escort carriers and their destroyer escorts known as Taffy 3. It was entirely due to the bravery, tenacity, and self-sacrifice of the sailors and airmen of Taffy 3 and Sprague's skillful maneuvering that Kurita did not smash that escort carrier task group. Kurita could have pressed on into Leyte Gulf and destroyed the transports and cargo ships there but instead put about and went north, a decision for which he has been heavily criticized, but one that turned a potential disaster into a victory for the U.S. Navy.

Lacking air reconnaissance and operating under radio silence, the Center Force operated in an intelligence vacuum, relying solely on visual sightings. The persistent attacks by carrier planes had led Kurita to believe an American carrier task force was north of his position. Afraid he would be trapped in Leyte Gulf with little room to maneuver, he turned north to attack this phantom fleet, believing that American forces were closing in on him. When he reached the San Bernardino Strait some hours later, he found an empty sea. Kurita was advised that he had just enough fuel to return to base in Brunei, which is what he did.[15]

On the morning of 25 October, Halsey and TF 38 attacked Ozawa's hollowed-out diversionary Northern Force. Ozawa had just one hundred aircraft to defend his fleet, and these were quickly dispatched by Mitscher's veterans. By that afternoon, Mitscher's planes had sunk *Zuikaku*, the last remaining veteran of the Pearl Harbor attack, and the carriers that had eluded him and Spruance four months earlier. It was the decisive carrier victory that Nimitz and the aviation clique had long desired.

In war, the enemy always has a role in determining the outcome of a battle. Here was the signal difference between Halsey's victory at Leyte and Spruance's at the Philippine Sea. By taking a defensive posture, Spruance and TF 58 were assured a victory, and the decisions made by Ozawa only affected the magnitude of that victory. However, Halsey's victory in the north would have been forever tarnished if Kurita had decided to press on and wipe out the landing forces at Leyte Gulf. The political repercussions of such a disaster, coming two weeks before the 1944 presidential election, would likely have resulted in radical changes in the command structure of the Pacific War and the ruination of Halsey's career.[16]

Halsey's defense of his single-minded pursuit of Ozawa was to point at the results of his victory. He forever denied having blundered. MacArthur, who was ashore at Leyte, was under no illusions about what the outcome might have been: "Should the naval covering forces allow either of the powerful advancing Japanese threats to penetrate the Leyte Gulf, the whole Philippine invasion would be placed in the gravest jeopardy. . . . It was fraught with disaster. . . . [Kurita's] powerful naval guns could pulverize any of the eggshell transports . . . and destroy vitally needed supplies on the beachhead. The thousands of U.S troops ashore would be isolated and pinned down helplessly between enemy fire from ground and sea."[17]

The decisions made by Spruance at the Battle of the Philippine Sea and Halsey at Leyte reflected their very different personalities and command styles. When Admiral Ozawa was interrogated after the war, he described Spruance with a Japanese term that could be translated as "cautious," a moniker that Spruance did not particularly like but that also connoted thoughtfulness—a tendency toward careful, logical, and orthodox military thinking. The Japanese believed that on this basis, they could predict Spruance's actions. On the other hand, Ozawa described Halsey as "impulsive," making his actions harder to predict. Halsey demonstrated this to great effect through his actions during the Solomon Islands campaign, which kept the Japanese continuously off balance. However, they could easily predict that waving the red flag in the form of Ozawa's depleted carrier force would be irresistible to "Bull" Halsey.[18]

While Spruance never commented in public on Halsey's decisions at Leyte Gulf, he was pleased by the outcome. At the end of October, he wrote to Margaret, "We have been following with great interest the action of the Philippines. . . . Mitscher and Bill Halsey did a fine job on the outfit that came down from Japan. The heavy force that came through San Bernardino and fell on our CVEs at daylight got off with much less damage. Why any our CVEs escaped to tell the tale nobody knows. The Japs had them then and there, sinking two CVEs, two destroyers, one DE and then let them go. What happened during this whole action was just what I was expecting off Saipan and trying to prevent—being drawn off westward while part of the Jap fleet came in around our flank and hit the amphibious force at Saipan. . . . They still have enough heavy ships left, however, to be, with their shore based air, a formidable outfit if we get over confident. That is something which I am not given to, however."[19]

Spruance also wrote to his old friend Johnny Hoover, expressing his concern about the losses of ships in the ongoing Philippines campaign from the new kamikaze attacks, which included the sinking of the escort carrier USS *St. Lo* (CVE 63) and the damaging of three others. "This suicide method of attack," Spruance wrote, "is very sound and economical warfare especially suited to the Japanese temperament. Unless we can think of some tactical counter to it, perhaps we should stop fighting the products of Japanese aircraft factories . . . and take our carrier air into the center to knock out the factories themselves." Spruance expressed his doubts about the effectiveness of the Army Air Force's "precision" bombing from 30,000 feet: "That might work for large areas but is too slow and inaccurate to take out specific targets." The Iwo Jima operation would provide Spruance with an opportunity for some strategic bombing, Navy style.[20]

Spruance was getting bored with life on shore as he waited for the Philippines campaign to progress enough to release the Third Fleet back to him for Detachment. Most of the problematic planning tasks were handled by Turner's and Holland Smith's staffs. The previous operations provided a ready template for Art Davis and the Fifth Fleet staff to develop the overall operation plan for Detachment. There were many more ships involved, but the basic organization was similar. Iwo Jima was to be a rehearsal for Okinawa, and it was intended that the Fifth Fleet roll from Detachment directly into Iceberg. "I do not have enough work thrust upon me to keep me busy," he wrote to Margaret, "and I am too lazy to dig up work for myself. . . . I feel obliged to keep office hours and reading a book during office hours would not sit well. In other words, I am getting restless to get on with the war."[21]

With time on his hands, Spruance managed to return to his old routine of daily walks and weekly visits to the beach with his staff for swimming. His evenings were often occupied with entertaining old friends and shipmates, attending dinner parties hosted by local high society types, meeting congressional delegations, and standing in for Nimitz when he was away from headquarters. "I am getting to be a regular social butterfly," he wrote Margaret on Christmas Eve, "and it is high time I got out and did some fighting."[22]

The Fifth Fleet's Operation Plan 13–44 was released on 31 December, with D-Day set for 19 February 1945. The basic plan was somewhat simpler than the previous operations as there was just one main objective: "Capture, occupy, and defend Iwo Jima, (and) develop air bases on that island." Spruance, however, added a critical secondary objective to "reduce Japanese naval and air strength and production facilities in the Japanese homeland." At long last, the carrier forces would be unleashed to attack the Japanese Home Islands for the first time since the Doolittle Raid three years previous. Spruance planned to use TF 58 to attack the airfields and aircraft production facilities in and around Tokyo.[23]

There were three basic elements to the plan for Detachment. The first was the Joint Expeditionary Force, once more under Vice Adm. Richmond Kelly Turner, assisted by Jesse Oldendorf, now also a vice admiral thanks to his victory at Surigao. There were three task forces under Turner's command. TF 53, the Attack Force commanded by Rear Adm. Harry Hill, consisted of the attack transports, LSTs, and the landing craft that would carry the Marines ashore. Supporting the assault were ten escort carriers, forty-four transports, eighteen attack cargo ships, sixty-three LSTs, ninety-nine LCIs, and dozens of destroyers, minesweepers, tenders, and other support vessels of TF 52, the Amphibious Support Force commanded by Rear Adm. William H. P. Blandy. The Gunfire and Covering Force, TF 54, which included seven veteran battleships, plus the fast battleships *North Carolina* and *Washington*, would provide naval gunfire as directed, under Rear Adm. Bertram J. Rodgers. Under Turner for the last time was the redoubtable Holland M. Smith in command of the Expeditionary Troops, consisting of Maj. Gen. Harry Schmidt's 4th and 5th Marine Divisions tasked with the initial landings on D-Day, and the 3rd Marine Division under Maj. Gen. Graves B. Erskine, as the reserves. Aside from three companies of DUKW amphibious trucks, the Army troop presence during the assault phase of the operation was minimal.

The second element was Marc Mitscher's Fast Carrier Force, TF 58, which, as before, included four carrier task groups with eleven fleet carriers and five light carriers. Under Mitscher was Vice Adm. Willis Lee commanding TF 59, the Striking Force, now with eight fast battleships and a flanking force of nine light cruisers and thirty-four destroyers. The third element consisted of the task groups directly under Fifth Fleet control, as well as the Search and Reconnaissance Group and the Anti-Submarine Group. Logistics, as always, remained a major concern for Spruance, and he assigned the Logistics Support Group, ServRon 6, commanded by Rear Adm. Donald B. Beary, to accompany the fleet. This group had six escort carriers to provide replacement aircraft, plus a number of fleet oilers and ammunition ships. Two of the latter were specially equipped to transfer bombs and ammunition while underway. Spruance mentioned this need to King and Nimitz during their meeting on Saipan, and the Bureau of Ships developed a workable solution. Altogether, Spruance had more than six hundred ships of all types under his command.[24]

"Iwo Jima" translates to "Sulphur Island," a fitting name, as that mineral was its primary export and its smell permeates the place. As part of the Tokyo Prefecture, it would be the first piece of sovereign Japanese territory to be assaulted by the Allies. When Spruance first told Smith that Iwo Jima was the objective, he replied, "It will be the toughest place we have had to take. I don't know what anybody wants it for, but I'll take it."[25]

There were valid reasons why this hunk of volcanic rock had to be taken. Located some 670 miles due south of Tokyo and nearly halfway between the Home Islands and the Marianas, it was large enough to build runways capable of supporting heavy bombers. The B-29s of the XXI Bomber Command of the 20th Air Force had been operating from Tinian since late November, and an air base located halfway to Japan would provide an excellent place for damaged bombers and bombers running low on fuel to land. Its location also put it within the operational range of the P-51 fighters that the Army Air Force wanted to use to escort the B-29s on their runs over Japan. Seizing the island would also deny the Japanese use of the airfields there and eliminate the radio and radar installations that gave early warning of incoming bombing raids.

Iwo Jima is eight square miles of volcanic rock and sand, described as resembling a burned pork chop, five miles across at its widest point. At the southern tip of the "chop" is Mount Suribachi, a volcanic vent rising 556 feet above sea level with commanding views of the entire island. The southeastern side of the island has a strip of beach more than 3,000 yards long. Unlike previous operations, there was no coral reef, which permitted LSTs and LCVPs to come right up to the water's edge to unload. Just beyond the beaches are a series of terraces created by wave action and volcanic uplift. The ground continues to rise from here for another 700 yards to the central area of the island, which is relatively flat and was dominated by the runways of Air Field No. 1. North of this, the island widens, with the ground rising to the Motoyama Plain and Air Field No. 2, and thence to a barren, broken terrain of gullies and deep defiles at the north end of the island.

In June 1944, Lieutenant General Kuribayashi Tadamichi arrived on the island to assume command of the garrison. He decided to follow the example of the defense of Peleliu and use the terrain and geology of the island to his advantage. The volcanic rock was soft enough to be excavated with hand tools, and he directed the construction of bunkers deep underground, interconnected by an elaborate network of tunnels that linked them with natural caves and the heavily reinforced concrete pillboxes and blockhouses on the surface. These were carefully camouflaged and equipped with steel doors that could open and close rapidly to conceal firing positions. The landing beaches and the areas beyond were registered for indirect mortar and artillery fire, and boat guns and heavy artillery emplacements were located to pour fire on the eastern beaches from Mount Suribachi in the south and from an old quarry on the north end.

MacArthur's Philippines campaign took longer than anticipated, giving Kuribayashi additional time to bolster his defenses. Despite the continuing harassment by air and convoy sinkings by American submarines, by February 1945, Kuribayashi had managed to move more than 16,000 army and 7,000 naval forces to the island, including twenty-two tanks, nearly four hundred heavy artillery pieces and large mortars, one hundred 75-mm or larger antiaircraft guns, more than two hundred 20-mm and 25-mm antiaircraft guns, and almost seventy antitank guns. The Combined Fleet had failed to save the defenders of the Marianas, and Kuribayashi was under no illusions about his fate or that of his troops. Kuribayashi forbade his men to waste their lives in mass suicide attacks, telling them that if they were to die for the emperor, then "each man will make it his duty to kill ten of the enemy before dying."[26]

Spruance and his staff moved aboard *Indianapolis* and on 14 January set sail for Ulithi, where they arrived on 25 January. Halsey arrived the same day aboard *New Jersey*, and two days later, the Third Fleet became the Fifth Fleet again. Spruance asked Maj. Gen. Curtis E. LeMay, USA, who had just taken command of the XXI Bomber Command, to fly in from Tinian to discuss how his superbombers might support Detachment. Mindful of Holland Smith's comments, Spruance took the opportunity to ask LeMay, "What do you think about the value of Iwo Jima?" LeMay answered immediately, "Oh, but it's going to be of tremendous value to me. Without Iwo Jima, I couldn't bomb Japan effectively." The nearly 3,000-mile round trip from Tinian forced the bombers to reduce their payloads to carry enough fuel for the mission. Iwo Jima could be used to refuel bombers making the return flight.[27]

Indianapolis departed Ulithi on 8 February for Saipan, where Spruance met with Turner, Holland Smith, and Harry Hill to finalize the details for Detachment. Holland Smith and his Marines had been working on the assault planning since early October. When the Marine planners looked at the latest reconnaissance photos, the number of defensive positions and gun emplacements had actually increased since the heavy bombardment campaign began in October. Smith and his generals wanted to hit these with "a superabundance of fire," laid on with precision, something that took careful aerial spotting. They objected to the fact that the operation plan called for just three days of preliminary bombardment and requested that the naval bombardment last at least ten days. Spruance turned them down, citing the fact that his gunfire support ships did not carry enough ammunition for a bombardment of such duration as well as to have enough on hand for the planned prelanding bombardment on D-Day. Sending the ships back to Ulithi for replenishment would unacceptably delay the landings. Spruance also sought to maintain a degree of tactical surprise, fearing that a prolonged bombardment might allow the Japanese time to marshal a coordinated air and surface counterattack. The Marines, however, felt that their concerns had once again fallen victim to "naval expediency."[28]

Spruance departed Saipan on 12 February and rendezvoused with TF 58, heading for a position east of the Bonin Islands two days later, where they met Beary's fleet oilers and refueled. They then shaped a course to approach Tokyo from the southeast. At dawn of 16 February a fighter sweep was launched, followed by carrier bombers that hit the airfields and aircraft factories around Tokyo Bay. However, heavy rain and a low cloud ceiling hampered the operation, and the bombing was not as effective as hoped. The attacks were repeated the next day, but again bad weather limited the results. Nevertheless, Spruance reported that the carrier planes of TF 58 shot down 332 planes and destroyed another 177 on the ground while losing 49 in combat and another 21 operationally. Several airframe and aircraft engine plants were hit, and an escort carrier was sunk. He noted that the air defense was "non-aggressive" and that the Imperial Navy made no response. TF 58 then withdrew south to support the Iwo Jima operation, which by then was well underway.[29]

The ships of TF 54 arrived offshore at 0600 on 16 February, and together with the escort carriers of Blandy's TF 52, they began the scheduled three-day preliminary bombardment. The island had been carefully divided into zones, each assigned to a specific ship, for general bombardment. The gunfire support ships were stationed on both the east and west sides of the island. Bad weather in the form of rain squalls and low clouds made aerial spotting difficult, and to conserve ammunition Blandy ordered his ships to fire only when a target had been clearly identified. When a ceasefire was ordered at 1800, the ships retired beyond the range of any surviving shore batteries. An accurate assessment of the results was hampered by poor visibility.

Clearing skies the next morning gave Blandy some hope that better results could be obtained as the bombardment resumed. Minesweepers swept the boat lanes, followed at 1100 by UDT frogmen, whose job was to look for underwater obstacles. They were supported by twelve LCI(G)s firing rockets to suppress any small-arms fire directed at the divers. For the most part, Kuribayashi's gunners had held their fire up to this point, but thinking perhaps that the invasion was in progress, heavy artillery fire now erupted from all along the eastern side of the island, revealing previously undisclosed positions. Enduring nearly an hour and a half of fire, all twelve of the LCI(G)s were heavily damaged, with one a total loss. Despite the severity of the previous air and naval bombardments, it was clear that the defenders still had tremendous firepower at their disposal.

Blandy now directed that all naval gunfire be concentrated on the landing zones and the areas behind the beaches and on identified targets at the base of Mount Suribachi and high ground north of the beaches. Taking advantage of the good weather, carrier planes strafed, bombed, and dropped napalm; however, as the Running Summary noted, the "majority of known installations apparently remain intact."[30]

On the third day of the preliminary bombardment, poor weather conditions again prevailed, but the sheer scale of the bombardment began to have some effect. Rodgers ordered four of his veteran battleships and one cruiser to move within as little as 1,800 yards of the eastern beaches and concentrate their fire on the base of Suribachi and the rim of the quarry. When the firing ended at 1830 on 18 February, Blandy estimated that most of the coastal guns and the dual-purpose 5-inch guns on the east side had been silenced and that 80 percent of the blockhouses and more than half of the nearly one hundred concrete pillboxes had been destroyed or heavily damaged. He advised Turner that due to the weather, there was still ammunition allowance available. He recommended another day of bombardment but noted that the landings could proceed the next day "if necessary."

Holland Smith remained apprehensive, and the burden of sending his beloved Marines into the maw of Kuribayashi's well-prepared defenses weighed heavily on his spirits. At a press briefing that night, Smith, with Secretary of the Navy James V. Forrestal standing beside him, gloomily predicted that of the 60,000 troops being sent ashore, one in four would become a casualty. As it turned out, Smith underestimated the losses.[31]

Early on D-Day, Monday 19 February, Rear Adm. Harry Hill and TF 53 arrived with more than 450 ships carrying the three Marine divisions along with their equipment, supplies, and the landing craft to transport them to the beaches. The first wave of eight battalions mounted the LVTs lined up on the tank decks of the LSTs and waited for the word to depart. The weather had cleared, the seas were relatively calm, and the air temperature was 68 degrees F—a perfect day for an invasion. The bombardment began again at 0640. Spruance had arrived aboard *Indianapolis*, bringing *North Carolina* and *Washington* to add their considerable firepower. At 0730, they were joined by dozens of LCI(G)s firing rockets and mortar rounds onto

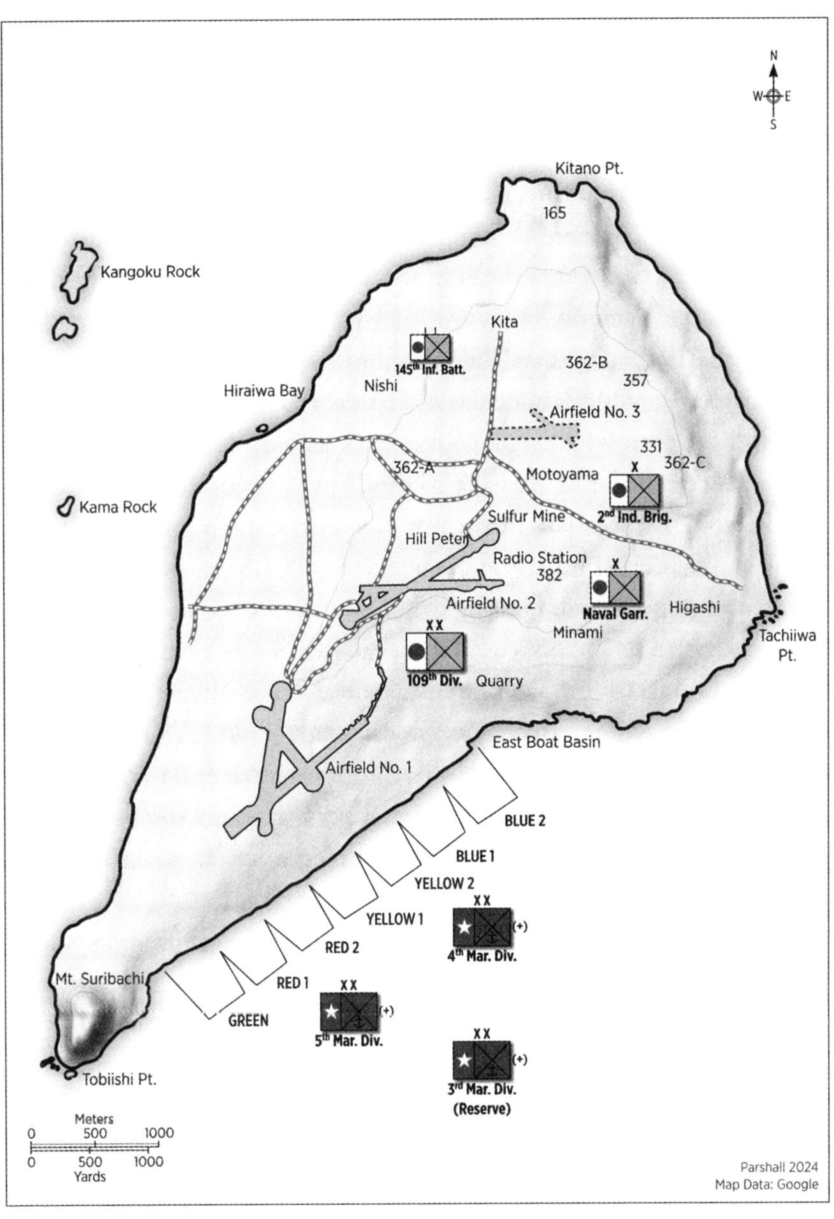

MAP 12. The Invasion of Iwo Jima, 19 February 1945

the beaches and slopes of Suribachi. At the same time, the LVTs began to take their place along the Line of Departure, which was located two miles offshore. The bombardment lifted at 0800 to allow the carrier planes to make two passes over the island and resumed again at 0825. At 0830, the Amtracks left the Line of Departure, and as they neared the beaches the naval gunfire became a rolling barrage reminiscent of an earlier age, designed to stay 400 yards ahead of the approach. The first LVTs hit the beaches just before 0900.[32]

The 5th Marine Division landed on the Green and Red beaches closest to Suribachi. The 28th Regiment was on the extreme left, tasked with moving across the narrowest part of the island to cut Suribachi off from the rest of the Japanese defenses. The 4th Marine Division landed on the Yellow and Blue beaches, the latter closest to the quarry. Their job was to move inland and take Air Field No. 1, then pivot north. There was, however, an unexpected impediment. Getting to the first terrace required the landing forces to climb a steep slope covered with loose volcanic sand. While some LVTs could traverse the slopes, most could not, and the Marines had to advance inland on foot. Succeeding waves came in on LCVPs, and after forty-five minutes, a total of 9,000 Marines were ashore. The Marines likened moving through the deep volcanic sand to walking through a grain elevator, and as they soon discovered, digging foxholes was an exercise in frustration. Wheeled vehicles quickly bogged down in the loose sand, and tanks lost their tracks. As the Marines came over the terraces and moved inland, they were met with little opposition but a smattering of machine gun fire from local defenders on their immediate front. Waiting patiently until the landing areas were crowded with men, machines, and landing craft, Kuribayashi gave the order at to begin firing at 1000. The Japanese heavy mortar and artillery gunners opened fire, their weapons preregistered to hit the landing zone, with the 4th Marine Division on the right bearing the brunt.[33]

By 1035, the 28th Marines had crossed to the island's west side and begun to prepare to assault Suribachi, but the intensity of fire prevented them from making much headway. To their right, the other Marine units also attempted to move across the island. Many of the pillboxes and blockhouses were still intact and had to be taken out one by one with a combination of grenades, satchel charges, and flamethrowers. The tanks that made it ashore were quickly pressed into service to provide point-blank fire support. Army DUKWs driven by African American soldiers braved the intense fire to land Marine artillery that promptly went into action. By the end of D-Day, six Marine infantry regiments and six artillery battalions totaling more than 30,000 men had landed, but they had also suffered heavy casualties. Most of the Japanese heavy artillery on the slopes of Suribachi was destroyed, but indirect fire from the north of the island continued to fall on the beaches, now congested with broken vehicles and wrecked landing craft. Despite the shelling, supplies and men kept moving ashore, and the wounded were evacuated to waiting hospital ships. The Blue and Yellow beaches were closed to traffic due to the amount of wreckage that had accumulated there.[34]

Savage fighting continued for the next three days, with the Marines making slow progress against an enemy determined to fight to the last. Tank-infantry teams assaulted the caves, pillboxes, and blockhouses. Marines with flamethrowers advanced under the cover of suppressive fire to shoot liquid flame into the open embrasures, followed by grenades and high explosives. To their dismay, positions to their rear that they thought had been cleared often came back to life. The strong points were interconnected with tunnels and had multiple entrances and exits so that new troops could replace their dead comrades. For the first time in the Pacific War, the Marines encountered antipersonnel mines carefully laid in the likely avenues of advance. But as the days wore on, the volume of defensive fire slowly slackened as positions were knocked out and defenders were killed. By the night of 20 February, Air Field No. 1 was overrun, and the Red and Green beaches had been cleared so that the DUKWs and LSTs could continue to land troops and supplies.[35]

While Spruance watched the invasion from the bridge of *Indianapolis* and followed the progress of the Marines on the radio, his mind was on the next operation. He provided Nimitz with an ambitious schedule for the continuation of Jamboree, as the operation to bomb Tokyo was named, to include additional missions to hit Kyushu and Okinawa, set to begin on 25 February. Nimitz cautioned that sufficient time had to be allowed for TF 58 to rest and replenish at Ulithi, and there could be no delay in commencing Iceberg. On 21 February Secretary Forrestal came aboard *Indianapolis* to congratulate Spruance on the operation's progress. Spruance showed him the aerial photos of the bombing of Tokyo, which surely must have gladdened the Secretary's heart.[36]

Near sunset of 21 February, it was the turn of the sailors of TF 58 to suffer an attack as the fleet was hit by fifty kamikaze aircraft. Taking advantage of the low visibility, five attacked the escort carriers of TG 52.2, damaging USS *Lunga Point* (CVE 94) and sinking USS *Bismarck Sea* (CVE 95), with the loss of 318 men. The venerable *Saratoga* was also hit, badly damaging her flight deck and causing fires on her hangar deck. The big veteran survived but was knocked out of the war, retiring to Bremerton for repairs. A minelayer and two LSTs were also damaged.[37]

In Spruance's mind, these losses reinforced the need to strike the Home Islands again, as he told Mitscher the next day. "Destruction of engine plants Tokyo area remains our most important objective if enemy air strength is the be checked at source," Spruance wrote in his dispatch. "Events such as those this area last night can be eliminated only by attack at the source as well as on forces already in operation." Spruance was anxious to get TF 58 on the move again. A few hours later, he sent a message to Nimitz telling him that while the dogged resistance on Iwo Jima was likely to delay the date when the airfields would be up and running again, he believed, based on reports from Turner and his own staff Marine officers, that Iwo Jima could be left without direct fleet support.[38]

On the evening of 22 February, Spruance departed Iwo Jima to join TF 58 for the next Tokyo mission. As they sailed north toward Japan they encountered heavy weather, and the storms damaged four destroyers. As before, they destroyed any picket boats along the way, and although the Japanese were aware of their approach, they were helpless to make any serious naval response. Bombing runs on two aircraft engine plants were made on 25 February, but the bad weather hampered the operation and the attacks scheduled for the next day were called off. Radford's TG 58.4 headed for Ulithi while Mitscher took his three other groups to raid Okinawa on 1 March and obtain photo reconnaissance. They then sailed south to join Radford at Ulithi on 4 March for maintenance and replenishment in preparation for Iceberg.[39]

As TF 58 steamed toward Tokyo, an event on Iwo Jima marked a watershed in the assault. On the morning of 23 February, Marines of the 28th Regiment carefully picked their way up the slopes of Mount Suribachi, which they had neutralized the day before. On reaching the crest they found a piece of water pipe, a remainder of one of the island's rainwater catchments, to which they attached the national flag, "Old Glory," and at 1020 they raised it for all to see. Their progress had been closely watched from below, and upon seeing the flag go up, spontaneous cheers erupted from every Marine on the island. Across the entire fleet, ships' sirens and whistles sounded. Forrestal, who had gone ashore with Holland Smith that morning, said as they watched, "Holland, the raising of that flag on Suribachi means a Marine Corps for the next five hundred years."[40]

The Seabees had carved roads leading out of the landing areas and into the island's interior. By 25 February, they had sufficiently repaired the runways of Air Field No. 1 to land light OY-1 spotter aircraft, followed by transport and cargo planes. Work had progressed sufficiently under sporadic mortar fire that on 4 March the first B-29, "Dinah Might," made an emergency landing, refueled, and flew on to Tinian.[41]

In the forenoon of 3 March, Spruance reported to Nimitz: "Situation ashore much better and success assured. Assume you concur with departure TF 58 this general area as planned on completion of fueling today." By then, after horrific fighting and mounting casualties, the Marines had pushed through the main defensive line and eliminated the bulk of the defending forces. But thousands more remained, dug deep into the rock on the island's north end. One aerial observer described the battle scene as unlike any other, with Marines moving over the surface against an unseen, underground enemy.[42]

General Schmidt called a halt on 5 March so that his Marines could rest and regroup. Spruance went ashore that day for the first and only time. Harry Hill sent his admiral's barge to pick up Spruance and Art Davis, from which they transferred to an LCT bringing cargo ashore. They landed on the western beaches and found the southern end of Iwo Jima swarming with men and supplies. They walked over to Air Field No. 1, where DC-3s were evacuating the wounded back to Guam. He spoke with a man who had been wounded just hours previously and a Navy nurse who attended to the evacuees on the plane. Spruance and Davis were driven in a jeep up to Air Field No. 2, but as this was within range of Japanese mortar fire they did not tarry long. At the 5th Marine Division headquarters, Spruance conferred with its commander, Maj. Gen. Keller E. Rockey. The reality of war was driven home when, during their meeting, it was learned that one of Rockey's most trusted battalion commanders had just been killed.[43]

Spruance and Davis returned to *Indianapolis* and departed for Guam at 1600. Iwo Jima was declared secured on 16 March, but pockets of Japanese defenders still fought to the last. Early on the morning of 26 March, a group of several hundred Japanese, reportedly led by Kuribayashi and his remaining staff officers, infiltrated the Marine lines and attacked a rear area encampment, killing dozens of sleeping pilots and men of the VII Fighter Command and wounding many more until stopped by the Marines of the 5th Pioneer Battalion. Kuribayashi's body was never identified.[44]

The butcher's bill for Detachment was staggering, and for the first time, the total American casualties exceeded those of the Japanese. In thirty-six days of fighting, 6,479 Marines and Navy corpsmen had been killed and another 18,378 wounded, with more than 22,000 Japanese soldiers and naval personnel estimated to have been killed. The ratio of killed in action was similar to that of Tarawa but on a far greater scale.[45]

While on Guam, Spruance visited one of the base hospitals there and was touched by the sacrifices that had been made to take Iwo Jima. "Seeing our badly wounded, especially the men who will suffer permanent disability," he wrote Margaret, "takes a lot of enjoyment out of a successful operation. I understand some of our sob fraternity have been raising the devil about our casualties on Iwo. I would have thought by this time they would have learned that you can't make war on a tough, fanatical enemy like the Japs without our people getting hurt and killed. I recommended both Iwo and the next operation. . . . It's going to be very expensive to us, but the result should be of the greatest value in pushing the war along." He told her that he was mailing home a copy of Joe Rosenthal's iconic photo of the Marines raising the flag on Suribachi, calling it "the finest photo this war has given us. . . . When we settle down I want to have this photo framed." Spruance added prophetically, "Some first-class sculptor should do this in bronze; it is so perfect."[46]

CHAPTER 14

OPERATION ICEBERG

The Capture of Okinawa

OKINAWA IS THE LARGEST ISLAND of the Ryukyu archipelago, also known as the Nansei Shoto, a group of islands that extend south from Kyushu to the northern coast of Formosa (modern-day Taiwan). While Okinawa was a prefecture of Japan proper, it was not part of the empire until annexed in 1879, and its indigenous people were treated as second-class subjects. Since it was located just over 325 miles from the Japanese mainland, both sides knew that the island provided an excellent base to stage an invasion of the Home Islands. Whoever occupied it could also control the sea lines of communication from the south and cut off Japan from the oil and raw materials needed to run its war machine, as well as access to imported food staples such as rice, upon which Japan depended. The vast effort that the Allies put forth to take Okinawa, and the fury of the Japanese in its defense, was indicative of the strategic importance of the objective.[1]

Okinawa is sixty-six miles in length, from Hedo Point in the extreme north to Ara Cape at the south, containing some 460 square miles of mostly hilly broken limestone rock, with the northern and southern halves of the island connected by the narrow Ishikawa Isthmus. The island's northern half is very rugged and sparsely populated, while south of the isthmus has most of the agricultural land and population, which numbered approximately 800,000 in 1945. On the east side lies the wide Nagagusuku Bay, with its many small islands, offering a large, sheltered anchorage. The southern third of the island features a series of high limestone ridges that run roughly from northeast to southwest. On the highest and most central of these ridges is Shuri Castle, the ancient capital of the Ryukyu Kingdom, overlooking the port of Naha to the southwest.

Spruance's Operation Plan 1–45 for Iceberg, the capture of Okinawa and the northern Ryukyus, was released on 3 January, with the landing date, L-Day, set for 1 April 1945. For this operation, there were two basic elements in the Fifth Fleet, the first being Spruance's TF 50, which included Mitscher's TF 58, whose primary task was to isolate the objective from attack and reinforcement by Japanese naval and air forces. The second element was the Joint Expeditionary Force, TF 51, under Vice Adm. Richmond Kelly Turner, comprising the troops themselves and the vast armada of ships that carried them, provided naval gunfire, and offered close air support.

Lt. Gen. Simon Bolivar Buckner Jr., USA, was now in command of the Expeditionary Troops, comprising the Tenth Army, a force combining the Army's XXIV Corps, commanded by Maj. Gen. John R. Hodge, and the Marine Corps' Third Amphibious Corps, commanded by Maj. Gen. Roy Geiger. Buckner had been slated to command the Tenth Army for Operation Causeway, but when that was canceled, the troops and resources were reassigned to Iceberg. In addition, the Joint Chiefs wanted the Army to assume the primary responsibility for the land campaign on Okinawa as a rehearsal for the main event, Operation Olympic, the invasion of Japan.

Four naval task forces under Turner's command supported the amphibious assault. TF 53, the Northern Attack Force commanded by Rear Adm. Lawrence F. Reifsnider, consisted of the attack transports, LSTs, and the landing craft slated to carry the Third Amphibious Corps ashore. TF 55, the Southern Attack Force under Rear Adm. John L. Hall Jr., would land the XXIV Corps. In direct support of the landings were the twenty-one escort carriers, fifteen light cruisers, dozens of destroyers, minesweepers, tenders, and other support vessels of TF 52, the Amphibious Support Force commanded by Rear Adm. William H. P. Blandy. The Gunfire and Covering Force, TF 54, under Rear Adm. Morton L. Deyo, would provide naval gunfire as directed from its ten veteran battleships, thirteen cruisers, and thirty-four destroyers and destroyer escorts. Marc Mitscher's TF 58 included four carrier task groups with eleven fleet carriers and six light carriers. Vice Adm. Willis Lee aboard *South Dakota* retained command of TF 59, the Striking Force, with eight fast battleships, eleven light cruisers, and twenty-three destroyers. *Indianapolis* was also part of this group but could be detached as the commander of the Fifth Fleet saw fit for duties elsewhere. Altogether, Spruance had nearly nine hundred ships of all types under his command, the largest invasion fleet yet assembled in the Pacific War.[2]

Spruance and Turner aboard *Indianapolis* arrived at Ulithi on 9 March 1945 to meet with Mitscher and discuss his schedule of operations. On the evening of 11 March, Spruance and TF 58 got a foretaste of things to come when USS *Randolph* (CV 15) was hit by one of two twin-engine kamikaze planes while at anchor in the Ulithi lagoon, damaging her flight deck and wrecking a number of aircraft. They appeared without warning and caught the air defense crews flat-footed. Fortunately, the damage was such that she could be repaired by ServRon 10 at Ulithi, but exactly when she could rejoin TF 58 was uncertain. Based on Mitscher's recommendation, Spruance requested that CinCPac release four additional escort carriers to compensate for this and other carriers lost during the Luzon operation. The scale of close air-support operations required for Iceberg and the suppression of the airfields on Kyushu required that replacement aircraft and pilots be made available as soon as possible.[3]

Spruance's nemesis in the campaign was an old adversary whose name was probably not even known to him: Vice Admiral Ugaki Matome. Ugaki had been Yamamoto's Chief of Staff at Midway and had commanded the First Battleship Division of the Combined Fleet from the bridge of the *Yamato* at the Battle of the Philippine Sea. Following the defeat at Leyte, his fleet was disbanded, but he found new employment as the commander of the Fifth Air Fleet, based at the Kanoya air base on Kyushu. His remit was to defend the Nansei Shoto, the Southwest Islands, and Kyushu from Allied invasion, utilizing the Special Attack Units, including the kamikaze "Divine Wind" suicide aircraft, as his primary means of attack. That a longtime battleship admiral should command such a force and have been reduced to such tactics was emblematic of how far the Imperial Japanese Navy had fallen. While Ugaki might have preferred an epic battleship duel, he nevertheless fully embraced the ethos of samurai self-sacrifice. He was also realistic enough to see that the only path open to Japan was to wear down American resolve and hope for a negotiated peace. "I have to break through this crisis with diehard struggles," he declared in his diary.[4]

Unbeknownst to Spruance, the mysterious attack on *Randolph* at Ulithi had been one of the first fruits of Ugaki's offensive to destroy the American carrier fleet before it could attack. It was a bold plan but poorly executed. Twenty-four Yokosuka P1Y Ginga twin-engine bombers, each carrying an 800-kg bomb capable of sinking the largest ship, had set out on 11 March for a 1,600-mile, one-way suicide mission to attack the Fifth Fleet anchored in Ulithi lagoon, hoping to destroy the carriers in one fell swoop. Less than half even reached the lagoon, and only two raiders managed to find a target thanks to poor training, poor weather, and darkness. The attack was considered a failure when snoopers from Truk overflew Ulithi the next day and found the American carrier fleet intact. The Japanese naval aircrews had once been the masters of night attacks, but those experienced flyers were now gone, and Spruance's luck had prevailed again. A frustrated Ugaki resolved to do better in the future.[5]

TF 58 sailed from Ulithi on 14 March, and while underway Spruance received the news that TF 113, the fast carriers of the British Pacific Fleet commanded by Vice Admiral Sir H. Bernard Rawlings, RN, would be joining Iceberg. Admiral Sir Bruce Fraser, RN, the commander of the British Pacific Fleet, had been seeking a more active role in the Pacific War since the beginning of the year. After some back and forth with Admiral King and some lobbying by Nimitz, it was decided that Rawlings' five British carriers could be best utilized operating as an adjunct to the Pacific Fleet, albeit with their own supply and logistics. King had preferred the British Pacific Fleet to operate against the Japanese forces in Southeast Asia, but the request by Spruance and Mitscher for additional carriers may have finally decided the issue. Rawlings' force was, however, subject to recall with seven days' notice should King decide to use them elsewhere.[6]

The Royal Navy's carriers joined Iceberg at a propitious time. Unlike during previous operations, where the Japanese defenders were far from their core territory, Okinawa was within range of airfields on Kyushu and Formosa, as well as many others scattered throughout the islands of the Ryukyu archipelago. While the Allies could isolate Okinawa with a ring of steel, the Japanese were still able to ferry aircraft into the battle through bases in China and directly from the factories in the Home Islands, where aircraft production was given top priority. The job of TF 113, now designated

TF 57, was to defend the operation's southern flank and suppress the airfields on Formosa and in the Sakishima Islands of the southern Ryukyus.[7]

TF 58 began striking the airfields on Kyushu on the morning of 18 March from a position about 75 miles south of the Home Island of Shikoku. The strike planes encountered little opposition when they arrived over the airbases on Kyushu, as on the previous night Ugaki had located the four task groups of TF 58 and had already dispatched his planes, a combined force of Special Attack Units and regular bombers, to attack Mitscher's force. While the Americans bombed and strafed at will, Ugaki's raiders found their targets. *Enterprise* of TG 58.2, *Yorktown*, and USS *Intrepid* (CV 11) of TG 58.4 were hit but remained operational for the remainder of the day. The damage to *Enterprise* and *Intrepid*, however, was such that they were sent to Ulithi for repairs.

The battle continued the next day as TF 58 continued to target the naval installations on Honshu, where they found and bombed the battleship *Yamato* in Kure harbor, as well as other warships, docks, and fuel storage facilities. However, the carriers of TF 58 suffered far worse damage from the Fifth Air Fleet. *Wasp* of TG 58.1 had a 250-kg bomb penetrate her hangar deck to explode in a crew galley below, killing more than one hundred men. USS *Franklin* (CV 13) of TG 58.2 was hit by two such bombs which penetrated the hangar deck, hit the fueled and armed aircraft there, and caused massive damage. The cruiser USS *Santa Fe* (CL 60) was damaged as she came alongside to help extinguish the fires and take crewmen aboard. *Franklin* was nearly abandoned, but at Spruance's insistence, she was saved. Regaining steering control, she slowly sailed back to Ulithi under her own power in company with *Santa Fe*, "down by the tail but chin up," but her damage was so great that her war was over. She had lost nearly 800 crew killed and 265 wounded, in addition to fifty-nine aircraft. With five carriers out of action, Mitscher reorganized TF 58 into three task groups and headed for Okinawa to support the preparatory bombardment.[8]

Turner's task forces were now converging on Okinawa, coming from Pavuvu, Saipan, Luzon, and Ulithi. The first to arrive on L-7 were Blandy's TF 52, the Amphibious Support Group, and Deyo's TF 54, the Gunfire and Covering Force. As Blandy's carrier planes began

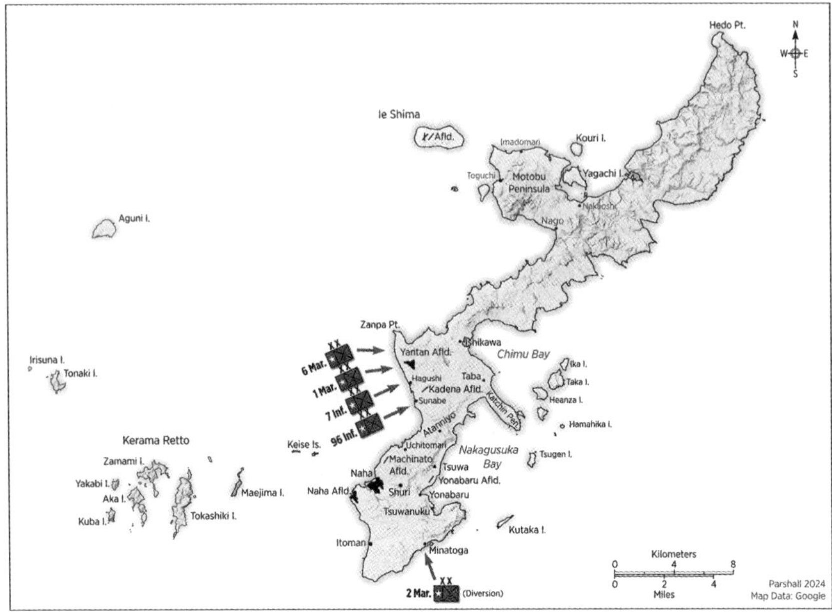

MAP 13. The Invasion of Okinawa, 1 April 1945

aerial bombardment, Deyo's veteran battleships and cruisers began the most extensive and intense naval bombardment of the war. Minesweepers scoured the shallow waters off the proposed landing beaches on the west coast of Okinawa and the islands of Kerama Retto, finding and destroying several hundred mines.

Kerama Retto was to be seized and occupied as a prelude to the main landings. This group of small islands, some twenty miles due west of Naha, was ideal as a safe anchorage for the ships of the Joint Expeditionary Force and a secure base for logistics, repair, and maintenance during the operation. The minesweepers and UDT teams found little in the way of mines or beach obstacles, and the 77th Infantry landed on 26 March against minimal opposition. The island group was secured three days later. A seaplane base was quickly established to provide long-distance search, antisubmarine, and Dumbo air rescue patrols.[9]

On L-1, two battalions of 155-mm artillery from the XXIV Corps were established on Keise Shima, a group of four islets six miles from Naha. From here, the Long Toms could provide artillery coverage over the landing zone and a large sector of the southern end of Okinawa. A ring of radar pickets, located 15 to 100 miles offshore, was established at sixteen points around Okinawa using destroyers and minesweepers. Aboard each were fighter director teams to vector the carrier-borne CAP to meet any incoming flights of attackers. As will be seen, they not only provided vital early warning, but they also absorbed the brunt of the suicide attacks.[10]

The initial kamikaze attacks continued daily, weather permitting, but on a relatively small scale. Early on 31 March, Spruance experienced the first of two such attacks on one of his flagships, as *Indianapolis* was engaged in shore bombardment of the landing zone along with the rest of TF 54. Four raiders attacked the shore bombardment group; three were shot down, but one made it through. Charles Barber was on the forecastle when he saw the plane roll over and dive on the ship. It hit the port side aft and bounced off, but the 250-kg bomb it carried sliced through *Indianapolis*' side, through the condenser room and the double bottom, and exploded under the ship. The two portside and the inner starboard side propeller shafts were damaged. Nine men were killed, including Barber's yeoman, and twenty were wounded. Operating on just the outer starboard propeller, she limped into the anchorage at Kerama Retto for repairs. Spruance and Capt. Emmet P. Forrestel, his operations officer, transferred to *New Mexico* several days later. Left behind with the rest of the administrative staff, Barber recalled that he felt like a sitting duck, as *Indianapolis* was one of the largest ships in the anchorage and, therefore, a prime target.[11]

Early on the morning of 1 April, Easter Sunday, the Northern and Southern Attack Forces arrived on the west side of Okinawa, and the transports and LSTs took their positions with respect to their targeted landing beaches. The wide beaches on the west coast of Okinawa, centered on the village of Hagushi, were considered the best place to land four infantry divisions abreast simultaneously. The Hagushi beaches were also in close proximity to the two main airfields located at Kadena and Yontan, a primary objective of the first phase of the assault. The previous day, the UDT teams had blown up more than two thousand wooden stakes driven into the reef in front of the Hagushi area. The shore bombardment commenced again at 0408 on Turner's order, and at 0700, the Marines of the Third

Amphibious Corps and GIs of the XXIV Corps debarked their transports and boarded the waiting LVT(A)s and DUKWs.

The bombardment had blasted large gaps in the seawall that planners feared would impede the landing. As the landing craft approached the beaches, carrier planes repeatedly strafed the landing zone and dropped napalm. From left to right, the 6th Marine and 1st Marine Divisions of the Third Amphibious Corps landed north of Hagushi, while the 7th and 96th Infantry Divisions of the XXIV Corps landed to the south. The first waves hit the beach at 0835, meeting only a desultory fire from scattered mortars and a handful of shore batteries. The LVT(A)s drove through the gaps in the seawall, disgorged their human cargo, and then returned to the Line of Departure for more. The succeeding waves of infantry were joined by tanks arriving aboard LCMs or driven ashore with floatation devices. The divisional artillery arrived soon after and set up their gun batteries.

All four divisions quickly moved inland without any meaningful opposition, finding the few remaining defensive works manned by service troops and home guards but little evidence of the Imperial Army. By 1300, the Marine and Army divisions had moved past their initial objectives and overrun both the Yontan and the Kadena airfields. As the Marine divisions pushed east to Nagagusuku Bay and north to the Ishikawa Isthmus, the 7th Infantry captured Kadena and headed east on the flank of the 1st Marine Division. The 96th Infantry Division swung south to block any counterattack against the landing zone. Within eight hours, 50,000 troops had landed across a front 15,000 yards wide and 4,000 to 5,000 yards deep, taking extremely light casualties. Across the front, the Americans dug in for the night, expecting a counterattack that never came. The big question on everyone's mind was: where was the Imperial Japanese Army?[12]

The main Japanese military force on Okinawa was the 32nd Army, which consisted of two regular Imperial Army divisions reinforced by independent regiments and battalions, totaling an estimated 77,000 men, split evenly between infantry and artillery units. A naval base force, estimated at 3,500 strong, was composed of mostly service troops untrained for infantry combat but who could be effectively pressed into service to defend fixed fortifications. A force of poorly trained Okinawan reservists known as the *Boeitai*, numbering around 20,000 men, were integrated into Imperial Army units or hastily organized into home guard battalions. Non-uniformed laborers and other civilians drafted into service could add another 20,000 men. Altogether, the Japanese defenders totaled more than 110,000 men.[13]

These forces were commanded by Lieutenant General Ushijima Mitsuru, an experienced commander who knew that his enemy possessed overwhelming firepower and that it was futile to fight in the open or attempt to disrupt the landings. He resolved instead to follow the example of General Kuribayashi in the defense of Iwo Jima by committing his forces to a defense in depth within a system of heavily fortified caves and fortifications carved out of the rugged limestone ridges of the southern third of the island. Here, Ushijima would wait with the bulk of his forces until the Americans advanced into his preregistered killing zones.

Another reason the Tenth Army did not encounter heavier resistance during its initial push was that the Japanese had moved a number of troops and artillery units to respond to a faux landing demonstration by the 2nd Marine Division, much the same as they had done at Tinian. On L-Day and again on L+1, they boarded landing craft and made a run at the beaches on the island's southeast coast, only to turn around and reembark. By L+3, the Tenth Army had reached its objectives on the island's east side. The 6th Marine Division pushed north up the Ishikawa Isthmus, meeting little organized resistance as the 1st Marine Division mopped up scattered home guard units in the central area. Their progress slowed as they outpaced their logistics train, which was hampered by the poor road network. The 96th and 7th Infantry Divisions were now abreast and beginning to run into increasing resistance from Ushijima's blocking forces as they advanced to the south.[14]

Spruance was disappointed to learn that *Indianapolis*, the ship he had called home for the last two and a half years, would have to return to the West Coast for repair. On 5 April, the day he moved into *New Mexico*, he wrote to his wife, "Up until today the fighting has been minor in nature, but it will not continue so, as there are many thousands of [Japanese] troops on Okinawa and undoubtedly they will put up a stiff fight and have to be killed." Neglecting to mention the attack on his flagship, he continued, "We have had a steady dribble of [Japanese] attacks, from moonlight nights to daylight, against our ships. It is annoying and ships get hit, but nothing they have been able to do so far is sufficient to affect the final result of this operation."[15]

The "steady dribble" was about to change, as the next day Ugaki's Fifth Air Fleet joined the first in a series of combined Imperial Navy and Army mass air attacks known as the *Kikusui*, or "Floating Chrysanthemum," attacks. Admiral Turner reported that 182 planes attacked the pickets and ships in the Kerama Retto roadstead in twenty-two separate attacks, sinking three destroyers, a minesweeper, two ammunition ships, and an LST, and heavily damaging nine destroyers, two destroyer escorts, a minelayer, and a number of other ships. Turner reported that his CAP shot down 55 raiders and destroyed another 35 by ship antiaircraft, with the damage done by 24 successful kamikaze strikes. TF 58 reported downing 249 of the attacking planes. All told, sixty ships were lost or damaged in this, the largest of the Kikusui attacks, with nearly 700 Japanese aircraft involved. Even though several of Ugaki's pilots reported "I am crashing on a carrier," none were damaged. Nevertheless, the cost was high in terms of ships and personnel.[16]

The first Kikusui attack was supposed to be part of a coordinated operation code named Ten-Go (Operation Heaven) that included simultaneous attacks on the American forces at Okinawa from land, sea, and air. Goaded by the emperor, the IJN general staff decided that the Combined Fleet, now a mere shadow of its former self, had to participate in some meaningful way in the offensive. They agreed that the honor of leading the sea attack must go to *Yamato*, the pinnacle of Japanese naval construction, in company with the light cruiser *Yahagi* and eight destroyers as escorts. The superbattleship was to attack the landing forces and then beach herself near Hagushi to become a mighty fortress of steel. With American air power thus diverted, Ushijima's 32nd Army would stage a counterattack against the U.S. Tenth Army.

The ability of the Imperial General Headquarters to coordinate such an ambitious operation was severely impacted by the intense, nearly daily, B-29 bombing raids. So it was that the fateful sortie did not get underway until late in the day of 6 April when it was spotted by the submarine USS *Threadfin* (SS 410) exiting the Bungo Strait and heading south at high speed. After *Threadfin* lost contact, the exact location of the *Yamato* strike force was not known, and it was possible that it could either continue south or swing west. To meet this threat, Spruance ordered additional submarines posted south of Kyushu, directed TF 58 to maintain its station northeast of Okinawa, and ordered Deyo and TF 54 to be prepared to form a battle line in the East China Sea west of Okinawa.[17]

Deyo prepared a dispatch with his detailed order of battle consisting of the battleships *Idaho*, *New Mexico* (with Spruance aboard), and *Tennessee*, which would engage the "Orange battleline" at "moderate ranges" of 17,000 to 22,000 yards, the effective range for their 14-inch guns, as his two cruiser divisions and destroyers made flanking torpedo attacks. Curiously, while Deyo copied Spruance on the dispatch, his primary addressees were Admirals King and Nimitz. Perhaps he was hoping for authorization from them to engage in what might have been one of the greatest battleship slugfests of all time.[18]

Sadly for the black-shoe admirals, it was not to be. By the time Deyo's dispatch had been received, *Yamato* was no more. Search planes from *Essex* located the force southwest of Kyushu at 0825 on 7 April, on a course heading west, away from TF 58 and into the East China Sea, and reported this to Mitscher. A flying boat shadowed the force and maintained visual contact, confirming that *Yamato* was still within range of the carriers. Around 1000, Mitscher provided the latest contact report and asked Spruance, "Will you take them or shall I?" Spruance replied immediately, "You take them."[19]

Deyo was counting on taking *Yamato* under two fires with his force, and while he might have prevailed, it was also likely that he would have taken some, perhaps even considerable, damage. Given that *Yamato*'s 46-cm main guns could hit at a range more than twice that of Deyo's specified "moderate range," this meant that TF 54 would have to maneuver under fire for some time before opening fire in return. *Yamato* also had a six-knot speed advantage over Deyo's veteran battleships, meaning she could theoretically stay beyond the effective range of Deyo's 14-inch guns for as long as she wanted. Ever the logical thinker and pragmatist, Spruance decided that his carriers should do the job and preserve the gunfire and covering force fully intact, allowing it to continue doing what it did best: supporting the ground troops and providing antiaircraft defense to the fleet.[20]

Mitscher had 380 planes in the air by 1015, with the first wave finding *Yamato* at 1232. The carrier planes worked over the superbattleship and her escorts for nearly two hours, hitting her with ten torpedoes and at least five 1,000-lb bombs until she capsized and sank at 1423. As she rolled over, munitions in her forward magazine exploded, tearing her in half. *Yamato* rapidly disappeared below the waves, taking more than 3,000 of her crew with her. The cruiser *Yahagi* and four destroyers were also sunk. During the attack, the Strike Force was left without any friendly air cover even as hundreds of Japanese planes converged on Okinawa. *Yamato* had been refitted with extensive antiaircraft defenses, but these proved ineffective. Mitscher lost only ten carrier planes.[21]

While these events unfolded, Nimitz was already thinking about Olympic, the invasion of Japan. On 5 April, he sent a dispatch for King's eyes only with his suggestions for the command structure, which revealed his opinion of his top two commanders. "It is my view that in Olympic the country will be best served if Spruance controls the amphibious phases which require meticulous planning," he wrote, "while Halsey is employed in offensive covering operations both of which will be coordinated by me. . . . Thus each will be employed in the field in which he is best qualified."[22]

King replied a few days later, telling Nimitz that the amphibious command structure had to be decided upon soon to meet the projected November schedule and allow enough time for coordination with MacArthur. "I agree with your view that this command should be (the) Fifth Fleet team of Spruance and Turner. . . . They should therefore be disengaged from Iceberg as soon as practicable. To this end I suggest that Halsey take overall command about one [*sic*] May and that Turner pass amphibious command to Hill or Blandy not later than one May."[23]

When King wrote this, there was some optimism that Iceberg might indeed wrap up ahead of schedule. The 6th Marine Division moved north with little opposition, reaching Hedo Point on 13 April. Several days later, the Marines began a push to clear the Motobu Peninsula, where they met fierce opposition from a battalion of troops under Colonel Udo Takehiko. However, this was overcome, and the peninsula was secured by 20 April.

The 77th Infantry landed on Ie Shima on 16 April and secured the island and its airfield five days later. Buckner's Army divisions, however, were faring less well in the south and were now in vicious combat with Ushijima's troops. The fighting was similar to Peleliu and Iwo Jima, with progress measured in hundreds of yards, requiring intense artillery barrages followed by infantrymen using flamethrowers, explosives, and close combat to drive the defenders from their caves and tunnels.

In the same period, Spruance's ships were hit with three more Kikusui attacks at intervals of four to five days apart, each with four to five hundred aircraft. Most of these were shot down, but those that got through were causing severe damage, mainly to the pickets. Most of the kamikaze pilots, many of whom were Army flyers, had little training in ship recognition and typically went for the first American ship they encountered. It was estimated that during the period of 18 March to 13 April over 1,800 Japanese aircraft had been destroyed. Yet more were to come.[24]

The raid on 12 April marked the first use of the Ohka, also known as the Cherry Blossom, a rocket-powered 600-kg bomb that is essentially a human-guided missile air-launched from twin-engine Ginga bombers. Fortunately, the bombers with such a payload were slow and difficult to maneuver; most were quickly shot down by the defending Hellcats. One did score a hit on USS *Mannert L. Abele* (DD 733), a radar picket from TF 54. Already crippled by a kamikaze, *Abele* was hit amidships and was ripped in two by the powerful blast, her shattered aft and bow sections rapidly sinking, leaving some 250 survivors clinging to the wreckage. The terrific speed of these flying bombs made them impossible to shoot down but also very difficult for their pilots to control. Despite their tremendous potential, they had little impact on the battle, and were called "baka" or "fool" bomb by the Allies. Ugaki's bomber crews reported sinking a battleship, a typical exaggeration of the sort that continuously misled the Japanese into thinking they were inflicting far greater damage than in reality. Ugaki even went so far as to believe that their "success" had triggered the death of President Roosevelt on 12 April.[25]

Suppressing Japanese air power over Okinawa became a major concern of both the Fifth Fleet and CinCPac. Not since Guadalcanal had an amphibious operation been so harassed from the air. Spruance wanted

TF 58 to conduct another fighter sweep on the Kyushu airfields, but Mitscher told him that doing so would require him to be at least two days away from Okinawa. On 10 April, Nimitz requested that Spruance provide him with a local estimate on the feasibility and timeframe for having eight air bases operational on Okinawa. Spruance went ashore on 14 April to inspect the ongoing work to repair and expand the four fields already under American control. He met with the Army engineers and reported that a shortage of building materials, adverse weather conditions, and poor roads were slowing progress.[26]

Spruance followed up with an urgent request: "Scale and effectiveness of many mass suicide air attacks and rate of ship loss and damage are such that we must use all available means to prevent future attacks." He recommended that all available long-range bombers and fighters be directed to hit the airfields on Kyushu and the feeder airfields on Honshu and Shikoku. TF 57 was scheduled to retire to Leyte for repairs and replenishment, and combined with a Tenth Army offensive planned for 19 April, TF 58 would be taxed to its limits in providing air support over Okinawa. "I wish to do everything possible to insure that preventable losses and damage to fleet units do not slow tempo of future operations," he wrote.[27] This certainly got Nimitz's attention, and results soon followed. In response to Nimitz's request, General LeMay agreed to have a portion of his XXI Bomber Command diverted from their ongoing bombing campaign of Japanese cities and industries to hit Kyushu "for as long as CINCPOA considers present emergency to exist."[28]

On 19 April, Buckner began a major offensive to break through the Japanese lines, bringing up the 27th Infantry to reinforce the XXIV Corps. Twenty-seven Army and Marine artillery battalions opened up along a five-mile-wide front for one of the longest and most intense artillery barrages of the war, with close air support from TF 52 and TF 58. It seemed to those watching that nothing could have survived such an onslaught, but the Japanese genius for tunneling and fortification proved more than adequate to withstand the attack. The three Army divisions made scant progress and took heavy casualties as the defenders returned to their machine guns and gun emplacements, replying with mortars and heavy artillery.[29]

Nimitz arrived from Guam on 22 April to assess the situation and determine how to expedite the conclusion of Iceberg. With him came Forrest Sherman and Gen. Archer Vandegrift, the commandant of the Marine Corps. After landing at Yontan, Nimitz and his party went out to *New Mexico* in the Hagushi anchorage to meet with Spruance for dinner. They witnessed the ongoing fourth Kikusui firsthand as eighty planes attacked the Fifth Fleet with eleven raids. The destroyer USS *Isherwood* (DD 520), on picket duty, was hit but was able to limp into Kerama Retto for repairs, while the minesweeper USS *Swallow* (AM 65) was hit and sank. Standing on the deck of *New Mexico* watching this air battle unfold was likely the closest that Nimitz came to actual combat during the war.[30]

The next day, Spruance accompanied Nimitz and Vandegrift to tour the occupied areas and meet with Buckner, who had moved his headquarters ashore from the command ship USS *Eldorado* (AGC 11) the previous week. Nimitz told Buckner of the importance of concluding operations on Okinawa as soon as possible so the fleet could be released for the next operation. Buckner reminded Nimitz that the land campaign was an Army affair and, in so many words, he should butt out. Nimitz reminded him who was in overall command and replied calmly but icily, "I'm losing a ship and a half a day. So, if this line isn't moving within five days, we'll get someone here to move it so we can all get out from under these stupid air attacks."[31]

Later, they accompanied Buckner to the headquarters of Roy Greiner, the Third Amphibious Corps commander. Buckner intended to move the Third Amphibious Corps into the line to relieve the weary and depleted Army divisions, a proposal that Vandegrift readily endorsed. The Marine Corps commandant suggested to Buckner that the 2nd Marine Division, which in the interim had returned to Saipan, be brought back and landed for real on the southeast coast, thus opening a second front. Buckner told him that General Hodges and the Tenth Army staff had thoroughly studied the idea and concluded that the Japanese defenses were too strong: "It would be another Anzio, only worse." Nimitz and Sherman agreed, at least for the time being, but Vandegrift and the Marines were never truly convinced. As it turned out, the grinding combat continued for another two months, with the Marines doing a large share of the fighting, and the issue became another bone of contention between the services.[32]

After returning to Guam, Nimitz reported what he had found to King. Sites for eight airfields had been identified, but the difficulties experienced by the Tenth Army in its campaign to eliminate the Japanese 32nd Army prevented a swift conclusion for Iceberg. As per his discussions with Buckner and Vandegrift, the Third Amphibious Corps would move into the line to the right of the XXIV Corps, relieving the 27th Infantry. Based on his conversations with Spruance and Turner, Nimitz suggested that the operations to occupy the islands north and south of Okinawa be deferred and that the resources be allocated to Okinawa to expedite its capture. King agreed almost immediately.[33]

On 1 May, the 1st and 6th Marine Divisions of the Third Amphibious Corps took up positions on the right of the line, and the depleted 27th Infantry was withdrawn to assume garrison duties. The 77th Infantry replaced the 96th Infantry, which retired for rest and replenishment. These moves proved timely, as on 4 May General Ushijima began an ill-advised general counteroffensive. In support of this, many Japanese artillery batteries were brought out into the open to fire more effectively on the American positions. Small amphibious landings were attempted on both the east and west sides of the island in an attempt to infiltrate behind the lines of the Tenth Army. These landing forces were quickly annihilated, and American counterbattery fire destroyed half of the guns available to the 32nd Army—guns that had previously been unreachable in their underground redoubts. Likewise, Ushijima's infantry assault was met with a skillful application of firepower and ultimately failed, resulting in heavy casualties.[34]

The fifth Kikusui operation was launched simultaneously with the 32nd Army's offensive, resulting in two destroyers sunk and an escort carrier damaged. Attempts were made to hit the Tenth Army's rear areas with conventional bombers, but these were driven off or shot down. TF 57 had just returned from Leyte to resume operations in Sakishima Retto when the carriers HMS *Formidable* and *Indomitable* were hit. However, thanks to their armored flight decks, they suffered limited damage, and both carried on with flight operations soon after. The U.S. Navy took note, and all future American aircraft carriers would be built with an armored deck.[35]

The continuing and persistent Kikusui attacks were a major headache for Spruance. The latest Japanese attacks had come from the southwest, and Spruance complained to Nimitz that MacArthur's command was not doing enough to suppress Japanese air forces in southern Formosa and China: "We suffered considerable losses in screening vessels in sundown attacks yesterday made by Formosan planes." Nimitz requested action, and MacArthur followed through, telling his air forces to get on the ball. Spruance also requested that the B-29 attacks on Kyushu be increased.[36]

On 5 May, Spruance went ashore again to assess the airfield construction situation, but he was not happy with what he saw. He expressed his frustration to Buckner that the maximum deployment of fighters was "being hampered by lack of adequate bulk storage of avgas and a too strict adherence to schedule in base development." According to Spruance, the Army's airfield engineers were holding up tactical fighter deployment by insisting on expanding the runways at Yontan and Kadena to accommodate B-29 bombers. Unsurprisingly, the 20th Air Force took exception to this. Nimitz had to step again in to exert his authority, telling the Air Force brass, including LeMay, that the runways would be extended in due course, but "after consideration of the requirements of all forces involved in attaining the overall strategic objective in the war against Japan . . . at the present time at Okinawa the requirements of tactical aircraft take precedence over those of 20th AF."[37]

The war in Europe ended with the signing of the Instrument of Unconditional Surrender by Grand Admiral Karl Dönitz on 8 May 1945. No mention of the event appeared in the Running Summary, however, and the war in the Pacific carried on. The sixth Kikusui attack commenced on 11 May and lasted several days, as long as the weather conditions were favorable. Mitscher's flagship *Bunker Hill* was hit in rapid succession by two Zeros that morning, one of which succeeded in putting a 250-kg bomb through the flight deck, setting off numerous fires from fueled aircraft on the hangar deck below. The wing and engine from the second kamikaze landed in the flag office, narrowly missing Mitscher but killing many from his staff. Mitscher was forced to transfer his flag to *Enterprise*, which was hit again on 14 May while TF 58 was conducting a night strike against Ugaki's Kanoye airbase. The attacking Zero made a near vertical dive, crashing through *Enterprise*'s flight deck with a 500-kg bomb just aft of the forward elevator. The resulting explosion sent the elevator several hundred feet into the air, but as flight operations had ceased and the fuel lines had been purged, *Enterprise* was spared the catastrophic fires that had gutted *Bunker Hill*. The war was over for both ships, however. Mitscher had to transfer his flag again, this time into *Randolph*, which had rejoined TF 58.[38]

The lack of fighter protection may have been more a matter of perception than reality. Japanese suicide planes had learned to evade early detection, sometimes coming in low, under the radar, or in company with high-speed bombers that dropped "window," the aluminum chaff that could defeat radar detection with false echoes. At other times, such as the attack on TF 58, they utilized low cloud cover to their advantage. They had also learned to attack at dusk when the daytime CAP was landing and before the night fighters were in place. It was at just such a time that Spruance had another brush with fate.

The twelfth day of May had been quiet for *New Mexico*, spent providing on-call fire support. Late in the afternoon, she went over to Kerama Retto for ammunition resupply and returned to the Hagushi anchorage at dusk. As *New Mexico* was about to drop anchor, two kamikaze pilots, having avoided radar detection, came in from the west and dived on the ship. *New Mexico*'s antiaircraft gunners put up a wall of fire, but as was often the case, despite being damaged beyond any recovery the momentum of their dives carried the suicide aircraft into their intended target. One overflew and crashed close aboard on *New Mexico*'s port side, but the second hit squarely amidships on the starboard side, just abaft the bridge superstructure. The plane tore a hole through the superstructure and landed in the air uptakes, while the bomb it was carrying went through the superstructure deck and exploded on the deck below.

Spruance had just left his cabin and was on his way forward to the flag bridge along the second deck when the plane struck. Had he taken his usual route along the main deck and up to the superstructure deck he might have been among the fifty-four men killed, one of whom was an enlisted man on his flag staff. Gil Slonim also narrowly missed being killed. The majority of casualties came from a group of four 20-mm gun tubs mounted adjacent to the stack. Loose ammunition from the ready supply lockers tumbled into the main uptake and into fireboxes below, where it cooked off and damaged three of the ship's boilers.[39]

The operation had been plagued from the start by periods of bad weather, which was a curse for the Marines and GIs, who had to contend with mud, but a blessing for the Fifth Fleet, as the poorly trained kamikaze pilots usually only flew in clear skies. The prevailing bad weather at the end of May thwarted Ugaki's seventh Kikusui attempt. However, from the perspective of the defending Japanese troops, bad weather was most welcome, as it limited the use of American close air support. General Ushijima took the opportunity to withdraw the remains of his 32nd Army from the battered fortifications under and around Shuri Castle, which the Tenth Army was threatening with envelopment, and conducted a masterful withdrawal south into the next and final line of defense. The Marines occupied the ruins of the ancient castle and raised the flag there on 29 May. More than 30,000 Japanese troops were now compressed into an area of only eight square miles. It took nearly another month of what Buckner called "corkscrew and blowtorch" tactics, alternating the use of high explosives against caves and pillboxes followed by flamethrowers, to root them out and secure the island.[40]

On 27 May, Admiral Halsey arrived, and the Fifth Fleet became the Third Fleet again. Vice Adm. John S. McCain Sr. relieved Marc Mitscher, and TF 58 became TF 38. Spruance's time commanding Operation Iceberg was nearing its end. Spruance's previous biographers have claimed that the reason for this unusual relief of top commanders before the completion of Iceberg was that Nimitz was concerned that they were becoming burned out by the unremitting stress of combat operations. There was clearly some concern, as Secretary James Forrestal, after he visited Iwo Jima, directed that Commo. Morton D. Willcutts, M.C., be attached to Spruance's staff as the Fifth Fleet Medical officer to keep an eye on the health of Spruance and his officers.[41]

The Fifth Fleet had been at sea for more than three months, and the effects of continuously being in harm's way and overseeing operations that resulted in the death and wounding of tens of thousands of men were indeed having an impact. Kelly Turner, in particular, found solace in the bottle, often drinking to excess in the evening but managing to bounce back in the morning without ill effect. Spruance covered for Turner and was not concerned about his performance but was sorry to see his friend in such a state. During this period Charles Barber, Spruance's flag secretary, claimed that he never saw Spruance tired or weary from his responsibilities. That was not true in Barber's case, however. Thirty years his boss' junior, Barber recalled, "I was worn out by the time we left. . . . As we sailed from Okinawa, I felt a relief I could not describe."[42]

As previously related, the early relief of Spruance and Turner was also foreordained, as King and Nimitz had wanted both men to be relieved by 1 May. In early May, Nimitz had sent Spruance a dispatch emphasizing the need to end the amphibious phase of Iceberg as soon as possible so that Turner could turn over the operation to Buckner and return to Guam to plan Olympic, but due to the unexpected ferocity of the Japanese defense of Okinawa, this had to be delayed. Soon after, Spruance told Carl Moore in a letter that he and Kelly Turner were due to leave before the end of May to return to Guam to plan the next operation. Writing to Margaret soon after his return to Guam, Spruance expressed his regret at having left too soon. "I was sorry to leave Okinawa before the job was finished," he wrote, "but the powers-that-be decided otherwise. Both Kelly and I have other things to do. . . . I am in fine shape in every way, so I don't need any rest. On board ship I usually managed to get exercise every day and I lost very little sleep on account of the night air attacks."[43]

By mid-May, the outcome of the battle if not its timing was certain, and Nimitz felt safe in replacing Spruance with Halsey, who could be counted on to do what he did best: pounding the Japanese. Nimitz wanted the best brains in the Navy with him to plan the invasion of Japan. Spruance departed Okinawa in *New Mexico* on 28 May as the eighth Kikusui attack raged and arrived at Apra Harbor on 1 June. Ugaki's suicide attacks continued into June, but with much less impact as he resorted to using obsolete trainers and seaplanes that had little chance of survival if engaged in aerial combat. The 32nd Army was slowly beaten into oblivion but resisted to the end. General Buckner was killed by a Japanese antitank gun while visiting the front on 18 June, and Roy Greiner took over temporary command of the Tenth Army. By 21 June, however, organized resistance had ended, and that same day, Ushijima committed ritual suicide in his bunker.

The Battle of Okinawa was the first of Spruance's operations where the number of Navy personnel killed was greater than those of either the Marines or the Army. In all, 4,907 sailors and naval airmen were killed and another 4,824 wounded. A total of 34 ships and smaller craft were sunk, but none more significant than a destroyer. Another 368 of all types were damaged, and 763 carrier-based aircraft were lost to all causes. The Marines, meanwhile, suffered 3,443 killed, missing, or died of wounds, and more than 16,000 wounded. Army casualties amounted to 3,931 dead and more than 15,800 wounded. The exact totals of Japanese casualties were not known, but it is estimated that more than 131,000 Japanese soldiers and naval personnel were killed, and for the first time a significant number, almost 11,000, surrendered or were captured. Sixteen Japanese warships had been sunk, including the superbattleship *Yamato*, and more than 7,830 aircraft were destroyed. The civilian population is estimated to have suffered as many as 150,000 killed. The Japanese military's willingness to die for the Emperor was expected, but their disregard for the fate of their civilians was a chilling preview of what might be expected when the Home Islands were invaded.[44]

CHAPTER 15

THE DEFEAT AND OCCUPATION OF JAPAN

SPRUANCE RETURNED to Guam on 1 June. Together with his staff members Emmet Forrestel, Dr. Morton Willcutts, and Art Davis, he moved into a comfortable four-bedroom house that had been built for flag officers on "Nimitz Hill," located not far from Apra Harbor. It was set at 600 feet above sea level, and Spruance found the cool breezes there a welcome relief from the hot and stuffy flag cabin in *New Mexico*, which was scheduled to return to the West Coast for repairs. That same day, Admiral Nimitz, at the CinCPac Advance Headquarters nearby, presented Spruance with a commendation awarding him the Navy Cross. In a very informal setting, Nimitz pinned it on Spruance's chest, with Kelly Turner and Forrest Sherman looking on. The citation read, in part: "For extraordinary heroism as Commander Fifth Fleet in action against enemy Japanese forces during the invasion and capture of Iwo Jima, Volcano Islands, and Okinawa, Ryukyu Islands, from January to May 1945."[1]

Spruance was impressed at the amount of reconstruction that had been done in Guam since the previous year, with significant improvements to the harbor, Orote Airfield, and the built infrastructure throughout the island. He resumed his daily walks in the hills, usually accompanied by Dr. Willcutts. Although it was rumored that there were still Japanese stragglers in the vicinity, this never worried them, as they were well protected by Marine guards, and the Japanese only seemed to come out at night to scrounge for food.

As Spruance was preparing to leave Okinawa, the Joint Chiefs of Staff issued their directive for Olympic on 25 May, calling for the invasion of Kyushu with a target date of 1 November 1945. Significantly, Gen. Douglas MacArthur was given primary responsibility for the operation, while

Nimitz was placed in a secondary role, leading the naval and amphibious forces. The 20th Air Force would continue to provide strategic air support under the direction of the Joint Chiefs of Staff, independent of either MacArthur or Nimitz. With input from the CinCPac staff, MacArthur's staff had already been hard at work preparing the plans for Operation Downfall, the overarching plan for the final defeat of Japan, and issued their staff study for Olympic a few days later.[2]

Disturbed by the ferocity of the fight still raging on Okinawa, Nimitz sent a dispatch for King's eyes only late in the afternoon of 24 May recommending that Olympic should be postponed until sometime in 1946 "unless speed is considered so important that we are willing to accept less than the best preparation and more than the minimum casualties." A close blockade of the Home Islands and the intense air bombardment campaign would still be maintained to keep maximum pressure on the Japanese.[3]

Nimitz's recommendation may have come after discussions with Kelly Turner, who had just returned from Okinawa. While King and Admiral Leahy, the de facto chairman of the Joint Chiefs, preferred a naval blockade to an invasion, speed was indeed "considered so important" that postponing the invasion was unlikely. Gen. George C. Marshall, in particular, was concerned that due to the increasing public war weariness and the staggering monthly cost of the war, waiting out the Japanese was not a viable option. As the Joint Chiefs worked by consensus, King could not change the directive without convincing the others. If they could not agree, it would be up to the president to decide the final course of action.[4]

Harry S. Truman was sworn in as president immediately following Roosevelt's death on 12 April 1945. Having often been excluded from Roosevelt's war councils, he spent some time getting up to speed. In late May he had a meeting with his good friend former president Herbert Hoover, who relayed to Truman his concern that an invasion of Japan would result in potentially horrendous casualties, ranging from 500,000 to 1,000,000 men. Hoover had gotten his information from sources inside the War Department. Deeply concerned, Truman requested that the Joint Chiefs verify the projected casualty estimates. At a meeting on 18 June, General Marshall provided his estimate that American casualties would fall in a range between 31,000 to 41,000 killed and wounded, based on the

Army's experience on Luzon and the assumption that only eight Japanese divisions defended Kyushu, totaling about 350,000 troops.[5]

Admiral Leahy was skeptical of this figure and thought the likely casualties would amount to 35 percent of the troops committed, as on Okinawa. Since MacArthur's plan called for landing fourteen divisions and 766,700 men, an invasion might result in more than 200,000 casualties. Surprisingly, King went along with Marshall, agreeing that there was more maneuver room on Kyushu and that the fighting there would be more akin to that on Luzon. Furthermore, the Joint Chiefs stressed that taking Kyushu provided a better base to strangle Japan into surrender. In the end, Truman did not receive a firm estimate, but was satisfied with the apparent unanimity of the Joint Chiefs and their assertion that Olympic offered the most economical means "in effort and lives" to end the war. Operation Olympic was given the green light, but Truman reserved the right to reconsider future landings.[6]

MacArthur's staff study for Operation Olympic specified landing the Sixth Army, composed of three corps of three infantry divisions each, at three separate landing sites in southern Kyushu. Two divisions would be sent ashore where needed in the initial assault, with another two held in reserve afloat, for a total of thirteen divisions. The three corps would not attempt to capture all of Kyushu but would instead establish a defensive line across the island roughly one-third of the way north. This would provide the area needed to establish air bases to support Operation Coronet, the invasion of central Honshu. The landing sites were chosen as those best suited for landing three divisions simultaneously; however, due to the mountainous and volcanic nature of southern Kyushu, there were simply no other good options. The areas surrounding the three sites were relatively flat but were heavily used for agriculture and covered in rice paddies. Beyond these areas, the terrain became extremely hilly and then mountainous, with narrow valleys and few natural avenues of advance, making Okinawa look relatively tame by comparison. In reality, there was extraordinarily little room for maneuver. The Imperial Army planned to take full advantage of the defensive opportunities that such terrain offered.[7]

When Spruance arrived at CinCPac headquarters, he joined an ongoing conference with MacArthur's staff, who had come up from Manila to review and discuss the shipping for Olympic. This would be on a scale never seen before, requiring the movement of more than 800,000 troops, 140,500 vehicles, and nearly 1.4 million tons of equipment. In addition to the initial assault troops, these totals included the rear-echelon service troops, military government personnel, and the Far East Air Force (FEAF) that would follow.[8]

Spruance wrote to his wife Margaret that he was so busy he did not know when he could return home for leave, despite Nimitz having urged him to do so since his arrival on Guam. Nevertheless, it did not take much prodding for him to agree to join Nimitz on a flight back to San Francisco on 23 June, when Nimitz was scheduled to meet with King for their last conference. During the long flight, Nimitz and Spruance undoubtedly discussed Okinawa, which had just been declared secure, and the hideous cost of that operation in terms of men and ships. They may have also discussed an unusual message from the Joint Chiefs that Nimitz and MacArthur had received the week before. They were told to prepare plans "to take immediate advantage of favorable circumstances, such as a sudden collapse or surrender, to effect an entry into JAPAN proper for occupational purposes." With much to contemplate, Spruance went home to California for a well-earned but all too short respite with his family and returned with Nimitz on 4 July.[9]

Throughout June and July, the strategic bombing of Japan by LeMay's B-29s continued daily, weather permitting. By the end of July, most major cities in Japan had been hit multiple times, with notable exceptions including Kyoto, the cultural center of Japan, and the Imperial Palace in Tokyo. The effort shifted to smaller cities, particularly those with critical industrial facilities or rail and transportation hubs. On 3 July, the Joint Chiefs sent a top-secret dispatch to Nimitz, MacArthur, and Hap Arnold, instructing them that, in addition to Kyoto, three other cities—Hiroshima, Kokura, and Niigata—were not to be attacked. Although not explicitly stated, these cities were reserved for what was termed "special treatment"; that is, they were potential targets for the use of atomic bombs.[10]

In early July, Halsey and TF 38 began a bombardment campaign against mainland Japan, one with a definite strategic purpose. On 14 and 15 July, the carrier planes of TF 38 hit targets in northern Honshu and the ports of southern Hokkaido where locomotives, rolling stock, and rail ferries used to transport coal shipments to the south were destroyed, creating a major disruption to Japan's energy supply. The fast battleships of TF 38 and TF 37 conducted shore bombardment of coal liquefaction facilities, coke plants, and steel mills along the northeast coast of Honshu, an undeniable sign that Allied sea power reigned supreme in the waters of Japan. Curiously, no effort was made to intercept the attacking aircraft. The Japanese were hoarding their aviation assets for another purpose.[11]

Nimitz then ordered Halsey to knock out what remained of the Imperial Japanese Navy. From 18 to 28 July, his carrier planes hit the naval facilities at Yokosuka, Kobe, and Kure. The attack on 24 July resulted in the sinking of the hybrid battleship/carrier *Hyūga* and the damaging of her sister *Ise*, as well as the sinking of the carrier *Amagi* and the heavy cruisers *Tone* and *Aoba*. The battleship *Haruna* was only damaged, but the planes of TF 38 returned four days later and sank her. A number of other warships received varying degrees of damage, and by the end of July, most of the remaining Combined Fleet had settled into the mud of the Inland Sea. This achievement, however, came at a terrible cost, as sixty-four carrier planes and their aircrew were lost, mostly from the heavy antiaircraft fire defending Kure.[12]

On 16 July, *Indianapolis* departed Mare Island bound for Tinian, her repairs and refit having been completed. She carried a top-secret cargo whose purpose remained unknown to her crew. After a record-breaking high-speed run, she arrived on 26 July, unloaded her cargo, the components of two atomic bombs, and then departed on 29 July for Leyte. She never arrived, having been torpedoed by the Japanese submarine *I-58* just after midnight on 30 July. It was not until 3 August that her fate became known and her surviving crew were rescued. Spruance had considered rejoining his old shipmates for the journey south to meet with MacArthur's staff, but once more, his luck had intervened.

In late July, the Joint Chiefs advised Nimitz, MacArthur, and Gen. Carl Spaatz, USAAF, commander of the newly formed Strategic Air Force located on Tinian, to prepare plans in the event of a sudden surrender of the Japanese government. Based on previous warnings, both MacArthur and Nimitz had already prepared plans for just such an event, with MacArthur's named Operation Blacklist and Nimitz's Operation Campus. On 27 July, Nimitz provided King and the other commanders with his simplified plan in three phases. The first phase would be an emergency naval occupation of Tokyo Bay, followed by the deployment of naval occupation forces throughout Kyushu and Honshu in the second phase, all in preparation for the third and main act, the occupation of mainland Japan by the U.S. Army.[13]

During this period, the Imperial General Headquarters had not been idle. They recognized that Kyushu was likely to be the next target for invasion. Nor was it difficult for them to identify which beaches offered the best locations for landing, and they planned their defensive strategy accordingly. They called this Ketsu-go, the Decisive Operation. Its main objective was to inflict maximum American casualties to force a negotiated end to the war on more favorable terms. Unlike previous operations, they now intended to attack the troop transports and landing craft as they approached the landing areas with *kaiten*, human-operated torpedoes; *koryū*, suicide midget submarines; *shinyō*, suicide motor boats; and of course kamikaze aircraft. The Japanese had been hoarding thousands of aircraft and large quantities of aviation fuel for just this operation, hidden in cleverly camouflaged locations away from the airfields that were obvious targets. As he wargamed and planned the operation, Admiral Ugaki noted with some satisfaction, based on reports taken from the American press, that in the Kikusui attack of 11 May, two of his suicide planes had heavily damaged the carrier *Bunker Hill* and Mitscher had barely escaped death. Ugaki resolved to dedicate more special attack aircraft in the next operation.[14]

The landings would be opposed at every possible stage: at the beaches as at Tarawa, in carefully prepared defenses in depth as at Iwo Jima and Okinawa, and in the hills and valleys beyond the range of naval artillery where the Imperial Army would keep its main strength. By August, it had moved more than fifteen divisions and 900,000 men onto Kyushu. In addition, tens of thousands of civilian "volunteers," men and women, were conscripted to serve as cannon fodder to distract attention and absorb American firepower.[15]

On 2 August, Nimitz sent a warning to all units that "a special operation will be conducted by the 509th Bomb Group on 4 or 5 August" and that all ships and aircraft of the Pacific Fleet were to maintain a distance of 50 miles from Nagasaki, Kokura, and Hiroshima during a period of four hours before to six hours after of the time of the operation, which would be announced later. However, the "special operation" did not get off the ground until the early morning of 6 August. At precisely 0815, the first atomic weapon was detonated over the city of Hiroshima.

Spruance had first learned of the atomic bomb in late July. On 25 July, Capt. William S. Parsons, the Navy's liaison and ordnance expert for the Manhattan Project, arrived to oversee the assembly and use of "Little Boy," the gun-type fission bomb that would be dropped first. He briefed Nimitz, Spruance, LeMay, and Edwin Layton on the weapon and showed them a film of the Trinity test at Alamogordo, New Mexico. Layton told the assembled brass that although the Japanese militarists knew they were beaten, they remained hell-bent on fighting to the death. As a trained biologist and a man of science, Emperor Hirohito might understand that here was a way out that would permit him to surrender and save face. This was also understood at a higher command level, as Tokyo and the Imperial Palace had been kept off the list of atomic bomb targets.[16]

Spruance's staff were working feverishly on completing the Fifth Fleet's operational planning for Olympic, oblivious to the possibility that the war might end very soon. Charles Barber recalled that they were working toward a deadline of the first week in September for the draft to be completed when Spruance gathered him and the rest of the staff on the veranda outside his office in early August. He read to them a dispatch describing the atom bomb, stating that B-29s would drop it on two targets in Japan and that it had the equivalence in explosive power to 20,000 tons of TNT. Most of them struggled to comprehend what this meant. After Spruance read the dispatch, he returned to his office without further comment, leaving them wondering.[17]

At around the same time, the survivors of the torpedoing of the *Indianapolis* were found and were being transported to hospital facilities, with some coming to Guam. As Spruance visited his old shipmates, he was much moved by the suffering they had endured. Spruance knew *Indianapolis* was vulnerable as one of the "tin-clad" treaty cruisers. He once told his staff, going into the Iwo Jima operation, that due to the additional antiaircraft armament, radio, and radar gear that had been added, her metacentric height had been significantly reduced, and that one good torpedo hit would cause her to capsize quickly. He might have been trying to frighten young officers like Charles Barber, but the reality of that prediction made manifest was terrible to behold.[18]

The buildup of Japanese forces on Kyushu was becoming apparent to American intelligence, and they began to warn that the opposition there was likely far greater than previously anticipated. Furthermore, the areas north of Tokyo now appeared to have been stripped of active air units, offering perhaps a better option for an operation. Marshall asked MacArthur to analyze this information, which MacArthur dismissed as "greatly exaggerated," arguing that "the situation repeats that of the Philippines campaign." Citing the limited response to the recent attacks made by TF 38 on Kyushu as proof, MacArthur gave his full-throated endorsement of continuing with Olympic as planned. "In my opinion," he told Marshall, "there should not be the slightest thought of postponing the Olympic operation. . . . It is very probable that the enemy is resorting to deception."[19]

MacArthur's preference for invasion was never tested, however. As Marshall and MacArthur exchanged dispatches, the Soviet Union declared war on Japan and began a massive operation along the Manchurian border. On 9 August, the second atomic bomb was dropped on Nagasaki. Emperor Hirohito met with his closest advisors, the Supreme Council for the Direction of War, and after some debate, instructed them to offer a Japanese surrender accepting the provisions of the Potsdam Conference, conditioned on the retention of the Imperial Throne. He told those assembled that victory through a decisive battle had often been promised, but "the experiences of the past, however, show that there has always been a discrepancy between plans and performance." Given the awful destructiveness of the new bombs, "the time has come when we must bear the unbearable."[20]

The Japanese transmitted their terms through the agency of the neutral Swiss and Swedish. The American response followed within hours, agreeing to the retention of the emperor, but with the requirement that his rule and that of the Japanese government would be subject to the

Supreme Commander for the Allied Powers (SCAP) and the will of the Japanese people. Furthermore, the country would remain occupied until the provisions of the Potsdam Declaration were fulfilled. These included the repatriation of all Japanese military forces from occupied territories, Japan's complete disarmament, the prosecution of war criminals, and the establishment of a democratic government.

After some tense days when it seemed that the extreme elements of the Japanese military might attempt a palace coup, the Allied terms were accepted, and at noon on 15 August, the Japanese people heard for the first time, via a radio broadcast, the voice of Emperor Hirohito reading a prerecorded script telling them of the surrender. This was astounding news for the vast majority of people who, despite their cities being reduced to burnt-out ruins and the daily presence of hostile aircraft overhead, still believed the official propaganda line that they were winning the war. Many Japanese officers, caught in the paradox of the shame of surrender versus obedience to the Emperor's direction, chose suicide instead.

One of those choosing an "honorable death" was Vice Admiral Ugaki Matome. Ugaki believed he was duty-bound to follow the example of the many young men who had already sacrificed themselves at his command. Having not yet received a direct order to stand down, at 1600 on 15 August Ugaki, wearing a plain uniform without insignia, bade his staff farewell with a sake toast, climbed into a waiting Suisei (Judy D4Y), and led a final kamikaze attack to strike the American shipping at Okinawa. The attack never materialized. Having taken off late in the day, the flight arrived at Okinawa in the dark and was attacked by waiting night fighters. The cockpit of a shattered plane was later discovered on an island north of Okinawa with the remains of a man corresponding to Ugaki's description, but a positive identification was never made.[21]

That same day MacArthur, who had just been designated the Supreme Commander, Allied Powers, announced a cessation of hostilities. Cdr. Edward Spruance was on Guam enjoying some relaxation at the camp set up there for submariners. He was walking with his father when they heard great shouting and cheers from nearby Quonset huts. News of the surrender had just been broadcast. However, it did not come as a great surprise to the elder Spruance. He expressed his satisfaction but showed no other emotion, and they continued their walk. Charles Barber and the staff were making copies of the Olympic plans for an upcoming conference with MacArthur's staff in Manila. They were due to sail the next day. When they heard the news, Barber told the yeomen to cease their work. Barber paused to let the news sink in. He felt a deep inner satisfaction, but soon set to work again, as Olympic was now be superseded by Campus and the occupation of Japan.[22]

On 16 August Spruance, Barber, and the rest of his staff went aboard *New Jersey*, headed for Manila. The Japanese needed time to transmit the surrender terms to their various commands and receive acquiescence from their commanders. MacArthur also insisted that representatives of the Japanese government meet him in Manila first to finalize the arrangements for the surrender ceremony and the initial occupation. MacArthur and Nimitz would accept the Japanese surrender simultaneously, with MacArthur accepting it on behalf of the Allied powers and Nimitz on behalf of the United States. President Truman directed that the ceremony occur on the deck of USS *Missouri* (BB 63), named for his home state, which his daughter Margaret had christened in 1944.

Spruance arrived in Manila on 21 August. He spent the next day at Sixth Army Headquarters with Gen. Walter Krueger, discussing the arrangements for the occupation of Japan. As part of Operation Blacklist, the Fifth Fleet's mission was to patrol the Japanese coast west of latitude 139° E, clear the avenues of approach of the many Japanese and American mines, and transport the Sixth Army to its designated landing sites. In the first phase, the First Corps would be loaded in the Philippines and its three divisions landed at Nagasaki and Sasebo on the western coast of Kyushu. The Fifth Amphibious Corps would arrive from Hawaii and the Marianas to land its three Marine divisions at Osaka and Kobe and then move inland to Kyoto. Halsey's Third Fleet would remain essentially the same, with TF 38 occupying Tokyo Bay and remaining available to provide air support if needed. The Third Amphibious Corps would land the Eighth Army in and around Tokyo, while Vice Adm. Thomas Kinkaid's Seventh Fleet moved the Tenth Army from Okinawa to occupy Korea.[23]

On Thursday 23 August, Spruance was scheduled to meet with MacArthur and then have lunch with the general and Mrs. MacArthur.

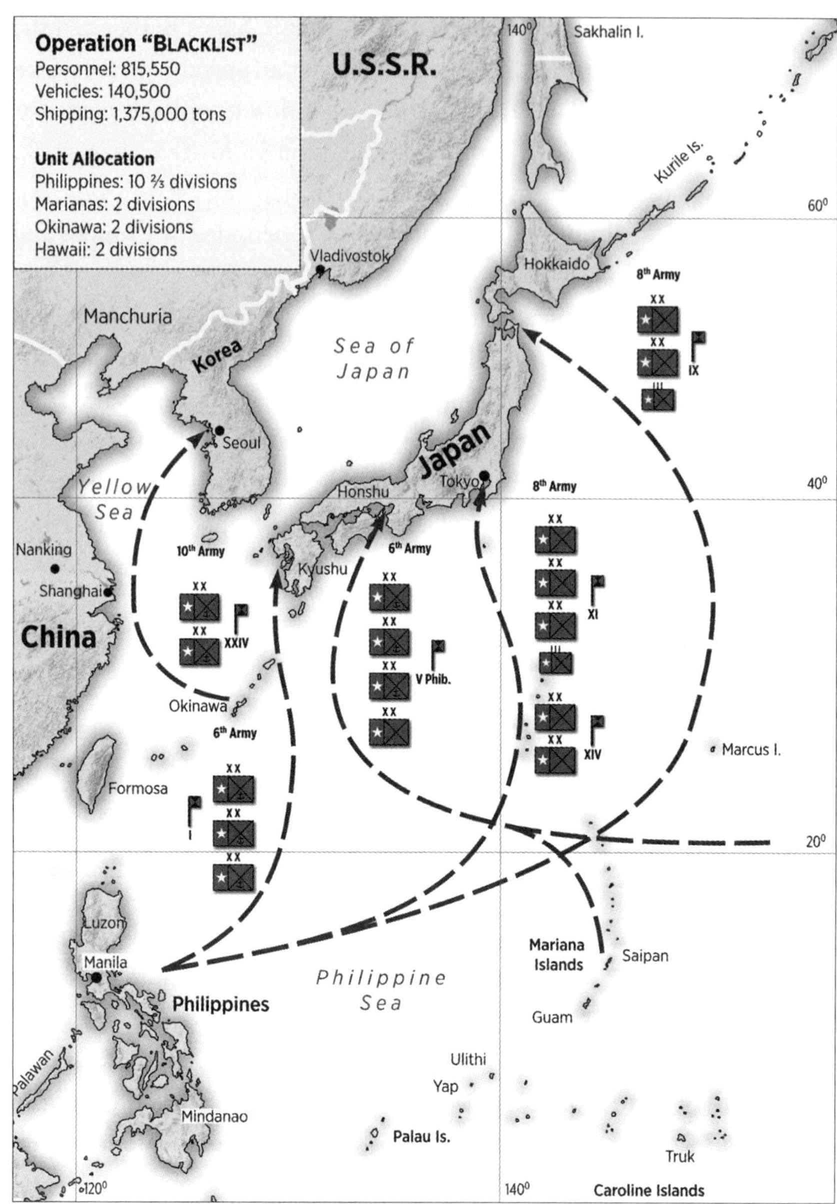

MAP 14. Operation Blacklist Phase 1

Charles Barber recalled Spruance nervously pacing the foredeck of *New Jersey* in anticipation. Spruance was not predisposed to like MacArthur, and indeed, one of the few times Barber had seen him angry was during Operation Flintlock, when MacArthur moved his forces to take the Green Islands without informing him. Spruance had never met the man, but like most senior Navy men, he did not care for what was seen as MacArthur's tendency for self-aggrandizement and his continuous competition for resources, which often seemed to come at the expense of the Navy. Spruance was told that the general liked to talk and talk and might never let him get a word in edgewise. On this occasion, MacArthur listened, and Spruance did most of the talking. Despite any preconceptions he may have had, Spruance fell entirely under the charm of the Supreme Commander. When he returned, he remarked to Barber, "He wasn't so bad." Spruance later wrote to his wife Margaret, "General MacArthur impressed me as a very able and broad gauge man. His ideas on how the Japanese should be treated I am entirely in accord with."[24]

MacArthur's plan to maintain the connection between the Imperial Throne and the people of Japan was an idea that Spruance fully endorsed. "If the Japanese want an emperor of great honor and sanctity, that's their business," he wrote Margaret. "Our business is to see that they are in no position to run amok again and not to tell them they must have some kind of government they are not used to and don't want."[25]

Spruance had another change of heart in Manila, this time regarding publicity and the press. In the forenoon of 25 August, Spruance had a press conference aboard *New Jersey* with thirty American, British, Australian, and Chinese reporters. He held forth for more than an hour and answered their questions with his thoughts on the occupation and the postwar future. Spruance believed that in the postwar period, the U.S. Navy would need to be drastically reduced in size to save costs. Besides the Royal Navy, there were no others that could challenge American maritime control. He spoke well of the Japanese as tough fighters; in his opinion, Japan had to be re-educated to prevent another "rampage," but they should be given a chance to rebuild their economy and reestablish friendly relations with the nations of the world. In Spruance's opinion, the United States should retain the hard-won bases in the Carolines and Marianas but avoid having bases on the Asian mainland. This also applied to Okinawa. It was of obvious strategic value, but retaining it was "potentially explosive" internationally, and its fate should be left to diplomatic negotiation.[26]

"I rather enjoyed the experience," Spruance wrote to his wife. "Now that the war is over the situation regarding publicity is greatly changed, and I recognize it." His comments, however, were not well received at the headquarters of the U.S. Fleet. As soon as Spruance's comments hit the papers, King sent Nimitz an angry dispatch with a copy to Spruance, categorically refuting much of what was said. "It is essential," he told Nimitz, "that the American position should not be handicapped or embarrassed by ill-advised expressions of opinion on such matters by commanders in the field. Desire you should issue appropriate instructions regarding the foregoing." Nimitz wasted no time in complying, sending a dispatch to all flag officers reminding them that "questions as to the disposition and use of captured or occupied territory are political ones to be determined by responsible officials of the government" and in so many words, to keep their opinions to themselves.[27]

After additional meetings with Krueger and Kelly Turner, Spruance went aboard *New Jersey* and sailed for Okinawa, where he would stay for the formal surrender ceremony in Tokyo. MacArthur had been taken aback when Spruance told him he had not been invited, but Spruance assured him that Nimitz must have had his reasons for not including him. Nimitz was already considering Spruance to be his replacement as CinCPac and likely wanted him, as the third highest-ranking naval officer in the Pacific, to be out of harm's way in case of some last-minute perfidy by Japanese fanatics. However, the instrument of surrender was duly signed on the deck of the *Missouri* in Tokyo Bay on 2 September without incident. The next day, the Eighth Army began its occupation of Tokyo and the Kanto Plain as troops of the 11th Airborne Division were flown in from Okinawa.[28]

On 4 September, Emperor Hirohito addressed the Japanese Diet in person and ordered his people to comply with the terms of the surrender and to cooperate with the Supreme Commander, with the goal of rebuilding the nation. He stressed the need for self-discipline and endurance as necessary to regain the trust and friendship of the world community. His address was widely reported and played an instrumental role in initiating the peaceful occupation of Japan.[29]

While the Eighth Army was occupying central Honshu, Spruance traveled to Wakayama on the southwest coast to assist in the evacuation of POWs and to observe the ports that he would use to land the Sixth Army. In the forenoon of 17 September, Spruance arrived at Yokosuka Navy Yard, which was now established as the U.S. Navy's primary base in Japan. There he met Bill Halsey, and together they visited the Eighth Army Headquarters and then Yokohama Prison, where those accused of war crimes were awaiting trial or movement elsewhere. In the latter category was Josef Meisensinger, the Gestapo liaison at the German Embassy, known as the "Butcher of Warsaw" for the heinous crimes he committed in Poland and who was to be sent there for trial. "He was a fat slob and a bully," wrote Spruance, who had no doubt about the outcome of his trial: "[his] morale was completely shattered and [his] execution will rid the earth of vermin."[30]

After several farewell parties for Halsey, which left the outspoken and pugnacious admiral "feeling no pain," Spruance officially relieved his old friend on 20 September. A number of the ships of the Third Fleet also departed for Okinawa as part of Operation Magic Carpet to transport troops back to the United States, while the remainder, now the Fifth Fleet, controlled the waters surrounding Japan. Spruance took the opportunity to visit *Mikasa*, the flagship of Admiral Tōgō, now encased in concrete as a memorial. At Nimitz's direction, Marine guards had been placed around her to prevent looting by souvenir seekers. Spruance had studied Tōgō's actions at the Battle of Tsushima while at the Naval War College, and the ship was "of particular interest" to him as he had met the famous admiral on board her in Yokohama Harbor during the cruise of the Great White Fleet in 1908.

By late September, the Eighth Army had established a strong presence in Tokyo, and the Sixth Army commenced its movement into Honshu. Krueger had established his headquarters in Kyoto, and Spruance flew down to meet him on 12 October to discuss the demilitarization of Japanese naval facilities. From the air, the awful results of the B-29 bombing campaign were clear to see: Tokyo, Nagoya, Osaka, and Kobe were mostly a heap of ruins. Kyoto, however, remained largely untouched. After his meeting, Spruance toured the ancient Imperial Palace complex and came away impressed by the simplicity and beauty of traditional Japanese architecture.

Krueger had told him that the majority of the people in Kyoto were friendly to the Americans and pleased to be rid of the militarists. So successful was this transition that when Spruance resumed his habit of daily walks in the countryside around Yokosuka, he could do so without an armed escort. He walked along the coast for miles, through small fishing villages and past areas of verdant cultivation that reminded him of Puerto Rico. At first, he found the people he encountered to be cautious and aloof, but the children came around quickly. Initially shy, they soon greeted him with smiles and happy chatter. Their parents also began to soften. "If the common people hated us," he told Margaret, "it would certainly show in the attitude of their children." This was an experience that the occupiers found throughout Japan as they met their defeated enemies with respect and treated them as fellow human beings, in stark contrast to how the Imperial Japanese Army had treated those who had fallen under their control.[31]

In late October, Nimitz asked Spruance to meet him in Pearl Harbor. Nimitz had just returned from a triumphal victory tour stateside, but despite the adulation of the public, he was having problems with Secretary of the Navy James Forrestal. Fleet Admiral King had recently announced his intention to retire by the end of the year. The office of the Commander-in-Chief, U.S. Fleet (COMINCH) had just been abolished, and henceforth the top billet in the Navy would be that of the Chief of Naval Operations, the CNO. King had expressly requested that Nimitz replace him as CNO, and Nimitz had expressed his desire to take on the position, but Forrestal was stalling. Worse, there were hearings in the Senate discussing the consolidation of the armed services into one department, an idea long favored by the Army but one which would likely be to the detriment of the Navy.

Nimitz had a plan. He had orders to return to Washington to testify before the Senate Committee on the Armed Services, but first he wanted to make Adm. John H. Towers the commander of the Fifth Fleet and bring Spruance back as the Deputy CinCPac and POA. This would ensure that Towers, a Forrestal favorite, would be sidelined on the other side of the Pacific so that when Nimitz was made CNO, Spruance and not Towers could replace him as CinCPac. Spruance told Nimitz that he would be pleased and honored to fill that post for as long as Nimitz wanted him there, but if he were to go ashore again, he wanted to be made the President of the Naval War College. Congress had recently changed the retirement age for flag officers to sixty-two from sixty-four years of age, and such an appointment was just what Spruance wanted to close out his career. Nimitz agreed.[32]

While Nimitz returned to Washington, DC, Spruance flew back to Yokosuka. In accordance with Nimitz's orders, at 1000 on 8 November, Spruance's flag came down from the masthead of *New Jersey* and Towers' was raised. Spruance was back in Pearl Harbor the next day. On the flight back, there was a stopover at Wake Island, and Spruance had a brief reunion with his old aviation officer from the CruDiv 5 days, Capt. Earl Junghans, the base commander. On his return, Spruance was chagrined to discover that Nimitz's fate and his were still up in the air. He did not have long to wait, however. On 20 November, after a heart-to-heart meeting with President Truman, Nimitz's appointment as CNO was confirmed, as was Spruance's appointment as CinCPac and CinCPOA.[33]

Fleet Adm. Chester W. Nimitz returned to Pearl Harbor, and on 24 November, on the deck of USS *Menhaden* (SS 377), one of the Pacific Fleet's newest submarines, he was relieved by his old chief of staff and comrade in arms. Spruance knew that his time in the job would be short-lived. Vice Adm. William S. Pye had been appointed President of the Naval War College in 1942 and had officially retired in 1944, but was brought back on active duty for the duration of the war to continue in that post. Now that the war was over, he was scheduled to end his duty there in early 1946, opening the way for Spruance to replace him. Given the dearth of housing in Honolulu and the likely short duration of his tour, Spruance told his wife that there was no sense in her moving out to join him. In addition, their daughter Margaret was in the last stages of her tuberculosis treatment in Monrovia. Spruance came to California on Christmas leave on 22 December. His wife remembered her husband was "very relaxed and very relieved" to be home. They visited friends, and Spruance managed to get a set of new tires that he had scrounged put on their old car.[34]

Admiral Towers relieved Adm. Raymond Ames Spruance as CinCPac on 1 February 1946. Spruance returned to Monrovia and began to pack for the move to Newport, Rhode Island. While his daughter stayed in sunny southern California to complete her recuperation, Raymond and Margaret Spruance began their road trip back east on 10 February. They took their time, stopping in Indianapolis along the way, and reached Coasters Harbor Island and the gates of the U.S. Naval War College on 1 March 1946.[35]

CHAPTER 16

POSTWAR AND EPILOGUE

WITH HIS RETURN to the Naval War College, Spruance was back where, twenty years earlier, he had embarked on the study of how to defeat the Empire of Japan. That mission was now accomplished, and his new task would be to reorient the Naval War College's curriculum to equip future flag officers with the knowledge they would need to confront new adversaries in the post-war atomic age. Spruance had been there less than two weeks when he set about revising Admiral Kalbfus' *Sound Military Decision*. When he had seen Charles Barber reading it, Spruance had referred to it as "a jungle of words." Now he would cut away the overgrowth and simplify it. The resulting *Naval Manual of Operational Planning, 1948*, issued by the CNO, used the basic "Estimate of the Situation" form and modified it for use by all of the armed forces. It remains the ancestor of the U.S. Navy's current operational planning document.[1]

The Naval War College class of 1947, which began in June 1946, saw the resumption of the full eleven-month course for both the Senior and Junior classes. The one hundred students included not only the usual Navy and Marine Corps line and staff officers but also Army and Air Force officers and, for the first time, a student from a foreign navy. Spruance brought Capt. Henry E. Eccles in to teach logistics, and for the class of 1948 a separate logistics class with its own curriculum was added. During Spruance's tenure, the *Naval War College Review* began publication, officials from the State Department were brought on board to lecture on foreign relations, and historians such as Capt. Samuel E. Morison, USNR, lectured on naval operations in the Second World War.[2]

War-gaming maintained its pride of place, but the problems and the overall slow pace of game mechanics needed to be updated for modern warfare involving jet aircraft, fast submarines, and nuclear weapons. Under Spruance, the staff made plans for a new electronic maneuver board to simplify game play and enhance real-time decision making, but the Naval Electronic Warfare Simulator (NEWS) that incorporated these features would not be up and running until 1958.[3]

A significant portion of Spruance's time at the War College would be spent elsewhere, giving lectures and preaching the one faith in which he truly believed: the importance of sea power to the continued success and freedom of the United States, as well as the irreplaceable role of the U.S. Navy in maintaining it. The first instance involved the very existence of the Navy as a separate entity, when he testified before the Senate Naval Affairs Committee on 10 July 1946. The long-simmering interservice rivalries for resources and ultimate authority, which had been contained by President Roosevelt, a known Navy man, were now coming to a head under President Truman. As a senator, Truman had advocated for a unified military to avoid another fiasco such as the failure of both the Army and the Navy to prevent the Pearl Harbor attack. Throughout much of the war, Gen. George C. Marshall had advocated for the unification of the War and Navy Departments into a "Department of Common Defense" with a single cabinet-level secretary and a general staff of senior officers. A new U.S. Air Force would assume all land-based military aviation functions and the Marine Corps would be reduced to little more than the ancillary service it had once been, providing base security and the occasional naval landing party.

In his testimony, Spruance reiterated the importance of the Navy in ensuring that the nation's "first line of defense" began at the far side of the surrounding oceans and not on America's shores. Spruance believed that a centralized bureaucracy would stifle the administration, planning, and innovation necessary to each service branch's unique function. He stated that, based on his war experience, a fleet without a land-based air force, trained to operate with naval forces and under a unified command, was like "a boxer with one hand tied behind his back." Citing examples from the Battles of Midway and the Philippine Sea, Spruance told the committee that naval operations move so fast and are so dependent on coordinated communication that "teamwork is essential." He noted the failure of the

Army's high-level bombers to sink or damage enemy warships, despite their often extravagant claims, and argued that successful naval operations depend on an integrated, combined-arms force operating under a common doctrine. Finally, Spruance stated his belief that any new legislation must include the retention of the Marine Corps as a joint operations force.[4]

Struggling with a limited budget in the era of postwar austerity, Spruance also made a case for the importance of the War College that is as relevant today as it was nearly eighty years ago. "The War College operations," he wrote to Vice Adm. William M. Fechteler, the Chief of the Bureau of Personnel, "is of such importance to the Government and the people of the United States that no effort should be omitted in the furtherance of War College work. The amount of public expenditure . . . is so small compared to other public expenditures, and the results of the higher instructions [*sic*] of the minds of leaders in naval actions is so important in the saving of materials and lives that any investment in the annual War College appropriations is in itself economy."[5]

While in Los Angeles for the Navy Day celebrations in 1947, Spruance took the opportunity to do some househunting on the Monterey Peninsula, an area whose pleasant weather and proximity to the sea greatly appealed to him. He purchased a Spanish colonial-style house in the Del Monte Forest near Pebble Beach, where he and Margaret would move in the summer of 1948. With the statutory retirement age now set at sixty-two years, Spruance knew he would be retiring on his birthday, 3 July 1948. He requested a slightly earlier retirement date of 1 July 1948, the date set by Congress when all officers would revert from the temporary ranks they held during the war to their permanent rank, which for Spruance was Rear Admiral. With the earlier date he would retire as a four-star admiral.[6]

Spruance need not have worried as in June 1948 Congress awarded him the permanent rank of admiral at full pay, a rare privilege. In some ways, this was done in compensation for the fact that he was not given a fifth star and the rank of Fleet Admiral like his friend Bill Halsey. Congress has authorized only four five-star billets, and the first three went to William H. Leahy, Ernest J. King, and Chester W. Nimitz. In late 1945, King had been asked by Secretary Forrestal to provide his analysis of which serving four-star admiral should get the last billet. In King's opinion, it came down to Halsey and Spruance. Unable to decide, Forrestal went to President Truman, and Halsey was selected based on his seniority and the fact that he had been at sea several years before the war started.[7]

Considering his career of sterling service, the Navy hierarchy treated Spruance rather shabbily on his retirement. He had hoped that he would be given a chance to remain as president of the War College for three years, but no extension on his retirement date was offered, nor was he given the opportunity to remain onboard after his official retirement as his predecessor Admiral Pye had done. Nor did Secretary Forrestal see fit to arrange a farewell ceremony. When Assistant Secretary John N. Brown II came to address the graduating class of 1948, he took steps to remedy this oversight and added remarks lauding Spruance's achievements on his own initiative. As Spruance and Margaret drove away from the president's house and over the causeway to the mainland for the last time on 1 July 1948, an honor guard of Marines saluted him as the band played, and the assembled War College waved him off. Spruance showed no emotion, but his wife knew he was disappointed. It was a bittersweet parting.[8]

In late 1951, Spruance was called out of retirement to serve his country again, this time as ambassador to the Philippines, a former colonial territory torn apart by a burgeoning communist insurgency fueled by the corruption of the ruling oligarchy. As ambassador, Spruance was instrumental, with the help of the State Department and the Central Intelligence Agency, and in the face of fierce opposition from the entrenched elites, in securing the election of Ramon Magsaysay, a man of integrity beloved by the common people, as the third president of the Republic of the Philippines. Magsaysay's election in November 1953 was seen as free and fair, and it played a decisive role in the collapse of the communist insurgency. A grateful Magsaysay ensured that the Philippines would remain a staunch ally of the United States.[9]

During his three years as ambassador, Spruance demonstrated a deep concern for the welfare of the Filipino people, and his integrity and leadership in that position significantly bolstered the credibility of the United States during an era of rapid communist expansion in the Pacific Rim. He was an exemplar of how a retired military leader could provide valuable service to his country in times of peace. Looking back more than ten years later, Spruance wrote, "Personally, I have always been rather proud of the way things went in that 1953 election."[10]

Spruance resigned from his position in April 1955 and returned to his home in Monterey to resume his well-earned retirement. He often claimed that he hated writing and so avoided writing a memoir as many another old warrior had done. Spruance was, however, more than willing to write long letters in his clear hand commenting on various naval histories sent to him for review. In 1955, he wrote the foreword to *Midway*, the English-language edition of the Japanese account of the battle written by Fuchida Mitsuo and Okumiya Masatake, former Japanese naval commanders, praising it for completing the historical picture. It would not be until many decades later that additional scholarship from Japanese sources revealed that their account was tainted by self-interest.[11]

In 1965, Congressman Burt L. Talcott, who represented Monterey, lobbied Congress for a fifth star for his storied constituent. While he appreciated the effort, Spruance told historian E. B. Potter that nearly twenty years later, few would much care anymore. "So far as my getting five-star rank is concerned, if I could have it along with Bill Halsey, that would have been fine." However, he told Potter, "If I had received it instead of Bill Halsey, I would have been very unhappy over it. . . . I have always been very grateful that I was privileged to play the part I did in the Pacific during the war, and it makes me very happy that when historians such as Sam Morison and you prepare the record of the war, you seem to approve of what I had a hand in doing."[12]

Spruance's lifelong insistence on healthy living kept him going when others of his generation had already passed on, but as he aged, his eyesight dimmed, and his once sharp mind became less so. He developed cataracts and underwent surgery to remove them; he also endured the discomfort of hard contact lenses. Nevertheless, he remained engaged, enjoying his family, corresponding with his old friends, and developed a love of gardening in retirement. He freely discussed the battles he had fought whenever someone sought him out, usually on the anniversary of the Battle of Midway.

In May 1969 Spruance's pleasant life was upended when his son Edward was severely injured in a car crash and died several weeks later. While

Edward had perceived his father as a somewhat cold and aloof parent, once Edward became a successful naval officer, his father treated him more as an equal and a confidant. As Spruance grew older, he became increasingly dependent on his son for help and advice, and so Edward's death came as a stunning blow. His wife Margaret recalled that he lost all interest in life and withdrew into a shell, carefully concealing his crushing grief. His health deteriorated, and he became bedridden. Raymond Ames Spruance died at home on 13 December 1969. He was buried in the Golden Gate National Cemetery beside his old friends and comrades Richmond Kelly Turner, Chester W. Nimitz, and Charles A. Lockwood.[13]

Looking back on the flag officers who had served under him, Fleet Admiral King said that "as to brains" Raymond Spruance was the "the best flag officer in the Navy in every way," while Fleet Admiral Nimitz, who perhaps knew Spruance best, said of him that he was "the admiral's admiral." The epitaph of Spruance written by Samuel E. Morison, while often quoted, perhaps describes him best and deserves repetition here:

> He envied no man, regarded no one as a rival, won the respect of all with whom he came in contact, and went ahead in his quiet way winning victories for his country.[14]

DECORATIONS AND CITATIONS OF ADMIRAL RAYMOND A. SPRUANCE

Navy Cross
Distinguished Service Medal
Gold Star in Lieu of Second Distinguished Service Medal
Gold Star in Lieu of Third Distinguished Service Medal
Army Distinguished Service Medal
Navy Commendation Medal
Presidential Unit Citation
Cuban Pacification Medal
World War I Victory Medal with "Overseas" Clasp
American Defense Service Medal with "Fleet" Clasp
Asiatic-Pacific Campaign Medal
Navy Occupation Service Medal with "Asia" Clasp
Honorary Companion of the Bath (Military), by Great Britain
Gold Cross of the Chevalier of the Order of the Savior, by Greece
Grand Officer of the Order of Leopold with Palm, by Belgium
Croix de Guerre with Palm, by Belgium

NOTES

PREFACE

1. Forrestel, *Admiral Raymond A. Spruance*, 109.
2. Forrestel, xi.
3. Buell, *The Quiet Warrior*, 239.
4. W. Hughes, "Clear Purpose, Comprehensive Execution," 125.
5. Potter, "The Command Personality," 25.

PROLOGUE

1. MSC037.1_13_20, Letter, Oliver to Buell, 5 August 1971, 6.
2. Oliver to Buell, 7. Layton's office was actually on the first "deck," but the rest of the intelligence staff, including Lt. Cdr. Joe Rochefort, worked below in what was called "The Dungeon."
3. MSC037.1_1_4, Letter, Spruance to E. P. Forrestel, n.d. (November 1962), 5.
4. Oliver to Buell, 7.
5. Potter, *Nimitz*, 85.
6. Lundstrom, *Black Shoe Carrier Admiral*, 225–26.
7. Carlson, *Joe Rochefort's War*, 352–3; Layton, *And I Was There*, 430–3. The ship types and numbers are taken from Commander-in-Chief, United States Pacific Fleet, "Operation Plan No. 29–42," 27 May 1942. Layton attributes the quip to Cdr. Richard Ruble, *Enterprise*'s navigation officer.
8. Operation Plan No. 29–42.
9. Operation Plan No. 29–42, "Letter of Instructions," 28 May 1942.

CHAPTER 1. LEARNING THE ART OF COMMAND

1. W. Hughes, "Clear Purpose, Comprehensive Execution," 124, quoting a letter from Baer, 17 April 2007. See Clausewitz, *On War*, Book 1, chapter 3.
2. MSC037.1_1_01, Letter, Raymond A. Spruance (hereafter RAS) to E. B. Potter, 4 February 1959.
3. The typical class size would shrink by 20 to 30 percent by the time of graduation due to such attrition.
4. MSC037.1_10_2_01, Interview with Margaret Dean Spruance (hereafter MDS).
5. Potter, *Bull Halsey*, 94. MSC037.2_1_12, Letter, RAS to MDS, 23 September 1945.
6. MSC037.1_10_2_01, Interview MDS, November 1971.
7. MCS037.1_10_2_01, Interview MDS.
8. Ingram was also entered into the College Football Hall of Fame for his game-winning touchdown against Army in 1906.
9. MSC037.1_10_2_01, Interview MDS.
10. MSC037.1_10_2_01, Interview MDS.
11. MSC037.1_10_2_02, Interview MDS. What exactly this entailed remains a mystery.

12. MSC037.1_10_2_03, Interview MDS.
13. MSC037.1_11_2, Letter, Capt. Wilbur M. Lockhart (Ret.) to Buell, undated.
14. MSC037.1_11_2, Lockhart to Buell.
15. MSC012_1_13, Official Navy Correspondence, 1919–1923. MSC037.1_12_20, Fitness Reports, 1919–1924. Halsey consistently rated Spruance as "excellent" in every category.
16. MSC012_1_13, Official Navy Correspondence, 1919–1923. MSC037.1_12_20, Fitness Reports, 1919–1924.
17. Robison, "The Part of Engineering in Command."
18. MSC037.1_10_2_02, Interview MDS. MSC037.1_12_21, Fitness Reports, 1924–1929.
19. MSC037.1_11_3, Letter, Vice Adm. William L. Rees (Ret.) to Buell, March 22, 1972.
20. MSC012_1_14, Official Navy Correspondence, 1924–1927.

CHAPTER 2. LEARNING THE ART OF WAR

1. Buell, "Spruance and the Naval War College: Part 1," 38.
2. RG-04_31_01, "Memorandum for the Senior and Junior Classes of 1927," 1239-A, 8. War with England and other powers was considered as well.
3. Hattendorf et al., *Sailors and Scholars*, 72. Buell, "Spruance and the Naval War College: Part 1," 41. See also Spector, *Professors of War*, 117–18.
4. Miller, *War Plan Orange*, 36, 116.
5. MSC037.1_14_5, Research Cards, Note Card 4. The records of this problem are found in RG-04, Files 1380 and 1381. See also Evans and Peattie, *Kaigun*, 129.
6. Miller, *War Plan Orange,* 116. MCS037.1_14_5, TBB Research Cards. Dunlap died in France in 1931 in a tragic accident, cutting off a promising career.
7. RG13_07_27_01, Cdr. Raymond A. Spruance, *Thesis on Command*, 11 September 1926, 4.
8 "Mississippi III (Battleship No. 41)," DANFS, Naval History and Heritage Command.
9. MSC037.1_11_6, Letter, Capt. Paul R. Coloney to Buell, 3 April 1972, 2.
10. MSC037.1_11_6, Letter, Nealy A. Chapin to Buell, 11 April 1972, 3–4.
11. Nofi, *To Train a Fleet for War*, 122.
12. MSC012.1_15, Letter, Bureau of Navigation, 30 January 1931; Buell, "Spruance and the Naval War College: Part 2," 39.
13. Potter, *Bull Halsey*, 135. King had been a member of a board in 1919 that recommended that all future flag officers attend the Naval War College. King did not graduate with the class of 1933, as he was made the chief of the Bureau of Aeronautics in April 1933.
14. MSC037.1_10_02_03, Interview MDS, 3–6. Potter, *Bull Halsey*, 126–27.
15. MSC037.1_12_22, Fitness Reports, 1929–1936.
16. MSC037.1_11_8, Letter, Capt. David R. Hull to Buell, 18 January 1972.
17. Nofi, *To Train a Fleet for War*, 190. MSC037.1_12_22. Fitness Reports, 1929–1936.
18. Buell, "Spruance and the Naval War College: Part 2," 39.
19. Evans and Peattie, *Kaigun,* 448–50.
20. MSC037.1_10_02_03. MSC037.1_12_22, Fitness Reports, 1929–1936.
21. MSC012_2_13, R. A. Spruance, "Lecture on Tactics—1936." Emphasis in the original.
22. MSC037.1_11_12, Letter, Vice Adm. George H. Fort to Buell, 13 November 1970. Emphasis in the original. Fort was captain of USS *North Carolina* during the Guadalcanal campaign and was a task force commander under Halsey.
23. MSC037.1_11_11, Letter, Cdr. Carlos A. Bailey to Buell, 7 November 1970. Letter, Capt. B. B. Wilson Jr. to Buell, 9 November 1970.
24. MSC037.1_09_06_01, Oral History of Margaret Spruance Bogart, 8.

CHAPTER 3. REAR ADMIRAL SPRUANCE

1. Hone, "Modernizing Battleships," 274–81.
2. MSC037.1_11_14.
3. MSC037.1_13_20, Letter, Robert J. Oliver to Buell, 17 September 1971, 3–4.
4. MSC037.1_11_14, Letter, Robert L. Savage to Buell, 16 May 1972.
5. MSC037.1_11_13, Letter, Rear Adm. E. J. Taylor Jr. to Buell, 23 April 1972.
6. Nofi, *To Train a Fleet for War*, 239–41.
7. MSC037.1_11_13, Letter, Rear Adm. C. H. Duerfeldt to Buell, 22 April 1972. Duerfeldt was testing the XPB2Y Mariner flying boat.
8. MSC037.1_11_13, Letter, Capt. Richard W. Garrity, MD, to Buell, 9 June 1972.
9. *Building the Navy's Bases in World War II*, 2:5–6.
10. MSC037.1_10_2_04, Interview MDS; MSC037.1_13_1, Fitness Reports, 1936–1948.
11. MSC037.1_11_16, Letter, Vice Adm. Harold W. Johnson, CEC, to Buell, 17 February 1972. Johnson was the officer in charge of construction in the Tenth Naval District. In early evaluations of the site Johnson had argued strenuously against Isla Grande but had been overruled.
12. King and Whitehill, *Fleet Admiral*, 311, 320–21. Buell, *Master of Sea Power*, 134–5. Buell recounts a humorous episode where Capt. Victor H. Krulak, USMC, demonstrated the new craft to King and it got hung up on a reef, a harbinger of things to come. The Higgins boat perhaps should have been named for Krulak, as it was he who suggested the design based on his observations of the Japanese *daihatsu* landing barges.
13. MSC012_1_16, Official Navy Correspondence, 1941–1944, Letter from Bureau of Navigation, Change of Duty, 2 July 1941.
14. MSC037.1_13_1, Fitness Reports, 1936–1948, Report of 25 March, 1941. MSC037.1_13_20, Robert J. Oliver typescript notes in reply to Buell, 5 August 1971, 2. Robert J. Oliver speculated that Halsey did indeed specifically request that Spruance be given the command of his cruiser division. A collaboration between Halsey and Spruance in this matter is the author's conjecture as there is no documentation of such.
15. MSC012_1_16. Letter, C. W. Nimitz to RAS, 12 August 1941.
16. Buell, *Quiet Warrior*, 99. Buell makes this statement based on his interview with Margaret Dean Spruance. Whether Spruance wanted to tell his wife that his job preference would certainly put him into harm's way is another question.
17. MSC037.1_09_06_2, Interview MDS, 4–5.
18. Friedman, *U.S. Cruisers*, 317. Gassed-up floatplanes, motorboats, and POL stored in the well deck/hangar area also contributed to these destructive fires.
19. MSC037.1_11_19, Letter, Vice Adm. Victor D. Long (Ret.) to Buell, 7 November 1971.
20. MSC037.1_11_19, Letter, Rear Adm. William M. McCormick (Ret.) to Buell, 12 October 1971.
21. MSC037.1_11_19, McCormick to Buell, 2.
22. Asada, *From Mahan to Pearl Harbor*, 282; Prange, *At Dawn We Slept*, 418.
23. Prange, *At Dawn We Slept*, 405–6. The Navy Basic War Plan, WPL-46-C, was the naval component of Rainbow Five.
24. Prange, *At Dawn We Slept*, 400–1.
25. Potter, *Bull Halsey*, 1–4. Halsey, *Admiral Halsey's Story*, 73–75. Rear Adm. Milo F. Draemel had command of BATDIV 1 that day.
26. Potter, *Bull Halsey*, 6–8.
27. MSC037.1_11_19, McCormick to Buell, 2.

28. The surface ships with the Strike Force included the fast battleships *Hiei* and *Kirishima*, both later sunk in the Solomons, and the cruisers *Tone* and *Chikuma*.
29. "Meet Captain Kidd," USS *Kidd* Veterans Museum, https://www.usskidd.com/explore-the-kidd/meet-the-man.
30. MSC037.1_09_06_02, Margaret S. Bogart Oral History, 7–8; MSC037.1_10_02_04, MDS Interview, 12–13.
31. Prange, *At Dawn We Slept*, 546–49. Prange quotes Yamamoto reportedly saying that Nagumo was like a thief who is brave during the robbery, but once it is done thinks only of escaping with the loot.
32. Lundstrom, *Black Shoe Carrier Admiral*, 42–45.
33. Halsey, *Admiral Halsey's Story*, 84. TF 8 wasted precious fuel sailing at high speed toward Johnston Island in response to a false alarm. Halsey believed he could have helped relieve Wake instead.
34. MSC037.1_01_04, Letter, RAS to E. P. Forrestel, n.d. (November 1962).

CHAPTER 4. THE EARLY CARRIER RAIDS

1. GB 122 (Green), January 02 1718, COMINCH to CINCPAC. The Makin raid of August 1942 found a small seaplane base manned by a support staff. After the raid it would be more heavily defended, but lightly compared to Tarawa.
2. GB 123–34, "Employment of Carrier Task Forces in January."
3. GB 55, Running Summary, 13 January; GB 186, 190, Running Summary, 25 and 27 January; GB 58, Running Summary, 21 January; GB 183, Running Summary, 23 January 1942.
4. Halsey, *Admiral Halsey's Story*, 89.
5. As the task groups were west of the dateline, the local date was 1 February.
6. MSC037.1_11_19, Letter, Rear Adm. William M. McCormick (Ret.) to Buell, 12 October 1971, 3.
7. NARA RG 38 2990147-14-16, Oral History, LCDR Earl A. Junghans, 12–13. Hereinafter Junghans. Junghans' 1942 estimates of the shells fired are given here and differ from those reported by Buell in *Quiet Warrior.*
8. Halsey, *Admiral Halsey's Story*, 93. In his memoir Halsey uses the tamer phrase "Haul Out with Halsey."
9. MSC037.1_13_20, Letter, Robert J. Oliver to Buell, 5 August 1971. Halsey, *Admiral Halsey's Story*, 93.
10. MSC037.1_1_11, Letters, RAS to MDS, 7 and 10 February 1942.
11. U.S. Navy History and Heritage Command, "The Raids on Wake and Marcus Islands."
12. MSC037.1_13_20, Letter, Oliver to Buell, 17 September 1971, 7–8. Junghans, 20. Junghans misidentified the planes as made by Kawanishi, the builder of the large four-engine seaplanes, but he clearly states they were of the same type as his SOCs.
13 Junghans, 21–25.
14. U.S. Navy History and Heritage Command, "The Raids on Wake and Marcus Islands."
15. MSC037.1_13_20, Oliver to Buell, 5 August 1971, 5. Ware and his section of four SBDs disappeared without a trace on their return to *Enterprise* after hitting the *Kaga* on 4 June 1942 during the Battle of Midway.
16. U.S. Navy History and Heritage Command, "The Raids on Wake and Marcus Islands"; Junghans, 23–25.
17. MSC037.1_1_11, RAS to MDS, 21 March 1942.
18. MSC037.1_13_21, Interview Notes, Robert J. Oliver, 5 October 1971, 4.
19. Hughes, *Admiral Halsey*, 165–66.

20. MSC037.1_01_04, Letter, RDS to E. P. Forrestel, n.d. (1962); Action Report: USS *Enterprise* (CV 6), Captain G. D. Murray to Admiral C. W. Nimitz, 23 April 1943.
21. GB 364, Running Summary, 17 April 1942.
22. MSC037.1_01_04, Spruance to Forrestal; Parshall and Tully, *Shattered Sword*, 42–43.
23. *Yorktown* also suffered several near misses that ruptured her oil tanks, causing her to leave an oil slick.
24. MSC037.1_13_21, Interview Notes, Robert J. Oliver, 5 October 1971.
25. Halsey, *Admiral Halsey's Story*, 105.
26. Washington was not entirely incorrect. The Japanese planned on assaulting Fiji after Operation MI. See Prados, *Combined Fleet Decoded*, 290.
27. GB Vol. 8/1_9, AIDAC from CINCPAC to CTF 16, no date. GB 480, Running Summary. Lundstrom, *Black Shoe Carrier Admiral,* 210–11, 562. There is no record of this cable in the Graybook; Lundstrom's source is private correspondence with Edwin T. Layton.
28. Layton, *"And I Was There,"* 415–16; GB 482, Running Summary, May 16, GB Vol. 8/ Midway Set 3/0031, CINCPAC to CTF 16, May 18; Halsey, *Admiral Halsey's Story*, 106.
29. Layton, *"And I Was There,"* 421–22.
30. MSC037.1_13_20, Oliver to Buell, 5 August 1971, 3.
31. Oliver to Buell, 5–6.

CHAPTER 5. THE BATTLE OF MIDWAY

1. Carlson, *Joe Rochefort's War*, 359.
2. Parshall, "What WAS Nimitz Thinking?," 12–13.
3. Operation Plan No. 29–42, Annex "2," Initial Area of Striking Forces; Hughes, *Admiral Bill Halsey*, 118.
4. Parshall, "What WAS Nimitz Thinking?," 9–10.
5. Lundstrom, *Black Shoe Carrier Admiral*, 226; Parshall and Tully, *Shattered Sword*, 44–45. As the authors point out, the Aleutians as a base for bomber attacks may have seemed far-fetched to the Americans, but to the Japanese it was a real concern.
6. Parshall and Tully, *Shattered Sword.* Some sources claim that six B-26 Marauders were sent.
7. MSC037.1_13_20, Letter, Robert J. Oliver to Buell, 5 August 1971, 10–11.
8. Oliver to Buell, 5 August 1971, 8–9; MSC037.1_11_17, Letter, W. E. Gallaher to Buell, 5 December 1971, 2. The Flag Shelter had been added by Halsey and was not originally part of *Enterprise*'s design.
9. Layton, *"And I Was There,"* 433.
10. Parshall and Tully, *Shattered Sword*, 97–99.
11. Lundstrom, *Black Shoe Carrier Admiral*, 235–36; Parshall, "What WAS Nimitz Thinking?," 13.
12. U.S. Navy History and Heritage Command, "Battle of Midway Army Air Forces." The true extent of the damage (or lack thereof) could not be assessed until IJN skippers were interviewed after the war.
13. Lundstrom, *Black Shoe Carrier Admiral*, 241.
14. Lundstrom, *Black Shoe Carrier Admiral*, 241–42. Enterprise Action Report, Serial 0133.
15. Oliver to Buell, 5 August 1971, 9–10. Lundstrom gives Browning the full credit for the decision, discounting Oliver's account. As Oliver was there, I prefer his version.
16. Lundstrom, *Black Shoe Carrier Admiral*, 244. See also Lundstrom's treatment of the 0900 launch myth in his introduction to Buell, *Quiet Warrior*, xiii.
17. Parshall and Tully, *Shattered Sword*, 135.

18. Parshall and Tully, 149.
19. Parshall and Tully, 156.
20. Parshall and Tully, 176.
21. Lundstrom, *Black Shoe Carrier Admiral*, 252–54.
22. MSC037.1_1_4, Letter, RAS to E. P. Forrestel, n.d. (November 1962), 6.
23. Slonim, "A Flagship View of Command Decisions," 85. The "snooper" was shot down by *Enterprise*'s CAP before it could repeat the contact; see Lundstrom, *Black Shoe Carrier Admiral*, 247.
24. Symonds, "Mitscher and the Mystery of Midway," 49–50; Lundstrom, *Black Shoe Carrier Admiral*, 248; Parshall and Tully, *Shattered Sword*, 271–74.
25. Lundstrom, *Black Shoe Carrier Admiral*, 251.
26. Symonds, "Mitscher and the Mystery of Midway," 50–51.
27. Fuchida and Okumiya, *Midway*, 196; Lundstrom, *Black Shoe Carrier Admiral*, 254.
28. Lundstrom, *Black Shoe Carrier Admiral*, 217; MSC037.1_11_17, Letter, William Buracker to Buell, 1 November 1971, 2.
29. Parshall and Tully, *Shattered Sword*, 223–26.
30. Parshall and Tully, 228–32. McClusky had ordered Best to attack *Akagi* at the same time as Best was reporting that he intended to attack *Kaga*, as per doctrine; they did not hear each other.
31. Lundstrom, *Black Shoe Carrier Admiral*, 261–62.
32. Parshall and Tully, *Shattered Sword*, 261–64.
33. Parshall and Tully, 274.
34. MSC037.1_11_17, Letter, W. E. Gallaher to Buell, 8 February 1972, 2; Symonds, *Battle of Midway*, 313. Ware's section was attacked by Zeros escorting the *Hiryu* strike on *Yorktown*, but they successfully fended off the attack. Ware was never seen again, but the crew members of a plane from his section were picked up by the Japanese and, after interrogation, brutally murdered.
35. Lundstrom, *Black Shoe Carrier Admiral*, 263.
36. Parshall and Tully, *Shattered Sword*, 296–97.
37. Lundstrom, *Black Shoe Carrier Admiral*, 266–68.
38. GB Vol. 8/Midway Set 5/0090, 050315 Z, COMTASKFORCE 17 to CINCPAC, 5 June 1942. Midway is located at GMT (Zone Zed) minus 12 hours, which equates to local time of 1515 4 June.
39. GB Vol. 8/Midway Set 5/0089, 050204 Z, COMTASKFORCE 16 to CINCPAC, 5 June 1942; Lundstrom, *Black Shoe Carrier Admiral*, 571n22, quoting letter from Richard Best to Lundstrom, 15 May 2000.
40. MSC037.1_11_17, Letter, W. E. Gallaher to Buell, 8 February 1972, 2; Letter, W. Fred Boone to Buell, 20 November 1971, 2.
41. Symonds, *The Battle of Midway*, 330–31.
42. Symonds, 332–33.
43. Parshall and Tully, *Shattered Sword*, 328–29.
44. Lundstrom, *Black Shoe Carrier Admiral*, 277.
45. Lundstrom, 277; MSC037.1_1_4, RAS to Forrestel, 8.
46. GB Vol. 8/Midway Set 5/0111, 060431 Z, CINCPAC to CTF 16, CTF 17, 6 June 1942.
47. MSC037.1_13_20, Letter, Oliver to Buell, 17 September 1971, 12.
48. MSC037.1_11_17, Letter, C. Wade McClusky to Buell, 12 November 1971; MSC037.1_11_18, Oliver Interview Notes, 5 October 1971.

49. Parshall and Tully, *Shattered Sword*, 364–65. "Scouting Squadron Six Action Report, 4–6 June 1942."
50. MSC037.1_1_7, Letter, RAS to E. B. Potter, 2 January 1960.
51. Lundstrom, *Black Shoe Carrier Admiral*, 286; Parshall and Tully, *Shattered Sword*, 366; MSC037.1_11_17, Newspaper Clipping, "Historic Battle of Midway Recalled by Adm. Spruance," *San Diego Union*, Monday, June 3, 1968, A-10.
52. Parshall and Tully, *Shattered Sword*, 367–68.
53. MSC037.1_13_20, Oliver to Buell, 17 September 1971, 12.
54. Parshall and Tully, *Shattered Sword*, 370–71.
55. Ugaki, *Fading Victory*, 155–57.
56. MSC037.1_11_17, news clipping, "Historic Battle of Midway Recalled by Adm. Spruance," *San Diego Union*, Monday, June 3, 1968, A-10.
57. GB Vol. 8/Midway Set 5/0121, 070756 Z, CTF16 to CINCPAC, 7 June 1942; MSC037.1_13_20, Oliver to Buell, 17 September 1971, 14.
58. Ugaki, *Fading Victory*, 158.
59. *U.S. Navy OP-20-G Memoranda and Reports Related to the Battle of Midway*, 094; Morrison, *Coral Sea*, 181–84.
60. MSC037.1_11_17, Letter, W. E. Gallaher to Buell, 5 December 1971, 2; Pearson and Allen, "The Washington Merry-Go-Round."
61. MSC012_2_4, "Battle of Midway, Forwarding of Reports," 16 June 1942, Serial 0144, Serial 0144-A. Uppercase used as in the original. Both copies contain pencil annotations.
62. See Symonds, "Mitscher and the Mystery of Midway."
63. MSC037.1_11_17, Letter, William H. Buracker to Buell, 1 November 1971; MSC037.1_11_18, Letter, Sherman E. Burroughs to Buell, 7 November 1971; Layton, *"And I Was There,"* 445.

CHAPTER 6. CINCPAC CHIEF OF STAFF, 1942

1. MSC012_1_16, Official Navy Correspondence, 1941–1944; Letter, RAS to E. P. Forrestel, 26 May 1963.
2. MSC037.1_11_20, Letter, P. C. Crosley to Buell, 1 April 1972, 2.
3. MSC037.1_11_20, Letter, L. J. Wiltse to Buell, 23 January 1973, 2. These attributes of Spruance's personality were mentioned by a number of former staffers that Buell contacted.
4. MSC037.1_1_7, RAS to E. B. Potter, 25 December 1961; Wiltse to Buell, 5.
5. Captain Gendreau became a close friend to Nimitz and Spruance. Tragically, he was killed in July 1943 aboard LST-343 attending the sick and wounded at Rendova.
6. Ugaki, *Fading Victory*, 172–74.
7. GB 605 (Pink), July 02 2200. COMINCH to CINCPAC, COMSOWESPACFOR, COMSOPAC.
8. Dyer, *Amphibians Came to Conquer*, 261–62.
9. Buell, *Master of Sea Power*, 218. See Layton, *"And I Was There,"* 141–42. Layton believed that the upper echelons of the Navy, which would have included King, "closed ranks" to protect one of their own.
10. GB 707, Running Summary, July 3; Dyer, *Amphibians Came to Conquer*, 272, 284. Dyer notes that no one on Turner's staff had any experience in planning amphibious operations either, but they managed to do so in short order.
11. *U.S. Marine Corps Tentative Manual for Landing Operations*, ch. 1, para. 1–29; *Landing Operations Doctrine*, Para. 201.

12. GB 1376 (Pink), January 02 0217, CINCPAC to COMINCH, Infeasibility of renewed offensives without air and sea superiority.
13. GB 1020, Conference Notes, 8 September 1943.
14. Symonds, *Nimitz at War*, 184.
15. GB 881 (Pink), August 20 1542, COMINCH to CINCPAC; GB 882, 20 145, CINCPAC to COMINCH; GB 887 August 29 0256, COMSOPAC to COMINCH.
16. Ugaki, *Fading Victory*, 227–28, diary entry for 8 October 1942. Prados, *Combined Fleet Decoded*, 382.
17. GB 1093, Running Summary, October 1942; Layton, *"And I Was There,"* 461–62. Layton was one of the staff who found Nimitz in his slippers and dressing gown about to turn in for the night. GB 895 (Pink), October 16 0937, CINCPAC to COMINCH; 16 0245, COMINCH to CINCPAC, "Your 16 0937 approved."
18. Potter, *Bull Halsey*, 160.
19. MSC037.1_1_4, RAS to E. P. Forrestel, 22 September 1963; MSC012_1_16, Travel Orders, 12 October 1942.
20. GB 897 (Pink), October 21 1400, COMINCH to Admiralty.
21. Trent Hone, *Learning War*, 192–97. Hone offers a compelling argument for Callahan's tactics and motivation in this battle. Callahan was aware of a Naval War College study that indicated that two or more cruisers had equal or greater fighting strength than a single battleship at ranges under 10,000 yards. Unfortunately, he was facing two battleships.
22. Hone, 200–1.
23. MDC037.1_11_21, Letter, Layton to Buell, 3 May 1972, 6. A transcript of the Japanese message traffic calling for a night action can be found in *U.S. Navy OP-20-G Memoranda and Reports Related to the Battle of Midway*, 113–18.
24. MSC037.1_1_02_06, Interview MDS, 1–2.
25. MSC037.1_1_7, Letter, RAS to E. B. Potter, 1 December 1964.

CHAPTER 7. CINCPAC CHIEF OF STAFF: PLANNING THE TRIDENT, 1943

1. GB 897 (Pink), October 27 0251, CINCPAC to COMINCH. Nimitz relayed Halsey's request to King.
2. Stillwell, *Battleship Commander*, 177–78. Van Allen was a brilliant physicist best known for his work on the magnetosphere and the discovery of the eponymous Van Allen Belt.
3. GB 1267, 1268, 1271, Running Summary, 3, 4, and 7 January 1943.
4. Combined Chiefs of Staff, *Casablanca Conference*, 11–17. The Casablanca Conference also included the provision of Unconditional Surrender of the Axis and the plan for round the clock bombing of the Third Reich.
5. GB 1277–1301, "Estimate of the Situation—Solomon Islands," 15 January 1943.
6. GB 1381–1383 (Pink), January 13 1130, COMSOWESPAC to CINCPAC, COMSOPAC.
7. GB 1347, "Notes on Conference Held at Nouméa," 23 January 1943; GB 1353, Running Summary, 28 January 1943.
8. GB 1434 (Pink), February 11 2237. CINCPAC to COMINCH, COMSOPAC; GB 1432, 1435, 1436m (Pink), February 1943, 09 2200 COMINCH to CINCPAC; 13 1250; 13 1400 COMINCH to CINCPAC. Copy to Halsey.
9. GB 1398–1409, "Memo for 16 February," 17 February 1943.
10. MSC-037.1_11_21, Letter, Edwin T. Layton to Buell, 3 May 1972. Layton attributed the tonsillectomy wisecrack to Capt. Thomas B. Hill, CinCPac Fleet Gunnery Officer.

11. MSC-037.1_01_11, Letter, RAS to MDS, 23 May 1943.
12. Morton, *War in the Pacific*, 394.
13. MSC-037–1–11–21, Photostat of *Minutes*, JCS 68th Meeting, Sunday, 21 March 1943, A20729–30. Spruance no doubt remembered the ineffectiveness of high-altitude bombing of moving ships.
14. GB 1473, 1474, GB 1496, 1497 (Pink), TZ WAR 291803, Joint Chiefs of Staff to MacArthur, Nimitz, Halsey.
15. MSC-012_1_16, Travel Orders; Buell, *Quiet Warrior*, 179.
16. *Bulletin No. 2, Battle Experience: Solomon Island Actions, August and September 1942*, 12–40, 12–46, 12–28.
17. *Bulletin No. 3, Battle Experience: Solomon Island Actions, October 1942*, 20–35; *Bulletin No. 4, Battle Experience: Solomon Island Actions, November 1942*, 28–70.
18. Reynolds, *Fast Carriers*, 72; Trent Hone, *Learning War*, 256–59.
19. MSC012_02_14_1, DeBaussel, *Paris Match*, 1965, "Interview with Admiral Raymond A. Spruance," 3–4. Given the twenty-plus years between events and interview, this should not be taken as a verbatim record of their conversation. Hereinafter DeBaussel.
20. DeBaussel, 6.
21. MSC-012_1_16, Official Navy Correspondence, 1941–1944. Spruance received his copy from Nimitz via a cover letter dated 14 June 1943. There was often a lag in the placement of such letters in the file; Spruance would have known for some time. Spruance was confirmed by the Senate on 28 May 1943. *Congressional Record*, 5070; GB 1536, Running Summary, 18 May 1943.
22. *Reminiscences of Admiral Raymond A. Spruance by Charles F. Barber*, NWC Oral History Program, 1996, 8. Hereinafter Barber Oral History. Barber had to find his replacement before his boss Admiral Bieri would release him for the duty.
23. GB 1527–41, Running Summary, May 1943. *Battle Experience: Assault and Occupation of Attu Island, May, 1943*, 48–7 to 48–12.
24. Smith, *Coral and Brass*, 103. See also GB1552 (Green), May 30 1150 and 1155. Some Japanese went to the food supplies where they "ate ravenously." A regimental command post and field hospital were overrun.
25. "Minutes of the 92nd Meeting of the Combined Chiefs of Staff, Washington, DC, 21 May 1943,"CCS, 431–37.
26. Smith, *Coral and Brass*, 104. Smith relates that he had come down with pneumonia while on Attu and was hospitalized on Adak. He makes no mention of the San Francisco conference, but the conference minutes record him as being present to report.
27. GB 1771, 1772 (Pink), July 20 2204. Three Parts. Joint Chiefs of Staff to CINCPAC.
28. Barber Oral History, 9.
29. "Admiral Charles J. Moore," Oral History Research Office, Columbia University, 1968, held at the Nimitz Library, U.S. Naval Academy, Annapolis, MD, 803. Hereinafter Moore Oral History.
30. MSC037.1_11_21. Letter, Adm. Roscoe F. Good to Buell, 11 May 1972. Good was CINCPAC Asst. Operations Officer until August 1943. Barber Oral History, 14.

CHAPTER 8. PLANNING OPERATION GALVANIC

1. Buell, *Master of Sea Power*, 366–67. Symonds, *Nimitz at War*, 184–85. According to Buell, Towers believed that King hated him, but in fact King had saved his career. Buell claims that Nimitz "came to hate" Towers, while Symonds says that they had a mutual "antipathy."

2. Moore Oral History, 809–13.
3. Moore Oral History, 814.
4. MSC037.1_1_11, Letter, RAS to MDS, 22 September 1943.
5. Dyer, *Amphibians Came to Conquer*, 603.
6. Reynolds, *Fast Carriers*, 81-2.
7. Smith, *Coral and Brass*, 109; MSC-012_1_6, Letter, Raymond Spruance to Emmet Forrestel, 2 March 1962.
8. GB 1786 (Pink), 6 August 1943, NR4907, Richardson to General Marshall; GB 1791, 6017 15 August 1943, Marshall to Richardson, Pass to CINCPAC.
9. Smith, *Coral and Brass*, 117, 118.
10. Moore Oral History, 825-26. In this often repeated bit from his oral history Moore seems to be quoting Smith verbatim, which seems unlikely.
11. MSC012_1_7, Letter to "Judge" Eller, 22 July 1966.
12. GB 1649, 1650, Running Summary, 6 September 1943.
13. Barber Oral History, 31.
14. Moore Oral History, 826–27.
15. Carter, *Beans, Bullets, and Black Oil*, 49–57.
16. MSC012_1-20, "Memorandum for Vice Admiral Spruance," 26 August 1943.
17. Forrestel, *Admiral Raymond A. Spruance*, 71. MSC-012_1_6, RAS to Forrestel, 2 March 1962.
18. Moore Oral History, 820–21. Moore said that McMorris was "disgusted" at this attempt to suborn him.
19. Dyer, *Amphibians Came to Conquer*, 618, quoting letter from Spruance to George Dyer. Also, see GB 1813, 1814, 1815 for CINCPAC's request, COMINCH approval, and change of D-Day date.
20. Moore Oral History, 822–23. King's response as related by Moore is unrepeatable in full. Note also that the transcript uses "Ujai" as the name of the atoll in discussion.
21. Reynolds, *Fast Carriers*, 84–85.
22. Evans and Peattie, *Kaigun*, 189–90; Prados, *Combined Fleet Decoded*, 487.
23. "Combined Fleet Ultra Secret Operation Order 41, 15 Aug. 1943" and "Combined Fleet Ultra Secret Operation Order 42, 15 Aug. 1943," Limited Distribution Translation No. 39, Part VIII, Combined Fleet Operation Orders, 4 June 1945, MacArthur Memorial Archives and Library RG 3, SWPA, ATIS, Box 153, 102-117. Hereinafter Op. Order 41.
24. Prados, *Combined Fleet Decoded*, 488; MacArthur Archives, RG-3, Box 153, Folder 39, Part VIII, Combined Fleet Operation Orders, 102. A copy of Koga's operation plans and other vital documents were recovered by Philippine guerrillas after Koga's seaplane crashed off Mindanao in April 1944 and sent by submarine to Pearl Harbor in May. See chapter 11.
25. Prados, *Combined Fleet Decoded*, 504. The 6th Base Force was headquartered on Kwajalein in the Marshall Islands. It was tasked with the defense of the Gilbert Islands as well.
26. Prados, 505; GB 1656, Running Summary, 13 September 1943.
27. Prados, 501–5. The Japanese also feared the Allies might take a northern route through the Kuriles, but as long as the Soviet Union remained neutral this seemed unlikely.
28. Reynolds, *Fast Carriers*, 87–88. An unfortunate result of the attacks on Wake was that ninety-eight American civilian workers taken prisoner when the Japanese captured the island were executed on the orders of the base commander.
29. GB 1674, Running Summary, 18 October 1943; Prados, *Combined Fleet Decoded*, 506–8.
30. Ross, *U.S. War Plans*, 287–91. Note that Abemama was often spelled as "Apamama" or "Apemama" in the documents of the time.

31. MSC037.1_1_11, Letter, RAS to MDS, October 1943.
32. MSC037.1_1_11, Letter, RAS to MDS, 8 November 1942, 1.

CHAPTER 9. THE TRIDENT STRIKES

1. Measurements by author from Map 67–45, Map of Bititu (Betio) Island, *Battle Experience: Supporting Operations before and during the Occupation of the Gilbert Islands, November 1943*. Hereinafter *Battle Experience—Gilbert Islands*.
2. Cheser and Doland, *Beyond the Reef*, 26.
3. Shaw, Nalty, and Turnbladh, "Gilberts Operation," in *Central Pacific Drive*, 29. Marine intelligence used the number of latrines seen on the aerial photography to arrive at their estimates, which were later corroborated by the body count.
4. Shaw, Nalty, and Turnbladh, 38.
5. Moon phase calendar, November 1943; McKiernan, "Tarawa," 38–49.
6. Alexander, *Across the Reef*, 2. This was the experience of journalist Robert Sherrod, who landed on Tarawa with the fifth wave; see Sherrod, *Tarawa*, 66.
7. Forrestel, *Admiral Raymond A. Spruance*, appendix III, Gilbert Island Operation, Task Organization (Skeletonized), 251.
8. Forrestel, 74.
9. MSC-037.1_11_22, Flag Log, USS *Indianapolis*, Operation Galvanic.
10. Reynolds, *Fast Carriers*, 99–102.
11. Sherrod, *Tarawa*, 61.
12. MSC037.1_11_22, Flag Log, USS *Indianapolis*, 20 November 1943; *Battle Experience—Gilbert Islands*, 67–14-15.
13. Cheser and Doland, *Beyond the Reef*, 52, 53.
14. Sherrod, *Tarawa*, 101.
15. Alexander, *Across the Reef*, 42–33.
16. Stockman, *Battle for Tarawa*, appendix D, Chronology, 75; Forrestel, *Admiral Raymond A. Spruance*, 95–96. The numbers given include men who died of their wounds later.
17. Dyer, *Amphibians Came to Conquer*, 665.
18. *Liscome Bay (CVE56)*, DANFS; Reynolds, *Fast Carriers*, 104–5. Towers would likely have included Chester Nimitz in this group.
19. Stockman, *Battle for Tarawa*, 76.
20. *Battle Experience—Gilbert Islands*, 67–1.
21. *Battle Experience—Gilbert Islands*, 67–7.
22. *Battle Experience—Gilbert Islands*, 67–103, 67–159–60.
23. *Battle Experience—Gilbert Islands*, 67–259.
24. COMINCH P-001, *Amphibious Operations during the Period August to December, 1943*, 7–7, 7–8.
25. *Battle Experience—Gilbert Islands*, 67–263.
26. Smith, *Coral and Brass*, 134; MSC012_1_6, Letter, RAS to E. P. Forrestel, 2 March 1963.
27. Moore Oral History, 860.
28. MSC037.1_1_11, Letter, RAS to MDS, 19 December 1942, 2.

CHAPTER 10. THE TRIDENT STRIKES AGAIN

1. GB 1803, 1804 (Pink). Joint Chiefs of Staff 012115 (September) to CinCPac; GB 1819 (Pink), October 22 1319 COMINCH to CINCPAC; 26 0519 CINCPAC to COMINCH, GB 1825 (Pink), November 09 0240, CINCPAC to COMINCH.

2. Reynolds, *Fast Carriers*, 115–16; Layton, *"And I Was There,"* 480–81.
3. Moore Oral History, 878. Spruance then referred to Majuro as "Moore-juro"; Layton, *"And I Was There,"* 481.
4. Heinl and Crown, *The Marshalls*, 30–32.
5. Heinl and Crown, 32.
6. GB 1703, Running Summary, 20 December 1943.
7. MSC037.1_1_11, Letter, RAS to MDS, 9 January 1944. The Damon House was part of a large estate near Honolulu used for recreation.
8. Reynolds, *Fast Carriers*, 121–22. Symonds, *Nimitz at War*, 267–68. Spruance was happy with Pownall's performance.
9. *Battle Experience: Supporting Operations for the Occupation of the Marshall Islands*, 70–18, 70–19. Hereinafter *Battle Experience—Marshalls*.
10. MSC037.1_1_11, Letter, RAS to MDS, 26 January 1944. Regrettably, the Seabees in their zeal also covered many of the improvised cemeteries containing the Marine dead.
11. *Report of the Flintlock Operation*, Commander, 5th Amphibious Force, 19 April 1944, N-7085A, 22.
12. Heinl and Crown, *The Marshalls*, 45.
13. Heinl and Crown, 70; Moore Oral History, 886. Spruance ordered Hill not to give Majuro this treatment as the facilities abandoned by the Japanese could then be put to immediate use. There were also many islanders still present.
14. Heinl and Crown, *The Marshalls*, 103.
15. *Report of the Flintlock Operation*, Intelligence Report, 18.
16. DeBaussel, 14.
17. Heinl and Crown, *The Marshalls*, 121.
18. Forrestel, *Admiral Raymond A. Spruance*, 104, 118.
19. GB 2310 (Pink), February 05 0623, COMAIRSOPAC to CINCPAC, COMCENPAC, COMSOPAC.
20. Moore Oral History, 889–92. Two of the fast battleships, *Indiana* and *Washington*, had collided during the bombardment of Kwajalein and returned to Majuro for repairs.
21. Prados, *Combined Fleet Decoded*, 534–35; "Japanese Battleships: Tabular Record of Movements (TROMS)," http://www.combinedfleet.com/senkan.htm. Prados notes the photos taken on 4 February were the first real glimpse of a *Yamato*-class superbattleship.
22. GB 1850, Running Summary, 5 February; GB 1854, Running Summary, 12 February.
23. Barber Oral History, 29–30; GB 1856, Running Summary, 15 February, COMSOPAC reports occupation of Green Island; MSC037.1_1_17, Buell Notes. Nimitz had given Halsey approval for the operation after Spruance had left Pearl Harbor and may not have informed Spruance, thinking it too minor to be a concern.
24. Moore Oral History, 896. Moore characterized Spruance's response as "indignant," which seems out of character.
25. MSC037.1_1_17, Letter, Charles Barber to E. F. Forrestel, 15 August 1965, 2.
26. "IJN Nowaki: Tabular Record of Movements"; Moore Oral History, 899–901.
27. Buell, *Quiet Warrior*, 255; Moore Oral History, 919–21. On the page previous to the citation Buell also posits that Spruance was seeking revenge for Pearl Harbor by flaunting the flag. It was not a "whim," in this author's opinion.
28. MSC037.1_1_11, Letter, RAS to MDS, 23 February 1944.
29. Heinl and Crown, *The Marshalls*, 70–77.
30. *Battle Experience—Marshalls*, 70–46, -47. Enemy Defenses as Determined after Occupation.

31. Heinl and Crown, *The Marshalls*, 128. "As cooly as if entering a home port" quotes a naval officer present.
32. Heinl and Crown, 169–72. Base defense and air unit casualties are not included. There were no naval casualties reported.
33. Carter, *Beans, Bullets, and Black Oil*, 118–26; Moore Oral History, 903; Forrestel, *Admiral Raymond A. Spruance*, 118.
34. GB 2312–14 (Pink), March 12 2319, JCS to MacArthur, Richardson pass to Nimitz, Halsey.
35. Moore Oral History, 940; Forrestel, *Admiral Raymond A. Spruance*, 119.
36. Prados, *Combined Fleet Decoded*, 548–49.
37. Prados, 550–51; Layton, *"And I Was There,"* 484–85; Bradsher, "The Z Plan Story."
38. MSC037.1_1_11, Letter, RAS to MDS, 24 May 1944; MSC037.1_10_02_06, Interview, MDS.
39. King and Whitehill, *Fleet Admiral King*, 536.

CHAPTER 11. THE MARIANAS AND THE BATTLE OF THE PHILIPPINE SEA

1. Frank, *Downfall*, 27–30.
2. *Battle Experience Supporting Operations for the Capture of the Marianas Islands (Saipan Guam and Tinian), June–August 1944*, 74–77. Hereinafter *Battle Experience—Marianas.*
3. Moore Oral History, 99–2; DeBaussel, 5; MSC037.1_1_7, "Notes made by Admiral Raymond A. Spruance for E. B. Potter," 4 January 1959, 9.
4 Layton, *"And I Was There,"* 485; Prados, *Combined Fleet Decoded*, 549–51. See also Moore Oral History, 1000–2.
5. "Z Operation Orders," Allied Translator and Interpreter Section, Southwest Pacific Area, Limited Distribution Translation No. 4, 23 May 1944, 1–6. Hereinafter Z Operation Orders.
6. Z Operation Orders, 18, 19.
7. Operation Order 76, Limited Distribution Translation No. 39, Part VIII, Combined Fleet Operation Orders, 4 June 1945, MacArthur Memorial Archives and Library RG 3, SWPA, ATIS, Box 153, 170, 174–6. This operation is more commonly referred to as "A-go." See Morison, 12–14. However, the ATIS translation of Op. Order 76 never uses that term.
8. See Prados, *Combined Fleet Decoded*, 567, for his discussion of the shuttle bombing tactics attributed to Admiral Ozawa.
9. The difficulties Toyoda faced are discussed in Japanese Monograph No. 90, "The A-go Operations." Most descriptions of the A Operation are based on this document.
10. Prados, *Combined Fleet Decoded*, 539–40.
11. Ugaki, *Fading Victory*, 395; Prados, *Combined Fleet Decoded*, 557.
12. *Battle Experience—Marianas*, 74–7; GB 2205–09 (Green) reports from TF 58 on carrier attacks 11 June–15 June.
13. Prados, *Combined Fleet Decoded*, 558; Hornfischer, *Fleet at Flood Tide*, 79.
14. Morison, *New Guinea and the Marianas*, 222–31; Prados, *Combined Fleet Decoded*, 563–64.
15. Ugaki, *Fading Victory*, 397.
16. Prados, *Combined Fleet Decoded*, 570; GB 1958, Running Summary, 14 June (Oahu date).
17. GB 2208, 14 0528 COM 5th FLT to CTF 58.
18. *Battle Experience—Marianas*, 74–11; GB 1957–8; Running Summary, 14 June (Oahu date).

19. GB 1958, Running Summary, 14 June (Oahu date).
20. Dyer, *Amphibians Came to Conquer*, 914. That Spruance informed Turner about the Z Plan intelligence is not documented, but given Turner's reaction this must have been the case.
21. Bjorge, *Hard Fighting in Saipan's Death Valley*, 9–10; Smith, *Coral and Brass*, 165. The 27th Infantry's unloading was cut short, and the 105th RCT's headquarters unit and much of the division's transport vehicles and tanks remained on the ships that moved to the sea.
22. *Battle Experience—Marianas*, Commander TF 58 report, 74–26.
23. Forrestel, *Admiral Raymond A. Spruance*, 136; Moore Oral History, 998.
24. Moore Oral History, 999; *Battle Experience—Marianas*, Commander TF 58 report, 74–27.
25. GB 1964, Running Summary, 17 June. *Cavalla* spotted the Japanese fleet at 2155 on 17 June but was unable to report until 0645 on 18 June (local); see Moore Oral History, 1009.
26. *Battle Experience—Marianas*, Commander TF 58 report, 74–28; Stillwell, *Battleship Commander*, 210–11.
27. Moore Oral History, 1003; *Battle Experience—Marianas*, Commander TF 58 report, 74–28, 29.
28. Moore Oral History, 1005; *Battle Experience—Marianas*, Commander TF 58 report, 74–30.
29. Ugaki, *Fading Victory*, 408; *Battle Experience—Marianas*, Commander TF 58 report, 74–30.
30. Morison, *New Guinea and the Marianas*, 259; "Battle of the Philippine Sea" Track Chart, Forrestel, *Admiral Raymond A. Spruance*, 141; *Battle Experience—Marianas*, Commander TF 58 report, 74–30.
31. *Battle Experience—Marianas*, Commander TF 58 report, 74–31. "Hey, Rube" was the traditional circus and carnival worker's rallying cry when confronted by hostile townfolk.
32. Morison, *New Guinea and the Marianas*, 247–48. See Ugaki, *Fading Victory*, 408. His times are earlier than those cited by Morison.
33. Morison, *New Guinea and the Marianas*, 268.
34. Morison, 269; Track Chart, Forrestel, *Admiral Raymond A. Spruance*, 141.
35. Ugaki, *Fading Victory*, 409. Ugaki thought it served them right. Moore Oral History, 1022. Moore says at least one was brought down by the *Indianapolis*' obsolete 1.1-inch guns, whose installation had bothered Spruance two years earlier.
36. Morison, *New Guinea and the Marianas*, 273–74.
37. Tully, Parshall, and Wolff, "Sinking of *Shokaku*."
38. Tully, "IJN Taiho." Tully's account differs in details from the standard histories but is based on Japanese records.
39. *Battle Experience—Marianas*, Commander TF 58 report, 74–32.
40. Morison, *New Guinea and the Marianas*, 285–87; Reynolds, *Fast Carriers*, 196; "USS *Enterprise* CV-6, Philippine Sea: June 19–20, 1944."
41. Symonds, *Nimitz at War*, 301; Reynolds, *Fast Carriers*, 230, for a facsimile of the letter of 19 June 1944 from Nimitz to Spruance.
42. Ugaki, *Fading Victory*, 413. The second transfer was when Ozawa moved aboard *Zuikaku* the next day.
43. GB 1965, Running Summary, 18 June; *Battle Experience—Marianas*, Commander TF 58 report, 74–32; Moore Oral History, 1016–17.

44. Moore Oral History, 1025–26.
45. Ugaki, *Fading Victory*, 411–12, quoting from Combined Fleet Telegram No. 192257.
46. *Battle Experience—Marianas*, Commander TF 58 report, 74–39.
47. *Battle Experience—Marianas*, Commander TF 58 report, 74–40.
48. Morison, *New Guinea and the Marianas*, 321.
49. MSC012_2_01, Letter, RAS to C. W. Nimitz, 4 July 1944, 3.
50. MSC037.1_1_11, Letter, RAS to MDS, 26 June 1944.
51. Ugaki, *Fading Victory*, 415–16, diary entry for 21 June 1944 (Tokyo time).

CHAPTER 12. OPERATION FORAGER COMPLETED

1. Some histories list Saipan as being seventy-two square miles in size, perhaps a simple but erroneous calculation of its length and width.
2. Shaw, Nalty, and Turnbladh, *Central Pacific Drive*, 260.
3. Shaw, Nalty, and Turnbladh, 309–11.
4. Moore Oral History, 1043–44.
5. Shaw, Nalty, and Turnbladh, *Central Pacific Drive*, 330–31.
6. MSC037.1_1_11, Letter, RAS to MDS, 26 June 1944.
7. Shaw, Nalty, and Turnbladh, *Central Pacific Drive*, 347.
8. MSC037.1_1_11, Letter, RAS to MDS, 8 July 1944.
9. Shaw, Nalty, and Turnbladh, *Central Pacific Drive*, 341–42. The attack shattered the U.S Army's 105th Infantry Regiment, accounting for about half of the Army's KIA on Saipan. Some sources put the number of attacking Japanese at more than 4,000.
10. Smith, *Coral and Brass*, 177–78.
11. Moore Oral History, 1062; Potter, *Nimitz*, 308–9.
12. King and Whitehill, *Fleet Admiral King*, 563. This was the fleet that Ozawa requested to be sent on 21 June. Moore Oral History, 1062–63.
13. MSC012_1_5, Letter, RAS to E. B. Potter, 28 March 1960.
14. Shaw, Nalty, and Turnbladh, *Central Pacific Drive*, 446–47.
15. Shaw, Nalty, and Turnbladh, 450.
16. Shaw, Nalty, and Turnbladh, 514–17.
17. MSC037.1_1_11, Letter, RAS to MDS, 15 August 1944.
18. Shaw, Nalty, and Turnbladh, *Central Pacific Drive*, 568.
19. *Sextant Conference Papers, CCS 397, Specific Operations for the Defeat of Japan, 1944*, 67. At the second Cairo Conference Adm. Ernest King and Gen. Henry "Hap" Arnold had a happy meeting of the minds, and Guam, Tinian and Saipan were specifically designated to be seized "for the strategic bombing of Japan proper."
20. Shaw, Nalty, and Turnbladh, *Central Pacific Drive*, 359. The name of Captain Oie, IJN, is also spelled "Oya." The authors claim there were 8,900 Japanese in defense of Tinian, but the numbers they cite and reported numbers buried do not add up, which is not unusual.
21. Hoffman, *Seizure of Tinian*, 131.
22. Shaw, Nalty, and Turnbladh, *Central Pacific Drive*, 369.
23. Shaw, Nalty, and Turnbladh, 370. Hoffman, *Seizure of Tinian*, 23. Appendix VII provides some fascinating insight to the origin of the choice of the White Beaches. Students at the Marine Corps Schools at Quantico had arrived at the same conclusions years earlier in their interwar studies.
24. Forrestel, *Admiral Raymond A. Spruance*, 152; Dyer, *Amphibians Came to Conquer*, 956–57. See also Moore Oral History, 1069–70.

25. Shaw, Nalty, and Turnbladh, *Central Pacific Drive*, 371–73. See also the U.S. Navy Seabee Museum, "Archivist's Attic."
26. Hoffman, *The Seizure of Tinian*, 41.
27. Shaw, Nalty, and Turnbladh, *Central Pacific Drive*, 391–99.
28. GB 2339 (Pink), August 10 0125, CINCPOA TO COM3rdFLEET, COM5thFLEET; Moore Oral History, 1072–73.
29. GB 2339 (Pink), August 10 0133, CINCPOA TO COM5thFLEET.
30. *Battle Experience—Marianas*, 74–75; *Report of Capture of the Marianas*, Encl.(A), Annex (3).
31. Smith, *Coral and Brass*, 201.
32. Hoffman, *Saipan*, 259, quoting a captured Japanese document: Captain Taisa Shimamura, IJN, "Tactical Lessons—Naval Shelling of Saipan," August 1944.
33. Ugaki, *Fading Victory*, 446.

CHAPTER 13. OPERATION DETACHMENT

1. DeBaussel, 21.
2. MacArthur, *Reminiscences*, 198.
3. Drea, *MacArthur's Ultra*, 153; GB 2347 (Pink), August GCT 23 2108, CINCPOA to COMINCH.
4. MSC037.1_11, Letter, RAS to MDS, 15 August 1944, 3. Davis was a highly experienced aviator who had commanded USS *Enterprise* during the Guadalcanal campaign. Moore believed King had it in for him and purposely withheld his promotion to rear admiral.
5. GB 2350 (Pink), September 09 0314Z, JOINT CHIEFS OF STAFF to NIMITZ, MACARTHUR.
6. GB 2353 (Pink), September 13 0230, 13 0300, COM3RDFLT to CINCPOA, CINCSOWESPAC, COMINCH; 13 0813, CINCPOA to CINCSWPA, info COMINCH, COM3RD FLT; GB 2354, 14 0316 MACARTHUR to CINCPOA, JOINT CHIEFS, info COM3RDFLT. The affirmation attributed to MacArthur was actually written by Gen. Richard Sutherland, as his boss was then at sea under radio silence.
7. U.S. State Department, Office of the Historian, *Foreign Relations of the United States, Conference at Quebec, 1944*, D179, "Combined Chiefs of Staff Minutes, September 13, 1944, 2:30 PM"; GB 2356 (Pink), September 14 1325 COMINCH to CINCPOA, COM3RDFLT; GB 2357 (Pink), September 15 0258 JOINT CHIEFS OF STAFF to NIMITZ, MACARTHUR, info HALSEY.
8. Hough, *Seizure of Peleliu*, 180–83.
9. MSC037.1_10_ 02_06, Interview MSD, 6; DeBaussel, 21.
10. GB 2362 (Pink), September 21 1042Z, MacArthur to CHIEF OF STAFF WAR Dept., info COMGENPOA, CINCPOA. In the same dispatch MacArthur also suggested moving directly from Luzon to the invasion of Japan after attacking the Bonin Islands.
11. DeBaussel, 21; MSC037_10_02_6, Interview MSD, 3, 4. Mrs. Spruance described them as "playing a little gambling game"—possibly acey-deucey, an old Navy favorite.
12. GB 2378 (Pink), October 03 2255, JOINT CHIEFS OF STAFF to MacArthur, Nimitz; GB 2379 (Pink), October 09 2200, and 09 2300, CINCPOA to COM5THFLT (and subsidiary commands).
13. Morison, *Leyte*, 58. MSC037.1_1_7, Letter, RAS to E. B. Potter, 25 December 1961.
14. Koyanagi, "With Kurita in the Battle for Leyte Gulf." Koyanagi makes it clear that Kurita and his staff did not like the idea of using such a powerful force against transports and cargo ships.

15. Ugaki, *Fading Victory*, 494–99; Prados, *Combined Fleet Decoded*, 684–86. Admiral Ugaki was on *Yamato*'s bridge with Kurita and witnessed the confusion of the battle off Samar. It was believed that the CVEs of Taffy 3 to the south were fleet carriers that would be too fast for the Center Force to chase. A battleship was reported on the eastern horizon, and gunfire flashes were seen to the northwest.
16. Toll, *Twilight of the Gods*, 304–6.
17. MacArthur, *Reminiscences*, 227–28. MacArthur blamed the divided command structure imposed by the president and the JCS as the cause of the near disaster. His solution was simple: place all of the Pacific theater under his command.
18. MSC037.1_1_7, Letters, E. B. Potter to RAS, 13 February, 20 February 1959; Letter, RAS to Potter, 21 February 1959.
19. MSC037.1_1_11, Letter, RAS to MDS, 31 October 1944.
20. MSC012_2_1, Letter, RAS to Vice Adm. J. H. Hoover, dated 30 November 1944.
21. MSC037.1_1_11, Letter, RAS to MDS, 2 December 1944.
22. MSC037.1_1_11, Letter, RAS to MDS, 24 December 1944.
23. "Commander Fifth Fleet Operation Plan 13–44, 31 December 1944," Annex A, Task Organization, Assumptions.
24. Forrestel, *Admiral Raymond A. Spruance*, appendix VIII.
25. DeBaussel, 22.
26. Garand and Strobridge, *History of the United States Marine Corps in World War II*, 455–61.
27. MSC037.1_1_12, Letter, RAS to MDS, 23 January 1945; DeBaussel, 22–23.
28. Garand and Strobridge, *History of the United States Marine Corps in World War II*, 491–92; DeBaussel, 24; Smith, *Coral and Brass*, 247.
29. GB 2751, 2752 (Green), February 18 2215, Com5thFlt to CINCPAC Adv HQ; *Amphibious Operations—Capture of Iwo Jima, 16 February to 16 March 1945*, 1–2. Hereinafter *Amphibious Operation Iwo Jima*. The numbers of aircraft claimed destroyed would be increased in Mitscher's later reporting.
30. GB 2542, Running Summary, 17 February; Garand and Strobridge, *History of the United States Marine Corps in World War II*, 498–99.
31. GB 2543, Running Summary, 18 February; Garand and Strobridge, *History of the United States Marine Corps in World War II*, 500–1; Smith, *Coral and Brass*, 253–54. Forrestal had joined Smith aboard USS *Eldorado* (AGC-11) at Saipan.
32. Garand and Strobridge, *History of the United States Marine Corps in World War II*, 501–4.
33. Alexander, *Closing In*, 14–15.
34. Garand and Strobridge, *History of the United States Marine Corps in World War II*, 525–27; GB 3019 (Pink), February 20 0600, CTF 51 to COM5thFLT.
35. GB 2546, 2547, Running Summary, 20 February; GB 3020 (Pink), 20 1230, CTF 51 to COM5thFLT.
36. Forrestel, *Admiral Raymond A. Spruance*, 185.
37. DANFS, *Bismarck Sea* (CVE-95); Saratoga V (CV-3).
38. GB 3023 (Pink), February 22 0647, COM5thFLT to CTF 58, passed to CINCPOA Adv HQ 220448; GB 3023 22 0801, COM5thFLT to CINC Adv HQ, info CTF 51, 58.
39. GB 2557, 27 February, Running Summary; GB 2559, 1 March, Running Summary.
40. Garand and Strobridge, *History of the United States Marine Corps in World War II*, 542.
41. GB 2774 (Green), March 01 0600, CTF 51 to COM5THFLTG is typical; Garand and Strobridge, *History of the United States Marine Corps in World War II*, 597.
42. GB 2779 (Green), March 02 2357, COM5thFLT to CINCPOA Adv HQ.

43. MSC037.1_1_12, Letter, RAS to MDS, 6 March 1945. Spruance did not identify the officer killed but it was most certainly Lt. Col. John A. Butler, the commander of the 1/27th.
44. Garand and Strobridge, *History of the United States Marine Corps in World War II*, 710.
45. Garand and Strobridge, appendix H.
46. MSC037.1_1_12, Letter, RAS to MDS, 13 March 1945.

CHAPTER 14. OPERATION ICEBERG

1. Although modern Okinawa is considered to be a Home Island, for this study the Home Islands are considered to be synonymous with "mainland" Japan: Kyushu, Shikoku, Honshu, and Hokkaido.
2. Morison, *Victory in the Pacific*, appendix I; Forrestel, *Admiral Raymond A. Spruance*, appendix IX; Stillwell, *Battleship Commander*, 249–50.
3. GB 2790 (Green), March 11 1216, 12 0950, Com5thFlt to CINCPAC Adv HQ; 2791 11 0800, Com5thFlt to CINCPAC Both HQ, COMAIRPAC.
4. Ugaki, *Fading Victory*, 536, diary entry for Saturday, 10 February, when Ugaki learned he had been appointed by the emperor to command the Fifth Air Fleet.
5. Ugaki, 549–51, diary entry for Sunday, 11 March 1945. Ugaki lamented the inexperience of his aircrews.
6. GB 3022, 3023 (Pink), February 21 1635, 1650, ComInch to CincPOA, Info CincBPF, CincSWPA; GB 3050 (Pink), March 14 1205, CincBPF to CTF 113, info CTF 112, CincPac Adv, Admiralty. Fraser orders Rawlings to report to Nimitz for duty in Iceberg.
7. GB 3052 (Pink), March 15 0658, (GCT) CincPOA to Com5th FLT. The spelling used at the time was "Sakashima." The group includes the Senkaku Islands.
8. GB 2578, 2579, 2580, 21, 23 March, Running Summary; DANFS USS Franklin (CV-13) "Big Ben."
9. GB 2582, 26 March, Running Summary; *Amphibious Operations—Capture of Okinawa, 27 March to 21 June 1945*, 1–1, 1–3. Hereinafter *Amphibious Operations Okinawa.*
10. Frank and Shaw, "Okinawa," in *History of the United States Marine Corps in World War II*, vol. V, 99.
11. Barber Oral History, 14–15; Forrestel, *Admiral Raymond A. Spruance*, 199.
12. Frank and Shaw, "Okinawa," 109–18.
13. Frank and Shaw, 43–55, 81.
14. GB 2596, 5 April, Running Summary.
15. MSC037.1_1_12, Letter, RAS to MDS, 5 April 1945.
16. GB 2601, 7 April, Running Summary; Morison, *Victory in the Pacific*, 197; Ugaki, *Fading Victory*, 572, diary entry for Friday, 6 April. The "Floating Chrysanthemum" refers to the war banner of the medieval warrior Masahige Kusonoki, considered to be the ideal samurai, loyal unto death to the emperor.
17. GB 2599, 6 April, Running Summary.
18. GB 3076 (Pink), April 07 0832, CTF 54 to COMINCH, CINCPAC BOTH, TF 54, info COM5thFLT. Given the dispatch time it would have been 1732 on 7 April in the East China Sea.
19. GB 2823 (Green), April 06 2337, CTF 58 to ATFC5thFLT, info CINCPAC, COM5Flt; GB 2824 (Green), April 07 0304, CTF 58 to COM5th FLT; GB 3076 (Pink), April 07 0105, COM5thFLT to CTF 58; Forrestel, *Admiral Raymond A. Spruance*, 205.
20. Morison incorrectly states that Deyo's battleships had 16-inch guns which had considerably longer range and hitting power, and that *Yamato* was therefore "fair game." Perhaps not. See *Victory in the Pacific*, 204. The fire control suite of *Tennessee* had been

modernized, enabling accurate fire out to 36,000 yards, but under *Yamato*'s maximum range of 45,960 yards.

21. GB 2600, 2600, 7 April, Running Summary, CTF 58 reports the Yamato attack; Morison, *Victory in the Pacific*, 205–9; "IJN Battleship Yamato: Tabular Record of Movement."
22 GB 3078 (Pink), April 05 0226, CINCPAC Adv to COMINCH, NIMITZ TO KING ONLY.
23 GB 3079 (Pink), April 09 1921, COMINCH to CINCPAC, KING TO NIMITZ.
24. GB 2612, 13 April, Running Summary.
25. Ugaki, *Fading Victory*, 582, diary entry, Thursday 12 April 1945; 584, diary entry, Friday 13 April 1945. Ugaki believed that the Japanese had succeeded in causing the U.S. government to fall and change administration, as the American success on Saipan had done to Tojo's government.
26. GB 3079 (Pink), April 10 044, CINCPAC to COM5thFLT; GB 2860 (Green), April 16 0834 COM5th FLT to CINCPAC ADV HQ, info to CTF51.
27. GB 2861 (Green), April 16 0847, COM5th FLT to CINCPAC ADV HQ, info to CTF51, CTF58.
28. GB 2865 (Green), April 17 1251, DECOMAF20 to CINCPOA ADV info 21BOMCOM, COM5th FLT.
29. Frank and Shaw, "Okinawa," 193.
30. Potter, *Nimitz*, 374; GB 2721 (Green), April 22 1315, CTF 51 to COM5thFLT.
31. Potter, *Nimitz*, 375.
32. Frank and Shaw, "Okinawa," 195–96.
33. GB 3096 (Pink), April 24 0838, CINCPAC to COMINCH; GB 3100 (Pink), April 25 1631, COMINCH to CINCPOA Adv.
34. Frank and Shaw, "Okinawa," 213.
35. GB 2637, 2639, Running Summary, 3–4 May; it should be noted that armored flight decks were standardized with the *Midway* class aircraft carriers laid down in 1943, based on Royal Navy experience earlier in the war. The performance of British carriers in the Pacific served to reinforce that decision.
36. GB 2890 (Green), May 03 2315, COM5thFLT to CINCPAC Adv, info CTF 51; 04 0204, CINCPAC Adv to CINCSWPA, info COMAF5, COM5thFLT; 04 1252 MACARTHUR to COMAAF, info CINCPOA ADV, COM5th FLT; GB 2893 (Green), May 06 0126, COM5thFLT to CINCPAC Adv.
37. GB 3223 (Yellow), May 06 1125, COM5th FLT to CINCPAC Adv; GB 2897 (Green), May 06 0129, COM5thFLT to CTF 56, info COMTAF . . . CINCPAC Adv; GB 2899 (Green), May 10 0752, DEPCOMAF 20 to CINCPOA PEARL, info CINCPOA ADV, COMAF20, COMGEN BOMCOM XX1; May 11 042, CINCPOA ADV to DEPCOM20AF, info COMGENTEN, COMGEN BOMCOM XX1. COMGEN BOMCOM XX, COMGEN 20AF.
38. Cox, "H-048-1."
39. MSC015_1, Letter, Spruance to C. J. Moore, 13 May 1945; DeBaussel, 26. Buell, *Quiet Warrior*, 388, relates that Spruance's staff found him manning a fire hose, fighting a fire ignited by the crashed aircraft.
40. Ugaki, *Fading Victory*, 616–18, diary entry, Friday 25 May 1945; Frank and Shaw, "Okinawa," 298. Willcutts reported in April 1945.
41. Forrestel, *Admiral Raymond A. Spruance*, 215; Buell, *Quiet Warrior*, 391. Later historians typically reference these accounts. See Symonds, *Nimitz at War*, 385. Forrestel was with Spruance on a daily basis during this period and would have had first-hand knowledge.

42. Dyer, *Amphibians Came to Conquer*, 1110–11; Barber Oral History, 18, 44.
43. GB 3223 (Yellow), May 03 0219, CINCPOA to COM5th FLT, NIMITZ TO SPRUANCE EYES ONLY; MSC015_1, Letter, Spruance to C. J. Moore, 13 May 1945; MSC037.1_1_12, Letter, RAS to MDS, 3 June 1945.
44. Frank and Shaw, "Okinawa," 369, appendix M. Many of the Japanese who surrendered were Okinawans drafted into service.

CHAPTER 15. THE DEFEAT AND OCCUPATION OF JAPAN

1. MSC037.1_1_12, Letter, RAS to MDS, dated 3 June 1945; "Raymond Ames Spruance," Modern Biographical Files in Navy Department Library, U.S. Navy History and Heritage Command.
2. GB 3143 (Pink), May 25 2158, JOINT CHIEFS OF STAFF TO NIMITZ, ARNOLD, MACARTHUR, WARX-87938. Regarding the high-level discussions taking place in Washington concerning the strategy to defeat Japan in 1945, see Kohnen, *King's Navy*, 419–25.
3. GB 3232 (Yellow), May 25 0517, CINCPAC ADV TO COMINCH, NIMITZ TO KING.
4. O'Brien, *The Second Most Powerful Man in the World*, 192–3, 341–3. Leahy was appointed Chief of Staff to the Commander in Chief in 1942, and as such presided over meetings of the Joint Chiefs. Leahy opposed both the invasion of Japan and the use of atomic bombs.
5. Giangreco, *Hell to Pay*, 75.
6. Frank, *Downfall*, 141–43. Marshall's estimate was based on the first thirty days of the operation and did not include naval losses.
7. "Staff Study, 'Olympic' Operations in Southern Kyushu," General Headquarters, U.S. Army Forces in the Pacific, 28 May 1945, Map, Annex 3(B)4, "The Operations Required." On this map Satsuma is identified as "Kagoshima Peninsula." The rugged terrain is clearly visible.
8. "Staff Study, 'Olympic,'" 10-R.
9. MSC037.1_1_12, Letter, RAS to MDS, dated 3 June 1945; MSC037.1_1_5, Letter, RAS to Emmet Forrestel, 3 October 1954; GB 3248 (Yellow), June 14 2307, JOINT CHIEFS OF STAFF TO MACARTHUR, NIMITZ, INFO ARNOLD. Based on Ultra and Magic decrypts it appeared that at least some civilian elements of the Japanese government were extending "peace feelers."
10. GB 3483 (Yellow), July 02 2226, JOINT CHIEFS OF STAFF TO MACARTHUR, NIMITZ, AND ARNOLD. Secretary of the War Department Henry L. Stimson specifically directed that Kyoto be spared to save its cultural legacy.
11. GB 3261–3263, Running Summary, 14 & 15 July.
12. GB 3391 (Pink), July 15 0728, CINCPAC ADV TO COM3RDFLT; GB 3275, Running Summary, 25 July; Tillman, "Halsey's Folly," 41.
13. GB 3497 (Yellow), July 26 1946, JOINT CHIEFS OF STAFF to MACARTHUR, NIMITZ, info SPAATZ, AGWAR, Navy Dept.; GB 3499 (Yellow), July 27 0920, CINCPAC ADV TO COMINCH, info MacArthur and Spaatz.
14. Ugaki, *Fading Victory*, 640, diary entry for Sunday, 1 July 1945.
15. Cox, "H-057-1."
16. Potter, *Nimitz*, 384; Layton, *"And I Was There,"* 492–93.
17. Barber Oral History, 34–35. There is no evidence of such a dispatch being issued in early August in the Nimitz Graybook. The first such discussing the atom bomb was dated 10 August. It may be that Spruance read something prepared just for the CinCPac staff.

18. Morison, *Victory in the Pacific*, 319, based on a letter from RAS to Morison, 25 December 1959.
19. GB 3509 (Yellow), August 07 1535, OPD WAR to MACARTHUR, passed by COMINCH to CINCPAC Adv; GB 3508, 3509, (Yellow), August 09 0443, CINCAF-PAC TO WARCOS, passed by COMINCH to NIMITZ, Nimitz eyes only.
20. Frank, *Downfall*, 295–96.
21. Ugaki, *Fading Victory*, 664–65; see "D4Y *Judy* Tail Code 701-122."
22. MSC037.1_13_26, Letter, Edward D. Spruance to E. P. Forrestel, 16 July 1963, 13; Barber Oral History, 52.
23. ADA 438112, *Basic Outline Plan for "Blacklist Operations,"* General Headquarters U.S. Army Forces Pacific, Maps, Annex 3C(2), 3C(3), 3C(4); Annex 5(g), "Summary of Provisions of CINCPAC Plan 'CAMPUS'"; MSC015.1_1, Letter RAS to Carl Moore, 30 August 1945.
24. Barber Oral History, 30; DeBaussel, 29; MSC037.1_1_12, Letter, RAS to MDS, 28 August 1945.
25. MSC037.1_1_12, Letter, RAS to MDS, 12 August 1945.
26. "Spruance for Cut in American Navy," *New York Times*, 26 August 1945; "Spruance Views Okinawa as Political Bombshell," *Press-Telegraph*, Long Beach, CA, August 26, 1945, from AP reports, 2.
27. MSC037.1_1_12, Letter, RAS to MDS, 28 August 1945; GB 3530 (Yellow), August 25 1548, COMINCH & CNO to CINCPAC ADV, info COM5THFLT; GB 3476 (Pink), August 27 0108, CINCPAC ADV TO ALL FLAG OFFICERS.
28. MSC037.1_1_5, Letter, RAS to Emmet Forrestel, 17 September 1964, 4.
29. Giangreco, *Hell to Pay*, appendix D, Operation Blacklist, 402.
30. MSC037.1_1_12, Letter, RAS to MDS, 23 September 1945.
31. SC037.1_1_12, Letter, RAS to MDS, 18 October 1945.
32. Potter, *Nimitz*, 407–7; MSC037.1_1_5, Letter, RAS to Emmet Forrestel, 17 September 1964, 5–6; MSC037.1_10_02_06, Interview MDS. Mrs. Spruance recalled that Nimitz was opposed to Towers replacing him as CinCPac and wanted her husband to have the job.
33. MSC012_1_17, Official Navy Correspondence, orders dated 3 November 1945.
34. MSC037.1_1_12, Letter, RAS to MDS, 14 November 1945; MSC037.1_10_02_06, Interview MDS, 6.
35. MSC012_1_17, Official Navy Correspondence. Spruance applied for per diem reimbursement for one person, and 3,240 miles at four cents per mile. Travel orders dated 18 April 1946.

CHAPTER 16. POSTWAR AND EPILOGUE

1. MSC037.1_12_04, NWC 1946–1948, Memorandum for the Staff, 12 March 1946; Barber Oral History, 31; *Naval Manual of Operational Planning, 1948*, RG04_168_08, Naval War College Archives; *Naval Operational Planning, NWP 5–01* (Office of the Chief of Naval Operations, Department of the Navy, Washington, DC, May 1998), 1–3.
2. RG 28–4A_18, "Current Plans and Activities of the Naval War College," August 1946.
3. McHugh, "Gaming at the Naval War College," 733.
4. RG 28–4A_16_01, "Statement Prepared by Admiral R. A. Spruance, USN for Delivery Before Senate Naval Affairs Committee, Washington, DC, 10 July 1946."
5. MSC037.1_12_4, Letter, RAS to Chief, Naval Personnel, 25 August 1947.
6. MSC012_1_18, Official Correspondence, Letter, RAS to Secretary of the Navy, 24 May 1948.

7. MSC012_1_19, Letter, Chief of Naval Personnel to Admiral Raymond A. Spruance, USN, 29 June 1948; MSC037.2_15_14, Fleet Admiral Ernest J. King, "Halsey's Five Stars—1944." King recalled that Congressman Carl Vinson, then the chairman of the House Naval Affairs Committee, backed Halsey for the fourth billet.
8. MSC037.1_10_02_06, Interview MSD, 8–9. The Browns were an old Newport, RI, family and good friends with the Spruances.
9. Andrew K. Blackley, "A True Sailor-Statesman," paper presented at the 2024 Society for Military History conference. See also "Philippines: The People's Choice," *Time Magazine*, November 23, 1953; Coquia, *Philippine Presidential Election of 1953*; Boot, *Road Not Taken*.
10. MSC037.1_12_7, Letter, RAS to Hugh B. Snow Jr., April 8, 1967.
11. See Parshall and Tully, *Shattered Sword*, 437.
12. "Five Stars Due Adm. Raymond A. Spruance," *Congressional Record of the 88th Congress*, 23144; MSC012_1_07, Letter, E. B. Potter to RAS, 11 January 1965; MSC037.1_1_07, Letter, RAS to E. B. Potter, 2 February 1965.
13. MSC037.1_10_02_01, Interview MDS; MSC937.1_09_02, Margaret S. Bogart Interview.
14. MSC037.2_15_14, Fleet Admiral Ernest J. King, "Comments on Flag Officers of the U.S. Navy"; Morison, *Two Ocean War*, 339.

BIBLIOGRAPHY

PRIMARY SOURCES

MANUSCRIPT COLLECTIONS AND ORAL HISTORIES

"Admiral Charles J. Moore," Naval History Project, Oral History Research Office, Columbia University, 1968. Transcript available at the U.S. Naval Academy Nimitz Library.

Command Summary of Fleet Admiral Chester Nimitz, aka the Nimitz Graybook, 7 December 1941–3 August 1945. Collection MSC-334_01_17_01, Naval Historical Collection, Naval War College Library, Newport, Rhode Island.

The citations for the Graybook give the Page Number (Color), Month Date Time, Addressee(s). Page color denotes security classification. Times are typically given as "GCT," Greenwich Civil Time, or Zulu 0. Running Summaries give the Oahu date or Guam date starting 23 January 1945.

Papers of Raymond A. Spruance, Collection MSC012, Naval Historical Collection, Naval War College Library, Newport, Rhode Island.

Papers of Thomas C. Buell, Collection MSC037.1, Naval Historical Collection, Naval War College Library, Newport, Rhode Island.

The citations for the Spruance and Buell papers give the collection, box, folder and sub-folder (where used) in this format: MSC012_Box_Folder_Sub-folder.

Reminiscences of Admiral Raymond A. Spruance by Charles F. Barber, Naval War College Oral History Program, 1996. MSC-382, OH-329, Naval War College Library, Newport, Rhode Island.

PRIMARY AND ARCHIVAL SOURCES

Defense Technical Information Center, Fort Belvoir, Virginia

ADA438112. *Basic Outline Plan for "Blacklist" Operations to Occupy Japan Proper and Korea after Surrender of Collapse: Annexes.* US Army Forces Pacific, Fort Shafter, HI, August 1945.

ADA637885. "Staff Study, 'Olympic,' Operations in Southern Kyushu." General Headquarters, U.S. Army Forces in the Pacific, 28 May 1945.

MacArthur Memorial Archives and Library, Norfolk, Virginia

RG-3 Records of Headquarters Southwest Pacific Area (SWPA) 1942–1945

"Combined Fleet Ultra Secret Operation Order No. 41, 15 Aug 1943." "Operation Order 76, 3 May 1944." Limited Distribution Translation No. 39, Part VIII, Combined Fleet Operation Orders, 4 June 1945, Box 153.

"Z Operation Orders." Allied Translator and Interpreter Section, Southwest Pacific Area, Limited Distribution Translation No. 4, 23 May 1944, RG3, Box 151, SWPA, ATIS, Current Translations No. 164–76, April–June 1944.

National Archives and Records Administration (NARA), College Park, Maryland

RG 38 2990147–14–16. Oral History, LCDR Earl A. Junghans.

The National Museum of the Pacific War, Fredericksburg, Texas
Digital Archive, World War II Document Collection
Battle of Midway Memoranda and Reports, OP-20-G.
Intelligence History of Japanese Naval Air and Fleet Units Active in JN-25. Vol. 1344, Ships S to Z.

The United States Army Command and General Staff College, Fort Leavenworth, Kansas
Ike Skelton Combined Arms Research Library
Ellis, Earl H. *Advanced Base Operations in Micronesia.* FMFRP-12–46. Washington, DC: Department of the Navy, 1921, 1996.
Marshall Islands Japanese Defenses and Battle Damage, N-7089. U.S. Army W. D. Mission Report, 1 March 1944.
Report by G-3 on Forager, N-3258-D, Enclosure C, Headquarters, Expeditionary Troops Task Force 56, 4 September 1944.
Report of Flintlock Operation, N-7085-A. Commander, Fifth Amphibious Force, Central Pacific, Reg. #30, 25 February 1944.
Report of the Capture of the Marianas, N-2966, Reg. #144, Commander, Joint Expeditionary Force, 25 August 1944.
U.S. Marine Corps Tentative Manual for Landing Operations, Ch. 1–7. Washington, DC: Headquarters, United States Marines, 1933.

United States Joint Chiefs of Staff, Joint History and Research Office
Sextant and Eureka Conference Papers, CCS 397, Specific Operations for the Defeat of Japan.
Trident Conference, "Minutes of the 92nd Meeting of the Combined Chiefs of Staff," Washington, DC, 21 May 1943.

United States Naval Academy, Nimitz Library, Annapolis, MD
Annual Register of the US Naval Academy, Class of 1905–1906.
Digital Collections
USNA Publications

United States Naval War College Archives
RG-04, Publications and Office Reports.
RG-13, Student Papers.
RG-14, Faculty and Staff Presentations.
RG-15, U.S. Navy War College Register of Officers, 1884–1979.
RG-28, Presidents Subject Files, Se-Sp, Box 4A.

U.S. Central Intelligence Agency, Freedom of Information Act Electronic Reading Room.

U.S. Navy History and Heritage Command
Dictionary of American Naval Fighting Ships (DANFS)
On-Line Reading Room
"Battle of Midway Army Air Forces," *Battle of Midway*, 2020.
Landing Operations Doctrine, United States Navy, FTP 167, 1938, Office of Naval Operations, Division of Fleet Training, United States Government Printing Office, Washington, DC, 1938.
"The Raids on Wake and Marcus Islands," *Early Raids in the Pacific Ocean*, 2020.

U.S. State Department, Office of the Historian, Washington, DC
Conference at Quebec, 1944, D179, "Combined Chiefs of Staff Minutes," 13 September 1944.

Foreign Relations of the United States, 1950, East Asia and the Pacific, Vol. 6.

Foreign Relations of the United States, 1951, East Asia and the Pacific, Vol. 6, Part 2.

Foreign Relations of the United States, 1952–1954, East Asia and the Pacific, Vol. 7, Part 2, Records of Official Correspondence of Ambassador R. A. Spruance.

World War II/Battle Reports and Analyses. Originally Issued by the United States Fleet, Headquarters of the Commander in Chief, Navy Department, Washington, DC.

Amphibious Operations during the Period August to December 1943, 1944.

Amphibious Operations: The Marshall Islands, January and February 1944, 1944.

Amphibious Operations: Excluding Marshall Islands: January–March 1944, 1944.

Battle Experience: Solomon Islands Action: August and September 1942, including Bombardment of Kiska, 7 August 1942. Secret Information Bulletin No. 2, 1943.

Battle Experience: From Pearl Harbor to Midway, December 1941 to June 1942, including Makin Island Raid 17–18 August, 1943.

Battle Experience: Solomon Islands Actions, October 1942, 1943.

Battle Experience: Solomon Islands Actions, November 1942, 1943.

Battle Experience: Solomon Islands Actions, December 1942–January 1943, 1943.

Battle Experience: Naval Operations, Solomon Islands Area, 12 July–10 August 1943, 1943.

Battle Experience: Assault and Occupation of Attu Island, May, 1943, 1943.

Battle Experience: Bombardment of Wake Island 5 & 6 October 1943: Dress Rehearsal for Future Operations, 1944.

Battle Experience: Battle off Cape St. George, New Ireland, 24–25 November 1943: Surface and Air Attacks on Nauru Island, 8 December 1943, 1944.

Battle Experience: Supporting Operations before and during the Occupation of the Gilbert Islands, November 1943 (First Major Stepping Stone Westward), 1944.

Battle Experience: Supporting Operations for the Occupation of the Marshall Islands including the Westernmost Atoll, Eniwetok, February, 1944 (Second Major Stepping Stone Westward), 1944.

Battle Experience: Battleship, Cruiser and Destroyer Sweep around Truk, 16–17 February 1944: Bombardments of Satawan and Ponape, 30 April–1 May, 1944, 1944.

OFFICIAL HISTORIES

Building the Navy's Bases in World War II: History of the Bureau of Yards and Docks and the Civil Engineer Corps, 1940–1946. Vol. 2. Washington, DC: US Government Printing Office, 1947.

Frank, Benis M., and Henry I. Shaw Jr. *History of the United States Marine Corps in World War II*. Vol. 5, Part 2, "Okinawa." Washington, DC: Historical Division, Headquarters, USMC, 1971.

Forrestel, Emmet P. *Admiral Raymond A. Spruance, USN: A Study in Command*. Washing ton, DC: US Government Printing Office, 1966.

Garand, George W., and Truman Strobridge. *History of the United States Marine Corps in World War II*. Vol. 4, Part 5, "Iwo Jima." Washington, DC: Historical Division, Headquarters, USMC, 1971.

Heinl, Robert D., and John A. Crown. *The Marshalls: Increasing the Tempo*. Washington, DC: U.S. Marine Corps Historical Branch, 1954. Repr., Nashville, TN: The Battery Press, Inc., 1991.

Hoffman, Carl W. *Saipan: The Beginning of the End*. Washington, DC: Historical Branch, G-3, Headquarters, USMC, 1950.

———. *The Seizure of Tinian*. Washington, DC: Historical Branch, G-3, Headquarters, USMC, 1951.

Hough, Frank O. *The Seizure of Peleliu.* Washington, DC: Historical Branch, G-3, Headquarters, USMC, 1950.

Miller, John Jr. *Cartwheel—the Reduction of Rabaul.* Washington, DC: Center for Military History, United States Army. Repr., 1968.

Morton, Louis. *US Army in WWII: The War in the Pacific: Strategy and Command; The First Two Years.* Washington, DC: US Government Printing Office, 1962.

Shaw, Henry I. Jr., Bernard Nalty, and Edwin T. Turnbladh. *History of US Marine Corps Operations in WWII.* Vol. 3, *Central Pacific Drive.* Washington, DC: Historical Branch, G-3 Division, Headquarters, USMC, 1966.

Stockman, James R. *The Battle for Tarawa: Marines in WW2.* Washington, DC: Historical Section, Headquarters, USMC, 1947.

SECONDARY SOURCES

BOOKS

Alexander, Joseph H. *Across the Reef: The Marine Assault on Tarawa.* Washington, DC: Marine Corps Historical Center, 1993.

———. *Closing In—Marines in the Seizure of Iwo Jima.* Washington, DC: Marine Corps Historical Center, 1994.

Asada, Sadao. *From Mahan to Pearl Harbor: The Imperial Japanese Navy and the United States.* Annapolis, MD: Naval Institute Press, 2006.

Boot, Max. *The Road Not Taken: Edward Lansdale and the American Tragedy in Vietnam.* New York: Liveright/W. W. Norton, 2018.

Buell, Thomas B. *Master of Sea Power: A Biography of Fleet Admiral Ernest J. King.* New York: Little, Brown, 1980. Reissue with introduction by John Lundstrom: Annapolis, MD: Naval Institute Press, 1995; paperback edition, 2012.

———. *The Quiet Warrior: A Biography of Admiral Raymond A. Spruance.* New York: Little Brown, 1974. Reissue with introduction by John Lundstrom: Annapolis, MD: Naval Institute Press, 1987; paperback edition, 2009.

Carlson, Elliot. *Joe Rochefort's War.* Annapolis, MD: Naval Institute Press, 2011.

Carter, Worrel R. *Beans, Bullets, and Black Oil.* Washington, DC: U.S. Navy Dept., 1953.

Cheser, S. Matthew, and Nicholas Doland. *Beyond the Reef: Tarawa and the Gilbert Islands. November 1943.* Washington, DC: Naval History and Heritage Command, Dept. of the Navy, 2020.

Clausewitz, Carl von. *On War.* Edited by Michael Howard and Peter Paret. Princeton, NJ: Princeton University Press, 1989.

Coquia, Jorge R. *The Philippine Presidential Election of 1953.* Manila, PI: University Publishing Company, 1955.

Drea, Edward J. *MacArthur's Ultra: Codebreaking and the War against Japan, 1942–1945.* Lawrence: University of Kansas Press, 1992.

Dyer, George. *The Amphibians Came to Conquer: The Story of Admiral Richmond Kelly Turner.* 2 vols. Washington, DC: U.S. Government Printing Office, 1971. Repr., FMFRP 12–109-I, U.S. Marine Corps, 1991.

Evans, David C., and Mark R. Peattie. *Kaigun: Strategy, Tactics, and Technology in the Imperial Japanese Navy, 1887–1941.* Annapolis, MD: Naval Institute Press, 1997.

Fisher, Stan. *Sustaining the Carrier War.* Annapolis, MD: Naval Institute Press, 2023.

Frank, Richard B. *Downfall: The End of the Imperial Japanese Empire.* New York: Penguin Books, 1999.

Friedman, Norman. *U.S. Battleships: An Illustrated Design History.* Annapolis, MD: Naval Institute Press, 1985.

———. *U.S. Cruisers: An Illustrated Design Guide.* Annapolis, MD: Naval Institute Press, 1984.

———. *Winning a Future War: Wargaming and Victory in the Pacific War.* Washington, DC: Navy History and Heritage Command, 2018.

Fuchida, Mitsuo, and Masatake Okumiya. *Midway, the Battle That Doomed Japan.* Annapolis, MD: Naval Institute Press, 1955; repr., 1992, 2001.

Giangreco, D. M. *Hell to Pay: Operation Downfall and the Invasion of Japan, 1945–47.* Annapolis, MD: Naval Institute Press, 2009.

Halsey, William F., Jr. *Admiral Halsey's Story.* New York: McGraw Hill, 1947.

Hattendorf, John B., et al. *Sailors and Scholars: The Centennial History of the U.S. Naval War College.* Newport, RI: Naval War College, 1984.

Hattendorf, John B., and Elleman, Bruce A., eds. *Nineteen-Gun Salute: Case Studies of Operational, Strategic, and Diplomatic Naval Leadership during the 20th and Early 21st Centuries.* Newport, RI: Naval War College, 2018.

Hone, Thomas C., and Trent Hone. *Battle Line: The United States Navy, 1919–1939.* Annapolis, MD: Naval Institute Press, 2006.

Hone, Trent. *Learning War: The Evolution of Fighting Doctrine in the U.S. Navy, 1898 to 1945.* Annapolis, MD: Naval Institute Press, 2018

———. *Mastering the Art of War: Admiral Chester W. Nimitz and Victory in the Pacific War.* Annapolis, MD: Naval Institute Press, 2022.

Hornfischer, James D. *The Fleet at Floodtide: America at Total War in the Pacific, 1944–1945.* New York: Random House, 2016.

Hughes, Thomas Alexander. *Admiral Bill Halsey: A Naval Life.* Cambridge, MA: Harvard University Press, 2016.

Hughes, Wayne P., Jr. *Fleet Tactics—Theory and Practice.* Annapolis, MD: Naval Institute Press, 1986.

Kennedy, Paul. *Engineers of Victory.* New York: Random House, 2013.

———. *Victory at Sea: Naval Power and the Transformation of the Global Order in World War II.* New Haven: Yale University Press, 2022.

King, Ernest J., with Walter Muir Whitehill. *Fleet Admiral King: A Naval Record.* New York: W. W. Norton, 1952.

Kohnen, David. *King's Navy: Fleet Admiral Ernest J. King and the Rise of American Sea Power, 1897–1947.* Atglen, PA: Shiffler Publishing, Inc., 2024.

Kuehn, John T. *Agents of Innovation: The General Board and the Design of the Fleet That Defeated the Japanese Navy.* Annapolis, MD: Naval Institute Press, 2008.

Ladd, Dean, and Steven Weingartner. *Faithful Warriors: A Combat Marine Remembers the Pacific War.* Annapolis, MD: Naval Institute Press, 2009.

Lansdale, Edward Geary. *In the Midst of Wars: The American Mission to Southeast Asia.* New York: Harper and Row, 1972. Repr., Fordham University Press, 1992.

Layton, Edwin T. *"And I Was There": Pearl Harbor and Midway; Breaking the Secrets.* New York: Quill, William Morrow & Co., 1985.

Leutze, James. *A Different Kind of Victory.* Annapolis, MD: Naval Institute Press, 1981.

Lundstrom, John B. *Black Shoe Carrier Admiral: Frank Jack Fletcher at Coral Sea, Midway, and Guadalcanal.* Annapolis, MD: Naval Institute Press, 2006.

MacArthur, Douglas. *Reminiscences.* Annapolis, MD: Naval Institute Press Bluejacket Books, 2012.

Mawdsley, Evan. *Supremacy at Sea: Task Force 58 and the Central Pacific Victory*. New Haven, CT: Yale University Press, 2024.

McCranie, Kevin D. *Mahan, Corbett, and the Foundations of Naval Strategic Thought*. Annapolis, MD: Naval Institute Press, 2021.

Miller, Edward S. *War Plan Orange: The U.S. Strategy to Defeat Japan, 1897–1945*. Annapolis, MD: Naval Institute Press, 1991.

Morison, Samuel Eliot. *History of the United States Naval Operations in World War II*. Repr., Annapolis, MD: Naval Institute Press, 2010. Vol. 4, *Coral Sea, Midway and Submarine Actions, May 1942–August 1942*; vol. 8, *New Guinea and the Marianas, March 1944–August 1944*; vol. 12, *Leyte, June 1944–January 1945*; vol. 14, *Victory in the Pacific, 1945*.

———. *The Two Ocean War*. New York: Little, Brown and Company, 1963.

Nofi, Albert A. *To Train a Fleet for War: The U.S. Navy Fleet Problems, 1923–1940*. US Naval War College Press, Historical Monographs 18 (2010). https://digital-commons.usnwc.edu/usnwc-historical-monographs/18.

O'Brien, Phillips Payson. *The Second Most Powerful Man in the World: The Life of Admiral William D. Leahy, Roosevelt's Chief of Staff*. New York: Dutton, 2019.

Olsen, A. N. *The King Bee: A Biography of Admiral Ben Moreell, Founder of the U.S. Navy Seabees*. La Vergne, TN: Trafford Press, 2007.

Parshall, Jonathan, and Anthony Tully. *Shattered Sword: The Untold Story of the Battle of Midway*. Washington, DC: Potomac Books, 2007.

Potter, E. B. *Admiral Arleigh Burke*. Annapolis, MD: Naval Institute Press, 1990.

———. *Bull Halsey*. Annapolis, MD: Naval Institute Press, 2003.

———. *Nimitz*. Annapolis, MD: Naval Institute Press, 2008.

Prados, John, *Combined Fleet Decoded*. New York: Random House, 1995.

Prange, Gordon. *At Dawn We Slept*. New York: McGraw Hill, 1981.

Reynolds, Clark G. *The Fast Carriers: The Forging of an Air Navy*. Annapolis, MD: Naval Institute Press; repr., 1992.

Ross, Steven T., ed. *U.S. War Plans, 1938–1945*. Boulder, CO: Lynne Reinner Publications, Inc., 2002.

Sherrod, Robert. *Tarawa: The Story of a Battle*. New York: Duell, Sloan, and Pearce, 1944, 1954. Fiftieth anniversary edition with preface by Robert Sherrod: Fredericksburg, TX: The Admiral Nimitz Foundation, 1993.

Sledge, E. B. *With the Old Breed at Peleliu and Okinawa*. New York: Ballantine Books Trade Paperback Edition, 2010.

Smith, Holland M. *Coral and Brass*. New York: Charles Scribner and Sons, 1949. Repr., FMFRP 12–37, Headquarters, USMC, 1989.

Spector, Ronald. *Professors of War: The Naval War College and the Development of the Naval Profession*. US Naval War College Press, Historical Monographs No. 3 (1977).

Stillwell, Paul. *Battleship Commander: The Life of Vice Admiral Wills A. Lee, USN*. Annapolis, MD: Naval Institute Press, 2021.

Symonds, Craig L. *The Battle of Midway*. New York: Oxford University Press, 2011.

———. *Nimitz at War: Command Leadership from Pearl Harbor to Tokyo Bay*. New York: Oxford University Press, 2022.

Toll, Ian W. *Pacific Crucible: War at Sea in the Pacific, 1941–1942*. New York: W. W. Norton, paperback ed., 2012.

———. *The Twilight of the Gods: War in the Western Pacific, 1944–1945*. New York: W. W. Norton, 2021.

Trimble, William F. *Admiral John S. McCain and the Triumph of Naval Air Power.* Annapolis, MD: Naval Institute Press, 2019.

Ugaki, Matome. *Fading Victory: The Diary of Matome Ugaki, 1941–1945.* Annapolis, MD: Naval Institute Press, 2008 [1991].

Zacharias, Ellis M. *Secret Missions: The Story of an Intelligence Officer.* New York: Van Rees Press, 1946.

PERIODICALS AND OTHER SOURCES

Bjorge, Gary J. "Hard Fighting in Saipan's Death Valley: The 27th Infantry Division's Experience in a Harsh Environment of Combat." Command & General Staff College, Fort Leavenworth, KS: Open Military Studies, Open MS-D-21-0012.

Bradsher, Greg. "The Z Plan Story: Japan's 1944 Naval Strategy Drifts into US Hands." *Prologue* 37, no. 3 (Fall 2005), https://www.archives.gov/publications/prologue/2005/fall/z-plan.

Buell, Thomas B. "Admiral Raymond A. Spruance and the Naval War College: Part I—Preparing for World War II." *Naval War College Review* 24, no. 3 (March, 1971): 31–51.

———. "Admiral Raymond A. Spruance and the Naval War College: Part II—From Student to Warrior." *Naval War College Review* 24, no. 4 (April, 1971): 29–53.

Cox, Samual J. "H-039–2: Typhoon Cobra—The Worst Natural Disaster in U.S. Navy History," 14–19 December 1944." Naval History and Heritage Command. December 2019.

———. "H-048–1: Kamikaze Attacks on U.S. Flagships Off Okinawa." Naval History and Heritage Command. 20 May 2020.

———. "H-057–1: Operations Downfall and Ketsugo—November 1945." Naval History and Heritage Command. January 2021.

Dyer, George. "Naval Amphibious Landmarks." U.S. Naval Institute *Proceedings* 92, no. 8 (August 1966): 50–60.

Hone, Tom. "Modernizing Battleships 40, 41, and 42 in the 1930s." *Warship International* 60, no. 4 (December 2023): 274–81.

Hughes, Wayne, Jr. "Clear Purpose, Comprehensive Execution—Raymond Ames Spruance (1886–1969)." *Naval War College Review* 62, no. 4 (2009): 117–29.

Immerwahr, Daniel. "Philippine Independence in U.S. History: A Car Not a Train." *Pacific Historical Review* 91, no. 2 (2022): 220–48.

Koyanagi, Tomiji. "With Kurita in the Battle for Leyte Gulf." U.S. Naval Institute *Proceedings* 79, no. 2 (February 1953): 119–33.

Lempke, Andrew E. "Lansdale, Magsaysay, America, and the Philippines: A Case Study of Limited Intervention Counterinsurgency." Art of War Papers, Fort Leavenworth: KS, Combat Studies Institute Press, 2012.

McHugh, Frances J. "Gaming at the Naval War College." U.S. Naval Institute *Proceedings* 90, no. 3 (March 1964): 48–55.

McKiernan, Patrick L. "Tarawa: The Tide that Failed." U.S. Naval Institute *Proceedings* 88, no. 2 (February 1962): 38–49.

Office of the Chief of Naval Operations. *Naval Operational Planning, NWP 5–01.* Department of the Navy, Washington, DC, May 1998.

Parshall, Jonathan B. "What WAS Nimitz Thinking?" *Naval War College Review* 75, no. 2 (Spring 2022): 92–122.

Pearson, Drew, and Robert S. Allen. "The Washington Merry-Go-Round." United Features Syndicate, June 12, 1942.

Potter, E. B. "The Command Personality." U.S. Naval Institute *Proceedings* 95, no. 1 (January 1969): 18–25.

Ransom, James P. "Bleak December." *Naval History* 35, no. 6 (2021): 26–33.

Reynolds, Clark G. "Admiral John H. Towers and the Origin of Strategic Flexibility in the Central Pacific." *Naval War College Review* 40, no. 2 (1987): 28–36.

Robison, John K. "The Part of Engineering in Command." U.S. Naval Institute *Proceedings* 49, no. 2 (1923): 240.

Seese, Robert J. "The Roebling Alligator." U.S. Naval Institute *Proceedings* 109, no. 12 (1983): 27.

Slonim, Gilven M. "A Flagship View of Command Decisions." U.S. Naval Institute *Proceedings* 84, no. 4 (1958).

"Spruance for Cut in American Navy," *New York Times*, 26 August 1945.

"Spruance Views Okinawa as Political Bombshell," *Press-Telegraph*, Long Beach, CA, August 26, 1945, from AP reports, p. 2.

Symonds, Craig L. "Mitscher and the Mystery of Midway." *Naval History* 26, no. 3 (2012): 49–50.

Tillman, Barrett. "Halsey's Folly." *Naval History* 39, no. 4 (2025): 36–41.

ONLINE SOURCES

Action Report: USS *Enterprise* (CV-6), Captain G. D. Murray to Admiral C. W. Nimitz, 23 April 1943. https://www.ibiblio.org/hyperwar/USN/ships/logs/CV/cv6-Tokyo.html.

"Commander Fifth Fleet Operation Plan 13–44, 31 December 1944," Annex A. http://www.ibiblio.org/hyperwar/PTO/Iwo/ComFifthFltOpPlan13–44/759.pdf.

Commander-in-Chief, United States Pacific Fleet. "Operation Plan No. 29–42." 27 May 1942. http://www.midway42.org/Features/op-plan29-42.pdf.

"D4Y *Judy* Tail Code 701-122." *Pacific Wrecks*. March 3, 2021. https://pacificwrecks.com/aircraft/d4y/ugaki.html.

"Japanese Battleships: Tabular Record of Movements (TROMS)." http://www.combinedfleet.com/senkan.htm.

Japanese Monograph 90. "The A-go Operations (May–June 1944)." http://www.ibiblio.org/hyperwar/Japan/Monos/pdfs/JM-90/JM-90.pdf.

Japanese Monographs, originally prepared by the Military History Section of the Headquarters, US Army Forces East, and distributed by the Office of the Chief of Military History, US Department of the Army, 1945–1947. http://ibiblio.org/hyperwar/Japan/Monos.

"Scouting Squadron Six Action Report, 4–6 June 1942." http://www.cv6.org/ship/logs/action19420604-vs6.htm.

Tully, Anthony. "IJN Taiho: Tabular Record of Movement." Rev. 19 June 2007. http://www.combinedfleet.com/Taiho.htm.

Tully, Anthony, Jonathan Parshall, and Richard Wolff. "The Sinking of *Shokaku*: An Analysis." N.d. http://www.combinedfleet.com/shoksink.htm.

U.S. Navy Seabee Museum. "Archivist's Attic: Conquering the Cliffs of Despair with the Doodlebug in WWII." https://seabeemuseum.wordpress.com/tag/doodlebug.

"USS Enterprise CV-6, Philippine Sea: June 19–20, 1944." http://www.cv6.org/1944/marianas/default.htm.

INDEX

Note: Photo insert images are indicated by p1, p2, p3, etc. Page numbers in italics indicate figures and tables.

ABOUT THE AUTHOR

ANDREW K. BLACKLEY is an independent scholar specializing in naval history, particularly the Pacific War. His work has been featured in *Naval History* and the *Naval War College Review*. He has presented research at the McMullen Naval History Symposium and the Society for Military History Annual Meeting. Blackley focuses on the evolution of U.S. Navy doctrine and the operational history of its leaders. *Wielding the Trident* is his first book, showcasing years of meticulous research and a passion for uncovering untold stories of naval leadership.

The Naval Institute Press is the book-publishing arm of the U.S. Naval Institute, a private, nonprofit, membership society for sea service professionals and others who share an interest in naval and maritime affairs. Established in 1873 at the U.S. Naval Academy in Annapolis, Maryland, where its offices remain today, the Naval Institute has members worldwide.

Members of the Naval Institute support the education programs of the society and receive the influential monthly magazine *Proceedings* or the colorful bimonthly magazine *Naval History* and discounts on fine nautical prints and on ship and aircraft photos. They also have access to the transcripts of the Institute's Oral History Program and get discounted admission to any of the Institute-sponsored seminars offered around the country.

The Naval Institute's book-publishing program, begun in 1898 with basic guides to naval practices, has broadened its scope to include books of more general interest. Now the Naval Institute Press publishes about seventy titles each year, ranging from how-to books on boating and navigation to battle histories, biographies, ship and aircraft guides, and novels. Institute members receive significant discounts on the Press' more than eight hundred books in print.

Full-time students are eligible for special half-price membership rates. Life memberships are also available.

For more information about Naval Institute Press books that are currently available, visit www.usni.org/press/books. To learn about joining the U.S. Naval Institute, please write to:

Member Services
U.S. Naval Institute
291 Wood Road
Annapolis, MD 21402-5034
Telephone: (800) 233-8764
Fax: (410) 571-1703
Web address: www.usni.org